GRADUATE EDUCATION IN THE UNITED STATES

THE CARNEGIE SERIES IN AMERICAN EDUCATION

The books in this series have resulted from studies supported by grants of the Carnegie Corporation of New York, and are published by McGraw-Hill in recognition of their importance to the future of American education.

The Corporation, a philanthropic foundation established in 1911 by Andrew Carnegie for the advancement and diffusion of knowledge and understanding, has a continuing interest in the improvement of American education. It financed the studies in this series to provide facts and recommendations which would be useful to all those who make or influence the decisions which shape American educational policies and institutions.

The statements made and views expressed in these books are solely the responsibility of the authors.

Books Published

Berelson · Graduate Education in the United States
Clark · The Open Door College: A Case Study
Cleveland · The Overseas American
Conant · The American High School Today
Corson · Governance of Colleges and Universities
Glenny · Autonomy of Public Colleges
Henninger · The Technical Institute in America
Medsker · The Junior College: Progress and Prospect
Pierson · The Education of American Businessmen

Graduate Education in the United States

BERNARD BERELSON

McGRAW-HILL BOOK COMPANY, INC.

New York   Toronto   London   1960

IN MEMORY

OF MY FATHER

GRADUATE EDUCATION IN THE UNITED STATES

Contents

v

PART THREE: CONCLUSIONS, COMMENTARY, AND RECOMMENDATIONS

APPENDIX

Introduction

Graduate education in the United States is now only about 85 years old and it is still in process of development. Since the establishment of graduate work at Johns Hopkins in 1876, the graduate school has lived through a number of phases in responding to a variety of educational and social pressures; it has become the major home of research and scholarship, and the training therefor; it has incorporated both foreign and domestic features in its organization and programs; it has affected and been affected by the undergraduate program; it has moved and sometimes been torn between scholarly and professional emphases; it has grown from a few disciplines in a few institutions to many in many; and it has always exercised its own influence at a pivotal point in the system of higher education.

It is no wonder, then, that graduate education has a controversial past, present, and future. Whether the issue is its organization, its balance among competing functions, its academic quality, its capacity to meet the demands of the imminent increase of students—whatever the issue, there is responsible controversy over the facts as well as the values involved. The issues are bound to be sharpened and re-argued in the years ahead, and decisions are bound to be taken that will affect the course of graduate study for the next academic generations.

Accordingly, this seems to be a particularly good time to review the state of graduate education. In general character, the study would concern itself with the first century of graduate work in this country, from 1876 to 1976, but it would focus on the period just past and just ahead. It would include a broad review of the history of graduate education and its institutions, not for its primary detail but in order to locate and interpret the major trends and issues now active. It would include some considered projection of what might happen to graduate education, not for the sake of forecast but in order to provide a proper basis for clarifying alternatives or making recommendations. It would stay as close as possible to the facts and it would make clear where they run out and personal interpretation enters in. It would try to keep actionable themes in the center of attention. The result would be a report on what has happened, is happening, will happen, and should happen to today's graduate school and graduate education.

1

The preceding paragraphs taken from the original proposal for this study can serve as an appropriate introduction to this report. They tell in broad outline what the report is about. In the remaining pages of introduction, I wish only to note some of the considerations that prompted such a study at this time, to describe how I went about doing the study, and to tell how the report is organized.

Graduate education has grown substantially since World War II and it will grow substantially in the next years, in anticipation of and reaction to the massive enrollments expected at the baccalaureate level in the 1960's. Graduate education has perhaps changed in character in recent decades and this is one reason that the system of graduate study has come under renewed scrutiny and controversy over both means and ends. A roll call of recent statements of what's right and wrong—usually the latter—would include the Committee of Fifteen report sponsored by the Fund for the Advancement of Education, the "white paper" of the Committee on Policies in Graduate Education of the Association of Graduate Schools in the Association of American Universities, the symposium in the March, 1959 issue of *The Journal of Higher Education*, reports by the President's Committee on Education beyond the High School, the Educational Policies Commission, the American Council on Education, the National Education Association, the Trustees of the Carnegie Foundation for the Advancement of Teaching, and several others. A number of disciplines have recently surveyed their own graduate programs or are doing so now—e.g., mathematics, psychology, history, economics, philosophy, English, chemistry—and a few institutions have done the same.

In the past few years, as an indication of the sputnik effect, education has become of major importance to the American public. The *New York Times* has signified its interest with many stories and columns devoted to the problems of graduate education; a few letters to the editor and an editorial have also appeared on the deficiencies of Ph.D. training. Even graduate students have become formally involved: a group at the University of Minnesota founded a quarterly journal devoted to the intellectual and practical problems of the *Graduate Student of English*, now in its third volume. In the last days of 1959, the Institute of Higher Education of Teachers College, Columbia University, issued a pamphlet on the *Graduate School and the Decline of Liberal Education* in which the former is once more cast as the villain responsible for the latter, and the Brookings Institution issued a conference report dealing with *Research on Graduate Education*.

Despite all the controversy, perhaps because of it, no comprehensive study of graduate education in this country has appeared in the recent past (except, perhaps, for Hollis's *Toward Improving Ph.D. Programs*, and that was limited in conception and, in data, to the 1930's). This does not mean that the topic has been neglected—far from it. The debate has been continuous and the positions strongly held. The assumptions have been various; the values ambiguous or in conflict; and the facts alleged, contradictory, scanty, or altogether absent.

Accordingly, I thought it might be useful to review the story from the beginning, state the problems, analyze the arguments, bring the facts to bear, and see what conclusions and recommendations were indicated. As it happened, the Carnegie Corporation also thought the job was worth doing, and the following report is the result.

I began the study in the fall of 1957 and spent most of the following two years on it. This is how I went about it:

First, I reviewed the history of graduate education in this country, consulted the current literature, and collected the data available from published sources on trends in degree conferrals, shifts by field and institution, and the like.

Early in the first year, I talked to a number of people who were in a position to see the problems of graduate education in some overview.

Throughout the two years, I attended meetings of various kinds in which graduate education was formally discussed.

Especially during the first year, I visited a number of universities where I talked with the graduate dean, the president, the dean of the undergraduate college, departmental chairmen, and faculty members about the problems of graduate education from the institutional point of view.

In the first year, I asked a number of distinguished people in the major academic fields to serve as my consultants on the problems as seen from the disciplinary point of view. I sent them a common set of questions about graduate education and then, six weeks or so later, talked with them at some length. Our talks were recorded and ran about two hours. Occasionally, when we could not conveniently meet, they submitted written responses. This set of material is referred to in the text as coming from the disciplinary consultants. The names of the consultants and the questions sent them appear in the Appendix.

Also during the first year, I began a few small studies designed to get at some important and controversial facts about graduate education, e.g., how long the dissertations are, how many holders of the doctorate published soon after they got the degree, and so on. The results will appear at the appropriate places in the text.

About the middle of the second year, I sent out five sets of questionnaires: to the graduate deans in 92 universities (the American members of the Association of Graduate Schools and about 50 other universities giving 10 or more doctorates a year), to a sample of all graduate faculty members in the same institutions, to a sample of the 1957 recipients of the doctorate, to the presidents of all liberal arts colleges and teachers colleges in the country, and to all industrial firms employing over 100 professional and technical personnel. The various questionnaires included many questions in common, so that these groups can be compared on many points. As for the validity of the returns, I need say here only that on the whole I consider the responses to be reasonably representative of the groups to whom the queries were directed; the detailed sampling data are presented in the Appendix, along with the questionnaires.*

In all, I read countless pages and collected numerous statistics, attended about 10 formal meetings, visited 20 or more institutions, secured about 45 disciplinary consultations, conducted 5 or so special studies, talked to over 150 people, and systematically collected facts and judgments from about 80 graduate deans, 1,800 graduate faculty members, 2,300 recent recipients of the doctorate, 600 college presidents, and 70 industrial representatives. I thus sought to look at the state of graduate education by institution and by discipline, in terms of what goes in, what comes out, and what happens in between.

In scope, I am concerned with those disciplines and fields that typically lead to the Ph.D. or its equivalent—by which I mean the arts and sciences (the physical sciences, the biological sciences, the social sciences, and the humanities) plus such neighboring professional fields as education, engineering, agriculture, and business. That is, I include all postbaccalaureate education except that in medicine and law, though they too enter occasionally for comparative purposes. Within that range, I concentrate somewhat more on the arts and sciences than on the professional fields and much more on the doctorate than on the Master's.

The report consists of three sections.

The first deals with the past: what has happened in graduate education in this country. In including this material, I do not pose as an historian of graduate work; I seek only to discern the limitations that the past imposes on the present and the lessons that it ought to teach. In any case, that section will provide a common background for what follows.

* Response rates were quite similar across all major groups except for a low return from humanists on the graduate faculty. (Sample sizes for all subgroups are given in the Appendix.)

I would hope that the report is not perceived simply as a survey of academic opinion. What the people involved think about the various aspects of graduate study is basic information for such a study, especially in view of the fact that disputants in the debate make contradictory assertions about the matter. However, I do not treat the data as providing the final word: at several points, as the reader will see, I myself disagree with the main tendency of academic judgment.

One further word about the data: since this report is offered not primarily as a research document but as a contribution to the consideration of policy, and since it is addressed not to the research fraternity but to a wide range of people interested in the topic, I have kept the technical details to a minimum in the text. In view of the nature of the subject and the decisions to be made, I have not considered it necessary to present the data in the fullest detail—so to speak, to the last decimal point.

The second section deals with the present and the near future: what is happening and will happen. This is the body of the report and it is organized along the lines of the major problems now active. In view of the general character of the study—covering so many different fields, so many different institutions, and so many different outcomes of graduate training—the discussion here is also necessarily general, but I trust that it is not more so than the problems themselves. Because of the nature of the case, I exclude any consideration of the curricular content of graduate programs in particular fields. Nor do I deal directly with the university's problems of financing graduate study (though I do deal with the student's) or with the related problems of physical plant, laboratory facilities, library resources, etc. Such exclusions still leave problems enough.

The third and final section sets forth conclusions, commentary, and recommendations: what should happen. This section rests directly on the preceding material, especially that contained in the second section, and is not read properly apart from it. The final recommendations are, of course, my personal suggestions as to the best course of action to be taken in the present situation. Regardless of how the suggestions may be judged, the factual and analytic material of the second section still remains to be taken into account. Hence, to my mind, it takes on a special importance in the total report.

As I began this study, I sought advice from experienced graduate deans as to the kind of study and report that would be most helpful to the field at this time. One dean advised me to "write a short, concise report with clear recommendations." Another advised me to "go out on a limb" in saying what ought to be done. The third advised me to "stick to the facts." I have tried to follow the advice of all three.

PART ONE

The Past

The critical year for graduate education in this country is 1876, when Johns Hopkins was founded. But the story really begins before that.

Over the past century or so, the development of graduate work has been marked by five phases:

The Pre-history: to 1876
The University Revolution: 1876–1900
Consolidation and Standardization: 1900 to World War I
Growth and Diversification: World War I to World War II
Revival and Reappraisal: since World War II

The Pre-history: to 1876

This was the period of struggle: of "aspiration, controversy, and experimentation" that led to the successful establishment of Johns Hopkins in 1876. It was the time of the "supremacy of the Master's degree" —an unearned Master's degree that was awarded only to the institution's own alumni, who qualified for it, as Richard Storr has said, "by staying alive and out of trouble for three years after graduating from college and by giving very modest evidence of intellectual attainments."

In the fifty years or so before 1876, and especially after 1850, there were several efforts to establish graduate education in American institutions and all of them failed—at Harvard, Michigan, Yale, Columbia, Pennsylvania, Western Reserve, University of the South, and Virginia, among others. But these unsuccessful attempts did prepare the ground for the inevitable start, at Johns Hopkins. As President Gilman acknowledged in his inaugural address, "We reap the lessons, while others bear the loss."

There is little point here in going into the detailed story of the early battles over graduate education, fascinating and revealing as they often are. The combination of high purpose and dedication, of hope and disappointment, of grand plans and mistaken strategy, of radical vision thwarted by conservative practicality—in short, that combination of traits attending most innovating movements of such scope was not absent here. Even a casual reading of White on the Cornell situation, or Tappan on Michigan, or Burgess on Columbia will remind anyone acquainted with academic politics that the familiar practices of today were by no means unknown in the nineteenth century.

The early skirmishes are still important, however, because some arguments and issues current now were apparent even then. For example:

The controversy and conflict involved in getting graduate study under way exhibited the resistance to change that traditionally characterizes educational institutions (and other institutions, too, for that matter). Many of the arguments used today against innovations in graduate study were used then against starting it at all: e.g., the always applicable position that scarce resources should not be put into new ventures when existing undertakings need to be improved; or the argument made in 1816 by the President of Harvard College to the effect that young men "must not be detained from active life, professions, etc., longer than now, nor may the expenses of our education be much increased"; or the argument that there would be no market for the product.

The tension between undergraduate education and the proposed graduate variety was strong and pervasive, especially since there was no experience with which to judge or work out the problems. The natural hostility of college faculties was only sharpened by the recognition that the new institution represented science and professionalization whereas they represented the classical curriculum and a "calling." Not to put too fine a point on the matter, a difference of interests existed, and college faculties resented and opposed the proposal of organized graduate study: that higher level to which, they feared, they would inevitably become the lower.

The increase in the body of knowledge, especially in science, was creating pressures that were too strong for the classical curriculum of the colleges to resist. Learning was expanding much faster than the college's program of studies; and since the one could not be stopped, the other had to give way. The choice was between expanding upward or outward. Since the latter would mean thinning out the existing college program, the existing vested interests were naturally opposed to that too. At the time, the expansion upward took off some of the immediate pressure, but not for long, for the products of graduate study soon returned to the colleges to devise their own programs of study there. In the end, of course, both expansions occurred. But already at this early date, the growing body of knowledge—growing unevenly among fields—was having its effect on the organization of higher education; and as we shall see, it has made for problems in graduate study ever since.

The "needs of the times" are always available as a weapon in arguments over educational policy and the phrase was used to prepare the way for graduate study. America was rapidly becoming urbanized and industrialized and there were needs of a practical, professional, and even vocational kind that the existing system of elite colleges could not fill. President Wayland of Brown complained in 1850: "Our colleges are not filled, because we do not furnish the education desired by the people. . . . We have produced an article for which the demand is diminishing. We sell it at less than cost. . . . We give it away, and still the demand diminishes." The Morrill Act of 1862 and the establishment of land-grant universities hastened the acceptance of "practical" higher education as against or along with the "academic" variety. The "spirit of the age" won out, as it always does: the victory itself decides what the "spirit" really was. (At the time a Yale professor remarked, one hopes ironically, that the demands of the spirit of the times were so numerous and so discordant that it was not easy to ascertain them distinctly.) Today's "need of the times" that strongly influences graduate study is, of course, the national security.

The hazy line between graduate education as pure learning and graduate education as professional training was in debate even before graduate study began. Partly this was due to the adaptation of the German model to American conditions. In Germany at the time, graduate study prepared for the professions of law, divinity, and the civil service, as well as for teaching; here it had a more limited outlet and a less narrowly professional one. It became apparent to some realists that graduate study, at least at the start, needed some mundane incentives—specifically, the "artificial stimulation" of fellowships—to add to the attractiveness of the life of the mind. There has been a continuing argument over the years between those who perceive graduate education as primarily "academic" and those who perceived it as primarily "professional" (in the narrower sense)—between graduate *education* and graduate *training*.*

So some characteristics and themes that pre-date the founding of graduate education in this country are still active today:

The normal resistance to innovation and change by established faculties

The tension between scholarship and professional practice as the primary objectives of graduate study

The impact of a fast but unevenly growing body of knowledge

The conflict between influences on educational policy from inside the academic community (the universities and the disciplines) and from outside ("the needs of the times")

* As a note on the currency of the issue: the March, 1959 issue of *The Journal of Higher Education* is completely devoted to a symposium on "Problems and Policies of Graduate Education." One article, by a graduate dean, is entitled "Professionalization of the Ph.D. Degree." The editorial deals with "Graduate Degrees as Professional Degrees," and in its last sentence concludes that "the M.A. and the Ph.D. are professional degrees."

During the intervening century, the form of such issues may have changed but much of their substance has remained. They have had an impressive historical vitality.

The University Revolution: 1876–1900

This period begins with the establishment of Johns Hopkins and ends with the establishment of the Association of American Universities. During this period events occurred that determined the character of American higher education for the twentieth century, and probably beyond.

As for graduate study, the period settled permanently the issue of *whether*. The forces pushing toward its establishment finally succeeded —the needs of the times, the pressures of science upon the classical curriculum, the patriotic competition with the German system, the dissatisfaction with the current character of collegiate instruction, the inherent attractions of advanced study. And these forces were first successful in a new institution with no traditions, programs, interests, or personnel to get in the way of the *higher* higher learning in America.

Programs of graduate study initially took root in three kinds of institutions: new ones like Hopkins, Clark, and Chicago; strong private colleges like Harvard, Columbia, Yale, and Cornell; and such strong public institutions on the rise as California, Michigan, and Wisconsin. Nowhere did the development come easily. In each established institution it took years to overcome local resistance sufficiently to make even a small start, and in each new institution the leader's vision of an exclusively *graduate* university lost out to the practicalities of the situation. Gilman and Hall quickly had to accommodate undergraduate colleges at Hopkins and Clark; and Harper was never able to build a graduate Chicago on top of a minor league of feeder institutions as he had planned.

But graduate education was established; in the end, perhaps, the leaders got more of it more quickly than they would have settled for. Once begun, there was no stopping it. The inherent case could not be denied. But the case had to be put, argued, exemplified, and funded. Happily, the cause had the services of a number of able, vigorous young educators who staked their energies and careers on its development: Gilman at Hopkins, Angell at Michigan, White at Cornell, Harper at Chicago, Hall at Clark, Eliot at Harvard, Burgess at Columbia. At the time they were leading the organization of graduate study at their institutions, these men were between thirty-five and forty-five years of age; all of them made their reputations on the wave of the university revolution.

The period settled not only the question of whether to begin graduate study but the questions of *what* and *how* as well. In the first place, it settled the issue of the highest degree—*that* one would be awarded, and *which* one it would be. The Ph.D. quickly won out, though it took thirty years or so to eliminate the honorary and unearned varieties. There was thus established the institutional form of recognition that has played such a central role in higher education ever since, though not always an uncontested one. President Lowell of Harvard later referred to the conferring of degrees as "President Gilman's one mistake, if it was a mistake; and if so, it was certainly not his alone. . . . If his main object was to develop original thinkers, men expected to contribute deeply to knowledge, who cannot be very numerous in any generation, he would have done better to confer on them no degree and let their productions speak for themselves." *

With regard to organizational matters, the period settled for over half a century the attempt to establish a separate graduate institution—i.e., a graduate university without an undergraduate college. Hall and Harper and Gilman wanted essentially this kind of institution but were unable to bring it off—partly for economic reasons, partly because of the pressures for "service to the community," partly because of the need to develop one's own supply of graduate students, and finally because of its very novelty and radical character. A graduate school based on the German model was placed on top of an undergraduate college based on the English model, and several people believe that this arrangement has plagued the system ever since. (Not until these very years will a purely graduate institution make its way, in the form of the Rockefeller Institute, and then in a small size, over a limited field, and with heavy subsidy.) Furthermore, though the graduate school was "on top" of the college, it was really subordinate to it for many years and in some respects it still is. Again, this is partly due to the economics of the situation: the larger and less costly undergraduate unit helps to support the smaller and more costly graduate program.

Adding graduate work as another layer led to further organizational decisions that characterize the situation today. For example, it quickly became the practice to intermingle the graduate and undergraduate faculties. Now intermingling is common, except for places like Columbia and Chicago, and it is being reconsidered at the one and softened at the other. Some people have argued that the practice has resulted in the inappropriate use of required class attendance, course examinations, grades, and lectures at the graduate level, the lower faculty taking its undergraduate procedures with it as it moved up the scale. Also asso-

---

* President Lowell later set up the Society of Fellows at Harvard with the clear purpose of countering the doctorate; at the start, the Junior Fellows were forbidden to work for degrees while under appointment, but now most of them take the Ph.D. The magic of the degree is apparently not to be denied, not even by the best young men at Harvard.

ciated with this problem is the practice of putting both graduate and undergraduate students in the same classes, often assigning them the same course requirements. (The symposium issue of *The Journal of Higher Education* carries an article on this "Dangerous Trend in Graduate Education.")

It also became common practice to consider the graduate faculty as a unitary one without distinguishing broad fields like the natural sciences, the social sciences, and the humanities (again with Columbia and Chicago as the exceptions, the former with three graduate faculties in the arts and sciences and the latter with four).

This decision tended to lessen distinctions by field—for example, in the language requirements—because the entire graduate faculty is involved in all decisions above the departmental level. During the nineteenth century, according to Professor W. H. Cowley of Stanford, about 10,000 Americans went to Germany for graduate study but relatively few went to France; as a result we ended up with the German model of a single graduate faculty rather than the French division by broad fields. One organizational consequence of all this, important historically and current today, is the relatively weak position of the graduate dean compared with the undergraduate dean on the one hand and the professional deans on the other. The graduate dean has much less control over the budget and appointments, two major ways of affecting educational programs; he is hence more dependent upon persuasion and enlightenment. Furthermore he must operate across an extremely broad spectrum of studies, most of them not similar to his own. Both of these practices—the failure to separate the graduate and undergraduate faculties and the failure to distinguish by field—stem largely from the Harvard reorganization of 1890 that was copied by state universities then growing into graduate stature.

The die was cast on the character of graduate study as well as on its organization. The battle already joined between the traditional curriculum and the new scientific learning was settled for good: the latter won, though the victory did not come easily. Like some other educational innovations, the introduction of the new scientific learning had partly to be "bought" into existence, e.g., in the earlier grants for the Sheffield School at Yale (of which, incidentally, Gilman was an early head) and the Lawrence at Harvard. At that, it took some time before such enterprises were considered quite respectable on their own campuses.

Science won in more ways than one. First, of course, scientific courses and subjects of study were accepted and in time became prominent. In addition, the "scientific approach" began to infiltrate other subjects: the social studies began to turn into the social sciences, literary studies became heavily philological and technical, and philosophy lost psychology to science and started on the positivistic road itself. As someone has pointed out, when America copied the German version of advanced study, it was unfortunately the period when the Berlin positivists were in the ascendancy. A recent recipient of the doctorate in English referred to the

> . . . unfortunate historical accident that the American graduate school arose as an institution in a period when the exact sciences were gaining great prestige, while traditional, class-linked humanistic culture was losing its efficacy as a franchise of high social status. Today, Latin has given way to mathematics as the international language of scholarship and the key to the most abstruse and most widely honored branches of learning.

It is always well to remember that the graduate school came into being under the pressures of science and that it has lived its whole life in an increasingly scientific and technological age. It is no wonder that the major critics of graduate study have come from the humanities and certain parts of the social sciences. In an important way, the institution has from the start been a scientific institution, and it is today.

Coupled with the role of science is the position of research, the activity that quickly became the *raison d'être* of graduate study and still is, despite decades of criticism from those concerned about the preparation of college teachers. The demands of research and training for research, culminating in the doctoral dissertation, have been at the heart of controversies about graduate study from the start.

Now this was not a settled matter in 1876, though it was by 1900. Not all of the early leaders of graduate education believed that research should be at the center of graduate enterprise. Tappan, Gilman, and White upheld the primacy of teaching and made a sharp distinction between college and university teaching. Hall and Harper upheld the primacy of research; the latter introduced a radically light teaching load at Chicago to allow time for research—eight to ten hours a week—and publicly proclaimed that promotion would depend "more largely" on research productivity than on teaching, a matter of constant contention in higher education. (What else, his contemporary opponents might have asked, could you expect of a man who did his doctoral dissertation on "A Comparative Study of the Prepositions in Latin, Greek, Sanskrit, and Gothic.")

The question was settled in a way that blurred the distinction between college and university teaching. In the Harvard reorganization of 1890, Charles Eliot established a single faculty for both functions. But at the graduate level, it was research that won out: if nothing else, how could one train research scholars without letting them participate in research scholarship? The logic of that situation quickly established research in the center of the stage in graduate education where it has been ever since.*

Science and research were not the only determining characteristics of graduate studies established in the late nineteenth century and persisting to today. The utilitarian ends of the enterprise were another. This was the period of the flowering of the land-grant state universities and the Morrill Act, for "the Benefit of Agriculture and the Mechanic Arts," and through them the insistence on making knowledge useful. That idea took effect not only in the public institutions devoted to the direct service of their agricultural, industrial, political, and professional constituencies; the great private universities also bowed to the ideal of applying learning to social needs.

In 1895, President Harper observed that "the most marked characteristic in the development of university life in the last twenty-five years has been the adaptation of its methods and training to the practical problems of the age in which we live," and he worked toward lowering the barriers between the academy and the world outside. Perhaps the best statement of the idea appeared in President Gilman's inaugural address at Hopkins. The opening of the university, he said, "means a wish for less misery among the poor, less ignorance in the schools, less bigotry in the Temple, less suffering in the hospital, less fraud in business, less folly in politics; and among other things it means . . . more security in property, more health in cities, more virtue in the country, more wisdom in legislation, more intelligence, more happiness, more religion." This was a tall order: the new learning was to be not only advanced but also made useful outside academic life. This tendency, too, has continued throughout the life of the graduate school.

The period furthered a basic change in the character of higher education, and the graduate school was in the forefront of the movement as the supplier of teachers and the model of learning. There were two major shifts, themselves interrelated and both deriving from graduate study. One was the professionalization of teaching as a career and the other was the further organization of the curriculum into subjects or disciplines, similar to those in which the teachers had taken their gradu-

---

* Although the university is still the home of research *training*, it may already have lived its short life as the dominant center for research itself. Before the graduate school, research went on in academies and societies devoted to particular subjects; since World War II, it is increasingly located in industrial and governmental research installations and, as a half-way measure on both sides, in the research institutes common on university campuses but not integrally a part of the instructional program. The fifty years from the 1890's to the 1940's may have constituted the "university era" in scientific research taken as a whole. However, the university is still dominant as the home of "basic research," though perhaps not so much as is generally assumed. For example, of all the authors in the leading learned journals in 22 disciplines and fields in recent years, only 65% were in academic life.

ate work. According to Professor Cowley, "professors teaching single subjects did not come upon the American scene in influential numbers until toward the end of the nineteenth century. . . . Even in state universities, clergymen held most teaching positions, many of them had become professors because of their failure with congregations, and American higher education took an impressive leap forward when laymen supplanted them." These developments fed back from the graduate school not only to the colleges but through them to the secondary schools as well: according to Paul Woodring, "High school teachers, like the college professors who taught them, came to think of themselves less as teachers than as historians, classicists, scientists, or mathematicians. This was something new in the educational world." Thus specialization, another fighting word in the controversy over graduate study today, entered the lists and won a secure place for itself. The battle thereafter was less to displace specialization than to find ways to contain it.

So graduate study, and everything associated with it, began to grow. Government support, both Federal and state, was matched by private funds—Rockefeller at Chicago, Clark at Clark, the Stanfords at Stanford, as well as in the established institutions of the East. Jobs were available in the growing educational establishment. The students who had been going to Europe began to stay home, attracted both by the quality of some of the emerging faculties and by the fellowships that, then as now, were apparently necessary to keep the supply coming. (Since Johns Hopkins had no A.B.'s of its own at the start, it offered fellowships to the better students of other universities, a novel practice at that time. What had started from necessity became a major factor in the institution's early success.)

In 1900 about 250 legitimately earned doctorates were conferred—a tiny number by today's standards but about double the number in 1890. By 1900 about 150 institutions were committed to graduate study—though less than a third of them to doctoral work—and were developing faculties and programs to that end. The universities were burgeoning; not only was graduate work being established in the arts and sciences but professional education was also undergoing scrutiny and repairs: Langdell introduced the revolutionary case method in law at Harvard in 1870 and out of the self-criticism of medical education came a report of the AMA Council on Medical Education in 1904 that prepared the way for the famous Flexner report in 1910.

With all this, the period marked the coming of age of professional learning in this country. No fewer than 15 major scholarly societies were established between 1876 and 1905, or one every two years: *

* Almost all of these are the basic associations, rooted in the disciplines. About fifteen to twenty years later the more *general* scholarly associations were founded—

1876   American Chemical Society
1883   Modern Language Association of America
1884   American Historical Association
1885   American Economic Association
1888   Geological Society of America
1888   American Mathematical Society
1889   American Academy of Political and Social Science
1892   American Psychological Association
1899   American Astronomical Society
1899   American Physical Society
1901   American Philosophical Association
1902   American Society of Zoologists
1902   American Anthropological Association
1903   American Political Science Association
1905   American Sociological Society

Learned journals were being established in every major discipline: *American Journal of Mathematics* (1878), *American Journal of Philology* (1880), *PMLA* (1884), *Modern Language Notes* (1886), *Quarterly Journal of Economics* (1886), *Political Science Quarterly* (1886), *Botanical Gazette* (1887), *American Anthropologist* (1888), *Journal of Political Economy* (1892), *Philosophical Review* (1892), *School Review* (1892), *Physical Review* (1893), *Journal of Geology* (1893), *Psychological Review* (1894), *American Journal of Sociology* (1895), *American Historical Review* (1895), *American Journal of Physiology* (1898). All of these have been central journals in their disciplines and have been active ever since.

In short, this period established graduate study and determined many of its enduring qualities. Its close was signalized in 1900 by the founding of the Association of American Universities. The call to the organizational session was issued in the names of the presidents of Harvard, Columbia, Johns Hopkins, Chicago, and California (which then conferred 55% of all earned doctorates) and went to the presidents of Catholic University, Clark, Cornell, Michigan, Pennsylvania, Princeton, Stanford, Wisconsin, and Yale (which conferred another 33%). Those 14, with nearly 90% of the doctoral production at the time, were charter members of what became the "class" organization of American institu-

---

the National Research Council in 1916, the American Council of Learned Societies in 1919, and the Social Science Research Council in 1923. Ten to twenty years after them, more *specific* societies were founded, as the disciplines developed more specialized branches and subbranches, e.g., in the social sciences, like the Econometric Society (1930), American Association of Physical Anthropologists (1930), Population Association of America (1932), The Society for the Psychological Study of Social Issues (1936), American Society of Criminology (1936), Rural Sociological Society (1937), The Society for Applied Anthropology (1941), Economic History Association (1941), The American Association for Public Opinion Research (1945), et al.

tions interested in graduate study. The invitation to the organizational conference, incidentally, referred first to the desirability "of representing to foreign universities the importance of revising their regulations governing the admission of American students to the examinations for the higher degrees" but it envisaged a broader role for the organization too:

> There is reason to believe that among other things the deliberations of such a conference . . . will (1) result in a greater uniformity of the conditions under which students may become candidates for higher degrees in different American universities, thereby solving the question of migration . . . ; (2) raise the opinion entertained abroad of our own Doctor's degree; (3) raise the standard of our own weaker institutions.

So it is by no means hyperbole to call this period one of educational revolution. In 1876 the college was at the top of the educational program with a largely ministerial faculty, a classical and tradition-centered curriculum, a recitative class session, a small student body highly selected for gentility and social status, an unearned Master's given to alumni for good behavior after graduation; and serious advanced students went abroad. By 1900, in a short twenty-five years, the university was firmly established in America and was leading the educational parade with its professional character, its utilitarianism and community-centered program, its stress on advancing learning, its new subjects of study, its seminars and laboratories and dissertations, its growing attraction for a new class of students—all capped by the earned Ph.D. Graduate education was on the road of growth and of increasing importance in American education: it was institutionalized in the graduate schools of the important universities, it had dedicated faculties, it had ambitious students, it had adequate funds, and it had an important mission. The face of American education would never be the same again.

Consolidation and Standardization: 1900 to World War I

The period from the founding of the AAU to World War I was one of small growth and great self-scrutiny—as it turned out, something of a plateau between the impressive start of the preceding quarter century and the rapid development of the next.

The plateau was a platform too. The easy independence of the first years could not be maintained now that the system of graduate education had grown even this large, and questions of quality and purpose, of programs and personnel, were more and more discussed as more and more people and institutions became involved.

Pressures for standardization and control began to arise in the 1890's, many of them from outside the universities. The Federation of Graduate Clubs, consisting of current and former graduate students, wanted the universities to protect the doctoral degree by taking steps to outlaw the unearned and honorary kinds and by doing something about the different standards for the degree at different institutions. The University Senate of the Methodist Episcopal Church, important for its support of colleges, resolved against the honorary version of the Ph.D. and for firm standards. The International Congress of Education called upon the presidents of the major universities to accredit graduate institutions, an invitation that they then, and the AAU later, were pleased to reject (although the AAU for years maintained an "approved" list of undergraduate institutions). The organization of the learned societies in the 1890's brought the formal voices of the disciplines into the discussion. All of this culminated in the formation of the AAU as the guardian of the values and practices of graduate study. Once it was set up, it became the natural forum for the debate that continues to the present.

It is instructive and often entertaining to review the discussions of the AAU in the first few years of its existence, at a time when only a few hundred doctorates were being awarded annually. There is hardly a topic active today that was not being debated then, and not infrequently in the same terms. Fellowships, the meaning of research, the character of the dissertation, the quality of the students, the foreign language requirement, the major-minor problem at the doctoral level, the proper examinations, the role of the Master's, preparation for college teaching, college-university relations, uniform statistics—all these topics came up in the first years of the AAU.

I am tempted to quote extensively from this early debate, so engagingly familiar is its sound. Almost every issue and argument rings the bell today. As one example, take this specific action: a few years ago, the Association of Graduate Schools in the AAU laboriously worked out an arrangement for simultaneous notification of fellowship applicants by April 1 and acceptance of awards by April 15; in 1906, fifty years before, the AAU agreed "(1) that the election of fellows be held as nearly as possible simultaneously, (say) during the week ending March 24 . . . and (3) that no person be asked to *accept* any such appointment before (say) April 1. . . ."

Let me sample the early discussion, to illustrate its concerns and its tone. At the 1901 meeting, Charles Eliot asked for greater "sifting" of the doctoral dissertation because of its excessive length; Nicholas Murray Butler complained "how frequently the same persons will offer themselves as candidates (for fellowships) at several institutions" and told what steps he had taken to stop the practice at Columbia; Henry Pratt Judson of Chicago asked rhetorically whether "the graduate school itself, after all, is not practically a professional school" and observed that the "demand for specialists as teachers is now so imperative that artificial stimulus for graduate work is no longer a necessity" (he referred to fellowships as "pre-doctorate bounties" and "a species of protective tariff on domestic learning"); and Alan Briggs of Harvard called for broader training for prospective college teachers.

In 1902 a report on the Master's degree debated whether it should be regarded as a terminal degree or a steppingstone to the doctorate; again in 1910 there was a survey of the "meaning" of the Master's in which it was pointed out that the thesis requirement was not general, that most recipients go into teaching in secondary schools, and that the degree is better in departments that do not concentrate on the doctorate. There was even a complaint, by Calvin Thomas of Columbia, that "the Master's degree is not conferred exclusively by universities that are worthy of the name and can be trusted to maintain a high standard under a regime of perfect liberty"—a complaint that would be echoed in many quarters today, on its fiftieth anniversary.

In 1905 a dean complained that "a man can hardly expect to get an appointment of a higher grade than instructor upon his record as a teacher alone." Three years later, Abraham Flexner was deploring that the university had sacrificed college teaching at the altar of research (though he himself did a great deal later, as a foundation officer, to promote research).

In 1906 President Eliot thought that "there was no question" that graduate students were less able than students of medicine and law and added that graduate study suffered by comparison with work in the major professional schools. In 1909, the year he became President of Harvard, Abbott Lawrence Lowell spoke of the "monstrous" numbers attending graduate schools and added that through the fellowship subsidy "we are in danger of making the graduate school the easiest path for the good but docile scholar with little energy, independence or ambition. There is danger of attracting an industrious mediocrity which will become later the teaching force in colleges and secondary schools." A few years later, David Starr Jordan unburdened himself: "Mr. Chairman, we are spending a great deal of money in this country, and a great deal of thought, on graduate work, and the results are very discouraging. . . . There are so many discouraging elements all along the line"— he mentioned the lack of qualified students to learn and of qualified professors to teach, as well as the narrowness and triviality of the dissertation—"that one is ready to accept almost any solution of the problem. . . ."

In 1908 H. H. Horne reported the results of a questionnaire addressed to the presidents of colleges and universities in New England, inquiring into their attitude toward work in education for prospective college teachers. The vote, as usual, was split. Eleven were encouraging and the other seven exhibited "various attitudes of non-encouragement."

In 1912 the Association turned again to the "Present Status of the Degree of Doctor of Philosophy in American Universities." Requirements are reasonably clear, said the main speaker, Dean Woodbridge of Columbia: the degree aims at advanced research but the "educational situation" works against that because of the inadequate preparation of the students on the one hand and the too great specialization of subject matter on the other. The result is "proficiency rather than scholarship." Four years later the Dean was back to complain that "graduate instruction . . . is not conducted . . . in a way which forces students into habits of independent study, reflection and inquiry. The atmosphere . . . is one of supervised, regulated, and controlled study."

At the same time, Dean West of Princeton was worried about "the most sordid and dangerous thing just now in our graduate schools," namely, that they are "attracting . . . men, not because they must be scholars, but because they want a job. Why is the degree made the be-all and the end-all? It is beginning to be known like a 'union card' for labor." In these years the members also discussed such contemporary topics as outside remunerative work by professors, the summer school and graduate work, the relation of academic and professional doctorates, the organization of research activities, research professorships, cooperation with industry, and the graduate school's failure to create a "society of scholars" within itself.

The recurrent character of the debate over graduate study can perhaps best be summarized by the frequent pleas for someone to settle the question of what the doctorate was *for*—as though another definition or statement of objective would suddenly clarify the entire enterprise. To anticipate somewhat, every decade provides a few examples:

1912   Dean Woodbridge, at the AAU: "Since the degree is conferred in Sanskrit and in animal husbandry, in philosophy and highway engineering, for what does it essentially stand?"

1928   Dean Heller, at the AAU: "Since the end of the 16th century it has been copiously written about . . . this stupendously unentertaining literature (inquiring into the when, why, whence, wherefore, and particularly the 'whomfor' of the Doctor's degree). . . . Nearly all those treatises attempted to settle the still somewhat open opinion—What does the degree really mean?"

1939   The advisory committee on the Isaiah Bowman report, in its introduction: "One of the most important problems . . . was the development of a clear statement of the functions of the graduate school."

1944   President Walter Jessup of the Carnegie Foundation, in his annual report: "American graduate education is in a rut. Its aims lack sharp definition from the point of view of professional ends as well as means." The general tone of his analysis is revealed by these three headings: "Confusion and Need," "The Confusion Aggravated," and "Wanted: Another Gilman."

1957   The report of the Committee on Policies in Graduate Education of the AGS: "This critical degree . . . now seems to offer nearly as many services as the A.B. itself. Current pressure forces us to examine our myth-enveloped Ph.D. with candor. What we see makes us look away with shock. . . . The basic flaw is: we have never clearly *defined* this protean degree" (their emphasis).

What always seems to be wanted is not so much acceptance of *a* definition as acceptance of one's own!

Nor was the debate limited to the AAU. From 1905 to 1908, the National Association of State Universities deliberated over the minimum standards for graduate schools (e.g., three years of work toward the doctorate, at least five departments offering the degree). A decade later, from 1916 to 1919, a committee of the AAUP, under the chairmanship of James Rowland Angell, reviewed "the knotty subject" and "ever-present problem" of the requirements for the Ph.D. degree in an effort to "reach some results representing a common understanding" and to "safeguard standards under existing conditions in American institutions" through the "explicit and unambiguous formulation of ideals." At least one ambiguity, however, the committee could not clear up: it did not make a recommendation as to the proper breadth of graduate work because "the Committee has not found it practicable to frame a satisfactory definition of a 'department.'" At the same time, another AAUP committee firmly supported the research aims of graduate study, and the discussions brought out a strong feeling, as Arthur Lovejoy phrased it, against "a tendency to which many institutions are tempted—that of having sham graduate schools." There are now "far too many," said another speaker, who proposed that 20 or 25 "real universities" were plenty. (There were then about two hundred giving the Master's degree and nearly fifty giving the doctorate.)

Finally, this was the period when the outside-but-near influences of the accrediting associations and the foundations were allegedly decisive in sending the colleges to the graduate schools by requiring certain numbers of degree holders for the faculty. Actually the story does not seem to be that simple, or that clear. As we shall see in a moment, there were complaints about this form of "snobbery" in the colleges during the very first years of the century, before the accreditors or philanthropists had arrived on the scene. In 1906, the Carnegie Foundation, seeking a way to define a "college" for the purposes of its pension and grant programs, borrowed the criteria used by the state of New York that required, among other things, the presence of at least six full-time professors on the staff (in 1922 raised to eight). Somehow the historical accounts have converted that requirement to six *Ph.D.'s*—in Hollis, for example, and through him, presumably, to the 1947 President's Commission on Higher Education. In 1909 the North Central Association set down its minimum requirements for college faculty: graduate study equal to at least that required for the Master's degree; graduate study and training in research equivalent to that required for the Ph.D. usually necessary. As late as 1923—and in line with the ACE standards of 1922 and the AAU of 1924—the North Central Association was listing two years of study in graduate school, presumably including the Master's, as a requirement for the collegiate faculty, with the Ph.D. or equivalent professional training required for heads of departments. Later, and currently, such counting of Ph.D. noses has largely been given up by the accrediting associations, though they are still being blamed for the alleged Ph.D.-itis of the colleges.

As far as the magic of the doctorate for college teaching was concerned, the issue had long been settled. In 1909 and 1910 Johns Hopkins and Yale tried to push a two-year Master's as the degree for college teachers with the idea of reserving the Ph.D. for the few genuine researchers. Said Joseph Ames of Hopkins to the AAU:

> In connection with the Doctor's degree, one of our great reasons for having a second higher degree was to emphasize clearly to the student that we intended to reserve the Doctor's degree, for one thing, for ability in original research. Men have abilities along different lines. . . . Our idea in using the Master's degree was to emphasize that dual character of intellectual work, and that we intended to have the Doctor's degree reserved exclusively for men who could do original investigating work. . . .

The plan did not take then, and it did not take when it was later reintroduced. Even at that time the Master's was being considered as a degree for secondary school teachers and as a consolation prize for those failing the doctorate. It could not be rescued for a higher purpose.

No one has characterized this degree situation better than one of the first disputants, to whom I gladly give the last word. In a way, he can serve as the representative of the many individuals who, in their private capacities, participated in the discussion of the new graduate education. As early as 1903 William James was concerned lest "The Ph.D. Octopus" crush the true spirit of learning in the universities. His observations and comments reveal so well the timelessness of some issues of graduate study —and they are set down with such style—that they deserve lengthy quotation:

Graduate schools are still something of a novelty, and higher diplomas something of a rarity. The latter, therefore, carry a vague sense of preciousness and honor, and have a particularly "up-to-date" appearance, and it is no wonder if smaller institutions, unable to attract professors already eminent, and forced to recruit their faculties from the relatively young, should hope to compensate for the obscurity of the names of their officers of instruction by the abundance of decorative titles by which those names are followed on the pages of the catalogues where they appear. The dazzled reader of the list, the parent or student, says to himself, "This must be a terribly distinguished crowd,—their titles shine like the stars in the firmament; Ph.D.'s, S.D.'s, Litt.D.'s, bespangle the page as if they were sprinkled over it from a pepper caster."

Human nature is once for all so childish that every reality becomes a sham somewhere, and in the minds of Presidents and Trustees the Ph.D. Degree is in point of fact already looked upon as a mere advertising resource, a manner of throwing dust in the Public's eyes. "No instructor who is not a Doctor" has become a maxim in the smaller institutions. . . .

America is thus as a nation rapidly drifting toward a state of things in which no man of science or letters will be accounted respectable unless some kind of badge or diploma is stamped upon him, and in which mere personality will be a mark of outcast estate.

Our higher degrees were instituted for the laudable purpose of stimulating scholarship, especially in the form of "original research." Experience has proved that great as the love of truth may be among man, it could be made still greater by adventitious reward. The winning of a diploma certifying mastery and marking a barrier successfully passed, acts as a challenge to the ambitious; and if the diploma will help to gain bread-winning positions also, its power as a stimulus to work is tremendously increased. . . . But the institutionalizing on a large scale of any natural combination of need and motive always tends to run into technicality and to develop a tyrannical Machine with unforeseen powers of exclusion and corruption.

To interfere with the free development of talent, to obstruct the natural play of supply and demand in the teaching profession, to foster snobbery by the prestige of certain privileged institutions, to transfer accredited value from essential manhood to an outward badge, to blight hopes and promote invidious sentiment, to divert the attention of aspiring youth from direct dealings with truth to the passing of examinations, —such consequences, if they exist, ought surely to be regarded as drawbacks to the system, and an enlightened public consciousness ought to be keenly alive to the importance of reducing their amount. . . .

Is not our growing tendency to appoint no instructors who are not also doctors an instance of pure sham? Will anyone pretend for a moment that the doctor's degree is a guarantee that its possessor will be successful as a teacher? Notoriously his moral, social, and personal characteristics may utterly disqualify him from success in the classroom; and of these characteristics his doctor's examination is unable to take any account whatever. . . .

The truth is that the Doctor-Monopoly in teaching, which is becoming so rooted an American custom, can show no serious grounds whatsoever for itself in reason. As it actually prevails and grows in vogue among us, it is due to childish motives exclusively. In reality it is but a sham, a bauble, a dodge, whereby to decorate the catalogues of schools and colleges. . . .

Men without marked originality or native force, but fond of truth and especially of books and study, ambitious of reward and recognition, poor often, and needing a degree to get a teaching position, meek in the eyes of their examiners,—among these we find . . . the unfit in the academic struggle for existence. There are individuals of this sort for whom to pass one degree after another seems the limit of earthly aspiration. Your private advice does not discourage them. They will fail, and go away to recuperate, and then present themselves for another ordeal, and sometimes prolong the process into middle life. . . .

We know that there is no test, however absurd, by which, if a title or decoration, a public badge or mark, were to be won by it, some weakly suggestible or hauntable persons would not feel challenged, and remain unhappy if they went without it. We dangle our three magic letters before the eyes of these predestined victims, and they swarm to us like moths to an electric light. . . .

The more widespread becomes the popular belief that our diplomas are indispensable hallmarks to show the sterling metal of their holders, the more widespread these corruptions will become. We ought to look to the future carefully, for it takes generations for a national custom, once rooted, to be grown away from.

Not only observant but prophetic as well. James's proposals for checking "the hold of the Ph.D. Octopus" were threefold: first, let the universities give the doctorate "as a matter of course . . . for a due amount of time spent in patient labor," like the Bachelor's degree; second, let the colleges and universities "give up their unspeakably silly ambition to bespangle their lists of officers"; and third, let able students bypass the degree when it interferes with their own independent study and let the faculty protect such students "in the market-struggle which they have to face." All of this in 1903.

The first two decades or so after the formation of the AAU, then, witnessed an elaborate and continuing debate of the objectives, procedures, and programs of graduate study—a debate that does not sound anachronistic today. Throughout the period the enterprise expanded. By World War I 10 more institutions had been admitted to the AAU, 8 of them state universities from the Middle West. The graduate school had consolidated its position in higher education: e.g., in 1900 about a third of the Ph.D.'s were still being given by colleges for off-campus work, or for none, and another 8 to 10% were honorary; by World War I this practice had virtually disappeared. The period further stabilized the standards of graduate study that still exist—the residence requirements, the foreign languages, the character of the dissertation.

In the period 1916 to 1918, the Ph.D. was given in a total of 149 separate "fields" in the major American institutions—about 45 of them major branches of learning, the remainder variants of one sort or another. In 91 of the fields, the degree was offered at only a single institution (e.g., in the animal husbandry that Dean Woodbridge had used as his example before the AAU in 1912, in architecture, classical archeology, fine arts, Oriental languages and literature, philology); and in another 22 fields it was offered at only two institutions (e.g., Germanic languages, history of art, paleontology). At the other end of the distribution were the central fields of graduate study at that time, in no case common to all 26 institutions included in this particular survey (Zook and Capen): chemistry was offered for the doctorate in 20 institutions; history in 19; botany in 17; education and physics in 16; mathematics and English in 14; economics, philosophy, psychology, and zoology in 13; geology in 12; political science in 11; and Latin in 10. As for institutions, Cornell offered the doctorate in 49 fields; Columbia in 38; Wisconsin in 34; Chicago in 31; Pennsylvania in 26; California, Johns Hopkins, and Michigan in 23; Illinois, Minnesota, and Yale in 21; and Harvard in only 15 (though on the whole broader ones).

The period was crucial less for growth in numbers than for growth in evaluation and self-recognition. By the early 1920's, the college's demands were sizable and the graduate school, after the standardization of this period, was in turn ready for a development of its own.

Growth and Diversification: World War I–World War II

On the bases laid by the elementary school were built the consecutive periods of growth of the educational layers above. First the high school, then the college, then the graduate school—about twenty-five years apart as the lower laid the groundwork for the upper, both in supplying the raw material and in demanding the product. The larger the high school enrollment, the more students there were to go on to college and the more high school teachers were required. The larger the collegiate enrollment, the greater the flow of students to the graduate schools and the greater the need for teachers from them.

The system of graduate education entered a period of great growth and diversification. From 1900 to 1940, everything in higher education was increasing in size, and far faster than the population of the age group most directly involved. The latter did not even double in these

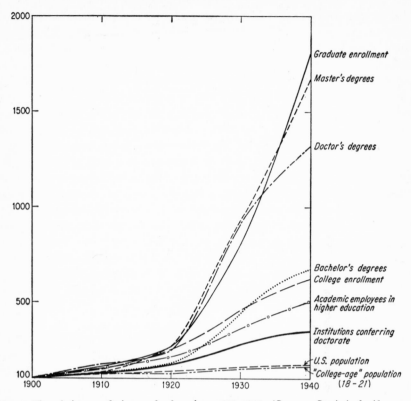

FIG. 1. Trends in population and education, 1900–1940. (*Source: Statistical Abstracts, Stigler, Office of Education reports.*)

four decades, but institutions offering the doctorate more than tripled, college faculties became five times as large, college enrollments six times, baccalaureate degrees seven times, and graduate enrollments and degrees from thirteen to seventeen times (Figure 1). Up to 1920, growth in higher education exceeded growth in the population at large, but in the following twenty years the gap became much wider. Adjectives like "tremendous," "phenomenal," and "unprecedented" have been used to describe the growth of the period, and the terms seem justified. The percentage of the population eighteen to twenty-one years of age that went to college rose from about 4% in 1900 to over 15% in 1940, and the percentage of baccalaureate holders who took graduate degrees went from about 6% before 1900 to around 10 to 12% from 1900 to 1925 and then to about 15%. In the twenty years from 1900 to 1920, earned doctorates increased by about 250%; in the twenty years from 1920 to 1940, they increased by over 500%. The prosperity of the 1920's no doubt stimulated this growth, but the depression of the 1930's did not retard it. The

Trends in population and education, 1900–1940
(Raw data)

	Population (000,000s)		Institutions conferring doctorate	Academic employees in higher education (000s)	Enrollments* (000s)		Earned degrees (000s)		
	U.S.	College-age (18–21)			College	Graduate	Bachelor's (and 1st-level professional)	Master's (and 2nd-level professional)	Doctor's
1900	75.9	5.9	25	29.0	237.6	5.8	27.4	1.6	0.25
1910	92.0	7.3	32	45.0	355.2	9.4	37.2	2.1	0.44
1920	105.7	7.3	44	62.0	597.9	15.6	48.6	4.3	0.62
1930	122.8	9.0	70	105.4	1,100.7	47.3	122.5	15.0	2.30
1940	131.7	9.8	88	146.9	1,494.2	105.7	186.5	26.7	3.29

Source: Statistical Abstracts, Stigler, Office of Education reports.

* It is virtually impossible to find data on enrollments and degrees that will stand up to every test, but I am confident that these data are valid enough for their broad purpose here. For the 1900 base figure for doctoral degrees, I have included only earned doctorates from "legitimate" institutions, omitting from the official figures almost 100 degrees awarded in that year by such colleges as Moravian, Columbian, New Windsor, American University of Harriman, and Taylor.

number of institutions giving the doctorate rose from about 50 in 1920 to nearly 100 in 1940 and the number giving the Master's from 200 to 300.

As for diversification, this was a period when the composition of the graduate student body changed for good—away from whatever remained of the nineteenth century's genteel tradition and social elitism, toward primary concern with simple intellectual quality. One result, as we shall see in a moment, was concern with the social manners and religious deportment of the *parvenu* graduate students. Another was the introduction of formalized testing procedures for admission: the Graduate Record Examination began in 1937 under the highest auspices—Harvard, Yale, Princeton, Columbia.

Moreover, the doctoral program was itself extended not only to more specialized fields within the arts and sciences but far beyond, to a number of professional fields: agriculture, business, education, engineering, home economics, journalism, librarianship, nursing, social work.

The growing specialization was also reflected in a growing body of knowledge, i.e., of scholarly and scientific literature. Verner Clapp reports that "the Royal Society of London recorded only 1,555 scientific journals for the whole of the nineteenth century; for less than half the twentieth, the *World List of Scientific Periodicals* lists 50,000." The publications flooded out not in just one large river—that would have been hard enough for graduate study to cope with—but in an increasingly large number of streams and tributaries. The journals founded before 1900 tended to be general to each discipline, and many of them still are. The newer journals established themselves on specialized segments. Take these cases, for example: in the humanities, *Speculum* (1925), *American Literature* (1929), *Philosophy of Science* (1934), and *Journal of Aesthetics* (1941); in the social sciences, *Econometrika* (1933), *Sociometry* (1937), *Public Administration Review* (1940), *Journal of Personality* (1932), and *Journal of Clinical Psychology* (1945); or in the physical sciences, *Journal of Applied Physics* (1930), *Journal of Organic Chemistry* (1936), *Bulletin of Mathematical Biophysics* (1939), and *Journal of Polymer Science* (1945). Bibliographical and abstracting services had to be set up to handle the flow of learning that came, directly or indirectly, from the graduate school.

Nor were the voices silent on this matter, either. An AAUP committee in 1922 wanted the learned journals strengthened and enlarged, but only those then in existence: "It is undesirable to increase the number." The consequences of training so many researchers who would want or try to contribute to the flow did not go unnoticed; long before, in 1905, Dean West of Princeton thought that "we have been yielding to one or two fallacies and one of them, being merely the excess of a good thing, is the idea that every professor must be a producer, more or less irrespective of the value of what he produces. And the flood of publications, say in some subsection of the vast field of biology, is swamping men. . . . The men who can read and criticize and review what has been turned out in the year are very rare." In many ways, growth in numbers and growth in knowledge have been twin pressures upon the graduate schools, and the latter may be even harder to control or live with than the former.

All these large changes brought again to the fore the perennial question of purpose and quality. For example, take the claims of the professions for an equal place in graduate study. The case of education was bitterly contested and finally settled in a half-inside, half-outside manner. Harvard decided in 1922 to give the doctorate for work in education—but not the Ph.D., only the Ed.D., and that practice prevails there today. At Chicago, only the Ph.D. is awarded, and at some universities, such as Columbia, both degrees are given, although for different programs. Similarly with doctoral programs in other professional fields like engineering and business: both the traditional Ph.D. and the professional doctorate in the field (D.Eng. or D.B.A.) are current.

In general, the professions were after the Ph.D.; as they grew in self-recognition, they looked to the university as the home of respectability as well as of knowledge and they sought the traditional doctorate both for its substance and as a symbol that they had arrived. The struggle was reminiscent of an earlier one: fifty years before, the classics had argued against the entry of science on the ground of inappropriate subject matter and method for "true learning," and now the academic arts and sciences joined together to use the same arguments against the professional newcomers. The debate was partly conducted on the line of standards versus service. Although the hard core of academic sentiment can always be found on the side of "standards," social pressures and funds are often found on the side of service, and it often wins out.

As another example, take the case of the preparation of college teachers. That was a live issue then, just as it is today, with the sharp growth in college enrollments and another increase ahead. Throughout the 1920's and 1930's, the discussions of the AAU returned to the topic: should there be two doctoral degrees, one for researchers and one for teachers? Should there be more direct training for teaching? Was the doctoral program too specialized? The conclusions, to the extent there were any, seemed to echo Wilbur Cross's diagnosis of 1925 that "there is no escape from the dual character" of the degree.

Also in 1925, Raymond Hughes, then president of Miami of Ohio, urged the Association of American Colleges to bring pressure on the graduate schools: "We (the AAC) represent some five hundred colleges

. . . which are the chief employers of the products of the graduate schools of America. . . . This being the case, it seems to me that we might have more weight in influencing the policies of the graduate schools, at least to a small degree, so that the teachers who come to us from them might be somewhat better fitted for the work for which we employ them." What did he want? Four things: the graduate school should (1) broaden the doctoral program and (2) provide more teacher training; but in addition—and this reflects the changing composition of the student body—it should (3) take some responsibility for the religious life of graduate students since many would be teaching in denominational colleges and (4) find a way to give the students some "social training" so that they would become "cultivated gentlemen," like the graduate students from Princeton. But the efforts to increase the teacher training element in doctoral work were defeated in the AAU as too "educationist" in nature, and Dean Cross pointed to another obstacle in reviewing Yale's attempt to develop the two-year broadly programmed Master's as the degree for college teachers: "The trouble lies in the name of the degree conferred. It is not a Master's degree but a Ph.D. that is wanted."

A Commission on the Enlistment and Training of College Teachers was set up in 1925 by the AAC, under the chairmanship of President Ernest Wilkins of Oberlin, and finally reported in 1929, in language of extreme discretion, that each graduate school should ask itself whether it is "doing all that it can rightly do to train its students for the profession of college teaching." Today's call to the graduate school was already old then: give training in teaching methods, admit only those with a "broad range of intellectual interest," give a course on the American college to intended teachers, don't stress research "unduly." From the AAC "hearty approval"; from the AAU and the AAUP, appointments of committees to look into the matter. The final outcome, according to President Wilkins' own appraisal much later, was failure; in Professor Cowley's judgment, "The Wilkins campaign ended without any substantial results other than the establishments of a few professorships of higher education."

Or for another example, take the overarching case of the quality of graduate study. In 1925, for the first time, there appeared an informal rating of graduate departments conducted by a faculty group at Miami under President Hughes. Another was done in 1934, this time under the auspices of the Committee on Graduate Instruction of the ACE, of which Hughes was chairman. The latter rating, based on the judgment of specialists in the various fields, indicated that about 20% of the graduate departments in the arts and sciences were "distinguished," another 35% were "adequate," and the remaining 45% were "inadequate." Although the proportions of all doctorates awarded by the "inadequate" departments was of course much lower, there was still a good deal of concern voiced about the level to which graduate education was falling under the impact of numbers—as, again, there is today.

The specifics cited were the familiar ones. People were concerned about the "huge numbers" of students (President Jessup of the Carnegie Foundation, 1939); about the "overexpansion" of programs that "has harmed the quality of graduate instruction in many cases and has served to depreciate the value of the doctorate" (John, 1934); about the "fashion for university teaching to be literal and unimaginative rather than colorful and inspired" (Ryan, 1939); about the students' spending time "not on the kind of work that would make them interested in research problems and skillful in the presentation of results, but in making up undergraduate deficiencies, for which they get graduate credit" (Dean Laing of Chicago, 1930); about the "fallacious assumption that one set of requirements will serve, and one runway of training suffice for all" (Henry Suzzallo of the Carnegie Foundation, 1930); about the "young men of undistinguished ability and indifferent personal traits who are diligently grubbing their way to the doctorate" (AAU committee report, 1933); about the growing standardization and regulation of graduate work that require a return to "the old flexibility" lest in a few more years the graduate school become merely "a continuation school" (Dean Cross, 1925); and so on.

The old refrain about the Master's degree was raised several times: the "existing confusion" at the beginning of this period (AAU, 1921) became "evident confusion" near the end (AAU, 1935); the "widespread dissatisfaction is justified" but the "immediate standardization of requirements is impracticable" (AAUP, 1932). An ACE committee in 1934, baffled by the academic and professional uses of the degree, threw up its hands: "Indeed, the Committee feels that it cannot adequately carry further the study of this large subject"—and suggested another study. Throughout the period, there were recommendations that the degree be considered simply an extension of undergraduate education and be administered accordingly, e.g., by Dean Keniston to the AAU in 1924 and by Commissioner Zook at the twenty-fifth anniversary of graduate study at the University of California in 1936. The last word on this subject is John's, from his 1934 review of graduate study: "The question was increasingly raised as to whether the degree was a preparatory research degree or one primarily concerned with subject matter expansion. The question is still a live one and doubtless never will be answered finally." While "never" is a long time, certainly the past quarter century has not proved him wrong.

On another front, in 1927, the North Central Association was worried about the undue extension of graduate work and in 1934 the AAU formally resolved that it "views with concern the growth of the number of institutions conferring the Ph.D. degree in fields in which . . . they are not adequately staffed or equipped for work"—but since no names were mentioned there was no need for any institution to think that the AAU meant it. At the very close of this period and the beginning of the post-war era, in 1945–1946, another major effort was made in the AAU to develop a national accrediting arrangement for graduate work; the Special Committee recommended such a program—it "could not much longer be deferred"—but after much discussion and revision the Association voted "no" by 15 to 13.

The entire situation was ventilated from time to time in studies and calls for studies. In 1927 and again in 1935 the AAU proposed inquiries into the present state of graduate education, with words like "comprehensive," "constructive," "searching," and "courageous" used to describe what was wanted. Neither one could be financed. Meanwhile, however, a number of other reports and pronouncements on graduate education did appear, so many that this was the second most-reported period for the graduate school—second only to the present. The statements were prepared by groups and individuals from a variety of disciplines, positions, and institutions; and were sponsored by a variety of educational associations as well as the Office of Education and interested foundations. For example:

1925   Hughes' *Study of the Graduate Schools of America,* a quality ranking

1929   Report of the Wilkins-chaired AAC Commission on Enlistment and Training of College Teachers mentioned above

1930   Flexner's *Universities: American, English, German,* attacking the service orientation of American institutions

1930   Gray, editor, *The Training of College Teachers; Proceedings of the Institute for Administrative Officers of Higher Institutions;* an early symposium on the topic

1932   Report of an AAUP committee on the Master's degree: "dissatisfaction," as noted above

1933   Report of an AAUP Committee on College and University Teaching: graduate schools should pay more attention

1934   Report of the ACE Committee on Graduate Instruction, including a ranking of graduate schools

1934   John's *Graduate Study in Universities and Colleges in the United States,* a broad review sponsored by the U.S. Office of Education

1936   Foster's *The Functions of a Graduate School in a Democratic Society,* a private venture proposing fewer, better graduate schools

1939   Bowman's *The Graduate School in American Democracy,* an essay by the president of Johns Hopkins; the outcome of the 1935 call for an investigation

1939 Ryan's *Studies in Early Graduate Education,* a history of the early years of Johns Hopkins, Clark, and Chicago; sponsored by the Carnegie Foundation for the Advancement of Teaching

1940 Horton's *The Graduate School (Its Origin and Administrative Development),* a doctoral dissertation

1944 Edwards' *Studies in American Graduate Education,* an analysis of whether students from accredited colleges do better in graduate school than those from unaccredited, plus a report on interviews with graduate faculty members at twelve universities; also sponsored by the Carnegie Foundation

1945 Hollis' *Toward Improving Ph.D. Programs,* based on an occupational analysis of doctorates from the 1930's and recommending more attention to the preparation of college teachers; sponsored by the ACE Commission on Teacher Education

—plus the normal amount of discussion in academic journals, proceedings, annual reports, meetings and conferences, professional papers, and all the rest.

Revival and Reappraisal: Since World War II

Whatever was growing in graduate education between the two world wars quickly recovered after the second and continued to grow, only more so. The demand for training and the supply of students, the institutions offering graduate work, the body of knowledge to be communicated, the professionalization of graduate study, the debate over the entire enterprise—all of these familiar trends were back in high gear by 1950 and they have continued to the present.

As for conferred degrees, the figures that seemed so "overwhelming" at the graduate level at the beginning of World War II were more than doubled five years after its end. Now they are well on their way to trebling. More doctorates were granted in this country in the past decade than in all the years up to then. The index of growth is revealing: using the number who got each degree in 1939–1940 as 100, here are the indexes for 1958–1959:

Bachelor's (and first level professional degrees)	206
Master's (and second level professional degrees)	260
Doctor's degrees	284

The higher the degree, the greater the increase.

Some leaders of graduate education were worried about the impact of numbers upon quality when the system produced 500, 1,000, 3,000 doctorates a year; what would they say today about the production of 9,000? The only real dip in the long-term curve of Master's and Doctor's degrees was caused by World War II, and it was quickly surmounted (Figure 2). Not only are more students becoming potentially available

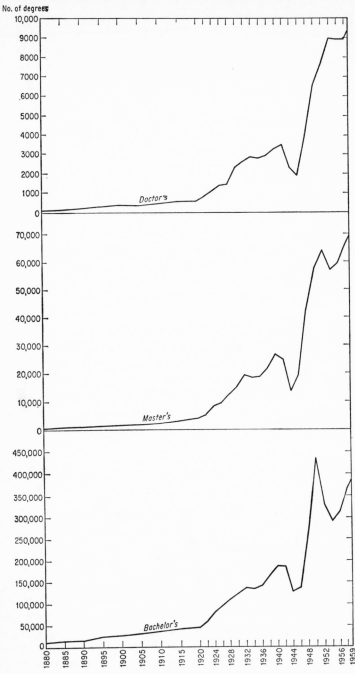

No. of degrees

FIG. 2. Earned degrees, 1880–1959. (*Source: Office of Education.*)

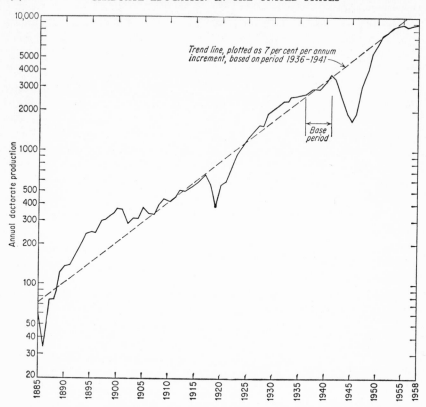

Fɪɢ. 3. Production of doctorates in United States universities, 1885–1958. (*Source: "Production of United States Scientists," by Office of Scientific Personnel, NAS-NRC, Science, March, 1958, p. 683.*)

for graduate study by completing the baccalaureate, but more of them are actually going on, stimulated by the social demands for trained personnel and the need for advanced training to qualify for many posts. In the first decades of the century, the Master's amounted to about 10 to 12% of the baccalaureates and the doctorates about 1.5%. Now the Master's are almost 20% of the baccalaureate figure and doctorates are up to about 2.5%. Since the 1920's, the Master's degrees have increased sharply under the pressure of staff requirements in the secondary schools, and only in this decade have the figures been stabilized at around 60,000 a year. Even with the progressively larger base, doctoral production has nearly doubled every decade since the beginning (Figure 3). These very years represent something of a plateau in the production of graduate degrees. The backlog of the war years has been worked off, and the crop of wartime babies who are about to become the "college bulge" will not reach the graduate school until the mid-sixties.

During the post-war period, one reason for the increase stemmed directly from that basic ingredient of educational growth: money. Graduate study received increasing support in this period from the Federal government—directly in fellowship funds and through the GI Bill, indirectly in research grants, housing loans, and other funds. The whole enterprise could not have prospered as it has without that support. Here it is necessary only to point out a simple but crucial fact: namely, that such funds were forthcoming because the graduate school had become a highly important institution from the standpoint of the national security.

As we shall see, this growth was handled not only by the traditional universities but by the newer entrants into graduate work. In 1940, about 100 institutions gave the doctorate and about 300 the Master's; in 1958 the figures were 175 and 569. There are a number of reasons for this development: the pressure of enrollments; the certification and promotional policies in the public school systems that encourage or even "force" teachers into graduate programs; the colonization of the underdeveloped institutions by ambitious products of the developed ones who then seek to make the colony a competitor of the mother university; the need to have graduate students as research and teaching assistants, partly in order to get and hold senior staff; the vanity, pride, and legitimate aspirations of institutions.

Once a university undertakes doctoral work seriously, it does not give it up again: the only drop-outs in this century have been the colleges giving cheap doctorates in the very first years. Just as the way for the academic man to get ahead was to earn the doctorate, the way for an institution to get ahead was to offer it. "There is no man who does not need to climb." Neither, apparently, are there many institutions—and in our educational system, climbing means getting into the big league of graduate, and especially doctoral, study.

Besides the increases in number of students and of institutions there was also an increase in the number of fields in which doctoral training was offered, thus reflecting further the expansion and proliferation of knowledge. If every distinctive name for the field of award is counted, there are now well over 550 "fields" in which the doctorate is awarded by one or another institution (but only one institution in almost 400 of them). This figure is directly comparable to the 149 fields in 1916 to 1918. Actually, of course, the number of "real" fields is much smaller: depending on how a "field" is defined, one gets between 60 and 80—all the others are variants, offshoots, or combinations.

The central fields in the arts and sciences are much the same as forty years ago: chemistry (doctorates now offered in about 110 institutions as against 20 in 1916 to 1918); physics (90); psychology, mathematics, history, and English (75 to 85 each); economics (65); philosophy (50);

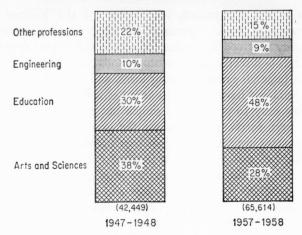

FIG. 4. Distribution of Master's degrees, by field. (*Source: Office of Education.*)

and so on. Similarly, the fields offered by particular institutions doubled in these decades: from an average of about 25 to 30 in the major institutions to about 55 to 60 in each of them.

The fields changed in complexion as well. Perhaps most notably, the professionalization of graduate study continued to grow. As for the Master's degree, even in this single decade, the tide of educational degrees became stronger (Figure 4). Ten years ago, 38% of the degrees were awarded in the arts and sciences as against only 28% in 1957–1958, and education is up by over half again, from 30% to nearly half of all Master's degrees.

The situation at the doctoral level is not so extreme, but there is a clear movement over the long run toward professional fields (Figure 5). From the early years of the century there has been a constant increase in the proportion of professional doctorates. According to present figures, over a third of all the doctoral degrees are in professional fields, and most of this relative growth has come at the expense of the historical center of higher education, the humanities, which have fallen from one-quarter of the total to about one-tenth.

Perhaps more important still, the growth of professionalized graduate work is not restricted to the awarding of doctoral degrees by professional schools and departments. There is more to the matter of professionalization in graduate work than that. If one defines as professional any high-level program that trains for practice or doing rather than for learning or teaching, then a substantial segment of the graduate work offered within some large traditional academic disciplines is professional in character—for example, the training for industrial practice in chemistry, for public administration in political science, or for clinical work in psychology. If such programs are accepted as essentially professional in character though not in label, then not many more than half the doctorates conferred in 1957–1958 were academic.

The debate continued. In the years since the war, there have been many important pronouncements on graduate education, in addition to the regular flow of journal articles, speeches, reports, committee meetings, etc. In 1946 Howard Mumford Jones proposed a double doctorate plan—one for teachers, one for researchers—in his *Education and World Tragedy*. In 1947 appeared the report of the President's Commission on Higher Education that gave a great deal of attention, most of it critical, to the graduate school. In the same year was held the Lake Mohonk Consultation on the Preparation of College Teachers and this was followed by the Poughkeepsie Consultation in 1948, which was in turn followed by the 1949 Chicago Conference sponsored by the American Council on Education and the U.S. Office of Education that produced the title "The Preparation of College Teachers." The Chicago Conference on "Improving College Instruction" was sponsored by the same two agencies in 1950. In the same year appeared an Office of Education Bulletin, *Toward Better College Teaching*.

After a breathing spell, the debate was rekindled in 1955 by the controversial report of the Committee of Fifteen, "The Graduate School Today and Tomorrow." The following year came another conference report issued by the ACE, this one called "Expanding Resources for College Teaching." The year after that appeared the "white paper" of the Committee on Policies in Graduate Education of the AGS and another report on another conference, "Staffing the Nation's Colleges and

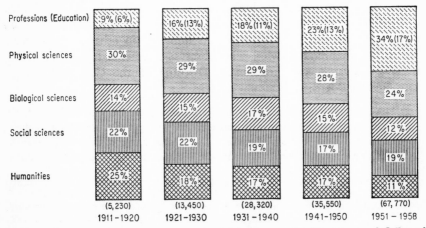

Fig. 5. Distribution of doctoral degrees, by field. (*Source: Wolfle report and Office of Education.*)

Universities," this one sponsored by the U.S. Office. In the past year or so there have been two more reports: the trustees of the Carnegie Foundation for the Advancement of Teaching devoted their annual meeting to "The Education of College Teachers" and the appropriate committee of the ACE issued yet another report on "Graduate Study for Future College Teachers."

Whatever else may be said, the idea that the graduate school has not been subject to scrutiny or criticism or that it has been remote from the mainstream of educational discussion is simply not true. The graduate school may have played its own game over the years, but it has not lacked for coaches, referees, and Monday morning quarterbacks.*

In addition to the standard motives for such discussions, historically tested and honored, there are two specific conditions that have called them forth in such numbers in the past few years. One is the sputnik. Only weeks after the satellite appeared, the report of the AGS committee that was so dramatically critical of the doctorate program was reprinted in full in the *New York Times*. It is hard to believe that this report would have appeared in the *Times* had the Russian satellite not appeared in the skies, especially since the document had only been submitted to the Association and was never approved by it. The other is the college bulge—the concern with what will happen to the quality of college teachers under the impact of the expected enrollments of the 1960's. These two pressures push in different directions, thus increasing the tension within the system: the sputnik effect calls for more emphasis on research and research training, the college bulge effect for more emphasis on the preparation of college teachers.

The result of all this has been to reinforce the position of the university as the leader of American higher education. Not only does it award twice as many baccalaureates as the liberal arts college, not to mention higher degrees, but it is increasing its influence in other ways as well. According to Frank Bowles, who observes American higher education from an advantageous position as Director of the College Entrance Examination Board:

> The university, responding to new problems, has expanded its influence along with its size and has now replaced the undergraduate college as the dominant unit in higher education. . . . Dominance in this case means domination of educational thought, the setting of academic patterns, de-

---

* The graduate school, of course, is not alone in being subject to such scrutiny. One of the marks of American education as a whole is the extent to which it is studied, surveyed, reviewed, committeed, and commissioned. The reports on secondary or collegiate levels are too numerous to mention But in the same period covered by this list, there were at least two full-scale reviews of theological education, four of business education, three of legal education, and five of medical education—most of them of much broader scope than the items listed.

termination of intellectual goals, the capacity to create an atmosphere of stability or of change.

The Legacy

In less than seventy-five years, the modern university, led by the graduate school, has come from nowhere to the position of leadership in American higher education. We should not forget how young the institution of graduate study was by World War II—hardly more than two generations old. Many of the students of the first graduate professors were themselves still active in 1940 and were only then beginning to turn the system over to *their* students. In that brief period, the graduate school had to accommodate itself to two large pressures: numbers of students, expansion of knowledge.

Along the way, graduate education picked up a number of distinguishing and durable characteristics. Tradition and precedent are important in all human institutions and by no means least in the conduct of educational affairs. It makes almost no sense to talk about present conditions as though they did not develop out of the history presented here, or as though reform of the present and future were not severely limited by the past.

The internal organization of the graduate school has, for the most part, been taken for granted by the graduate faculty—no matter what it happened to be. The intermingling of graduate and undergraduate students, the single administrative tent for all graduate fields, the relative weakness of the graduate dean, the grading and examining system, the German graduate school on top of the English college—by and large, all of these have been accepted as normal. It was as though only two organizational arrangements were considered natural by most members of graduate faculties: the one in force at the institution where they took their doctorate and the one in force at the institution where they taught. Since the two were usually of the same type—if not the same institution—no real question of appropriateness arose.

Underlying the entire enterprise and aggravating all other problems was the advancement of knowledge itself, with its inevitable specialization and proliferation. Some traditional fields were broken apart, like philosophy, and some new ones came into being, like biochemistry. Dean Woodbridge's observation was probably as true thereafter as it was when he first made it in 1912: "This fact (the growth of knowledge) is affecting university methods and university procedures far more profoundly than is generally recognized."

As for the highest degree itself, it is hard to exaggerate the importance attached to the Ph.D. As Richard Hofstadter has said, "The exceptional regard that exists for the Ph.D. in academic circles, where presumably most persons know better, has never been fully explained." The degree itself has often been in the way of proposed reforms; for example, a broadened and enriched Master's has never caught on as a degree for college teachers mainly because it was not the doctorate, and the two-track system at the doctoral level has sooner or later come up against the question of which track would get the Ph.D. and what, then, the other would get. "Everyone" has wanted the Ph.D.—other academic doctorates have always stood markedly lower in prestige—and no one has wanted formal distinctions within it. Given the range of fields in which it is awarded and the range of institutions that award it, there are inevitable distinctions made among degree holders—but they are made informally. There can be no question: despite all the easy jokes about the Ph.D., the "magic" of the degree is among the most important legacies in the entire system.

Another source of stability in the system has been the primacy of research. If there has been one dominant call to reform made to the graduate schools from the start, it has been to give more explicit attention to the preparation of college teachers. If there has been one dominant objective at the doctorate level, it has been research and training for research. The graduate school brought research into the universities, protected and fought for it there, and would not lower its claims. Partly this has been the victory of science; even science's term "research" has won out over "scholarship" or "learning" as the central undertaking. Moreover, it is important to recognize that the very people who have succeeded at the research game are running the show in the graduate schools, and it is hardly to be expected that they would voluntarily give priority to what the others want, i.e., those who have gone into college teaching. Here even more directly than in other professions, the recipients of one generation become the setters and guardians of requirements in the next, so that each new group of aspirants has to jump the hurdles "I had to face."

As a result, the graduate school has always been accused of abnormal resistance to change by those who had a reform to introduce. President Jessup of the Carnegie Foundation said in 1944 that it was "in a rut," President Keppel of the Carnegie Corporation called it "the sacred cow in American education," Professor Richardson likened it in 1930 to the prohibition amendment: anyone criticizing it was considered immoral, incompetent, and governed by questionable motives.

If the graduate school has not changed enough to suit its critics, it has not been through lack of controversy. The legacy also includes the debate itself. Like many other such debates, this one perhaps did not settle much. Some early problems of graduate study were simply outgrown, as with the internal migration of students or the relationships with foreign universities; and some were resolved by events, as with the publication of the dissertation, where printing costs largely settled the matter, or the Master's thesis, where the pressure of numbers was decisive.

Not many seem to have been settled by argument and agreement. The same issues have always been discussed, largely in the same way. What does the Ph.D. really mean? What is the place of the Master's? How can standards be maintained under the pressure of numbers? Why aren't the students better qualified? Why not give the preparation of college teachers more consideration relative to research, especially since college teaching is the prime occupation of the graduates? What can be done to counter the growing specialization of the disciplines? How can the doctoral dissertation be domesticated? How many institutions should offer doctoral work? And all of these must still be reckoned with today. *Plus ça change, plus c'est la même chose.*

The fact that the debate has been unchanging and indecisive does not necessarily imply that it should not be taken seriously. But how are we to explain the repetitiveness of the debate?

There are a number of explanations. Inherent in the system of higher education are some direct and lasting conflicts of interest—e.g., college teaching versus university research—and they give rise to the same issues from one academic generation to the next. The debate may remain the same but the debaters are different—and not all of them know how much of what they are saying has been said before. There has been no real way to measure the quality of the product, and disagreements could more easily be aired in the absence of the facts. From time to time new conditions have arisen that required the reappraisal of current practice and conception, as with the recurring "crises" of numbers.

But perhaps an historical function of the debate is not, and should not be, to find the "one best way" but rather to reveal and maintain a necessary tension and equilibrium within the system. Some of the central issues of graduate study—research versus teaching, service versus standards, professional versus academic training—are in fact insoluble when posed that way. The real question is not which side of the dichotomy is right, but rather how much of one to pay for how much of the other, or still more, how to keep them in a harmonious and productive relationship. From this point of view, the historical debate can be seen as another example of the operation of the academic pendulum. Let the pendulum swing too far in one direction and the advocates of the opposing point of view seek to reverse the direction or at least to retard the rate of movement.

But such observations, while they may help to explain the debate, do not settle any of the issues. In the end, the lessons of history are ambiguous. There are those who claim that so little has been done to meet the criticisms that naturally they have had to be made over and over again. On the other side are those who believe that the critics have simply been wrong, that they have been only the dissident minority found in any large system, and that cooler and wiser heads have been prevailing.

Whatever the case, this much at least is clear: what has happened in graduate education not only sets the stage for what is happening, but determines a good deal of the plot and selects many of the cast of characters as well. We cannot close our eyes to what has happened, or pretend it away; but if we can read its lessons correctly, we may be able to put it to the service of the present and the future.

PART TWO

The Present

The historical travelogue through the remote and recent past now lands us squarely in the present situation of graduate education. Whereas in the preceding section I tried to picture the development of graduate study in this country in broad brush strokes, in this section I mean to analyze the details of the important topics now in active controversy: to set out the problems and values involved and to marshal the arguments and the facts.

As we have seen, almost everything connected with graduate study has been considered a problem or issue at some time, by someone. I plan to take up the major matters of current importance under four major headings:

> Purposes
> Institutions
> Students
> Programs

All the questions worth discussing can find a place somewhere in this series: for example, the teacher-researcher issue under Purposes, the national distribution of graduate study under Institutions, the recruitment problem under Students, the duration of the doctorate under Programs.

Needless to say, these issues have a way of overlapping one another, since the fabric is all of one piece, but for purposes of clarity and precision it is necessary to deal with them one at a time. In the final section on Conclusions and Recommendations, I shall try to put the puzzle back together and show how the pieces fit together.

THE PURPOSES

The issue of purpose has been under discussion from the start. What is graduate training *for?* This has been a constant question, particularly from those who were dissatisfied with the current answer and who wanted one that was "clearer"—usually a euphemism for one more congenial to their own views. At bottom, this question of purpose has usually come down to the priority assigned to the preparation of college teachers as against the training of researchers, and that will be at the heart of my inquiry into the issue here. Besides that, there are questions about the professional or academic character of graduate study and about the uniformity or diversity in what the Doctor's degree "means," but they are subordinate to, as well as involved in, the central question of the teacher or the researcher.

The College Teacher Problem

If one criticism of graduate study has been made more frequently and intensely than any other, it is that the graduate school has not done right by the college teacher. The argument is especially prominent during periods of growth or anticipated growth in college enrollments, as in the 1920's and at present. Most of the recent conferring and pronouncing about graduate study has started, and usually ended, with this issue. Several conferences of the past decade, from Lake Mohonk in 1947 to the ACE of 1959, have centered on the graduate school and the supply of college teachers. The President's Commission of 1947 spanked the graduate schools quite hard on this issue: ". . . seriously inadequate . . . single-minded emphasis on the research tradition . . . not fully aware of opportunities and obligations . . . forcing all students into the mold of a narrow specialism . . ." and culminated in the peroration: "It is said that an entrenched priesthood will never reform itself; American graduate school faculties must demonstrate the falsity of this axiom." *

The Committee of Fifteen was similarly critical. The Carnegie Foundation report was no less concerned but was more judicious in recognizing that "the conflict is a real one. The graduate school is uniquely the place where individuals may be introduced to the highest standards of

---

* Although it is something of an *ad hominem* argument, it is worth noting, I think, that the authors of such reports and the participants in such conferences are *not* primarily from the liberal arts colleges themselves (not that college teaching does not belong to the universities too). Only four of the Committee of Fifteen were from the colleges, only four of the eighteen academic members of the Carnegie trustees, only five of thirty-nine participants in the 1958 ACE conference. Many of the more vocal critics of the graduate school on this score are university people who disapprove

scholarly investigation. It is also the primary producer of college teachers. It is inevitable that there should be some conflict between the two objectives." Whatever the particulars, however, on one central point there is agreement: this is A Big Problem confronting American education today.

What precisely is the problem? According to the critics, it is three-fold:

First, it is a matter of *policy:* the graduate school has wrongly given higher priority to research and research training as against preparation for college teaching.

Second, it is a matter of *program:* the graduate school is not selecting the right students in the first place and then not training them correctly. As to the latter, the program lacks (*a*) sufficient breadth and (*b*) sufficient training in teaching.

Third, it is a matter of *numbers:* the graduate school is not training enough people to staff the colleges in the next years of the expected "bulge" in enrollment.

There are other criticisms, and many variants on these, but as I read the literature, this is what it mainly comes down to. Clearly the programmatic and numerical problems are themselves intertwined—it would be no trick to get *enough* of *something*—but it is necessary to look at them separately in order to handle the complexities involved.

THE QUESTION OF POLICY

To begin with, the graduate school is now a multipurpose institution. It may not have been so in the beginning, but it became that some decades ago and it has become more so with the passage of the years, so that today the very range of the calls upon the graduate school is at the center of many of its problems. And the differing requirements of the various fields of graduate study complicate the matter still further.

What are the major tasks of the graduate school? In the questionnaire to the graduate faculties, I asked them, field by field, "to rank the major tasks in order of their importance," with this result:

---

of the prestige attached to specialized research training as against general education at the undergraduate level, or who dislike seeing the research-oriented faculty running the show, or who are themselves dissatisfied with the present character of their disciplines and what passes for scholarship therein. Some observers believe that such critics do not really know what is going on in the colleges or how the colleges feel about the matter, and some go so far as to suggest that the critics are trying to use the liberal arts college as a lever with which to change things they do not like in the universities. At the same time, it is only fair to add that there are in the graduate school a number of forceful proponents of the case for the fuller preparation of college teachers.

Average rank (1 = high, 5 = low)

	Phys-ical sci-ences	Bio-log-ical sci-ences	Social sci-ences	Hu-man-ities	Total Arts & Sci-ences	Profes-sional fields
Training college teachers	2.8	2.5	2.2	1.4	2.4	2.5
Training research scholars	2.0	2.1	2.0	2.7	2.1	2.7
Training professional practitioners	3.5	4.1	3.8	3.4	3.7	3.0
Doing basic research	2.5	2.5	2.9	3.5	2.8	3.4
Doing applied research	4.2	3.7	4.1	4.0	4.0	3.4
Total no. of cases (calcu-lated only for those rank-ing all five tasks)	260	178	301	110	849	463

Note: Here and throughout, these broad divisions include the usual disciplines; on the borderlines, geography and statistics are with the physical sciences, psychology and history with the social sciences, fine and applied arts with the humanities. The professional fields include education, engineering, agriculture, business, et al. (but not medicine or law).

Training research scholars and training college teachers emerge as the central tasks across the board, although basic research is considered more important than training college teachers in the physical sciences and equally important in the biological. Only in the humanities is the preparation of the college teacher clearly considered as the No. 1 priority.

Despite the fact that some of the tasks (e.g., training researchers and doing research) are not necessarily in conflict for the time of the faculty, the resources of the university, or the attention given to students, there still remains a sizable amount of disagreement with this assignment of priorities. Many more disagree with the first-place choice than agree; even in the humanities, over a quarter do not give first rank to the prepa-ration of college teachers. So to the extent that there is some conflict among the various objectives that cannot be resolved simply by the verbal combination of "the scholar-teacher," then we must face up to the fact that there are substantial disagreements within the graduate faculty on what graduate study is primarily for. That is not necessarily bad, but it is so.

Certainly the teacher and the researcher are in the center of the stage. What of the tussle between them? I went on in the survey to ask the graduate faculty this two-pronged question: "Consider the balance in doctoral study in your field, as between preparing for teaching and preparing for research. What is it now and what should it be?"

	Is now			
	More for research	*More for teaching*	*About equivalent*	*Can't say*
Physical sciences	79%	6	12	3
Biological sciences	74%	6	18	2
Social sciences	63%	15	18	4
Humanities	53%	23	20	4
Arts & sciences	68%	12	17	3
Professional fields	58%	21	17	4
	Should be			
Physical sciences	60%	5	28	7
Biological sciences	48%	4	45	3
Social sciences	37%	16	43	4
Humanities	25%	32	39	4
Arts & sciences	43%	14	38	5
Professional fields	32%	19	42	7

So preparation for research is now in the saddle in all fields, even in the humanities. But also in all fields, the present emphasis is now considered to be too much; and substantial proportions of the faculty, especially outside the physical sciences, say that they would like to redress the balance somewhat but, except for the humanists, not all the way. Research training still remains, outside the humanities (and still more strongly, education), as the dominant objective. The general feeling seems to be: more attention to teaching, but not so much as to shift the balance.

The attraction of research is not only greater in the more prestigious fields—the arts and sciences as against the professions, and the natural sciences within them—but also, and perhaps more importantly, in the more prestigious institutions: *

	Top 12 institutions	*Other AGS members, plus*	*Other universities*
Balance is more on research	72%	67%	62%
Balance should be more on research	55%	42%	33%

Their programs are more research-oriented now, and the faculty is more satisfied that they should be (i.e., they "lose" less from *is* to *should be*). And as the leading institutions, as well as large ones, they are more likely to lead.

A similar picture emerges from the faculty's responses to a more

* The basis of this classification is presented in detail in the section on Institutions.

sharply phrased proposition, but one not unrepresentative of much of the present criticism of the graduate school:

The graduate schools unduly stress research and research training at the cost of properly preparing college teachers

	Agree	Disagree	Can't say
Physical sciences	23%	62	15
Biological sciences	31%	55	14
Social sciences	31%	56	13
Humanities	37%	47	16
Arts & sciences	30%	56	14
Professional fields	44%	38	18
Top 12 universities	27%	56	17
Other AGS universities, plus	33%	53	14
Other universities	40%	43	17

Thus even the humanists do not quite agree with this indictment; only the professions do, with education strongly leading the way. Again, the top institutions are most opposed. As a group, about 35% of the graduate faculty agrees with the statement, and the figure is essentially the same for the graduate deans and the recent recipients of the doctorate. It is the college presidents who differ: about three-fourths of them feel that the graduate school is overdoing research at their expense, and thus the issue is sharply joined.

It is apparent that there is considerable disagreement among the people most concerned with what the graduate school does—the college presidents as against the graduate faculty and deans, the arts and sciences as against the professional fields, the physical scientists as against the humanists, the better or more prestigious institutions as against the lesser. Let us follow the argument, and the facts, a little further and see where they lead.

THE MARKET-RESEARCH ARGUMENT. The position underlying the programmatic and the numerical aspects of the problem is at basis what I would call the market-research argument. That argument is to prepare the product directly for its subsequent use.

Most doctorates go into college teaching and few make real contributions in research, so the graduate school should organize its training accordingly: that is the essence of the argument, and it is not a new one though it is always newly made. Professor Richardson of Dartmouth said it in so many words in 1924:

> The graduate school is utilized mainly for the training of college teachers and as such occupies a place much the same as other schools for the

training of professional men. . . . The guiding principle . . . is so obvious as to seem almost inane. A school for the training of college teachers should base its instruction on that purpose as its primary motive.

In the mid-forties, Hollis' basis for his suggestions *Toward Improving Ph.D. Programs* was a job analysis of the recipients of the degree in the 1930's: what was needed was "realistic differentiations in doctoral programs based on ascertained differences in job demands," which in the context clearly meant: more attention to college teachers, less to researchers. Only a year or two ago, Dean Hayward Keniston complained about "the anomalous situation that college teaching is the one profession which a man or woman may enter without any specific training for the tasks they are to perform. Schools of law and medicine aim at training lawyers and doctors; graduate schools aim at training in research, not at the preparation of teachers."

Now in so far as such arguments hold, as some come close to doing, that the graduate school should devote itself to the training of college teachers because that is the only place they are trained, to that extent the argument can be dismissed as simply begging the question. That is where they are trained, but it is also the only place where researchers are trained too, and increasingly, as we shall see, some types of practitioners as well. As a matter of fact, it is not quite the *only* place for college teachers, since some teachers colleges are now entering the field, but it *is* the only place for researchers. So college teaching cannot claim priority on that ground alone.

There is the further argument that college teachers are in themselves more important than any alternative product of the graduate school and hence should be given priority. This is such a subjective position, and so open to dispute, that it is seldom made so explicitly though as a belief it must certainly underlie the judgment of many critics. At the least, what with the growing importance of research in our national life in recent years, the argument seems weaker today than it was only a couple of decades ago.

To return to the central theme of the policy question, then, let us inquire into the two basic assumptions made: most do college teaching, few do research. Both of these are factual assertions, and hence amenable to testing by data. What do recipients of the doctorate do?

How Many Teach? To start with teaching, from time to time in the past some data on the employment of doctorates have appeared in the literature. The data have to be pieced together and may not be accurate to the last percentage point, but they are the best available, and, I think, valid for the purpose before us. From them, I have constructed the following picture of the proportions of doctorates who have gone into higher education:

Date	Approximate percentage of employed doctorates in college and university posts	From
Around 1900	70 to 80	Ryan on early doctorates from Johns Hopkins, Chicago, and Clark Walcott on Ph.D. recipients from 1885 to 1904 Chase on early Harvard doctorates Haggerty on early Chicago doctorates
Late 1920's	70 to 75	John on a sample of doctorates after 1924 Haggerty on Ph.D.'s from 7 major universities
1930's	65	Hollis on Ph.D.'s of the 1930's
1958	60	NRC data on all doctorates

Two important points emerge at once: first, holders of the doctorate are not now employed overwhelmingly in colleges and universities, but only a slight majority of them; and second, the long-run trend is running against the employment of doctorates in higher education. On the overall picture, then, the market argument, that was not persuasive enough to change the situation in the past, is even weaker today. If it was a good argument earlier, it is not as good now; if it was bad then, it is worse now.

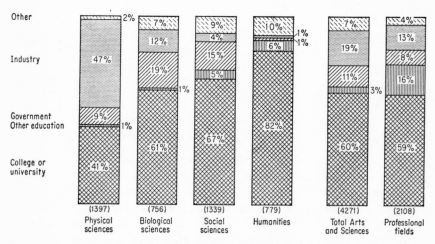

FIG. 6. Type of employment of 1958 recipients of the doctorate. (*Source: NRC data.*)

There are, of course, large differences by field: twice as large a proportion of humanists now go into higher education as do physical scientists (Figure 6). But it is precisely the scientific fields, in which the shortage of college teachers is alleged or expected to be most severe, that would be least subject to the market argument. They are increasingly moving in non-academic directions.

As a matter of fact, this decline in academic employment through the years does not simply reflect the extension of the doctorate to professional fields. The latter, indeed, are holding up in academic employment. It is in the arts and sciences where there are now fewer recipients of the doctorate going into higher education than did only two decades ago—the biological and physical sciences are down eight or nine percentage points, and the social sciences and humanities are down four or five percentage points, according to a comparison between employed doctorates in the 1930's and in 1958:

	Percentage of employed doctorates in academic jobs	
	Hollis data for recipients in the 1930's	*NRC data for recipients in 1958*
Physical sciences	50	42
Biological sciences	71	62
Social sciences	76	72
Humanities	93	88
Professional fields	76	75

At the start, non-academic employment was pretty well limited to the chemist, but now physicists and mathematicians are moving into industry, biologists and psychologists into government, and, while still small, growing numbers of sociologists and economists into economic life. Nor, incidentally, is the attraction outside academic life limited to the salary differential; there are other inducements as well: full time on research, technical assistance, good library and translation services, sabbatical leaves with full salaries, funds for attending professional meetings. As a university scientist observed: "The climate is often more academic there than here." So if one were going to model training on subsequent activity, much of the training in the graduate school, and especially in the sciences (where the problem is presumably most severe), would be directed away from academic teaching, not toward it.

But there is still more to the matter. The argument typically refers to preparation for "college teaching"—by which can be meant (*a*) college and university employment; (*b*) undergraduate teaching, whether in a college or a university; or (*c*) undergraduate teaching in a liberal arts college. The figures above refer to the first of these, but the argument really refers to the third—and there is a big difference between them. About 60% of the current recipients of the doctorate go into "college or university employment" but only 20% go into "undergraduate teaching in a liberal arts college." The rest go into university work, where they have the opportunity, and the ambition, to teach graduate courses for which research training is the *sine qua non*. As a matter of fact, three-fourths of the recent recipients in my sample are already handling graduate courses, within two years of getting the doctorate. Even at this early date, then, only 25 to 30% of the doctorates are undergraduate teachers mainly or entirely. Only in the humanities are they a majority, and then only about 55%.

Nor is the need for research training altogether absent at the college level either. Over a third of the 1957 doctors employed in the liberal arts colleges "teach or supervise" graduate students, typically at the Master's level. When the college presidents were asked whether they were "finding it necessary to develop more research opportunities and facilities for the faculty in order to attract top people in competition with the major universities," 36% said that it was "already true here" and another 46% that it was "not true yet, but probably coming." What is more, over 80% thought the development "a desirable one." Similarly, while only a few of the presidents believed that "the undergraduate teacher needs to be a productive research man (i.e., one who publishes papers in the learned journals) in order to be a good teacher," * almost every one thought that "the research training experience at the doctoral level, and particularly the dissertation, is necessary or desirable for the undergraduate teacher."

The rationale was expressed in typical terms by several of my consultants:

The president of one of the country's best-reputed colleges: "Research opportunities have been made available not in order to compete, but because of our deep feeling of the importance of research in maintaining the highest calibre of undergraduate teaching."

The former president of one of the country's best-reputed universities: "The undergraduate teacher needs scholarly opportunities for his morale and self-respect, and in order to keep from going to seed and becoming a completely routine teacher."

A biologist influential in the development of the undergraduate curriculum in the field: "The teacher shouldn't appear to the student as a professional teacher of his subject, but as a practitioner of it. If all his career eggs are in the instructional basket and he has no private chal-

---

* As contrasted with the graduate faculty, of whom nearly 40% thought he *did*—and more in the sciences and in the better institutions!

lenge, then he will go to hell, and teach old-hat stuff in obsolescent courses."

A university president identified with the problem: "The degree is right because it joins the concept of present knowing and future learning. In spite of all the complaints about the dissertation, the idea is important to good teaching. . . . No new program for preparing college teachers should be allowed to draw a false dichotomy between teaching and research."

So training in research in graduate school gets a firm vote of confidence at the college level, even training *for* it. There too it is wanted and needed.

The relevance of all this for the market argument is clear: if doctoral candidates are to be trained for what they are going to do after getting the degree, then training in research must be provided—yet the "over-emphasis" on research training is precisely what the present doctoral program is being criticized for and what the critics seek to replace.

Here is one of the lags in the debate over graduate study. College teaching, i.e., teaching of undergraduates, once was the major occupation of Ph.D.'s, but no more. As recently as the 1930's, about 60% of those going into academic employment went into colleges; now 60% of them go into universities. Nor have we seen the end of this trend, by any means. There are now twice as many regular faculty members in universities as in liberal arts colleges, well over twice as many Ph.D.'s on the faculty, and almost twice as many students. Since the "college bulge" will be absorbed far more by the universities than by the liberal arts colleges, the ratio will move still more in the direction of the universities. Furthermore, if for no other reason than their competition with the universities for good faculty members, the research emphasis in the colleges will grow too. Add to that the increasing national importance of research—not simply with respect to the national security but to a whole range of spheres from health to the economy and from technology to psychological and social well-being—and this seems an inopportune time for cutting down research training in the name of the undergraduate teacher.

Hence, the first assumption underlying the market argument—that since most recipients of the doctorate do undergraduate teaching, the research training of the graduate school is misplaced—does not seem to stand up.

How Many Do Research? I turn now to the second assumption: few do research. The argument is a familiar one. The Carnegie report referred to "some critics who have attacked the whole notion of research training implicit in the dissertation by pointing out that a high percentage of

Ph.D.'s do not make any published contribution after the thesis." In his vigorous attack on "The Ph.D. Stretch-out," Benjamin Wright, then President of Smith College, concluded that "it does seem reasonably clear that for most of those taking the Ph.D., the emphasis upon research in the degree has not led to productive scholarship, so far as that is evidenced by publications."

Now the debate cannot get far until we decide what par is or ought to be. How many is "few"? What is "a high percentage"? Does "most" mean 51% or more? This is a simple, even mundane, point. But until a figure is put in place of the vaguer qualitative terms, it is hard to join the issue properly. President Wright reported that "none of these studies [the ones he had seen] gives a higher estimate than 50 percent, while several indicate that not more than one-fourth of those who earn the Ph.D. ever publish anything which can be called research . . ." and he went on to speak of "the meager results obtained in what appeared to be the majority of instances."

Leaving aside the important consideration of the collective contribution of a relatively few, what is the magic number that would justify the research training given for the doctorate from this standpoint? No one knows, of course; that is the kind of judgment everyone must make for himself. Certainly those most immediately concerned have made the judgment: about 80% of the deans, faculty, and recent recipients (and even more from industry!) disagree with the statement that "doctoral training for research is inefficient and wasteful because so few recipients of the degree become productive researchers in the field."

Specifically, how many recipients of the doctorate have published in recent years? Here are some data that speak to the issue, even if they do not settle it.* I checked through the standard bibliographies and abstracts of nine disciplines to see how many recipients of the doctorate in 1947–1948 had published in subsequent years, how much they had published, and whether the publications seemed to derive directly from their dissertations. The argument sometimes runs to the effect that Ph.D.'s don't make enough "real" contributions or that their research is "trivial." As for the quality of what is published, I have only the fact that the titles were included in scholarly bibliographical services. Here are the results:

* I am not suggesting here that the subsequent publication record of the recipients of the doctorate is the only or the best justification for research training. As the Carnegie trustees pointed out, "published contributions are only one desirable consequence of research training. Other consequences are scholarly judgment, critical acuity, knowledge in depth, and a capacity to teach in an inspired fashion." Another that is particularly topical at the present time is the contribution of the sciences to the national security. Another, perhaps the basic one from which the others flow, is the long-range development of man's knowledge of himself and his universe.

	Published one or more titles	Published one or more titles other than the dissertation	Average number of publications per recipient	Publications with single authors
Chemistry	89%	87%	6.1	17%
Biology	86	77	5.7	30
Physics	82	77	4.9	33
Psychology	77	72	5.4	53
Mathematics	68	61	4.0	85
Philosophy	63	59	2.8	95
English	61	57	2.2	97
Education	56	51	2.4	80
History	34	19	0.5	96

Except for history—where the book is more likely to be the unit of publication—a majority in each field have published in the first eight or nine years after receiving the doctorate (and almost three-fourths of the total in these fields that make up two-thirds of all doctorates). Since more will publish, an increment of about 2% or so a year for the next few years over the entire group, the record will show fifteen years after the doctorate that from 80 to 90% of all recipients in the natural sciences will have published something of sufficient stature besides their dissertation to warrant inclusion in the scholarly bibliographical sources; more than three-fourths in psychology, more than two-thirds in mathematics, philosophy, and English, over half in education, and over a fourth in history. The situation in related fields is probably similar.

Clearly the "data disciplines" (chemistry, biology, physics, psychology) show up better than the "word disciplines" (history, education, English, philosophy), with mathematics, which is not quite either, in between. But again, except for history, the differences are not particularly pronounced, especially when the character of the fields is taken into account, including the tendency to joint authorship in the sciences. There is a strong inverse relationship between the percentage publishing, field by field, and the percentage of titles with single authorship. The break between the "data" and "word" discipline stands out most sharply, and the results make the record of fields like philosophy and English even more remarkable.

Considering the teaching load and the new family obligations many of these people carry, the lack of interest with which many began the training necessary to get their "admission badge" for college teaching, the inevitable mis-selections and mis-training occurring in any complicated human enterprise, and even the normal amount of dross found in scholarly publication—all in all, the score on publication is quite high.*

* In fact, a friend suggests that perhaps *too many* publish too much—under the pressure of the "publish or perish" dictum—rather than the other way around, thus adding only bulk to the scholarly literature.

Here again, a few other considerations must be added. The first is the growth of organized research activity *within* the universities. This has resulted partly from increases in knowledge and increased specialization of knowledge, partly from the national need and the availability of Federal funds. Whatever the cause, however, it has meant the emergence of a number of full-time academic researchers. The number is already substantial, according to figures collected by the Office of Education: over 32,000 in 1958 or over 10% of the resident instructional staff. Most of these researchers are in the sciences and engineering, though some research institutes are beginning to appear in the social sciences too (for example, the Institute for Personality Assessment and Research at Berkeley, the Bureau of Applied Social Research at Columbia, the Institute for Social Research at Michigan, the National Opinion Research Center at Chicago). This is largely a post-war development—there were only 6,600 in 1939–1940, or about 5% of the staff then, most of them in agricultural research—and although the number involved will be limited by the instructional needs of the institutions, such centers will certainly continue to provide an important employment outlet for doctoral recipients in some fields.

The second consideration is the growth of organized research activity *outside* the universities, in industrial laboratories and governmental installations. The organization in this country that employs most Ph.D.'s today is not Harvard or Yale or Illinois or Michigan. It is Du Pont. Furthermore, General Electric has more than twice as many Ph.D.'s on its staff as Princeton, Shell has more than MIT, Union Carbide or Eastman or IBM has about as many as Northwestern or Cal Tech.* As a matter of fact, industrial firms like these probably employ more Ph.D.'s today than all the liberal arts colleges in the country. As we have seen, non-academic employment in professional fields has held steady over the past twenty years, but it is precisely in the arts and sciences that it has increased. Most of the industrial firms I queried said that they expected the trend in employment of graduate degree holders to be "moderately up" over the next five years and almost none thought it would go down.† Research training is of course the desideratum.

It appears, then, that both of the major assumptions of the market argument are faulty: fewer than "most" are engaged in college teaching and more than a "few" publish research and scholarly titles. As a result, I conclude that the policy argument cannot in itself justify a radical change in the priorities presently assigned in the graduate training pro-

---

* The Federal government has more than any of these, about as many as the top 10 universities put together.

† As one industrial representative frankly said: "In the future, we expect to hire more and more graduates with advanced degrees, if for no other reason than many of the better men are available only at this level."

gram away from research training and toward the preparation of college teachers.

THE QUESTION OF PROGRAM

But that does not settle the matter, by any means. The critics of the graduate school on this score have more detailed complaints to make. Beyond the market argument over policy, there seem to be three programmatic criticisms made of the graduate school from the standpoint of preparing college teachers: (1) mistaken admission policy, so that the wrong students—or at least, not all the right ones—are allowed into the training system in the first place; (2) lack of sufficient breadth in the training program; and (3) lack of proper training in how to teach.

When I asked the college presidents "which three [of eight] qualities are most important for a college teacher," their answers were clear:

Knowledge of subject matter of his discipline	98%
Knowledge of how to teach	82
Interest in young people	68

Not another item got as much as 20% of the vote, including the one referring to breadth, "interest in fields outside his own" (14%). The candidate's interest in young people is a personal matter, not subject to graduate instruction, and hence is involved in the issue of student selection. The other two are directly connected with the graduate school's program of training: the what and the how.

SELECTION OF STUDENTS. According to this argument, the graduate school, in its dominating concern with research, admits students primarily or exclusively on the basis of one criterion: intellectual capability. That criterion may not be measured or judged well, and there are inevitable mistakes, but nonetheless the intent is to admit only those applicants who have the ablest, keenest minds. Now, this may be best for the advancement of knowledge, but it is not necessarily best for the advancement of college teaching. For that task, other qualities are needed: an interest in young people, the readiness to be a good citizen in the academic and local community, a pleasing personality, a better-than-average possession of the moral virtues. In so far as these do not come into play in the admission policies of the graduate schools, which is the first screening on the way to an academic post, to that extent the colleges subsequently lose out. So the argument goes.

Thirty-five years ago, a college president publicly asked the graduate schools to do something about the religious beliefs and the social manners of their students (Raymond Hughes before the AAC in 1924). Today, it takes a hearty critic indeed to argue in public against the sole use of intellectual capability as the criterion of admission, so fully accepted is it in academic circles. Occasionally, however, it is done, and there have been some calls, and some efforts, to devise "more adequate means of judging . . . the traits other than intelligence which characterize good teachers," as Oliver Carmichael said in a Carnegie Foundation report. More often, personal interviews are used for the purpose, as notably in the Woodrow Wilson fellowship program—and even there, of course, they are not *admission* interviews.

The question is really a part of two larger questions. The first goes to the central purpose of graduate study, and if that is conceived as research training and the advancement of knowledge, the issue of criteria other than intellectual for admission is no issue at all. The second goes to the means. Unlike medical or law schools, the graduate schools typically screen students more fully *after* admission than before. As part of its screening during the course of the program of study, the department or professor judges the candidate's suitability for teaching in general and the desired qualities in particular. This may not always be done well in the individual case, but the rationale is clear enough: admit by intelligence and screen for other qualities later.*

In the general argument about the preparation of college teachers, this is not a matter of major contention; almost no one really argues against the primacy of intelligence. Because of the reasons cited, most people are willing to leave the other qualities to subsequent selection rather than initial admission. In the end, the question is academic anyway: as we shall see, virtually everyone who applies to a graduate school gets into one, somewhere.

Hence, the answer to the question of how to get more people who are personally qualified for college teaching is the same as the one that would be given if the question concerned getting qualified people for academic administration or professional practice or anything else: get more good students. I shall deal with this problem in detail when I consider the matter of recruitment to the graduate school. The particular solution for college teachers is inseparable, I think, from the general one: if the graduate school gets more intellectually able students, it will have more who are qualified for and interested in each type of post for which it trains people.

The other two programmatic points are of greater urgency, if one can judge from the amount and intensity of the debate. As a summary of the criticism, consider this quotation from the Fund for the Advance-

* However the selection is done, the graduate school does get higher IQ's in its student body. According to the data brought together in the Wolfle report, graduate students in the arts and sciences have a median intelligence score about five points higher than college graduates and doctoral recipients are about twelve points higher. Half the Ph.D.'s have IQ scores equaled by only 7% of the population at large.

ment of Education, the convener of the Committee of Fifteen and an organization noted for its attention to the "college teacher problem":

> In one respect the situation as regards preparation for college teaching is the reverse of that for public school teaching. If the latter has tended to overdo methods at the expense of subject matter, the former has tended to concentrate on subject matter specialization to the neglect of teaching competence. It oversimplifies the matter to some extent, yet perhaps not too much, to say that the ideal of the scholar-teacher has suffered in our graduate schools, on the one hand, from too narrow a view of scholarship and, on the other, from an almost complete disregard of preparation for teaching.

As in all such matters, we must inquire into both desirability and feasibility.

THE PROBLEM OF BREADTH. This issue touches closely on the very conception of what graduate training is for. Is it to produce the man of wisdom and broad cultivation or the man of specialized skill? "More breadth" is a frequent cry, coupled with the derogation of "undue," "narrow," or "over-" specialization—the plain noun almost never appears by itself any more. And again the issue is not a new one: Dean Woodbridge of Columbia deplored "proficiency rather than scholarship" in 1912 and President Bowman of Johns Hopkins termed this the "most important" of the graduate school's problems in 1939.

In the first place, it is often difficult or even impossible to learn from the critics how broad "breadth" is supposed to be—except that it should be "as broad as possible," which of course it always is. Is it enough for an historian to know colonial history, or American, or modern European, or does he have to know the Middle Ages too, or the ancient world, or the Far East, or perhaps something of economics and political science? Should a psychologist cover experimental and physiological and personality and social and applied psychology, or should he know something of sociology too? How many fields of English literature make for a "broad" training, or is some philosophy needed too? The term is an attractive one—deceptively so; the problems arise only when it is specified, for what is depth to me may be narrowness to you and what is breadth to you may be superficiality to me.

This issue of breadth ties up with other issues of educational policy. For example, those who approve of survey or survey-type courses at the undergraduate level tend to want breadth at the graduate level. Those who value general education for undergraduates more highly than specialized study tend to want breadth; so do those who are particularly concerned with the teaching process, and those who subscribe to objectives other than the development of intellect. The smaller and poorer institutions tend to want breadth, so that fewer faculty members can cover a wide range of subjects.

The direct participants are split over the issue, though not evenly: they defend the present level of specialization in graduate training, though with little desire for any more, but at the same time they are somewhat concerned about the plight of wisdom in graduate training: *

		Graduate deans	Graduate faculty	Recent recipients
Doctoral programs are too specialized and narrow	Agree	23%	26%	24%
	Disagree	58	57	58
Doctoral programs are insufficiently specialized	Agree	3%	6%	7%
	Disagree	68	69	67
Doctoral programs stress techniques and skills too much, at the expense of broad understanding, cultivation, and wisdom	Agree	33%	36%	29%
	Disagree	46	49	54

Within the total group of graduate faculty, however, two distinctions must be made: throughout these questions the arts and science people are consistently more friendly to specialization than their professional colleagues, and the faculties of the top institutions more friendly than those of other institutions. Thus the cry for more breadth in graduate study lacks relative support in the sources where it is most needed.

But if more breadth is wanted, why isn't it provided? First, there are a few facts of life to be faced:

1. The doctoral program cannot take "too long." Already many people are concerned with "the Ph.D. stretch-out" and are seeking ways to shorten the training period, not lengthen it. Covering more material in the same amount of time makes for less thorough training. Yet:

2. Thoroughness of training is a prime desideratum. If in training for the doctorate the faculty has to choose between thoroughness over a lesser field and superficiality over a broader one, it will choose the former.

3. The pressure of the subject matter to be covered is toward increased specialization, not toward breadth, because the body of knowledge is constantly growing, and sharply so in some fields. As a result, according to a slight majority of the graduate faculty in the natural and social sciences, "doctoral candidates are now trained in a narrower portion of the total field than they were, say, before World War II." As a consequence, for

* The remaining cases in each tabulation, that would total to 100%, were undecided. In this and subsequent tabulations, unless otherwise stated, the faculty and recent recipient groups include both the arts and sciences and professional fields (i.e., education, engineering, agriculture, etc.). I distinguish between them wherever the differences are sharp or of particular interest, as in the text here. ("Recent recipients," of course, consists of the recipients of the doctorate in 1957 who responded to my survey.)

example, the place of the minor in doctoral study is being steadily diminished.

4. The research experience represented by the doctoral dissertation cannot be given up since it is a necessary ingredient of doctoral training, and research requires specialization.

5. The traditional disciplines—chemistry, psychology, history, mathematics, English, economics, philosophy, and the others—are the central units around which the undergraduate curriculum is organized now and will be for as far ahead as we can see. According to the college presidents, less than 10% of the teaching at their institutions is done "outside the discipline in which the instructor received his highest earned degree."

Given these considerations, it is hard to know where the time for further breadth can be found, either within or among disciplines.

A number of deliberate attempts have been made to achieve more breadth at the doctoral level, and many people are definitely sympathetic to the idea:

	Graduate deans	Graduate faculty	Recent recipients
Develop more interdepartmental and similar programs, as a way of broadening doctoral study	72%	69%	76%

Here again the arts and sciences and the better institutions are somewhat less convinced, and some respondents no doubt favor such programs as a way to shift the burden of breadth away from their own disciplines. About two-thirds of the college presidents also vote for "doctoral programs in broad subject fields . . . as preferable to traditional Ph.D. programs."

Now there are two kinds of interdisciplinary studies: interdisciplinary work by integration and interdisciplinary work by juxtaposition. One is the result of the natural development of the subject itself; the other is more artificial and forced.

As an example of the former, take biology today. In that field there is a trend that some might call a movement toward breadth, in the sense that lines between the disciplines are becoming dim and blurred. Botanists, zoologists, biochemists, and physiologists are moving back and forth among the traditional departments as a result of recent developments in the subject that focus attention on similar or closely related sets of problems. In a sense, it is greater breadth—the substitution of "biology" for the former group of specific disciplines—but it has not meant less specialization. This has been the sort of reduction or compression that can happen in science; a number of subjects have been pulled together by a scientific advance that redefines and reorganizes the subject matter and on the way discards some elements of the former arrangement in the process of surmounting them. This is hardly what is meant by the argument for more breadth in doctoral programs.

As for the "loss" of substance between the disciplines, a sociologist of science, Robert Merton, recently observed with particular regard to the behavioral sciences:

> The danger that important classes of problems will be lost to view as a result of great specialization seems not to have materialized as often as might be supposed. Perhaps this is because the danger, once recognized, has brought about its own counterpoise. One such offset is the growing collaboration among specialists. . . . When the multiple convergence of behavioral scientists upon the same subjects, problems and methods becomes sustained, this gives rise to new interdisciplines. Just as biochemistry, biophysics and chemical embryology emerged from the repeated criss-crossing of separate physical and life sciences, so have new mergers appeared in the behavioral disciplines. Psycho-linguistics, social biology and psychobiology, political sociology and social psychiatry, human ecology, ethnology and sociological history or, at the edges, such a composite as paleopathology are a few among the many bearing witness to this process of intellectual affiliation. In this way, the interstices between the specialties become gradually filled with new cross-disciplinary specialties. . . . For the most part, growing specialization has curbed rather than widened the separatism of the behavioral sciences.

But that process, too, does not satisfy the call for breadth.

Most of the recent experiments in breadth are of the second type: interdisciplinary work by juxtaposition. By and large, they have had an uneasy and not very successful life. Good students are, at the least, leery of taking a degree off the beaten track of the disciplines for fear that they will not find a proper berth when they are finished, and with reason. The better college employers are a little suspicious of the product. Getting and keeping good faculty members together is hard; the centrifugal forces pulling back to the department are strong. Often, after the first enthusiasm is over, the lack of discipline in the new combination begins to show itself. Even the lesser efforts, designed simply to give doctoral candidates a little more acquaintance with one another's fields, have not been notably successful.

The record does not seem impressive. In the past few years, for example, both Minnesota and Harvard have given up their doctoral programs in social science, and for the same reasons: they found few takers among the students, the ones they did get tended to be those students who could not make the grade in a regular department, the faculty was uninterested or even hostile, and the students could not be placed well. Chicago has, and has had for years, a number of broad doctoral programs in humanistic fields but they typically handle only a very few candidates. Syracuse has a large Doctor of Social Science program now nearing its fifteenth year of operation and still growing, but it is not fully accepted at its home base and a large proportion of its products have taken positions primarily concerned with secondary education, i.e., in teachers colleges. The programs for breadth in the humanities at Stanford and Claremont and Emory are perhaps too new to be judged, but the consensus I found in the field, often among sympathetic observers, was somewhat dubious largely on the ground of unavoidable thinness when the subject is spread so far. The efforts at Stanford and Vanderbilt to provide a layer of general education at the graduate level have hardly caught on. Many American Studies programs are considered undisciplined and synthetic, so that the student ends up knowing less than his fellows in American Literature or American History. It is the history of many such experiments that they are not viable once the establishing foundation grant is gone.

Within the disciplines, something along the lines of breadth also goes on. For example, there has been a development in English departments over the past few decades that comes close to what is meant. Formerly, under the influences traced in the historical section, graduate study in English was limited in several ways: nothing beyond the nineteenth century, nothing on American literature, heavy on philology, heavy on early languages such as Old English and Gothic, little on appreciation and criticism. Today the emphasis is on the other side: much more on appreciation and criticism, much more on recent and even contemporary literature, much less on linguistic origins or "scientific" lines of study. In fact, it is so much so that the older generation is wondering whether the pendulum has not swung too far too fast, and whether the *discipline* in literary study is being lost. This movement is presumably the kind of development that the critics of specialization would applaud, but the question now is whether it has gone too far.

The case is not clear, then, that radical innovations on a national scale to achieve more breadth in doctoral training are either desirable or feasible. There is simply a limit to the amount the candidate can know well, given the circumstances and the primary obligations of graduate study. To go beyond such a negative formulation, there is a good deal that remains to be said of a positive character about the virtues of specialization in doctoral training, especially when it is clearly located in time: it comes *after* years of general education—as a graduate dean said to me: "Can't they specialize *now?*"—and it comes *before* a lifetime of independent scholarship. As Dean Moody Prior of Northwestern says:

> Excellence demands specialization. . . . By the time one has reached
> the final and most advanced stage in his formal training, his task has be-

come too concentrated, his purpose too single-minded, to impose side excursions on him in the expectation that he will be taught a lesson which he should have learned long ago.

Despite everything that can be said about the arbitrary character of many of the present disciplines, a broader training does not seem to work well at the doctoral level. Apparently, for the purposes of scholarship, there is no substitute for the discipline of a discipline. Indeed, many leading graduate departments today do not really train their candidates in the discipline as a whole, simply because that is manifestly impossible in the time available; * even mature professors with a full career in the subject do not pretend to know it all. Depth *plus* breadth in graduate study does not seem to be practicable in time or money, and probably not in energy or capability, especially in view of the heavy increases in the amount of knowledge to be deep and broad in, simultaneously.

THE PROBLEM OF TRAINING IN TEACHING. The other major criticism of the graduate school is that it does not train students how to teach. There is substantial agreement with this proposition by every group involved:

Doctoral candidates preparing for college teaching don't get enough training in teaching while in graduate school

	Agree	Disagree	Can't say
Graduate deans	63%	31	6
Graduate faculty	53%	33	14
Recent recipients	47%	29	24
College presidents	77%	14	9

Once more, the differences within the faculty are perhaps instructive. The arts and science people are much less persuaded than are the professionals (about 90% of those in education agree) and the top institutions less than the others. Among the recent recipients, the issue is a standoff in the physical sciences and the humanities, both of which have large numbers of teaching assistantships. But over all, the criticism seems to stick.† However, the recent recipients do reject by 2 to 1 the associated assertion that "the atmosphere in graduate schools tends to lessen

* This goes for the undergraduate level too. The speaker at the 1959 ACE meeting who dealt with the topic reported that "the first, soundest, and virtually unanimously repeated recommendation is that natural science curricula must give up the debilitating fetish of subject matter coverage. It is no longer educationally sound to try to cover the entire spectrum. We must make judicious selection of subject matter."

† In fact, it sticks so hard that it brings into question the value of the teaching assistantship: no matter how long they spent as teaching assistants, the recent recipients are just as likely to accept the criticism. Since even three or more years aren't "enough," one suspects that it isn't considered "training."

If it were, incidentally, much of the argument would fall away. In the training of secondary school teachers, where "method" is taken to be important, about one-sixth the total training time is devoted to such preparation. If the teaching assistantship is counted as "training in teaching," the figure is higher at the doctoral level.

people's interest in and respect for undergraduate teaching" and even the college presidents are split about 50–50 on that.

What is being done, or what can be done, to remedy this apparent deficiency? There are two possible lines of action.

The first has to do with didactic course work, and it raises an issue on which the graduate faculty feels strongly indeed. That is whether anyone can be taught *how* to teach at the level of higher education as distinct from *what* to teach. The modal position of graduate faculty members is that the only, or by far the most important, need is to know one's subject and that there is nothing to teach about teaching at the level of higher education. On the other side, there are those who hold that there is a wealth of knowledge and know-how about the organization of courses, the philosophy of education, the learning process, the interests of young people, the effect of non-intellectual factors upon learning, the structuring of examinations, the housekeeping details of college teaching, etc., that now exist, that can be communicated, and that could improve the classroom performance of most college teachers, especially at the start of their careers.* A middle group holds that in a way both sides are right, but about different things; that is, that knowing the subject is enough to teach it to interested and self-motivated students (e.g., majors or graduate students) but not enough to teach it to other types of students.

Whoever is right, there is high agreement among the arts and sciences faculty that whatever training in teaching *is* provided in the graduate school shall not be provided by the department or school of education. Whether justified or not, there exists the strong conviction that graduate students shall not spend time on "methods" courses. There have been, and are now, some efforts in this direction but they are typically small and of low prestige.

Perhaps a more promising course, along these general lines, is concerned not with how-to-teach, in the literal sense, but with the setting within which the teaching takes place. Some observers consider it more important for intended college teachers to learn something of the history, the purposes, the problems, the "philosophy" of the liberal arts college,

---

* An experimental effort to set down such material in a concise, coherent form was made in the summer of 1960 by a group under the leadership of Ralph Tyler and O. Meredith Wilson.

Another experiment of this kind, considered a successful effort to apply the knowledge of education to the improvement of teaching in medical school, is reported in brief form by Stephen Abrahamson, "The Professional Educator and Medical Education," *Journal of Higher Education*, January, 1960, pp. 38–41; and *in extenso* by George E. Miller, M.D., and Edwin F. Rosinski, Ed.D., "A Summer Institute on Medical Teaching: Report of a Conference," *Journal of Medical Education*, May, 1959, pp. 449–495.

Descriptions of the major course programs now in operation are contained in A. D. Albright and John E. Barrows, *Preparing College Teachers*, University of Kentucky and the Southern Regional Education Board, 1959, section 2.

that is, for them to get an introduction to the institution they plan to serve. As a matter of fact, if they "had to choose" beween the two "as part of the preparation for college teachers in graduate school," twice as many college presidents say they would choose such instruction over instruction in how-to-teach (and still more in the better colleges).

The second, more prevalent, line of action is based on what appears to be economic reality, that is, to use a large number of graduate students as teaching assistants in sections, laboratory sessions, readerships, tutorships, etc. Hence there is and will be some built-in undergraduate teaching experience—not necessarily training—for a sizable proportion of doctoral candidates (at present, about two-thirds of them). The arrangement is apparently so necessary a part of the system, on both sides, that it is now becoming elaborated under the impact of rising enrollments, especially in the state universities. For example, Florida has recently established ranks within this category—the teaching associateship on top of the teaching assistantship—and has spread the salary equivalent from the lower instructors to the higher assistant professors. Other public universities, like California, are considering the same idea. In any case, the teaching assistantship is the means by which most universities work off whatever they consider their obligations on this score.

As such, the teaching assistantship is frequently considered to be faulty on at least three grounds: (1) not all potential teachers have the experience; (2) many have it far too long; and (3) the experience is insufficiently directed and planned.

(1) If universities or particular departments believe that training in teaching via the assistantship is desirable and necessary or want to be sure that all their potential teachers have it, then they must arrange it for *all* their graduate students. Some universities or disciplines now do, or think they should. For example, Tulane and Brown require some training in teaching for virtually all their doctoral candidates, and a recent national report on mathematics recommends that "departments of mathematics include the teaching of one properly supervised elementary course as a normal requirement for the Ph.D. degree." Such a requirement, incidentally, would be desirable for a second reason at least as cogent as the first, namely, to learn one's subject. That is in line with the academic commonplace, "You never really begin to learn your subject until you have to teach it to someone else." Whatever the virtues of this requirement, which I shall consider later, the climate is well-prepared for it: about two-thirds of the deans, the faculties, and the college presidents favor "requiring all doctoral candidates to do some undergraduate teaching, under supervision," and nearly that proportion of the recent recipients themselves. In this case, the arts and sciences are stronger for the proposal than the professional fields.

(2) How long can the assistantship be justified, as a training measure?

It appears to many that the typical period of service today is too long. Those recent recipients who held teaching assistantships did so for a median of over two years (and a mean of over three). By all accounts, the *training* value can be realized in less time. Beyond that period, it is a matter of presumed economic necessity on the part of the institution and/or the student. However convenient for departments or however inexpensive for institutions, it is fair to neither the graduate assistants nor their undergraduate students to maintain a "second class" staff in this way, on the rationale of providing training in teaching. As I shall try to indicate later, it may not be economic for the student, and perhaps not for the institution, either.

(3) If there is something to the experience as training, then presumably it requires some direction and planning; otherwise, why not get it simply on the first job? In some cases today, the assistantship is supervised; in more, it is only "supervised" or not even that. It is no secret that the teaching assistant, more often than not, now handles the dirty work in university instruction (one dean calls them the "intellectual dishwashers"). Leaving aside the fact that that is hardly the most pleasing introduction to teaching, the critics point out that it is by no means all that should come under the heading of training in teaching. What else is there? Counsel and supervision from a sympathetic senior professor; seminar discussions on the problems of teaching the subject at the undergraduate level; a range of teaching activities and not just the more mechanical requirements of chemistry sections and freshmen composition for the nth time. If, say the advocates, the introduction to teaching were taken more seriously as a training measure and not simply as an economic one, then the student would have to prepare course outlines, lead small discussion groups, give a few lectures, and otherwise test himself against the range of what a college or university teacher does.

Despite these problems with the teaching assistantship as presently administered, the people most directly concerned consider them useful. Almost two-thirds of the college presidents think that the experience made better teachers of their recent appointees, and fewer than 10% think it did not; the rest "can't say" one way or the other. Of those recent recipients who held a teaching assistantship and now teach undergraduates, over 80% think it was "really helpful." In the absence of any clear evidence that training in teaching, of whatever kind, makes doctoral candidates into better undergraduate teachers, we are forced to rely on the testimony of the participants and the plausibility of the arguments.

But it remains to make one more point about training in teaching that affects what the graduate school does. Several observers of the present situation conclude that training in teaching is more of the college's business—more than it has been, more even than the graduate school's. The graduate school has been called upon for decades to do this better, they say, but its attention is elsewhere and it will never do it very well. The colleges, on the other hand, have this as their major task, they have on their staffs men dedicated to teaching and good at it, they know what there is to know and they care. Individual colleges with their own "approaches" will need in any case to induct a new teacher to their way of doing things. Furthermore, the colleges are the only professional institutions that expect newly trained degree-holders to operate at full capacity without a breaking-in period on the ground. M.D.'s have a period of internship in a hospital, LL.B.'s and J.D.'s often have an apprenticeship in law, even Ph.D.'s in industry are usually given a special training period before they are expected to produce.

Hence, the argument concludes, the colleges should take more of the load on themselves. Only about half of them now have any kind of "formal arrangements for introducing new faculty members to the problems of teaching at your institution." In a proper division of labor, the graduate school might prepare the student in *what* to teach, and the college in *how*. As the dean of the college in a large university said, "There is a mistaken notion that training institutions produce the final product. The graduate product is 'unfinished' and the college should normally expect to provide the internship needed to produce the finished teacher."

For the time being, I conclude this discussion of the graduate school's preparation of college teachers by inquiring into the general evaluation of the situation. All in all, how well is it doing?

The important point in the answer is that the college presidents think it is doing better than the graduate deans or the graduate faculties. Half the presidents say the graduate school "is doing reasonably well . . . in both quantity and quality" as against less than a fourth of the graduate faculty and a sixth of the deans. Another quarter of the presidents think the graduate school "could do somewhat more, but not a great deal," and from a third to a half of the graduate school people "would be willing to do more, if a realistic program were put forward." In reply to another question, two-thirds of the presidents said that "despite some problems with it, the present doctorate program is a good one for college teachers."

As a matter of perspective, if nothing else, it is well to keep clearly in mind a primary fact. Beyond all the concern, the experiments, the argument and the recrimination, the prophecies of doom and the actual faults—beyond all that the present system of preparing college teachers is working reasonably well, in the judgment of the major employer. If one takes into account the complexity of the product and imperfections in human enterprises of this character, it is doing well indeed.

One reason the debate on this topic has been so long and on the whole so sterile is, apparently, that people like the Ph.D., what it stands for and what it represents, better than the critics know or imply. Improve it here and there, of course; it can always be better, just as anything can be, and especially anything in an intangible matter like education. At bottom, though, it is reasonably satisfactory.

But there is another reason, too. That is, I believe, that the critics have not really worked out an alternative program. A leading humanist, sympathetic to the problem, told me that "so far as I know, this school (i.e., those wanting to stress the preparation of college teachers) has no particular program, and it is usually on the defensive since ordinarily it seems to be attacking the standards for the degree and to be wanting to lower the standards." An undergraduate dean remarked that "the opponents of the research program haven't identified the right enemy. Simply to knock out research does not make people into good teachers."

Over thirty years ago Presidents Hughes of Miami and Wilkins of Oberlin called upon the colleges to state their case to the AAU. Over ten years ago, President Butterfield of Wesleyan opened the Poughkeepsie conference by suggesting that "the colleges should work out a statement of what they want the graduate schools to give them." Such a statement would have to deal with the particulars, not the slogans; would have to be workable within the economic realities of the system; would have to honor the going standards of graduate study; and would have to accept the demand of the colleges for the Ph.D. If it were produced—in itself, a big *if* since the colleges themselves do not agree on what is wanted—the graduate schools say they would seriously consider it.

THE QUESTION OF NUMBERS

In addition to the chronic concern with the qualitative problem of what the doctorate is or should be for the purposes of college teaching, there is currently an acute concern with the quantitative problem: How can we get enough? As for the spectacle of critics who deplore the present product yet desire much more of it, many of them feel not only that it is feasible to attack both problems simultaneously but even that it is necessary to do both at once. There is hardly another matter on the educational scene so much "viewed with alarm" as this one, especially in its predominant form: How can we get enough qualified teachers to handle the college bulge?

The expression of concern can be found almost at random in educational writings on this subject in recent years. For example, the kick-off speaker at the 1958 ACE conference began with "the most obvious thing I can say . . . (that) we shall not be able to produce anywhere near the number of Ph.D.'s that we need." The president of the ACE, in his summary of that conference, concluded that "the number of prospective doctors is clearly and grossly inadequate to provide the number of recruits needed for teaching posts in the future." The President's Committee on Education beyond the High School viewed "the cumulative deficit at the doctoral level (as) an alarming prospect." Perhaps the most widely distributed and quoted statement on the matter was made by the Committee of Fifteen: after referring in its section on "the quantitative problem" to the " 'tidal wave' " of coming students and the "appalling personnel problem" it will create, the Committee concluded: "To expect that by 1970 the proportion of college teachers holding the Ph.D. degree will have declined from the present 40 per cent to 20 per cent is not statistical hysteria but grass roots arithmetic."

Like almost everything else in graduate education, there is nothing particularly new in such "viewing with alarm." For example, in 1947, the President's Commission on Higher Education was also concerned:

> It is clear that the number of additional teachers required to man our system of higher education will be enormous. . . . The task ahead is of unprecedented magnitude. To provide the number of competent and well-qualified faculty personnel required by American colleges and universities is a problem of the first importance. It can be solved only by Herculean efforts.

The Commission, incidentally, was off in its projection for the 1960 faculty: 300,000 "teaching faculty" as against an actual figure of about 200,000 in 1958 (full-time equivalent of resident instructional staff). A participant at the Lake Mohonk Conference in 1947 stated that "it is unmistakably in the cards that fifty or sixty thousand teachers, to put it modestly, are going to be required" in the next five or ten years at the junior college level—where there are now less than 25,000 all told.

In anticipation of the post-war bulge, Walter Jessup called on the graduate schools, in the Carnegie Foundation report of 1944, to give "immediate and sharp attention to the future. . . . The minimal desideratum is that the graduate schools shall not be taken by surprise. . . ." Considering the attention currently being given the matter, certainly no one has an excuse for being taken by surprise this time. Rather, I think, the professional discussion of the subject has taken on the character of a Crisis. Hardly a discussion of higher education these days does not start with the "impending tidal wave" ahead, and the critical figures are used so often that they seem to gain credence by their very repetition.

Now the facts that we survived or even surmounted earlier crises, and that some of them failed to materialize, does not of course mean that we shall do as well with this one, should it actually come about. But before we can sensibly know what to do about the problem of getting enough teachers for higher education in the next years, we need to know how big a problem it really is. So it is necessary to look into the nature and magnitude of the alleged crisis, in order indeed to decide what is "grass roots arithmetic" and what "statistical hysteria."

This means that we have to take an excursion through the numbers of the future, however hazardous that journey is. I am reluctant to do so because of the uncertainties and dangers involved, but I feel it is necessary in order to put the numerical problem into perspective.

THE BASIC PROJECTIONS. To start with, there are four projections involved in this demand-and-supply analysis: (1) the projection of the "college-age" group in the general population; (2) the projection of the enrollment in colleges and universities; (3) the projection of the number of college and university teachers needed; and (4) the projection of the number of doctorates to be produced and the number who will go into higher education. All of these projections are based on two elementary assumptions: no major war, no major depression. Most of the projections limit themselves to the period ending in 1970 and hence so will I; not only are the projections difficult enough to make a decade or so ahead but no decisions about policy are likely to be made more than that far distant in any case.

The first projection, as to "college-age" population, is the one most readily and most reliably made: all the people who will come of "college age" from now to 1970 are already living and counted, and it requires only the demographer's actuarial tables to tell us how many of them will still be alive and in this country in the next years. The estimates are not infallible, but they are quite good and they certainly give us a satisfactory starting point. What do they indicate? As everyone knows, the birth rate increased during and after World War II and as a result more people are going to be in the "college-age" group, starting in the early 1960's. Specifically, the picture looks something like this (throughout this section, I shall use approximate figures, rounded off, to avoid the impression of high precision in such data):

1950 (actual)	8,900,000
1955 (estimated)	8,600,000
1960 (projected)	9,600,000
1965 (projected)	12,200,000
1970 (projected)	14,600,000

These are census estimates and projections: so far, so good.

The next step is to derive from the number of potential students the number who will actually end up in the classroom. This step requires the first guess: What proportion of the "college age" will go to college? Broadly speaking, there are two ways to make this estimate, one conservative and one liberal. The conservative one is that the same proportion will be attending college in 1970 as are attending now; the liberal one is that the upward trend of that proportion over the past years will continue at about the same rate or faster. These estimates probably provide the lower and upper limits of the range, and the correct figure is probably somewhere between them. What are the proportions?

Here is the first real chance to go wrong. Up to 1940 the proportions of the "college-age" group that were in college are generally agreed upon: about 4% in 1900, 8% in 1920, 15% in 1940, or about double every twenty years. But for the period since the war, the figures produced by different experts do not agree. Thus, for 1950, the widely-used *Teachers for Tomorrow* pamphlet of the Fund for the Advancement of Education says that the correct figure was 29.8%, the Educational Policies Commission says 30.2%, and Thomson, who framed the phrase "impending tidal wave," says 31%. They are in substantial agreement with one another, but in substantial disagreement with Seymour Harris who says that the figure was 22.0% and the Office of Education and George Stigler who say it was 19.65%.

Now these are large divergences in themselves, and even more serious when it comes to using them as the bases for projections to 1970. How can they disagree by as much as 10 percentage points, from roughly 30% to roughly 20%, when it is simply a matter of "grass roots arithmetic" to divide the numerator (how many students in college) by the denominator (how many people of "college age" in the population)? The answer is that Harris, the Office of Education, and Stigler omitted the number of veterans in colleges and universities in 1950 on the ground that they constituted an abnormal weighting of the student body; and over a third of all college and university students in 1950 were veterans.

How this is handled affects not only what base rate to start with, but also what increase to forecast in the rate. For example, in its alternate projection to the Office of Education, the *Teachers for Tomorrow* analysis assumed that the increase from 15.3% in 1940 to 29.2% in 1954 would continue at that rate of one percentage point a year and came out with a figure of over 44% of the age group enrolled in 1970; if veteran enrollment in 1954 had been taken into account, the curve of projection would have been flatter.

All of that has to do with the numerator. (I omit the further complication in the numerator of how to handle part-time students; they are typically included in all these estimates.) Yet the denominator requires a little scrutiny too. To this point, I have been putting the term "college age" in quotation marks because by no means all the students in colleges and universities are of "college age." In such projections, "college age" almost always refers to the number of people aged 18–21 in the population. But a large number of college and university students are *not* in that age bracket. Specifically, in October, 1958, with a total enrollment of 3.2 millions, about 1.4 millions, or over 40%, were either under 18 or, mostly, over 21. For 1958, the percentage enrolled was 35.7% of the 18–21 year group, but that does not mean that over a third of *that* age group was actually in colleges and universities. Here are the figures when *both* enrollment and population are classified by age, i.e., when the numerator and denominator refer to the same age group:

Percentage of the age group enrolled in colleges and
universities, October, 1958

	Men	Women	Both
14–17	1.4	1.8	1.6
18–19	26.7	21.7	24.3
20–21	20.7	12.9	16.9
18–21	23.7	17.3	20.6
22–24	11.7	2.6	7.2
25–34	5.1	1.3	3.2

The proportions are much lower but the base population has become much larger.* This would appear to be a more appropriate way to work with the ratios between age and attendance on which so many of these predictions are based. Use of this broader and more appropriate base yields projections a little smaller than the 18–21 population base alone.

Hence there are some delicate problems in deciding how to figure the present rate and even more in figuring out the proper projections. In addition to such matters, the latter should take into account what the colleges and universities themselves are going to do about increased enrollments. Most of these projections assume that institutions will take increasingly more students relative to the population that presents itself, as they have to this point. But if some institutions place a lower ceiling on their enrollments, toughen their admission policy, and select a better grade of students, then that in itself will tend to hold down the rate of increase †—only "tend to" however, because other institutions may then take up that slack and more, e.g., public institutions and junior colleges.

There are, in short, a number of imponderables in such projections. Actually the figures themselves imply as much since they cover quite a range. In general, the projections for 1970 enrollments have ranged from around 4.5 to about 6.5 millions: the ACLS and Wolfle from 4.3 to 4.6 millions, Harris 4.75, *Teachers for Tomorrow* 4.9 to 6.4, the President's Committee 6.0 plus, the NEA 6.2, the Office of Education 6.4, the Bayne-Jones Committee 6.4. On the whole, the later the estimate was made, the higher the figure.

If the true figure does no more than keep pace with the population increase, there will be 4.8 millions in colleges and universities in 1970 (according to a projection based on separate calculations for men and women and for four different age groups, and utilizing the 1958 enroll-

* These figures include a veterans enrollment of perhaps 10% of the total, but there is no real way to know how much of that is "abnormal" and hence to be discounted.

† For whatever it is worth, in their replies to the questionnaire, college presidents indicated that they did not expect to take on quite as many new faculty members in the next four years as they had in the past four.

ment rates). Beyond that, it is anyone's guess: if the over-all rate of en‐ rollment increases by five percentage points or so in the next decade (assuming some institutional restrictions on enrollment and some regression effect), then the figure will be between 6.0 and 6.5 millions. If the rate increases by twice that, there could be as many as 8 million students in 1970.

The next step is to convert the projections of enrollment into projections of the instructional staff needed to handle the enrollment. Typically, this is done by dividing the estimated enrollment by the estimated (or desired) student-teacher ratio. Now the latter varies with whether the figure used for the faculty represents the total numbers of different professional persons employed in institutions of higher education, or only the faculty for resident instruction in degree-credit courses at the college grade, or only the senior staff (instructor and above); and whether it is restricted to the full-time staff or whether the part-time is to be included, or alternately, whether the full-time equivalent figure is used. In 1958, for example, the student-teacher ratio ranged as follows:

Resident enrollment, college grade	3,585,000
Total number of different persons on professional staffs	348,500 or 10:1
Total faculty for resident instruction	260,500 or 14:1
Full-time equivalent of that faculty *	194,000 or 18:1
Full-time faculty equivalent and estimated full-time student equivalent	16:1

* The junior instructional staff of teaching assistants, etc., is estimated at half-time service, on the average.

It thus makes quite a difference which of these figures is used, if the determination of the student-teacher ratio is empirical rather than normative.

In addition, the projections will depend on what happens to this ratio under the pressure of increasing enrollments, and particularly the need to finance them. The trend is slightly upward; and it will continue upward, if for no other reason than simply because more of the coming enrollment will be handled in the public institutions. They had about 57% of the enrollment in the late 1950's; the Office of Education estimates they will have about 65% in 1970. The public institutions now have a student-teacher ratio from two to three units higher than the private. To the extent that the bulge is accommodated in junior colleges, even more so: the ratio is still higher there.

With all of this, one would expect the projections of total staff needed in 1970 to vary somewhat, and they do: from about 400,000 "full-time" teachers by the NEA, to about 500,000 in the "resident instructional staff" in the *Teachers for Tomorrow* pamphlet.

Next, the projection of how many *new* teachers will be needed, for specified enrollments and student-teacher ratios in 1970, also depends on what replacement rate is used to calculate how many of the present staff will still be teaching then (i.e., will not have died, retired, or quit the profession). That rate can range, say, between 3% and 6%; the actuarial rate for deaths and retirements is just under 2% annually and no one really knows what the quit-rate is. Here too we get a range in the estimates of new teachers needed by 1970:

Wolfle	172,000, from 1955
The President's Committee	180,000 to 270,000, from 1957
Teachers for Tomorrow	337,000 to 484,000, from 1956
Educational Policies Commission	375,000, from 1955
NEA	346,800 to 426,000, from 1959

or an annual average increment somewhere between 11,500 and 38,700.

Now let us take the last step and see how many doctorates are likely to be produced in these years. Here are the major estimates:

Wolfle	135,000, from 1954
Teachers for Tomorrow	121,000 to 135,000, from 1955
Office of Education	160,000, from 1959

or from 8,100 to 13,350 annually, on the average. These estimates are based on extrapolations of the curve of doctorate production or on the long-term trend in the relation of doctoral to lower degrees. The first thing to be said about such projections is that they are typically low only a few years after they are made:

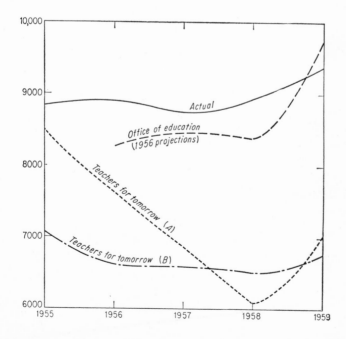

And Wolfle projected only 6,600 for 1960; the actual figure will be higher by nearly 50%.

Finally, not all doctorates go into higher education so that the total estimate has to be cut to the proportion likely to be recruited for academic faculties, that is, to the 60% we noted above, or perhaps a little less than that, in view of the long-term trend toward non-academic employment of doctorates.

ANALYSIS OF THE PROJECTIONS. What is to be made of all this? Are we really in a perilous situation, or is there a realistic chance that we can meet the situation? If this quick trip through the numbers of the future has done nothing else, it should at least have shown how many assumptions are involved in such projections and how much variance there is among them.*

It is easy to project a Crisis by selecting all the unfavorable assumptions, those on the high side for enrollments and teacher needs and those on the low side for teacher production. In this way, it is easy to say that we shall not come near getting enough doctorates for the faculties of higher education: for example, a student body in 1970 of 6.5 to 7 millions, a low student-teacher ratio, a teaching staff of almost 550,000, a high replacement rate, new teachers needed in the number of 450,000 or more, doctorate production of not over 135,000 of whom not over half go into academic life. When the matter is put that extremely, then the disparity between demand and supply is so great as to be insurmountable and we are faced with the dire prediction with which we started: a decline in the proportion of doctorates on college and university faculties from the present 40% to 20% in 1970.†

* For example, in the six months from December, 1958 to June, 1959, the NEA projection to 1970 of new full-time teachers needed declined from 426,355 to 346,800, or nearly a fifth. The estimated number of full-time teachers now in service went up from 200,000 to 250,000, the replacement rate went down from 7% to 6%, and the assumed student-teacher ratio changed at both ends. I cite this instance to illustrate the vagaries of projecting the Critical figures.

† This widely quoted conclusion from the *Teachers for Tomorrow* pamphlet— a conclusion with two *ifs* and a *may* in the original that became an expectation supported by "grass roots arithmetic" in the Committee of Fifteen report—is partly based on the equally widely quoted figures from the NEA studies of *Teacher Supply and Demand* that reveal that the proportion of doctorates on college and university faculties is, in the terms of the 1959 report, on a "precipitant down-trend." The main facts presented are that in 1953–1954 about 40% of the total full-time staff of the sampled institutions held the doctorate, and that the proportions of doctorates among "new teachers" since 1953–1954 were between 24% and 31%; in the four years since 1955–1956, when the samples of institutions were more nearly comparable, they have been within one or two percentage points of 25%. Leaving aside any sampling error and the outside possibility that the recruits are replacing a lower average level of faculty, I think it is important to make these two points: (1) Although the 40% and the 25% are being widely cited as evidence of the deteriorating quality of faculties in higher education, they are not directly comparable at all. One refers to *total* staff and the other to *new* teachers (i.e., those "newly employed teachers who the preceding year were *not so employed anywhere*"). The latter, being concentrated in the lower ranks, would have had lesser qualifications at any time. But if that were the

But is that a realistic expectation? I think not. Without retracing all the statistical steps taken to this point, let me try to recapitulate the situation. As I have tried to suggest, there is a good deal of room for judgment, and even for some revised computations. And the matter is of sufficient importance to warrant close scrutiny.

The population figures can be taken as given. As for enrollment, it may be that the two factors of concern for quality and lack of funds will hold down somewhat the larger projected increases in college and university enrollments. According to the private institutions, they plan to expand enrollment only enough to keep up with the population increase, though they may not be able to hold to that intention against the inevitable pressures. The public institutions will increase more, of course, but even there some limitations may come into play.* Suppose, then, that we end up somewhere short of the maximum estimates though well above the minimum—in short, for purposes of illustration, suppose for a moment that college and university enrollment in 1970 is of the order of 6 million.

What about the teaching staff? Assume that as part of the financial solution for such heavy enrollments we witness a softening of the present student-teacher ratio of around 15:1, remembering (1) that the ratio has

---

case, the query arises, how could the proportion for the total staff ever have risen to 40% or so? (2) It could have done so—and, in fact, it did—because people already on the staff got their doctorates. This is common practice and the pattern is clear: the doctoral candidate who completes everything except the dissertation, gets a teaching job (a "new teacher"), and then finishes the degree later. As a matter of fact, the 1959 NEA report itself shows that there are more of them than of the new recruits with doctorates. About one-fourth of the (sampled) doctorates of 1956–1958 *continued* in their college teaching jobs as against only about one-fifth who *entered* college teaching for the first time. So according to these figures, the total staff of higher education gains more doctorates from within than it recruits from the outside, yet the 25% figure reflects only the contribution of doctorates from the latter source.

Incidentally, the same report illustrates sharply the disparity between the present situation and the typical projection of requirements. On page 10 is a strong statement discarding the "theory" based on a student-teacher ratio as not having a "practical basis" and favoring a "realistic measure of the demand for teachers." On the same page the number of new full-time teachers employed by almost 90% of the institutions queried is 9,100 for the year 1958–1959 (to which, for comparison, must be added 1,650 new teachers in junior colleges, or a total of 10,750). Yet forty pages later the estimated number of new teachers needed for 1959–1960, based partly on a student-teacher ratio, is 26,900.

* Another alleviating consideration is the likelihood that a disproportionately large part of the increase will go into junior colleges where the student-teacher ratio is half again larger and the demand for doctorates on the faculty is far smaller—both factors that soften the demands of the situation. Furthermore, only about half the new teachers needed are in the arts and sciences, the core of college and university teaching, whereas over 60% of all doctorates are awarded in such fields. A substantial proportion of teachers will be needed in fields that are not typically considered to require the doctorate, at least in the same amounts, e.g., music, industrial and vocational arts, physical and health education, and perhaps home economics, library science, the health sciences, and speech and drama. These fields alone total close to 25% of the faculties of higher education.

increased over the long run, under the pressure of rising enrollments; (2) that the ratio is higher by two or three points in public institutions where perhaps as much as three-fourths of the increase will be handled in the next decade; (3) that some people actually advocate a higher ratio in a revised educational program, as for example the recent Ruml-Morrison plan that proposes a 20:1 ratio as economically suitable for the liberal arts college; and (4) that new educational techniques may extend the ratio.

Now whenever that ratio moves up by one student, the requirement for teachers at this level of enrollment falls by 15,000 to 38,000.* If we estimate the enrollment at 6 millions, here are what different ratios call for in total staff:

14:1	430,000
16:1	375,000
18:1	330,000
20:1	300,000

How many *new* teachers would these estimates require in the decade of the 1960's? Assume a 4% annual replacement rate; it probably will not be much larger because the better salaries in prospect will keep more people in academic employment, because the retirement age is now rising above sixty-five, and because the faculty today is heavy in the younger age brackets due to the recent increases. In that case, for a 6 million enrollment we shall require by 1970 about 250,000 new teachers to maintain a student-teacher ratio of 14:1, fewer than 200,000 for 16:1, and only 120,000 for 20:1. Since for the reasons indicated the ratio will probably rise a little, a figure of about 180,000 seems more appropriate than the official estimates of twice that, as listed above.

But even that figure needs qualification in order to get it into proper form for comparison with the number of doctorates produced. First, all these estimates include junior college enrollments and faculties. Yet such institutions are largely not staffed with doctorates. At present, the junior college employs about 10% of the total staff in higher education, and it will probably be a larger proportion in 1970. Not more than 10% of the junior college staff now hold the doctorate, but that too will grow. Assume that these two trends balance each other out. About 40% of the staffs of the four-year institutions now hold the doctorate.† So to hold

---

* Incidentally, here as elsewhere higher education has an important decision to make. If every additional thousand faculty members are on the average less able than the preceding one, then will the colleges and universities do a better educational job at this level with one more student per faculty member or with another 20,000 faculty members of lesser quality? It is not clear that the latter is the proper choice.

† One of the reasons for the seemingly large discrepancy in some of these estimates between the numbers of teachers needed and the numbers of doctorates to be awarded is that while the latter figure was usually cut to 60% or less to account for those going into college and university work, the former was not cut to 40% of the total to account only for those needed with doctorates in order to hold to the present rate.

our own we need *not* the full number of new teachers with doctorates, but only 37% of them, i.e., 40% of the 90% in degree-granting institutions and 10% of the 10% in junior colleges. And 37% of the total of, say, 180,000 means that about 66,500 doctorates would be needed for higher education during the 1960's.

Finally, how many will we get? If the present number of about 9,000 a year does not increase, then in eleven years we will have 99,000 new doctorates. If 60% stay in higher education, as at present, then we will come close to meeting this level of demand. But without doubt there will be many more than an average of 9,000 a year over the next years, if for no other reason than because the "college bulge" will itself become the "graduate school bulge" four years later. Moreover, almost every graduate school plans to expand in the next years. If the Office of Education projection is right—and it has been the closest this far—there will be a total of about 160,000 new doctorates in these eleven years, or enough to *raise* the proportion of doctorates on the staffs even if only half went into higher education and even with a lower student-teacher ratio.

Actually, of course, the system will have a good deal of freedom of choice—in admission policy, faculty recruitment and salaries, teaching methods, and the like. Within some sizable limits it can decide on how big it will be, and what the quality of higher education will be, as measured by such indices as the student-teacher ratio and the proportion of staffs with doctorates. But however such questions are decided and even given an enrollment of 6 millions, the over-all situation seems to me not a capital-C Crisis, but rather a small-p problem. If enrollment in 1970 is not much over 6 millions, if the Office of Education projection on doctorates is reasonably correct, and if the rate of 60% recruitment for higher education is maintained, then we have a good chance to increase the present rate of doctorates in the classrooms of higher education by 1970, not lower it.

Let us now take the final step and see what the situation would be with a still higher enrollment. If the Office of Education projections and the 60% academic recruitment hold up, we shall have about 96,000 new doctoral recipients for the faculties of higher education, or roughly enough to handle enrollments in 1970 of 6 millions at a student-teacher ratio of 14:1; 7 millions at a student-teacher ratio of 16:1; or 8 millions at a student-teacher ratio of 18:1.

What, then, does the numerical problem come down to? I conclude that the sense of Crisis that makes discussions of graduate education sound shrill these days is unwarranted and misleading. There is a problem, to be sure, but not one of the magnitude now commonly accepted, or at least commonly reviewed from the usual few sources. There is no reason to relax about the matter, but there is no reason to get tense about it either. The numbers problem in itself does not appear to justify major changes in the training program, nor to justify a shift of attention to quantity and away from quality.

Above all, it is well to keep some objectivity and perspective in viewing the matter. Forecasts have traditionally been pessimistic in this field. What is the problem? It is that within a fifteen-year period we shall be doubling our baccalaureate ranks. But baccalaureate degrees have doubled, or more, every fifteen years or so in this century—whereas doctorates have kept ahead of that pace by doubling every decade or so. The baccalaureate rate will slow down before the doctorate. Even over a sixteen-year period covering World War II, when doctoral production was way down, the proportion of doctorates on the faculties of accredited four-year institutions went up by 10%.

The numbers game is by no means lost.

The Problem of Professionalization

Beyond the problem of the college teacher, and complicating the matter of purpose even further, there is a serious issue about the basic conception of the doctorate. In a report on "The Professionalizing of the Ph.D. Degree" a few years ago, a committee of the Association of Graduate Schools (AGS) remarked that

> the entrance of the professional schools into the doctoral area, and the granting of the doctorate in liberal arts subjects for programs of study primarily aimed at the needs of a professional specialty are vastly complicating the problem of the character and aims of the Ph.D. degree. . . . If we are now going to award the degree for programs of study designed . . . to do any of the many things which need to be done and for which an advanced degree has become essential or desirable, then we will, on the one hand, confuse the issue as to what the degree means and we will, on the other, force a change in the demands which we make generally on the candidates for this degree since the same degree cannot for long make fundamentally different kinds of demands on the student within the same institution.

That wraps up a number of issues in one neat package: what is the degree for? who is it for? what does it mean? how pure should it be?

In the historical review of graduate study, I noted a trend toward professionalization in that (*a*) more doctorates were being given in the professional fields and (*b*) more doctorates of a professional type were being given within the academic disciplines. As I said there, if one defines as professional any high-level program that trains primarily for practice or doing rather than for learning or teaching, then a substantial segment of the graduate work offered within some large traditional academic disciplines is professional in character, e.g., the training for industrial practice in chemistry, for public administration in political science, for clinical practice in psychology. The borderlines are admittedly fuzzy—a chemist at Du Pont may be more academic in the best sense than many professors—but if such programs are accepted as essentially professional in character, then not many more than half the doctorates conferred last year were academic.

This development can be seen concretely in a number of fields, as academic interests have come more and more into contact with practical ones and as doctoral training has come under pressure to reflect this state of affairs. For example:

On the agenda of the recent conference on *Graduate Education in Psychology*, the most frequently raised question was summarized thus: "Can basic scientific and practical professional training be integrated?" Despite the location of clinical training in academic departments for over a decade, the issue is still somewhat controversial among psychologists.

The Yale pamphlet on *Graduate Training in Economics* reports that "panel members agree that the curriculum of graduate education in economics can no longer be organized exclusively about scholars; it has become essential to produce economists who can do, not just know." By doing, the report means not only research in business, labor, and government, but a "more operating capacity, where day-to-day decisions and advice are required without any formalized research work."

Public administration in political science trains people not only for academic positions, but also for operating posts in Federal and state governments.

According to a leader in the field, the course of modern physics has opened "many important areas to practical exploitation. Prior to 1900 such exploitation would have been carried out almost exclusively by individuals in other professions. At the present time there is a tendency for the physicist to become the expert practitioner in areas developed through fundamental research in the field."

The professional component in chemistry, if industrial practice can be so designated, is large and well-known.

Even in English, supposedly a "pure" academic subject, there is now a much closer relationship with the world of letters outside the academy than ever existed before. People move more easily between academic and non-academic pursuits; many academic people write for and edit the little magazines; and many are both academic scholars and professional writers, thus, as Wallace Stegner put it, "healing the breach (in) one general breed"—Stegner himself at Stanford, Trilling and Van Doren at Columbia, Nabokov at Cornell, Schorer at California, Brooks at Yale, Engle at Iowa, and several others. As I write, the dean of American critics, Edmund Wilson, is visiting professor at Harvard. In the field of literary study, this practice is perhaps the equivalent of professional practice.*

* Indeed, some people have suggested that the (alleged) historical decline of the humanities in this country, relative to the sciences and the social sciences, can be

But the other side of the coin is at least as noteworthy. That is the growth of work of an academic kind in professional schools and departments:

Medical research is increasingly biological in character. The number of Ph.D.'s on medical faculties is rising; they are more prominent than M.D.'s in preclinical instruction.

Engineering schools are increasing the amount of basic science in their advanced training. "The training that electrical (or electronic) engineers will receive in the future can be expected increasingly to emphasize the basic sciences at the expense of traditional engineering subjects . . . Those electronic engineers engaged in creative work commonly work side by side with physicists, mathematicians, chemists, metallurgists, etc. And their performance is measured by comparison with men having Master's and Doctor's degrees in these fields," says former dean Frederick Terman of Stanford. In a recent annual report, Lee DuBridge, the president of Cal Tech, calls their aim the development of "'scientific' engineers": "Applied science is changing so rapidly that specialized 'practical' courses are often obsolete even before they are given. A broad and basic training is more valuable in the long run—at least for students of high caliber."

The current developments at the Graduate School of Business of the University of Chicago are symptomatic in that field: "As each profession has grown increasingly complex, it has been recognized that a more general and theoretical education, based on scientific material and intellectual disciplines, is the only thoroughly practical preparation for the profession." This development is seen as a natural culmination of professional training that begins in all fields as simple apprenticeship, works through organized instruction in case studies and "best practices," and ends by anchoring itself in the underlying academic disciplines.

In short, we are now witnessing a long turn in post-baccalaureate study toward the mutual infiltration of academic and professional fields within the university. As academic fields are training more for their

---

attributed to their lack of a testing point in the real world—like engineering for physics, technology for chemistry, medicine for biology, the business cycle for economics, personality disturbance or intelligence tests for psychology, and so on. Howard Mumford Jones has said that since "the sole criterion of success in the humanities is an academic criterion, academicism is not held in check as it is in chemistry or political science, but on the contrary is encouraged." A century ago, the humanities had the check in the ministry. What happened, some think, was that the humanities in the graduate school retreated behind "scientific" studies of a narrow character and lost touch with the mainstream of modern thought and action. What is needed is to re-establish their position as the informed guides to questions of taste, philosophy, morals, and esthetics: to bring them back more into the world. Whatever the validity of the diagnosis or the prescription, certainly there is movement currently in the recommended direction.

equivalents of practice—or more precisely, perhaps, as more of their graduates are going into practice—so professional fields are using more academic material and academic personnel in their own programs. Many mathematicians and physicists are now found in schools of engineering, many biologists in schools of medicine and agriculture, many psychologists in schools of business and education, many sociologists in schools of social work.*

Nor is this rapprochement limited to the graduate school. In their pamphlet "Are Liberal Arts Colleges Becoming Professional Schools?" Earl McGrath and Charles Russell answered the question largely in the affirmative: their analysis shows much more professional and pre-professional preparation in the colleges today than some decades ago and at the same time more liberal arts material in the undergraduate professional program. A similar and earlier development changed the high school curriculum from the classical to the combined academic-vocational variety that is now accepted as the American standard. Frank Bowles puts the matter well:

> It is now about forty years since the idea of mass secondary education—then totally new—encountered the entrenched concept of secondary education as college preparation. In the end, both have won. Mass education is numerically stronger with its own curricular arrangements, but it has lost in a bid to control the curriculum. College preparation, numerically weaker, has been established as the primary task and is in the intellectual ascendancy.

The development at all three levels has been marked by much larger numbers of students and by a movement toward teaching as a profes-

---

* Beyond that, the relation of academic and non-academic work is revealed in the contributions from people in government and industry that appear in the learned journals. Here are the institutional affiliations of the authors in the leading journals, in 1958 (from a study described in the Appendix):

	Authors in government	*Authors in industry*
All fields	16%	15%
Chemistry	12	20
Physics	18	18
Biology	18	3
Psychology	18	5
Engineering	12	67
Agriculture	40	4

Even in the humanities—in language and literature, the classics, philosophy, the fine arts, and music—the authorship by non-academic people comes close to 20%.

sional job rather than a dedicated calling. Nor did this development at the high school level make for lower quality: comparative studies over a decade or more consistently show better performance.

But the seeming historical inevitability of this movement does not necessarily mean that it is desirable or right. The question has been concretely drawn in the case of the degree itself—should the Ph.D. be awarded in professional fields?—and has received various answers. As we saw, this issue first arose in connection with education, and has never really been settled: both the Ph.D. and the Ed.D. are given, sometimes in the same institution.

Some graduate deans strongly prefer that the professional fields use their own professional doctorates—Doctor of Business Administration, Doctor of Engineering, Doctor of Social Work, Doctor of Library Science—and leave the Ph.D. alone. For example, a former dean recently asked rhetorically: "Should not these groups now establish their own professional Doctors' degrees and set the requirements to produce the best-trained and most skillful practitioners? This would seem to me a more reasonable approach than the present effort to force the would-be specialists into the Ph.D. groove, or, more objectionable, to modify the Ph.D. requirement to fit their needs." A Columbia faculty committee, in connection with the recent educational survey of the university, concluded "that the professional schools should, in general, give professional doctorates rather than the Ph.D."

On the other side are those, like the authors of a report on the graduate program at Wayne State University, who dislike creating further splits within the university: "To call one type of work 'graduate' and the other 'professional,' or to hold that one is scholarly and the other is not, is to create dichotomies which are harmful to a university. . . . Insistence upon a high road and a low road can only have the effect of driving the professions further away from the disciplines or, conversely, further isolating the arts and sciences within their 'ivory tower.'" Indeed, a few people, like a former graduate dean at a leading university, feel that the sides should be held together not so much for the benefit of the professional schools as for the arts and sciences: "They are not the most vital part of the university these days, nor a special corner of it. Insofar as they hearken after the old arts and science tradition they are wrong: it is dead and cannot be resurrected."

Certainly the academic scene is different today in this regard. The "ivory tower" is hard to find in a large university these days—and so are some of the professors. They are in Washington testifying on scientific or economic policy or lobbying for Federal education measures, or in New York on a consulting or committee assignment, or in Paris for an international conference, or in India or the Near East or South America on a supervisory or advisory job for government or industry or one of the foundations. They make the headlines much more frequently these days and they are much more important on the national and international scene.

Indeed, this tide is now running so strongly that some people consider it a threat to the quality of university life and graduate study. Howard Mumford Jones has remarked the need for scholars to get away "from institutions that are supposed to exist for furthering fundamental thought" in order to find time to engage in some. Others have sadly or angrily noted the decline of the "community of scholars" and the sense of scholarly devotion in the big university of today, and the rise of administrative and bureaucratic values. As David Riesman has recently pointed out:

> Veblen argues that scholars were supported by businessmen in the guise of administrators; but I think most of us would today grant that professors are themselves apt to apply business standards to their work. . . . We academic people tend to judge ourselves as would a firm: does our university offer a full line; is it properly diversified; what is our Dun & Bradstreet rating in the proper accreditation association; how many students do we have?

As for graduate training, the fear is that the better professors are so busy off campus that their students are neglected at home. As a matter of fact, the graduate faculty itself indicates such a concern. I asked them whether "the load of work in administration, consultation, conferences, committee work, service jobs, etc., had increased markedly for you or your colleagues in recent years" and nearly three-fourths said it had.* To the further question, "Is this development interfering with graduate training, in your judgment, by taking you or your colleagues away from direct work with graduate students," about half said it had. The growing contact with the world of affairs has not come without its costs, though it is hard to see how the clock can be turned back.

The present uneasiness in the university is revealed in a paradoxical tension between how things are and how they ought to be. This is shown by the answers of the deans, the graduate faculty, and the recent recipients to the identical question put to each group:

---

* Not all of this, of course, is off the campus, but a substantial and no doubt an increasing proportion of it is. Everywhere one hears expressions of concern about the loss from teaching of excellent professors who become consultants to government or industry or foundations, who take on research programs with heavy administrative duties, or who take leaves of absence to pursue non-teaching chores elsewhere.

In the current debate over graduate education, there are two points of view about what graduate study is for—what its major aim or purpose is and ought to be. Put oversimply for sharpness, they are represented by these terms:

Professional conception		*Academic conception*
Training	as against	Education
Development of skills	as against	Development of wisdom
Development of depth	as against	Development of breadth
Specialist	as against	Cultivated man
Technical expert	as against	Scholar-teacher

Where do you think the emphasis now lies, and where should it?

Percentage of each group saying "more with academic conception"

		Emphasis does lie	*Emphasis should lie*
Graduate deans		41%	75%
Graduate faculty	Arts & sciences only	33	66
Recent recipients		48	63

Everyone strongly agrees that graduate study should be more academic.* (In fact, so do the faculty and the recent recipients in professional fields.) Then why isn't it? Partly, of course, because circumstances and the facts of university life are otherwise these days. Partly, I suppose, because this feeling only expresses a sentimental attachment to the "good old days" of more reflection and less pressure. But partly, I think, because it is primarily based on the symbols involved: "academic" sounds much better to academic people, and in the two closest comparative cases, "professional" has become something of a fighting word.

One of these has to do with the field of education itself—professional education as embodied in a school or department. The arts and sciences are traditionally suspicious if not contemptuous of what they call educationists and want to have little to do with them: not share their Ph.D. with education, not share their students for "methods" courses. Just as some people in education seek to label graduate degrees as "professional" (as in the editorial in the March, 1959 issue of *The Journal of Higher Education*), so the academics resist the tag (as in the AGS report cited above).

* Note that the difference between *is* and *should be* is about 35 percentage points for the faculty and deans and only half that for the recent recipients. Partly this is due to the latter's satisfaction with his training program, but partly too, perhaps, to the long-run trend: the recent recipients came through a system that had already moved in this direction, so that the disparity is less clear.

The other case has to do with the professional fields of medicine and law. They are held in high esteem but what is seen as their planned and relatively inflexible curricula are highly disapproved as models for graduate study. The issue was put by the Trustees of the Carnegie Foundation: "A good many critics believe that graduate education today is altogether too loosely organized and permissive, that it lacks well-defined objectives and invites students to dawdle. Critics point to the contrast in medical and legal education, in which tightly-knit programs designed to produce definite intellectual results absorb the student's entire time and offer few choices."

There are some academic people who believe not only that medicine and law draw the better students away from the biological and social sciences but that they train them more efficiently as well. But not very many: this is a question on which the graduate faculties feel more strongly than any other. Should "doctoral programs be 'tightened' and regularized, more like the training programs in medical and law schools?" Only 10% of the graduate faculty said "yes," 80% said "no." This response was the most intensely held position of any on a list of forty similarly worded statements. Recent recipients agree, and the graduate deans feel even more strongly about the matter: only one favors the idea. At the heart of this conviction is research and the dissertation: the graduate school is training scholars, not just (mere!) practitioners.* (Similarly with the other comparison: a reason for and consequence of the Ed.D. is that the traditional dissertation is replaced by reports of various kinds that, however useful they may be to an educational practitioner, are not research as the graduate school usually defines it.)

Beginning as far back as 1901, when Henry Pratt Judson first asked the perennial question—"Is not the graduate school itself, after all, practically a professional school?"—the graduate school has resisted the label, all the more so the closer the definition came to an existing professional school. Jacques Barzun may be right when he says that "graduate training has willy-nilly become a professional requirement," with the society demanding the Ph.D. for "hordes of college teachers, scientists, government servants, business consultants, linguists and other foreign affairs ex-

---

* According to an experienced graduate dean, for example: "The modish comparison of the Ph.D. (to its discredit) with the medical and legal programs of study disregards the differences in aim and traditional structure. The curricula for these professions are more completely standardized because they are determined by the needs of a single profession, they are guided by recommendations of professional associations, and they are shaped by the demands of state accrediting examinations. They can therefore be organized into a set body of courses and other educational experiences. The Ph.D., on the other hand, rests on a great variety of initial preparations, it aims at a progressive cultivation of independence and individuality, and it ends in a piece of investigation whose limits, while they may be practically circumscribed, cannot be arbitrarily fixed in advance without ruining its usefulness."

perts, statisticians and cyberneticists"—but the graduate schools resist and reject the implications.

Meanings and Alternates

It is clear, then, that the academic man rather than the professional practitioner is the graduate school's model of what it wants to turn out. But in the present complex situation, a single model will not do. The doctoral program is a multipurpose one, and the degree "means" many different things—by field, by institution, and by the use to which it is put.

How many things can the doctorate signify without losing its significance altogether? "The label Ph.D." said Jacques Barzun in his 1957 annual report as graduate dean at Columbia, "can no longer be said to denote anything very precise. . . . It is uncertain in its meaning. Whereas the lawyer is a lawyer, the physician a physician, the engineer an engineer, no one can predict what the Ph.D. knows or does: is he a scholar? a teacher? an educated man?"

Certainly the proliferation of degrees has somewhat attenuated the original meaning of the doctorate. The one side fears that this has weakened standards and debased the currency of the degree, as with the B.A. and the M.A. before it, and proposes the remedy of uniformity and singleness of purpose. The other side is less concerned with the diversity of meanings, and even of standards, on three grounds: (1) a variety of products is needed in a mass educational system and a complex society; (2) distinctions among types and qualities of doctorates are always made by informed people, and they are made informally and unofficially, as they should be; this harmless ambiguity enables the uneven parts of a single system to live together more congenially than clarity would permit; and (3) nothing can realistically be done about it anyway; the cure of legislated uniformity, the only feasible kind, would be worse than the disease.

Can a single program of study satisfy the many uses to which the degree is put? Many critics think it cannot, and that more specialized tracks should be laid down in place of the present single track to the degree. Now one reply to this is that in many fields at many places, perhaps in most at most, there is no single track beyond the basic core of disciplinary concepts and methods, i.e., the minimum necessary to identify the candidate as a member of the discipline. Beyond that, programs often diverge according to the interests and career plans of the candidate, so much so that candidates in the same department receive quite different courses of study and emerge knowing quite different things, e.g., the clinical psychologist as against the experimentalist, the public administrator as against the political philosopher, the various period specializations within history or literature, taxonomy or morphology in botany as against the newer chemical interests.

But these, while different tracks, are defined on the basis of further specifications of the discipline or subject matter, and not in terms of the uses to which the degree is put: research, teaching, practice. In this connection, I asked the graduate faculty about "the criticism of the graduate school that within departments it usually offers the same program of doctoral study for (these) three different kinds of people." Only about a quarter said that the "single program is seriously deficient and should be changed," and the remainder was evenly split between those who thought that "the single program is best for all" and those who believed that "the single program may not be best, but it's the only practicable one." What is more, this is another case where the arts and sciences and the top institutions feel somewhat more strongly about the matter:

	Best for all	Only practicable	Seriously deficient	Other
Arts & sciences	36%	34	21	9
Other professional fields	27%	40	22	11
Education	17%	22	46	15
Top 12 institutions	38%	32	21	9
Other AGS members, plus	35%	33	20	12
Other universities	27%	37	28	8

Again the "heart" of graduate work is less inclined to change the present arrangements on this score, and what might be a conflict in fundamental conception turns out to be accommodated to the general satisfaction of the graduate faculty (and the deans too, incidentally) in the name of common standards or practicality.

The extreme version of the multitrack position is the recurrent proposal that there should be two doctoral degrees, one for college teachers and one for researchers. The idea has been around for a long time but has never taken hold. Just after World War II, it was put forward again by two such different university men as William Kilpatrick of Teachers College and Howard Mumford Jones of Harvard. The latter has since turned away from the proposal and even the Committee of Fifteen, with all its concern over the college teacher, decided that the plan would not work. Everyone concerned—the universities, the colleges, and the students—would consider the new degree as a second-class one, with all its invidious distinctions. If the system had started this way, it might now seem natural to have two doctorates, separate but equal (if anything of this sort ever can be). As it is, the prestige of the Ph.D. has pre-empted the field. At least, the deans and the faculty, and for that matter the recent recipients too, are strongly opposed to the idea; only college presidents and people from departments of education favor it. The top institutions, where a new degree would probably have to start for reasons of prestige, are the most opposed of all.

Another "radical" proposal is currently being discussed in educational circles as a way out of the problem posed by the anticipated rise in college enrollments and in view of the alleged unavailability of Ph.D.'s, the unacceptability of the Master's, and the undesirability of the second doctorate. That is to invent a new two-year degree intermediate between the present Master's and Ph.D. and designed especially for the college teacher. It would correspond roughly to the period of the course work for the Ph.D. and the recipient thus might later be able to go ahead quite readily. However, the program would be a little broader, would not be so research-oriented, and would deal more with the problems and purposes of the liberal arts college. For prestige reasons, it would have to be called a doctorate—not the Ph.D. of course, but some other version, say, the Doctor of Liberal Arts or, by field, the Doctor of Social Science, Doctor of Humanities, etc.

There are three problems: (1) to get good institutions to offer such a program, (2) to get good students into it, and (3) to get good colleges to accept the product. A good university would hesitate to set up such a program because of the competitive disadvantage if its peers did not do likewise; the stigma if the experiment failed; but primarily because of the difficulty of finding enough, and prestigious enough, members of the graduate faculty to work on the program. Graduate students would naturally know that the professors think of this as an inferior degree to the Ph.D., not just a different one, and hence would hesitate to label themselves as inferior candidates even though they wanted to be college teachers and disliked the research emphasis of the regular Ph.D. program. And since the Ph.D. would be so much more negotiable, many would consider it a better investment to take the extra year or two, or even three, in order to get it. Finally, the colleges would have to take a chance on the new degree.

All three are formidable obstacles. Yet the graduate faculty opposes this proposal not nearly so much as that for a second doctorate of the regular variety, and nearly half the graduate deans actually favor it. Furthermore, the faculty in the humanities, where this could be the answer to the problem of research emphasis vis-à-vis undergraduate teaching of literature, is evenly split; and the better institutions are more favorably inclined than the others. As a matter of fact, in my own talks with only a tiny sample of academic opinion, I have met a number of administrators and faculty members in such fields as English, economics, chemistry, and biology, all at distinguished universities, who believe that this is the right course to follow; who would be willing, or even eager, to give it a try; and who in some cases have courses of study outlined for such a program.

Would the colleges take such people? What would they like to have? I put the question to the college presidents:

As you think of the problem of faculty recruitment at your institution over the next few years, how would you rank the following—first according to what you would like to have and then according to what you think you are most likely to have to take?

Average rank (1 to 6)

	Would like to have	*Most likely have to take*
Doctorate from major graduate school	1.2	3.3
Doctorate from minor graduate school	2.5	2.5
Holder of a new 2-year degree, intermediate between Master's and Doctor's, and specially designed for college teachers, from good institution	3.9	4.7
Doctorate from teachers college	4.0	3.9
Master's from university	4.2	2.5
Master's from good college	5.0	3.7

What they want and don't want is pretty clear: they want the best Ph.D.'s and they don't want the Master's (though they fear they will have to take it). If they cannot get enough university Ph.D.'s, they would prefer the proposed new degree over the alternatives.

In short, any revision of graduate study to prepare more, better college teachers is not likely to get far unless it comes to terms with two hard facts: (1) The graduate schools will not diminish their emphasis on research and scholarship. Blame it on blindness to other gods, on the national emergency, on professional inertia, on the heritage of copying the Germans in the first place—but there it is. (2) The colleges want Ph.D.'s. Blame it on institutional vanity, on the accrediting associations, on the magic of the degree, or on the fact that those who set the requirement are themselves products of the system—but there it is. As a recent example, take the conclusion of the 1959 Western Regional Workshop on Higher Education: "Though it was agreed that possession of such a degree does not automatically guarantee good teaching, there was a reluctance to depart from the goal of a doctoral degree as a critical qualification for college teachers."

The other side of that coin, referred to forty years ago by Dean West of Princeton as the "union card," is definitely visible to today's doctoral candidates and faculty, especially in the humanities and social sciences.

The proposition, "Doctoral work suffers because many students don't really want to be researchers but have to go through research programs in order to get the 'union badge' for college teaching," is agreed to by 70% of the recent recipients in the humanities and 55% in the social sciences (and similar proportions of the faculty), as against only 30% in the natural sciences and engineering.* Here is another striking difference between the word disciplines and the data disciplines—and, as noted in another connection, many people in academic life, especially on the science side of the campus, attribute it to the tendency in the social sciences and particularly the humanities to retill ground already covered.

Thus the debate over the very conception of doctoral study goes on: Is it one thing or several? Is it academic or professional? Is it supposed to produce the educated man or the skilled specialist? Is it for college teaching or for research? The debate is a mixture of dedicated conviction, alleged facts, clichés and prejudices, differences by field and type of institution, solid arguments, low motives and high ideals.

* That the union badge is even more important in the sciences elsewhere is indicated by the following lead and final sentences from a dispatch from Moscow to the *New York Times* of April 15, 1959: "The Soviet Union's scientists were told today that mere possession of a Doctor's degree would no longer guarantee a lifetime of luxury in the nation's top salary brackets. . . . The present system of payments to scientists in the Soviet Union put a priority on their having a degree." The article deals with the allegedly high salaries of academic personnel relative to holders of doctorates who work in production and with the tie-up of personnel in the academy because of the great pressure to process more and more doctoral degrees.

THE INSTITUTIONS

Historically, the national system of higher education has depended on a relatively few institutions to carry the load of graduate training. However, we are now in a long trend of decentralization in graduate work, a trend that has pretty well run its course for the Master's degree but is still active in the case of the doctorate. The story is suggested by these simple figures:

Up to the mid-1920's, the five most productive institutions (Columbia, Chicago, Harvard, Johns Hopkins, Yale) awarded about half the doctorates in this country.

In the 1930's, the five most productive (Columbia, Chicago, Harvard, Wisconsin, Cornell) awarded about a third of the doctorates.

In the 1950's, the five most productive (Columbia, Wisconsin, California, Harvard, Illinois) awarded well under a quarter of the doctorates.

But the story needs filling in, for involved here is one of today's lively issues: how will, and how should, the load of graduate study be distributed over the next years?

Growth and Changes in the System

As indicated in the historical review, the growth in graduate study was handled partly by the universities that got into graduate study early and partly by a series of newer entrants who saw doctoral work as an opportunity for national contribution, self-realization, or prestige. The growth of the system is the story of the rise of particular universities on the national scene. If we consider "genuine entry" into graduate study to mean the conferral of about 1% or more of the doctorates annually, here are the dates of entry (with the number of doctorates awarded in 1957–1958, the latest available year):

By 1900

Chicago (233)
Columbia (538)
Cornell (188)
Harvard (371)
Johns Hopkins (82)
Pennsylvania (155)
Yale (185)

By 1920

California (312)
Illinois (351)
Wisconsin (303)

By 1925

Cal Tech (54)
Catholic (107)

Iowa (158)
Iowa State (133)
Michigan (268)
Minnesota (221)
NYU (296)
Ohio State (261)
Princeton (105)
Stanford (187)

By 1930

MIT (153)
Northwestern (107)
Pittsburgh (96)

By 1940

North Carolina (73)
Penn State (126)
Purdue (216)
Southern California (147)
Texas (138)

By 1950

Indiana (199)
UCLA (164)

By 1955

Boston (89)
Maryland (102)
Michigan State (131)
Syracuse (80)
Washington, Seattle (115)

By 1920, there were only 10 institutions; by 1925, there were 10 more; and by 1955, 15 more than that. In 1900, there were only the 7 "great private universities"; of the next 13 entrants, 8 were public universities, all but 1 in the Middle West; and of the latest 12, 9 are public. By 1930, and for the most part much earlier, all the "national" graduate schools were established and in full operation; since 1930 have come the regional, state, and urban institutions, e.g., Washington in the Pacific Northwest, Southern California and UCLA for that area, North Carolina and Texas for different parts of the South, Purdue and Indiana and Michigan State in the Middle West, Boston for that urban center.

The comparable picture for the Master's degree is now so diffuse that it needs no such documentation. "Almost everybody" gives the Master's— that is, almost everybody but some dedicated and restrained liberal arts colleges. Because nearly half of all the Master's are awarded in education, three types of institutions are the leading producers: institutions with a heavy educational component, like Columbia (Teachers College) with 2,757 awarded in 1957–1958 or George Peabody with 578; urban universities with a concentrated clientele in education, like NYU (2,133), Southern California (973), Boston (842), Pittsburgh (753), or Wayne State (725); and state universities with a service to perform for their educational constituencies, like Michigan (2,081), Illinois (1,186), Wisconsin (1,124), or Indiana (1,103). As a result, some of the "great universities" that used to dominate the field have now fallen far behind. In 1957–1958, for example, Penn State gave more Master's degrees than Harvard, Temple more than Yale, Louisiana State more than Chicago, and Oklahoma State more than Cornell. Thus, the top Master's institutions are different from the top doctoral institutions, and that emphasizes the break between the two degrees.

The institutional picture has been changing in important ways. To start with, the traditional monopoly or near-monopoly of doctoral work has gradually worn away under the challenge of the newer entrants. It has been customary to say, and it still is, that despite the large numbers of institutions engaged in doctoral work, the overwhelming majority of degrees is granted by a handful of the great universities. Such universities still figure prominently in the conferral of doctoral degrees, of course, but not nearly so prominently as they did only a short time ago. In 1900, the 14 institutions in the AAU gave almost 90% of the doctorates; in 1958, the 39 institutions in the AAU gave only 70%. The top 10 in size gave 86% of the doctorates in 1900, and less than half that in 1958.

As the system has grown, the *relative* concentration has stayed about the same—a fourth of the institutions awarding doctorates gave about three-fourths the degrees in 1908, 1928, and 1958 (Figure 7)—but *which* institutions they are have changed. A year or so ago, Purdue gave almost as many doctorates as Chicago, Southern California about as many as

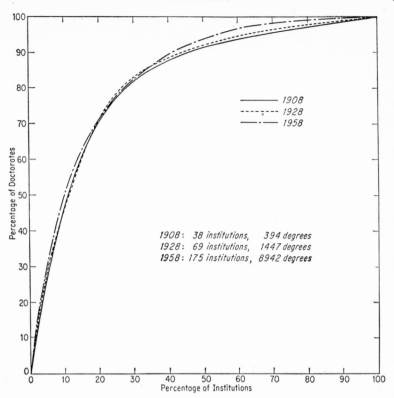

Fig. 7. Concentration of doctorates by institution—1908, 1928, 1958. (*Source: Office of Education.*)

Pennsylvania, Penn State more than Princeton, Indiana more than Cornell, Michigan State far more than Johns Hopkins or Cal Tech.

This trend has meant a movement of doctoral study not only toward the newer entrants but, concomitantly, of two other kinds. The first has been the gradual shift in the load of doctoral study from the private to the public universities. The numerical dominance of the private universities, so strong at the start, finally gave way only a few years ago to the long-run trend: more doctorates are now being given by the public universities (Figure 8). The private universities got to doctoral study first and it took some time for the public institutions to catch up. But now they have caught up, and since they are sure to grow faster in the years ahead than their private counterparts, it is not unlikely that a decade hence the private universities will be awarding not many more than two out of every five doctorates in the country.*

---

* The tension inherent in the situation, especially as it involves comparative tuition changes, was brought into the open in late 1959 by Lawrence Kimpton, Chancellor of The University of Chicago, in an address to the American Association of Land-grant Colleges and State Universities.

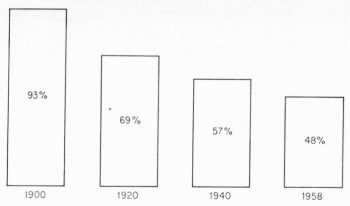

FIG. 8. Proportion of earned doctorates conferred by private institutions. (*Source: Office of Education.*)

The other development requires me to mention a fact of life in graduate education that, like other facts of life, is seldom discussed openly, even though it is of crucial importance. That is the fact that some universities are better than others—certainly better in faculty, in students, in products, in reputation, and probably better in program too. No one is yet able to *prove* to a sceptic's satisfaction that University *A* is really better than University *B*, especially when the sceptic is a member of the latter's faculty, but some way must be found to work with this slippery and controversial concept simply because it is necessary for the proper understanding of graduate work.

It so happens that as part of a general educational survey of the University of Pennsylvania in 1957, Hayward Keniston asked departmental chairmen in the arts and sciences throughout the country to rate the top departments in their fields. From their ratings, he constructed scores for the major departments; for the four broad divisions of the physical sciences, the biological sciences, the social sciences, and the humanities; and for the graduate school as a whole. Similar ratings were assembled in 1925 by Raymond Hughes and in 1934 by an ACE committee under his chairmanship, so that we can make a qualitative comparison over nearly thirty-five years.*

---

* Since such ratings are in dispute, and since I shall use a qualitative ranking based on them throughout this report, I append in a note to this section an extended statement about them that contains the classification used here. The reader might want to refer to it at this point. I appreciate why this is not a popular topic for public discussion, but I bespeak the willing suspension of passion for the sake of objective analysis of the present realities. I stand behind that great humanist who pointed out that the man who asks the question should not be held responsible for the answer!

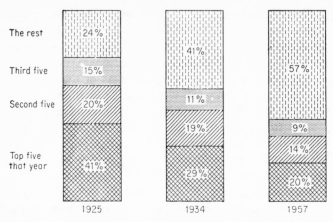

The rest

Third five

Second five

Top five
that year

1925   1934   1957

FIG. 9. Doctorates conferred by quality of institution.

Relative to the others, the production of doctorates by the better universities has been on a long decline. The dominance of the better universities, an historic feature of the national system of higher education, has gone down under the expansion and decentralization of the system (Figure 9).* In earlier times, the best universities also happened to be the leading producers of doctorates. Today, as doctoral study has spread out to more and more institutions, that is less clearly the case. In short, the concentration of doctoral study, especially in the "great private universities," has been greatly lessened and the trend has not yet run its course. This does not mean that the day of the great private university is over— far from it. Their quality is holding up, but their production is falling off relative to the system as a whole.†

* Actually, the situation is a little better when specific departments are considered rather than the university as a whole. In 13 of the major disciplines, the top 5 departments gave 30% of the doctorates a few years ago and the top 10 gave over 40%.
† Incidentally, there is an impression in the academic world that the traditional institutions give more doctorates in the arts and sciences and the newcomers more in the professional fields, but the differences are quite small:

	Proportion of all doctorates that are given in arts & sciences (1957)
Top 12 universities	71%
Other AGS universities, plus	71
Other universities	63
Private universities	73
Public universities	67
Established by 1930	70
Not established by 1930	70

Differences by field within the arts and sciences are perhaps more important: the

Actually, the relative quality of doctoral institutions has remained remarkably stable over the years. Of the top 10 in the Keniston rating today, 9 were charter members of the AAU in 1900, and the other, which happens to be the tenth in the quality rating, was admitted in 1908. Of the top 15 in quality today, all were members of the AAU by 1909. Of the top 10 in the 1957 rating, 9 were in the top 10 in 1925 and 9 in 1934. Of the best departments in 1925 and 1934, considered separately, about 75% were still among the best in 1957. No new institution that entered upon the doctoral enterprise in the past thirty-five years has been able to crash the top rank, relatively speaking, and most of the leaders have been around longer than that.

It takes a determined effort for an institution to move into the top ranks. Of the top 20 in quality in 1957, only 3 entered doctoral work, by the above definition, since the 1930's: UCLA (14th), Indiana (15th), and Washington (20th)—all public institutions. It is even hard to move into the top ranks quantitatively: of the top 20 in size of output in 1958, only 4 had entered since 1930: Purdue (11th), Indiana (12th), UCLA (16th), and USC (20th)—all aided by regional factors.

It is easy to add to the top institutions but hard to displace them. A major push can move an institution ahead in a decade or so but it typically takes more like a quarter century to get into the top ranks. As for the top 10, no newcomer has displaced the institutions that were established in graduate study decades ago. To those people who worry about the maintenance of standards and deterioration of quality under the impact of numbers, this should be a comforting thought. There may be more and more doctorates of lower and lower average quality; but the top institutions are still turning out important numbers of presumably the better doctorates. Will they be able to exert as much influence on the national system, as leaders and as models, when they give a third or fewer of the degrees as when they were giving two-thirds or more? Probably not. But will they be able to exert *enough* influence? Some deans of private institutions are pessimistic about their prospects, but I am not, at least not for the next few decades. The spiral of quality begetting quality will certainly run that far.

THE CURRENT SITUATION

What this long-run trend of decentralization implies, of course, is that the public universities, the lesser institutions, and the newer entrants are now growing faster than their opposite numbers. That is indeed the case.

---

physical sciences are equally prominent in all types of institutions, the social sciences and particularly the humanities are stressed more in the old, private institutions (the "Ivy League" influence), and the biological sciences in the newer, public ones (the "ag school" influence).

Using 1947–1948 as a base—it is the post-war year when doctoral production reached the pre-war level—I have calculated the relative increase in doctoral production for each of the major institutions and arranged them in descending order of growth over the past decade (Figure 10).

First, the public universities are growing much faster than the private ones. The only private universities on this list that expanded much faster than the system as a whole are urban institutions like NYU, Boston, Southern California, and Syracuse. The "great private universities" tend to cluster at the lower end. On the other hand, the large increases were made by such public institutions as Indiana, Michigan State, Washington, Maryland, Purdue, and UCLA.

The top institutions in quality are growing more slowly than the others. In part, of course, this is a matter of "attained maturity": the institutions that started first, whether public or private, reached or approached their limits first. True, the established institutions started from higher bases in 1947–1948; but it is also true that they have encountered some ceilings to their growth, and the others are now catching up. Some private institutions have deliberately remained small, despite the pressures for size, and have justified their position by claiming the maintenance of standards, e.g., Northwestern with 107 doctorates in 1957–1958, Princeton with 105, Johns Hopkins with 82, Cal Tech with 54. Others are smaller still: Brown, 42; Vanderbilt, 37; Washington (St. Louis), 32; Tulane, 21. In the present situation of graduate study, it is difficult for a small university to exert strong influence on the national scene; certainly Johns Hopkins was more influential some decades ago than it is today. Hardly any public institution stays small if it can help it.

Finally, the entrants since 1930, both public and private, are growing much faster than the established institutions. What is more, these 35 institutions, taken as a group, have not been increasing as fast as the others, that is, as those "coming" institutions that have committed themselves to the development of doctoral programs and are moving ahead fast. For example, in the years from 1954–1955 to 1957–1958, no fewer than 10 additional institutions gave 200 or more doctorates each, not enough to gain admittance to the earlier list, but close: Missouri (294), Florida (285), Duke (282), Rutgers (275), Rochester (265), Fordham (240), Kansas (239), Colorado (237), Nebraska (211), and Louisiana State (201). Almost all of them are still growing. And not far behind them are 5 more, also growing: Utah (197), Oregon State (196), Western Reserve (194), Denver (189), and Oklahoma (189). Most of these institutions entered into doctoral study on any scale only since the war: in 1940, Missouri, Duke, Rochester, Fordham, Nebraska, Western Reserve, and Louisiana State gave 23–25 doctorates each, but Colorado gave only 13, Rutgers 10, Kansas 8, Oklahoma 5, Oregon State 4, Florida 1, and Utah and Denver 0.

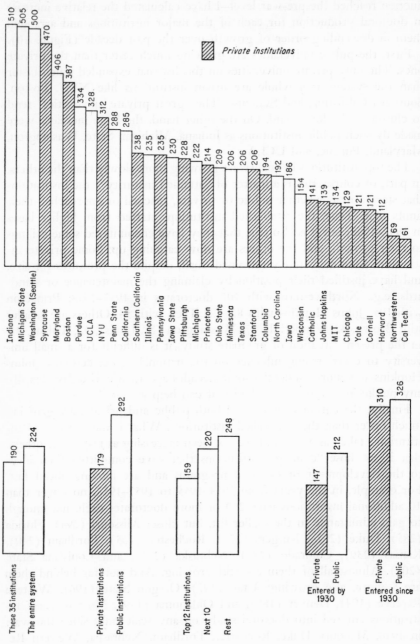

FIG. 10. Growth in doctoral production, 1947–1948 to 1957–1958, by major institutions. (*Source: Office of Education.*)

So the institutional resources for doctoral study have been gaining steadily and give no sign of slackening. A group of the small and fast-growing institutions still not in the center ring under the doctoral tent increased their share of the total production from 4% in 1947–1948 to 28% a year or two ago. The evidence is not yet in on how many of them will have staying power, but most of them have a good deal going for them, including determination and funds. All of this, incidentally, is a hopeful commentary on the numbers problem.

EXPANSION—AND STANDARDS

As the long-run trend continues, it contains the short-run answer to the important question: where is the expansion of graduate education in the next years going to take place? The answer is: everywhere, but mainly in the public institutions, in those below the top rank, and in the newer entrants.

First, let us look at recent enrollment trends. Since 1950, graduate enrollment has grown faster than the undergraduate, and doctoral enrollment has grown faster than total graduate enrollment, at all types of institutions. But the public and the newer ones have been growing faster at the doctoral level than the private and established places. Nor are the top institutions quite keeping pace with the others, especially at the Master's level. The traditional institutions, as I said, are now closer to

Growth in enrollment, 1950–1958
(Median figures; 1950 = 100)

	Undergraduate	Graduate	Doctoral
Total group	105	122	138
Top 12 universities	107	106	139
Other AGS universities, plus	100	115	132
Remaining universities	107	147	150
Private universities	89	119	134
Public universities	118	126	147
Established by 1930	99	102	127
Not established by 1930	107	147	150

their ceilings; the others are the growing institutions and they will be carrying an important part of the growth in the next decade or so.

This is clear from the graduate deans' own estimate of the situation. When they were asked, "About how much could your institution expand (doctoral) enrollment within your present facilities and without lowering standards?" and "How much should you?," their answers clustered approximately as follows:

	Medians	
	Could	Should
Total group	20–25%	15–20%
Top 12 universities	10–15	10–15
Other AGS universities, plus	25	20
All other universities	20–25	25
Private universities	20–25	15–20
Public universities	20–25	20–25
Established by 1930	15–20	15
Not established by 1930	25	20–25

The farther down in the university hierarchy, the larger the proportion of both *could* and *should*. The latter figures are always lower due to the natural tendency of deans to be cautious wherever standards are involved. For that matter, the graduate faculty substantially agrees with the deans in these estimates of *could* and *should*, with the further point in their case that the professional fields are 10–15 percentage points higher than the arts and sciences. As with institutions, so with fields: the latecomers are growing faster.

When the deans were then asked, "About how much expansion in graduate and doctoral enrollments at your institution do you expect over the next five years?," their answers were as follows:

	Medians	
	Total graduate enrollment	Doctoral enrollment
Total group	20%	20%
Top 12 universities	15	15
Other AGS universities, plus	20	15
Remaining universities	25	25
Private universities	15	15
Public universities	25	25
Established by 1930	15	15
Not established by 1930	25	25

These estimates are inevitably rough and approximate, but they are instructive, coming from the people closest to the situation. Again there is an expectation of more graduate students down the line, though there is not a great deal of difference at the doctoral level, where the top institutions will place even more emphasis relative to the Master's over the next years of pressure for the product.*

If the deans are right in these estimates, and the attrition rate remains about the same, the universities will confer a total of about 11,000 doctorates in 1964 as against the Office of Education's latest estimate of 12,700. But again, the deans are likely to be cautious in such an estimate, in the name of standards, and to temper their expectations with their wishes. If one takes that into account, together with the pressures for expansion, the figures hang together quite well.

Where *should* the expansion take place? For those who believe that the established and coming institutions will not or cannot rise to the challenge, the bugbear of graduate education, the teachers college, enters the scene. Here is the threat that worries many people today. Should the universities fail to produce the needed doctorates to staff the faculties of higher education, they fear that the teachers colleges will step into the breach, as they did decades ago training secondary and elementary school teachers when the liberal arts college "abdicated" its "responsibility." † This fear is common in today's discussion of the matter. The Committee of Fifteen and the trustees of the Carnegie Foundation expressed concern over the prospect, and the graduate dean at Harvard recently commented on the matter with his customary style:

> I do not wish to discuss this grave problem in a tone of general and tactful comity. The truth is that either institutions of liberal arts will supply the needed teachers . . . or else professional schools of education will hungrily jump in, with the same celerity that enabled them to found and staff normal schools in order to supply the late nineteenth century's need for elementary and secondary school teachers (when, be it remembered, the liberal-arts colleges, in an indifferent snobbism, abdicated this venerable privilege and duty).

* Actually, something of the same sort can be seen in the colleges' estimates of their enrollments five years hence. The top colleges expect to be about 25% larger, the lesser colleges about 35%, and the teachers colleges about 45%. In other words, if all these expectations are realized, the pressure of numbers will be accommodated disproportionately in the "lesser" and newer institutions of higher education. And as we shall soon see, this means that the expectations of the producers and the (academic) consumers of the doctoral product are pretty well in balance, by type of institution.

† Incidentally, as a graduate dean points out, if the liberal arts college *had* then taken on the task, it would not now be the liberal arts college we know. "It may very well have been the best thing for the country that the colleges decided not to destroy themselves in the interest of training the thousands of new teachers being demanded. Had they done so to the extent required by circumstances, they would have been ruined. They could not have met the need without reducing their requirements for admission or success or changing the course of study and increasing their numbers. As it is, they were preserved and are today a very vital part of our educational system. Their preservation has exercised a fine influence on the institutions that did take over the functions of training teachers."

The prospect does not alarm me, for a number of reasons.* In the first place, I do not expect it to happen. As I have suggested, I think that the numbers problem has been overstated and that it can be, and will be, handled satisfactorily within the present framework of graduate universities. Second, the "teachers colleges" are not teachers colleges any more; they are becoming state universities with staffs and programs and ambitions in the arts and sciences similar to those of general institutions. According to Paul Woodring:

> Today, virtually every subject taught in any liberal arts college is available in some of the better teachers colleges and is taught by men and women with the same academic background as professors in universities and liberal arts colleges—teachers who hold Ph.D. degrees from universities and whose professional commitment is to an academic discipline rather than to education as a profession.

Third, to the extent that such institutions do produce doctorates in the next decade, they will be needed in a whole range of American institutions that, for reasons of economy and prestige, cannot expect to get staffed by people from the top institutions. Fourth, they will not produce many doctorates in any case; as I have tried to show, it takes a long time to get tooled up to a substantial rate of production. Of the 64 institutions that awarded no doctorates in 1947–1948 but did in the last decade, only 2 can be said to have made the grade: Connecticut with 37 doctorates awarded in 1957–1958 and Florida State with 39.

Some people have been hoping that the "marginal producers" of strong Master's degrees will become active enough at the doctoral level to take some of the pressure off the established institutions. But that too seems an unlikely prospect. The only institutions that now give large numbers of Master's but no doctorates are those specializing in education, such as the state colleges of California and some Middle Western states and certain less prestigious urban institutions.

At the doctoral level, the national supply over the next years will have to be produced by the institutions already well in business. Nor is that prospect displeasing. In one sense, it might be said that the system has expanded too far already—in the sense that many institutions give very few degrees and might be said not to have real doctoral programs, even though they are listed as doctorate-conferring institutions. Of the 180 universities that conferred doctorates in the period 1936–1956, over half averaged 5 or fewer a year. The situation is improving somewhat: of the 175 institutions that conferred 1 or more doctorates in 1957–1958, only a third gave fewer than 10.

* Nor am I alarmed over the imminent prospect of off-campus graduate work. For the present, that is limited to the Master's and to the professional fields of education and engineering, and I do not look for its extension to the arts and sciences, much less to the doctoral level. For the time being, at least, the opposition is too strong.

Most observers, I suppose, would agree that a certain size is required for good graduate work—in order to have a sufficient group of students for their mutual stimulation,* a faculty large enough for proper specialization, and the necessary facilities. At present, it seems clear, not all doctoral institutions meet reasonable standards in this regard. At the top universities, that award the doctorate in an average of 52 fields, there are 10 or more doctoral candidates in residence in an average of 33 fields, or 60 to 65%. At the other institutions, the corresponding figures are 27 and 12, or 45%.

Or consider the spread of doctoral programs relative to degrees awarded: an average of only a little over four degrees were awarded in 1957–1958 per doctoral program offered in the arts and sciences. Chemistry is high with about nine degrees per program. Such fields as economics, mathematics, philosophy, history, biochemistry, botany, geology, geography, physiology, political science, sociology, zoology, and German are all under the average of four degrees per program offered. Some of the very small producers can perhaps justify doctoral programs on the grounds of strong specialities or geographical isolation, but very few.†

Actually, there is already some concern about the expansion of doctoral study on the part of both the deans and the graduate faculties. "Do you think that some institutions not really qualified for doctoral work are jeopardizing standards by expanding too rapidly?" "Yes," say three-fourths of the deans and over half the faculty. The surprising point here is that the responses of the graduate faculty are almost identical regardless of the level of institution. Everyone is responding, apparently, with an eye to those institutions below his own! As for fields, the physical and biological sciences are less critical on this score than the others; their standards are more settled. Along the same line, incidentally, the graduate faculty believes that "doctoral students at different universities do not get essentially the same training, in quality and scope." Here, the split in opinion is not particularly sharp, 52 to 32% with the remainder undecided. In this case, the physical sciences and the professions feel less strongly on the matter, and there is a clear institutional difference of the obvious kind.

---

* I asked the recent recipients whether as graduate students they had learned "a great deal from one another." About three-fourths said they had—a little more in the sciences, a little more in the top places (where the better students are). As a matter of fact, when I went on to ask: "When you get right down to it, and taking everything into account, did you learn more from your fellow students or from your professors?," only about three-fourths said their professors. Most of the others said the score was about even.

† It is considerations like these that lead to the fear that the requirement in the National Defense Education Act that fellowships go only to "new or expanded" programs would tempt more institutions to innovate unduly or to overexpand, even though it would not be very profitable for them to do so.

The ideal solution is pretty well agreed on:

	Graduate deans	*Graduate faculty*
Would be desirable to limit doctoral training to the major established institutions, if possible	6%	17%
Established institutions should be filled first, then other institutions should expand as necessary	72	50
Newer entrants into doctoral training should be encouraged to expand right now	16	23
Can't say	6	10

Here the field differences are negligible, and the faculty in institutions outside the AGS are only 10 percentage points more sympathetic to expansion.

As an economist wrote me: "It is uneconomical and inefficient to have a great many centers of graduate education which produce only a few doctorates a year each. Graduate training is a decreasing cost industry. . . ." Would it be better if there were more doctoral students per program, even if that meant fewer programs offered? Almost certainly yes. Can such redistribution of students be accomplished, given the realities of the situation? Almost certainly no.

To say the least, more students are needed more than more programs. Since there is no centralized agency that can set policy, let alone administer or enforce it, each institution on the doctoral market will decide for itself on expansion, with relatively little concern for what others are doing, except, perhaps, for a few near or dear to it. What comes out will be the national distribution of the doctoral load. That is one of the glories of the diversity of American higher education—or one of the costs, depending on how you look at it.

It seems to me, then, that the opportunity and the burden in the next years rest squarely on two groups of institutions: those already well-established and those newcomers that have given evidence of seriousness and potential. The former will continue to carry the brunt of the load, but the latter will carry more and more of it, as they have in recent years. In addition to the old stand-bys, it is that group that is critical in the next decade or so, say, the institutions that entered doctoral study, by the definition given above, in the past twenty years and those near that threshold. They are the ones, especially the newer and more regional of them, that should be encouraged to expand and improve their doctoral training to meet the needs of the next years. Harvard, Columbia, Chicago, Yale among the private universities, and California, Michigan, Wisconsin, and Illinois among the public ones, will continue to lead the parade, probably in both senses. The next decade should see the further emergence of institutions like UCLA, Michigan State, Washington at Seattle, Oregon and Oregon State, Texas, Rochester, Penn State, Rutgers, Duke, Tulane, North Carolina, Vanderbilt, Florida, Colorado. If the need is met, these two broad classes of institutions will have to do the job. If they do not, the need will not be met.

The anticipated expansion of doctoral study in or to a new class of universities has always raised concern about standards in those institutions already well established (even though most of them once had to struggle upward in the same way). But it is important not to lose sight of the benefits, both locally and nationally, of the moderate expansion of doctoral study.

Locally, the effect is generally to improve the institution, not simply at the graduate level but throughout, because of the attraction of graduate students and a better faculty. As Sir Hugh Taylor, former graduate dean of Princeton and now president of the Woodrow Wilson National Fellowship Foundation, has said:

> It is a commonplace that the satisfactions of the academic life to members of the faculty are enhanced by that master-disciple relationship which comes with a vigorous, healthy program of scholarship and research at the graduate level. Good faculty rightly demand the opportunities that come with good graduate students. . . . Given this association, the whole tone of undergraduate instruction can be raised to a higher level. This has been found true not only in the universities but also in the better colleges of the country.*

Not all the universities that have been in doctoral study for at least twenty-five or thirty years can be called great institutions—though all the great ones are in that group—but most of them are probably better than they would be without it. Graduate study helps institutions grow in quality, as all those now at the top once had to do. Over the next years, several public universities will successfully compete with the top private ones in salary levels and will build up their faculties accordingly, as indeed they have been doing in recent years.

Nationally, the need will more nearly be met and the entire system strengthened by a moderate expansion. In the past few years, two distinguished retired deans have made the same point—the need for more good graduate centers. Sir Hugh Taylor feels strongly that the national

---

* The other side of the coin was argued by Ralph Fields of Teachers College in the 1958 ACE meeting: "It has been the history of institutions as they have taken on programs above that which they originally started, that the new program has always received the greater attention in the years that come. The junior college that shifts into a four-year program very soon gives up those unique aspects of the program that it started as a two-year institution. As a four-year institution goes into graduate work, will there be a tendency that it will take attention away from what the institution has set up as its primary purpose?"

need "cannot be served . . . by a round dozen of prestige institutions"; and Dean Keniston concludes that we need "at least twice as many" as the present "fifteen or twenty centers."

Most people who worry about expansion are worried about falling standards. However, there are some saving graces in the situation. The longer a university works at doctoral study, the better grade of students it can attract and the higher its standards come to be. The better institutions today have been around a long time. Furthermore, everything in graduate study, in science and in scholarship, is communicable and hence can be and has been disseminated from the stronger to the weaker institutions.* As a knowledgeable educator said to me: "They can do things at Kansas now that used to be done only at Harvard."

What is more, as I shall show in a moment, the better institutions have for years been colonizing the weaker ones. In the beginning, only the better ones were producing many doctorates and through the years they have been among the major producers. Since as a class they could not absorb all their own doctorates, their graduates have gone elsewhere— largely to other universities where doctoral programs were offered sooner or later, with their own participation and often leadership. So over the years the weaker institutions have been strengthened by a supply from those up ahead. This filtering-down process throughout the national system has now located sizable contingents of doctorates in institutions of lesser quality than the institutions from which they secured their own doctorates, as we shall soon see. Put another way, substantial proportions of the faculties of lesser institutions were trained at the better places. If the qualification of the faculty's training is one measure of institutional merit, then that is now spread more widely than it was even a few decades ago.

We must also recognize that differences in standards, or at least in the realization of standards, are virtually inevitable in a system of higher education as diverse and as massive as ours. When more and more universities move into doctoral training, the range and variation tends to increase. Fifty years ago, when doctoral training was limited to a handful of the "great universities," they could maintain an even set of standards: partly by exchanging faculty members, partly by staying in close touch simply by reason of small numbers and personal relations. Now,

---

* I tried to get at this by checking the institutions in which the authors of leading texts were trained or are now employed, but due to the competition of the textbook market, I was unable to get a reliable list of what the leading textbooks are. My guess is that this is an important way in which the top institutions influence the lower ones. David Riesman, in his *Constraint and Variety in American Education*, remarks that "it is fascinating, in the leaflets put out by textbook publishers giving the names of colleges that adopted the particular book, to trace the spread of highbrow thinking into the academic hinterland: there are many books which are used virtually throughout the snake-like procession."

however, the enterprise is too large, too dispersed, too differentiated for that. In addition, one of the main means for exposing quality has long since disappeared, namely, the requirement to publish the dissertation. Hence standards differ, and that fact is a source of great concern to most observers of the situation.

Why should it be? Here we return to the issue of the "meaning" of the degree: "because the doctorate will come to mean different things, just like the Bachelor's degree." But why not? As a matter of fact, it does already, and people accommodate to the situation with little difficulty. "Everyone knows" that a doctorate from Harvard or Berkeley or Columbia or Chicago does not mean the same thing as a doctorate from newer and less prestigious institutions. "Everyone" also differentiates the Ph.D. by field—a Ph.D. in mathematics counts more than one in, say, sociology—and, indeed, most informed people distinguish between fields at the same institution ("history is good there but psychology isn't") and even between major professors in the same department ("he got his degree with X"). As a matter of fact, of course, the same differentiation is made even at the Bachelor's level: a degree from Oberlin or Swarthmore or Wesleyan means more than the same degree from a small denominational school in the South. Indeed, there may well be greater variation at the collegiate level than the graduate.

A crucial fact in the situation is a paradoxical one. It is that the production of more second-class doctorates, even though they may lower the national average, does not affect the production of first-class doctorates. We shall have as many and more of the latter *plus* the former as well. And at the doctoral level, large numbers are now needed. Not only that, but different kinds of doctorates too, by reason of another consideration that is central to the doctoral enterprise.

The System of Stratification: Its Operation and Effects

The graduate school is one of the most important distributors of talent in American life. It is a critical rung in the academic career ladder—in some ways, *the* critical one.

What the sociologist would call social stratification, complete with social mobility, exists within the system of higher education at the doctoral level, on the basis of the differences in (perceived) institutional quality. Just as a person's eventual position in society depends on the class he was born into as well as on his own talent, so his eventual position in higher education depends on the standing of the (parental) institution where he took his doctorate as well as on his scientific or scholarly capabilities. In each case, a good deal depends on what step of the ladder you start from. This is not to say that "class" is everything and talent nothing, any more than that is the case in other departments of life. But it does matter.

Logan Wilson observed years ago that in academic life no one could expect to rise much above the level of his graduate school, and Theodore Caplow and Reece McGee recently documented the same theme in their analysis of hiring practices in *The Academic Marketplace:*

> The initial choice of a graduate school sets an indelible mark on the student's career. In many disciplines men trained in minor universities have virtually no chance of achieving eminence . . . The handicap of initial identification with a department of low prestige is hardly ever completely overcome. The system works both in channeling students into graduate school and then in channeling them out into jobs. Thus it affects where students come from and where they go to.

Those are the central questions: where do graduate students come from and where do they go? This is where the graduate school operates as a big device for screening academic talent—indeed, all intellectual talent outside law, medicine, and the creative arts.

To begin with, the winners of the national fellowship programs end up largely at the top graduate schools. In fall 1959, for example, about 60% of the Woodrow Wilson Fellows and nearly 75% of the National Science Foundation Fellows went to the top 12 universities, which have only about 35% of the total doctoral enrollment. Such concentration has been a matter of great controversy in recent years, so much so in fact that both agencies have taken countermeasures. NSF has provided other kinds of fellowship funds that can in effect be administered locally and the Woodrow Wilson fund one year placed a ceiling on the number of its fellowships that can be awarded to any institution, with the sole effect of holding down the number going to Harvard. (The limitation is now voluntary.)

Some people close to the situation, incidentally, think that the national programs have worked to the disadvantage of the moderate schools and the less-than-top-grade students by sending some of the latter to the top institutions, where they have trouble, instead of to the schools where they more appropriately belong. A distinguished humanist who had been involved in the Wilson program thinks that draining off the superior students to the top places means that

> . . . the average graduate school will lower standards just to avoid failing out a high proportion of its students without a degree. There will always be some competing institutions whose standards are low enough to attract students away . . . The money poured into smaller graduate schools for prestige, a phenomenon of the post-war years, may go to less and less qualified students if the best are drained off. Then there will be

pressure to give degrees to a reasonable number of these students; and the fat is in the fire.

Furthermore, the better schools have a better chance to select the better students; they have more applicants and generally the first choice among them. But at the same time, precisely because they are the *national* graduate schools, they register fewer of those admitted:

	Percentage admitted of those applying	Percentage registered of those admitted
Top 12 universities	48	53
Remaining universities	71	72

The better students apply to several of the better schools, are admitted to a few of them, but then can register at only one. The lesser institutions are more regionally based: they admit large proportions of their applicants in order to have graduate students, and large proportions of their applicants actually register since they have applied to only the admitting institution or perhaps one other. Thus the problem of multiple applications is a problem only at the very top of the pyramid, and as more and more students apply for graduate study in the years ahead, the rich will get richer in the sense that the top universities will have even more of the top talent to select from.

As a result, the baccalaureates from the better undergraduate schools generally go to the top graduate schools. A current study on the financing of graduate work carried out by the National Opinion Research Center for the Associated Research Councils collected data from a national sample of graduate students in the arts and sciences. Here is the relationship between where they got their baccalaureate and where they were attending graduate school:

	Institution of Bachelor's degree * Graduate students				
Graduate school	*High universities*	*Better colleges*	*Middle universities*	*Other colleges*	*Low universities*
High	63%	50%	22%	21%	17%
Middle	23	40	69	50	29
Low	14	10	9	29	54
Total no. of cases (= 100%)	393	151	483	1,093	466

* This classification of institutions is the one used by NORC and differs slightly from mine, but the categories are essentially the same and so is the classification of individual institutions. In this case, high universities are the top 10 in Keniston; middle universities are the other AGS members; low universities are all others. The "better" colleges are those high on the Knapp-Greenbaum list. The classification of graduate schools is the same as for universities.

Students who take their Bachelor's degree from the top universities have the best chance, nearly two out of three, of getting into the top graduate schools—another kind of in-breeding—and those from the best colleges are next, with a 50–50 chance. Students from all other institutions have about the same chance—only one in five. And so on down the line, with extensive in-breeding by class of university. (In-breeding by individual institution accounts for about 25% of the university baccalaureates who go on to graduate school.) Where one takes his Bachelor's has a good deal to do with where he takes his graduate work. (I am told that there is a similar relationship, especially in the East, between one's secondary school and admission into the better colleges; so the chain of career effect can extend back that far.) On the whole, more students move up than down.

That is the picture for all graduate students in the arts and sciences—Master's as well as Doctor's, those who will finish as well as those who will not. The picture is about the same for recipients of the doctorate:

Recent recipients of doctorate
Institution of Bachelor's degree

Institution of doctorate	Top 12 universities	Better colleges	Other AGS, plus	Other colleges	Other universities
Top 12 universities	70%	39%	23%	25%	25%
Other AGS, plus	19	39	62	48	37
Other universities	11	22	15	27	38
Total no. of cases (= 100%)	321	279	444	517	564

As it happens, students from the lower institutions who get into the top places are more likely to finish their degree programs. Put another way, it is the especially able student who jumps that institutional gap, and he is more likely to get the degree. Moreover, the proportion of in-breeding, i.e., doctoral recipients who got their baccalaureate at the same institution, goes up sharply at the top and middle universities, to about 40%. Those institutions apparently can select the best prospects from among their own undergraduate students, on the basis of personal familiarity, more effectively than students from other places, so far as completion of the degree is concerned (assuming, of course, that their own do not get preferential treatment, consciously or not).

For the graduate faculty, the picture is still sharper.* In every case,

---

* Consistently across the board, the total faculty of colleges and universities stands between the figures for recent recipients and those for graduate faculty, in each of these categories.

Graduate faculty
Institution of Bachelor's degree

Institution of doctorate	Top 12 universities	Better colleges	Other AGS, plus	Other colleges	Other universities
Top 12 universities	84%	60%	41%	38%	46%
Other AGS, plus	11	34	54	45	31
Other universities	5	6	5	17	23
Total no. of cases (= 100%)	375	137	366	242	354

regardless of where they took their baccalaureate, they are more likely, by 15 percentage points or so, to have taken their doctorates at the top universities. Here the in-breeding by institution has the steepest range of all: from nearly 60% at the top (i.e., 60% of the graduate faculty in the top universities got their baccalaureates and doctorates at the same institution) down to only about 15% at the bottom.

The odds are clear: the chances of taking one's doctorate at the top universities are two out of three if the baccalaureate is taken there; about two in five if it is taken from the best colleges; and about one in four from anywhere else. In-breeding by quality of institution is also evident; that is, those who took their Bachelor's degrees from the second layer of universities tend to take their doctoral degree there, and similarly for the third layer. Moreover, in every case, there is more movement *up* the academic hierarchy, from Bachelor's to Doctor's, than there is down.

Why does it matter where people take the doctorate? Leaving aside anything else, it matters because the institution where a person gets the doctorate has a determining effect on where he ends up. The higher the institutional level of the doctorate, the higher the subsequent post in academic life (and probably outside it, too, though I have no data on that). Here are the figures for the recipients of the doctorate in 1957:

Where recent recipients took their doctorates

Their present academic position	Top 12 universities	Other AGS, plus	Other universities
Top 12 universities	28%	6%	5%
Other AGS, plus	15	24	9
Other universities	27	23	42
Better colleges	10	13	7
Other colleges	20	34	37
Total no. of cases (= 100%)	458	566	268

A similar picture emerges for the graduate faculty—remarkably similar when one considers that they are on the whole more highly selected.

Where the graduate faculty took their doctorates

Their present academic position	Top 12 universities	Next 10 universities	Other AGS, plus	Other universities
Top 12 universities	38%	15%	11%	8%
Next 10 universities	13	37	6	6
Other AGS, plus	20	19	44	12
Other universities	29	29	39	74
Total no. of cases (= 100%)	854	299	235	175

Where one ends up, by these institutional classifications, depends a great deal on where one starts out with his doctorate.

In this case, unlike the earlier one, there is much more movement down, from the doctorate institution to the present position, than there is up. A current recipient of the degree from one of the top universities has better than one chance in three to get into a top university or college, as against one in five or even one in ten for doctorates from other institutions. An established member of a graduate faculty similarly has a 2½ to 5 times better chance to land at the top if he manages to start there.* Whether it is due to better selection of talent, better training, better visibility, or mere personal relations—or all of these together—the hard fact remains. It is thus of critical importance for a doctoral student ambitious for an academic career to gain admission to a graduate school toward the top of the prestige ladder.

When people go to graduate school, then, they go out and up: *out* to institutions of rank similar to their own undergraduate institution, *up* to institutions generally considered better. When they leave graduate school, they go out and down.†

Through the years, then, the top institutions have been staffing the

---

* Furthermore, there is even a tendency for people from the top institutions to hold higher academic rank (in-breeding omitted):

	Proportion with tenure positions	
Highest earned degree from	Graduate faculty	General college and university faculty
Top 12 universities	85%	68%
Other AGS universities, plus	83	57
Other universities	73	43

† In addition, students tend to stay in their own regions and within the public/private sphere. Of the recent recipients in academic jobs (leaving aside in-breeding), 68% of those from public institutions are employed in public institutions as against 50% of those from private institutions. Roughly the same difference characterizes the faculties as well. The public/private distinction may be softening, but the grooves are still there.

others with personnel, and through them, with skills and standards.* The top 12 universities, by this classification, have produced over half the graduate faculty in all American universities, even though their doctoral production was never that high. As for the total faculty of the country's colleges and universities, here is their institutional origin:

	Present faculties of: *						
Received highest earned degree from:	Top 12 univs.	Next 10 univs.	Other AGS, plus	Other univs.	Best colleges	Better colleges	Other colleges
Top 12 universities	85%	47%	44%	31%	44%	33%	21%
Next 10 universities	9	38	13	15	19	16	11
Other AGS, plus	2	8	31	17	15	19	23
Other universities	1	6	7	28	7	12	23
Other	3	1	5	9	15	20	22
Total no. of cases (= 100%)	187	253	297	274	261	354	347
In-breeding (i.e., highest earned degree from own institution)	47%	27%	20%	15%	5%	6%	4%

* These data were secured primarily from the faculty lists in college and university catalogues. Incidentally, just as William James implied nearly sixty years ago, it is the lesser institutions that are quicker to list the degrees of their faculty members. Information on the sampling is given in the Appendix.

The top 12 universities have supplied themselves first and foremost, but beyond that have exported enough talent for nearly half the faculties of the better universities and the best colleges, about a third of the other universities and the better colleges, and even a fifth of the remaining colleges. In every case, they have provided more staff members to other classes of universities than the latter have provided for themselves.† In the system as a whole (and weighting these figures to proper faculty sizes in the various classes), the top 12 universities have provided some-

* Not always to the comfort of the local students, incidentally. Here is the observation of a recent doctorate in English from a strong Middle Western state university: "There is another very touchy problem, namely, the low reputation in which students at the home institution are held by imported faculty from Harvard, Yale and—alas— Chicago and Northwestern. The home-grown crop are mediocre—and faculty tell students so—compared to the bright boys among whom the professors took their degrees. The twining ivy, from wherever imported, frequently chokes the local plants."

† This needs to be taken into account in connection with the issue of standards or qualifications of newer entrants into doctoral study. One reasonable question to ask is: how many of their graduate faculty came through the major doctoral programs? If the cut-off point, for example, is put at securing the degree from the top 22 institutions, then the "other universities" are now only about 10 percentage points behind the "other AGS, plus."

thing like 35% of the staff of American higher education. They have been at it for a long time, of course, but even so the record still seems impressive.

Their in-breeding, incidentally, is high—naturally high since they have been the major producers: the oldest and best institutions always have had more in-breeding than the others. This may place a new light on the concept that is usually given a negative connotation in academic circles. (In-breeding is always "too much" just as specialization is always "undue.") As a class, they have had to in-breed, as a statistical consequence of their dominant position as producers.* Across the system as a whole—if such a figure makes any sense—the proportion of in-bred faculty is about 15%.

The System and the Future

Frank Bowles of the College Entrance Examination Board has written convincingly of the "university community" that ties together the colleges and universities. "Thus, when a college prepares a student for university work and sends him to a university, the college becomes in a sense a part of the university to which its student has gone. Some colleges have in this sense membership in many universities, some have membership in a few." He believes that this decade has witnessed the "merger of two systems of education"—the pre-Civil War private system and the post-Civil War public one—that now "have common standards, common ends, a common pool of students, and in effect have established a single system of education. Columbia now competes with Michigan and California as it used to compete only with Yale and Harvard."

In an informal way, we have what might be called a national system of higher education. At the very top are the best, "national" universities. For their graduate schools, the input consists of the best students from themselves and the best colleges, plus award-winners and their equivalents from other places. The output is taken first to staff themselves and the best colleges, and then to staff the rest of the system as far as the supply lasts. And so on through the layers of lesser universities and regional universities. In this sense, increased production down the line, even if it is of lower average quality, is useful in staffing other institutions still further down the line who cannot afford or attract the products of the best institutions. Deploring this situation amounts to complaining about salary scales in lower academia, objecting that prestige means too much to

---

* As my associate, Albert Gollin, points out, these data reveal the time lag in in-breeding. Only about 15% of the recent recipients are kept on, in each class of institution, but the figure builds up as they are recalled to the home institution in later years. To some people, the latter situation, in which a man receives considerable experience elsewhere after getting his degree, does not amount to "real" in-breeding.

people, trying to repeal the law of propinquity, or regretting that there are not more bright men.

Over the next years, as the competition for students and staff increases, the differences among institutions may sharpen. From 1955 to 1959, according to the NEA data, the universities held steady in the proportion of doctorates among the new teachers taken on to the staff. It was the municipal universities (a small segment), the state colleges, and to a lesser extent the liberal arts colleges that went down. That is probably a preview of the wave of the future. The top institutions will keep more of their own best products: they have first chance at them and they have personal relations on their side. In general, doctorates will be attracted first to the universities—where they already are and know their way around, where salaries are better, where research is encouraged, where research and library facilities exist, where the teaching load is less, where the prestige is high, and so on. In fields where industrial employment is possible they will be attracted to that because of salary and research inducements.

The best colleges will be able to compete with the best universities in prestige and in salaries. They have the added inducements, for some, of a smaller size and a more pleasant environment. Furthermore, they will not need many people: they are small and they will not expand as fast as the total system.

But most liberal arts colleges are already feeling the pressure in this regard, and will soon be feeling it even more. I asked the graduate deans, graduate faculty, and college presidents whether "under the pressures of the years ahead, the liberal arts colleges will be able to attract, on the average, only the less able Ph.D.'s in competition with the universities and industry." About three-fourths of them thought that it was "already happening" or "probably will happen"—the graduate school people heavier on the former (especially in the sciences), the college presidents evenly split between "already" and "will." It is perhaps natural for the graduate school to think that it is keeping its own best students, but even the college presidents acknowledge that this is a problem for them now and that it is likely only to grow.* Indeed, some observers

* I also asked the college presidents whether they thought "the graduate universities tend to keep their better Ph.D.'s and recommend only the others to the colleges." About half couldn't say, and the rest split evenly between "yes" and "no." But the presidents of the better colleges were much more likely to agree, and no doubt to resent it.

Incidentally, many people believe, as Frederic Ness put it, that "many men will come to liberal arts colleges to teach because they themselves initially went to such a college," but the figures do not bear this out. According to Frank Kille's recent study of the baccalaureate origins of college faculty, about a third came from liberal arts colleges—which is close to their total baccalaureate proportion. Oberlin is the only college in the top 30 producers of college faculty, with respect to their Bachelor's degrees.

of American higher education, like Frank Bowles, think that this de-velopment

> will mean that the liberal arts colleges, which have been the single most important factor in our social and cultural development, will be hemmed within a constricting intellectual perimeter which will in time force them into the uncomfortable position of being an anachronism. In terms of their past, in terms of their ideals, they will be a splendid anachronism, but they will become an anachronism for all their splendor.

The smaller and poorer institutions will suffer relative to the others: they will get fewer of the better doctorates. Already about two-thirds of the graduate faculty in the arts and sciences and the graduate deans have "serious questions about the quality of some of the academic insti-tutions to which doctorates go—in terms of what they can offer in in-tellectual opportunities, academic atmosphere, etc." Some deans, in all seriousness, question whether many small, undistinguished colleges can expect the abler doctorates, given their low salaries, high teaching loads, poor libraries, and the rest. As one told me, "we ought to tell the small colleges that we simply aren't producing for that market." *

As for the "lesser" and regional universities, they will increasingly have to grow their own. That brings us full circle, for as we saw ear-lier in this section, that is precisely what they are doing. The other in-stitutions *are* growing faster than the established ones. We are already witnessing a gradual decline in the traditional feeder system at the grad-uate level, as universities have kept their own students to build up their own programs. Only a few decades ago, for example, Washington and Oregon and Oregon State used to send their best students in certain fields to Berkeley and Stanford for doctoral training, and some Middle Western institutions would send theirs to Columbia and Harvard. Now

---

* The colleges know, of course, from which graduate schools they have chances of getting faculty members. I asked the college presidents "which three or four schools you generally try first," and their responses sharply revealed the system of stratification:

	Top colleges			Other colleges			Teachers colleges		
	Near	*Not near*		*Near*	*Not near*		*Near*	*Not near*	
Top 12 universities	30%	34%	64%	25%	11%	36%	20%	5%	25%
Other universities	27%	9%	36%	54%	10%	64%	65%	10%	75%
			N =			N =			N =
	57%	43%	105	79%	21%	568	85%	15%	146

The top colleges go to the top universities, whether near or not. The others go to the nearest institutions.

they keep them at home. Here the interests of students and institutions are sometimes in conflict. From the standpoint of the student with national ambitions, it is disadvantageous. From the standpoint of the regional institution, it is the only way to move ahead quickly in developing its graduate school.

Administration and Organization

At their meeting two years ago, the presidents and the graduate deans of the AAU universities held a symposium on "The Ambiguous Position of the Graduate School Dean." Most observers, I think, consider it just as ambiguous after that discussion as before, mainly because ambiguity is inherent in the situation as universities are now organized. As a former dean put it, "the graduate school is a residual organization."

Administrative and organizational problems have characterized graduate work so long that most people have become used to them. The subordination of the graduate school to the undergraduate college, the intermingling of graduate and undergraduate students in the same courses, the uneven struggle between the dean's office and the departments, the weakness of a dean with no budgetary or appointive authority—these matters have been remarked by generations of commentators on the graduate scene.

Jacques Barzun, when a graduate dean, referred to the graduate faculty as "the amiable anarchy" and Professor Cowley has characterized the graduate school as a collection of small professional schools (i.e., the departments) held together by their devotion to research and the magic of the Ph.D. degree. Someone has said that "you can't build up the graduate dean any more than you can the Vice President of the United States," and in the AAU symposium a representative of the deans, Roy Nichols of Pennsylvania, put the common plight very well:

> The graduate dean (is) in an anomalous position. In terms of the usual connotation of the word, he is not a dean at all. He has a faculty, to be sure, but he does not recruit it, pay it, or promote it. He cannot effectively either reward or admonish it. He cannot deal effectively with department heads in a direct face-to-face relationship in any realistic atmosphere of academic negotiation. The department heads know, and he knows, that they must look to other deans for new appointments, promotions, increases of salary; they must negotiate elsewhere than in his office. . . . In fact, it seems only too apparent that the graduate dean can, in certain instances, be described as little more than a registrar and student counselor. Yet he and his part-time associates are responsible for the highest quality of the university instruction and for the carrying out of some of the most difficult objectives of higher education.

—and, it might be added, some of growing importance, absolutely and relatively.

In the typical university, even the large graduate university, the undergraduate dean "outranks" the graduate dean partly because of history (he was there first), partly because of size (he has more students and gets more tuition for the institution), and partly because of primacy (he has under him what is usually defined as the major task of the institution). The graduate dean has a voice in academic matters but usually it is only an advisory and consultative one. Compared to the professional deans in medicine and law, he has much less authority. In only a very few institutions is the organization radically different: Chicago is the notable example—in effect, it has a graduate dean for each of the major divisions of knowledge, with a budget and appointive power.

As a matter of administration, the graduate school usually has jurisdiction over the award of the Ph.D. wherever in the university it is given, and less often, over other graduate degrees as well.* The major policies and practices in graduate study are "actually determined, regardless of formal regulations," in the following way, according to the graduate deans:

Mainly by the graduate school	By both	Mainly by the department
Residence requirement	Amount of course work	Character of doctoral dissertation
Foreign language requirement	Student admission	Type of general examination
Membership in graduate faculty	Master's degree requirements	

Thus the graduate school is left (1) with determining membership in the graduate faculty, which is *pro forma* in many cases and a matter of departmental recommendation in others; the graduate school can veto, but every such veto costs something in peaceful relations, frequently more than it is worth; (2) with setting the residence requirement, largely

* Some rapidly growing professional schools, like engineering and business, chafe a little under this arrangement and will increasingly sue for independence in the next years in another struggle between "standards" and "self-determination." The obvious compromise, for them to give their own doctorate rather than the Ph.D., is generally unacceptable because it is the Ph.D. that is wanted. As these pages were being written, such a conflict was in process at one of the great universities. The business school sought a permanent seat on the committee controlling the Ph.D. program. The proposal was supported by representatives from engineering, medicine, pharmacy, and education and opposed by those from arts and science. The proposal failed by one vote, when the law school representative sided with the latter group. But the issue is not dead.

a paper requirement that is becoming even less consequential; and (3) with determining the foreign language requirement—small wonder that it is so in contention. As to the joint responsibilities, the department typically makes the decision and the graduate school ratifies or implements it. The graduate school admits students, to be sure, but the departments really select them (what one disapproving university president describes as "something amounting almost to a guild system with restriction of entry at the departmental level"). Even the Master's degree requirement is passing to the departments, reflecting what is happening to the status of that degree.

Indeed, some people seriously propose that under the circumstances the graduate school should abdicate to the departments, thus placing formal responsibility where the actual power is. In any case, how can a dean know enough about the specialized problems and qualifications of English, engineering, economics, mathematics, zoology, history, chemistry, psychology, and all the rest to do more than ask a few questions and ratify the judgment of the departments? (Some departments are so large and diversified that, as one faculty member put it, "the heads are bumping together there too!")

Under the circumstances one might expect the graduate deans to be discontented and restless, but on the whole they are not. Some deans are appointed as a reward for seniority or earlier distinction, especially when the office is more honorific than substantial. Sometimes top men will not take the post because of its clerical character and lack of real opportunity. But there is no basis for the minor legend in academic circles that the tenure of the graduate dean is extremely short—just long enough for a man of vision to find out how little he can do. The graduate deans are not particularly short-lived: the present group have been in office an average of about seven years. As nearly as I can tell, they do not hold office for a shorter period than the dean of the college or, for that matter, the president himself.

As for their attitudes toward the situation, only one dean in five thinks that "the office of graduate dean at your institution does not have enough authority to do the job properly" although about a third say it "would be better for graduate study if the office were strengthened." By and large, the graduate deans themselves appear to accept the situation as it is. One told me that in view of the absolute requirement for persuasion and consent in a university of strong and independent departments, all he could get was a "paper authority" in any case. Another—who recently put through a basic change at his university—thought that it was desirable to have one important office on the campus without power, as a safety valve for the tensions and conflicts inevitable among other centers of power within the university. Most graduate deans are, or soon become, realists: it may not look good on an organization chart, but it works.

Solutions have usually been local and personal in character (often, indeed, resting on the personal relations between the dean and the president): a strong dean who makes things work, by skill in negotiation or force of character or reputation; or a weak dean who lets things work. The "radical" remedies that have been proposed correspond to these types: make the graduate deanship into a strong, full-time administrative post, with staff, authority, budget, and power; or abolish it, and handle the clerical work through the registrar, the practices through the departments, and the general policies through an advisory council. In this respect, the proposal is reminiscent of the foreign language requirement: build it up or do away with it.

The formal solution of separating the graduate and undergraduate faculties is rejected by three-fourths of the graduate faculty and almost 90% of the deans (in reply to the proposition: "Graduate work would be done better if the graduate faculty did not also have to handle undergraduate work."). Chicago is cited as the critical experiment: it created two classes of faculty on the same campus; the plan failed and is now on its way out. The example of the "isolated and insulated" professional schools, *in* the university but not *of* it, is also cited in this connection.

But if intermingling of faculty is generally approved, the related issue of intermingling graduate and undergraduate students in the same classes is less widely accepted. This is another problem of long standing: in 1927 an officer of the ACE reported to the AAU, in disapproving terms, that between 25% and 40% of the courses taken by graduate students were senior college courses; and only last year *The Journal of Higher Education* published an article on this "Dangerous Trend in Graduate Education." Here the entire graduate faculty is split almost exactly 50–50 on the proposition: "The practice of having graduate students and undergraduates in the same classes lowers the quality of graduate instruction." But the arts and sciences agree less than the professions, and within them the data disciplines less than the word disciplines. What is perhaps of more importance, the recent recipients agree a little more—having just been subjected to the practice.*

Given the difficult administrative position of the graduate dean, his

---

* Incidentally, the arguments for the practice usually are that such a separation would be bad for the *undergraduates*. Here, I think, is a case where the hold of tradition can easily be demonstrated. Suppose that graduate work had always been purely graduate in character and that an educational report now recommended that about a third of the courses be joint with undergraduates in order to save money and upgrade the seniors. Think of the outcry that would arise in the name of standards, and from many of the same people who now tolerate or approve the situation as "the natural thing at this institution—works very well!"

person becomes more important. Because of the research emphasis of the graduate school and the research reputation of the sciences, a disproportionate number of graduate deans are likely to be physical scientists these days:

Academic field of dean

Physical sciences	27
Humanities	17
Social sciences	14
Biological sciences	9
Professional fields	9

Whether the academic allegiance of the deans makes much difference in the administration of the graduate school is hard to say, though in this instance it would seem to reinforce the claims of research and of science. In any case, the fact that the deans come from the field where most outside funds have been available in recent years is, I take it, not coincidental.

But another characteristic of the deans is perhaps more important. From my observations over the past few years, I have come to recognize two basic types of deans, plus a third who combines qualities of both. One is the conservative dean who has lived with the problems of the graduate school and the solutions thereof for a long time, who has settled into the situation effectively, who knows how much tolerance there is within the system and never tries to outreach it, who seems indifferent to criticism because he has heard it all so many times before. The other is the newly appointed radical reformer who sees all the problems anew (as someone said, "Graduate professors see their responsibilities only when they become graduate deans"), who searches anew for the solutions, who is impatient to *do* something, nationally as well as locally. Then there are the deans who combine the better qualities of both.

All types are involved in what has become of growing importance in recent years, namely, the national organization of graduate study. The history of the AAU, and more recently the AGS, is interesting not only for its contribution to the debate over graduate study, but also for its central place in the politics of graduate study.

The subject is too long, too complicated, and in some respects too confidential to go into here. It is enough perhaps to say that the AAU began as the organization of the presidents, was taken over for a long time by the graduate deans, and was taken back by the presidents about ten years ago. Now only the chief executive officer of the university can attend the AAU meeting—no substitutes allowed—and more than one president describes it as their private club in which confidential matters can be privately discussed, as is natural and desirable for such a crucial office. For the graduate deans, the Association of Graduate Schools in the Association of American Universities was established, and the two organizations usually spend one joint session together in their otherwise separate annual meetings.

It is no secret that the marriage has been uneasy on both sides, though neither has quite wanted to sue for divorce. Leaving aside the personal relations of president and dean, the major issue has been the size of the national organization: the presidents have wanted to keep the size down, the deans to expand. Just within the past year, a strong minority of deans tried to force the issue, but without success: for the time being the associations will hold together, and at about the same size (currently 41 members, 2 of them Canadian).

The minority envisaged a strong, comprehensive, central organization of graduate schools that would include every institution giving many doctorates (that is, two to three times the present membership). It would have a full-time secretariat and would serve as forum, clearinghouse and information center, researcher and data collector, public representative and spokesman, lobbyist, perhaps standardizer of non-academic regulations—but *not* evaluator or accreditor. In a way, this could signal the further coming of age of graduate study in this country. But it lost out, at least for the present, to the current arrangement plus regional federations throughout the country.

NOTE ON QUALITY RANKING OF INSTITUTIONS

A number of objections can be made to ratings like the Keniston one: the lag in judgments of departments moving up and down in quality, so that the rating may be a few years behind reality; the overlooking of quality in professional schools as against arts and science departments, to the possible disadvantage of public institutions where, e.g., biological talent may be located in schools of agriculture; poor sampling; insufficient information on the part of the departmental chairmen; the bias of the chairmen toward their own institution or that from which they took their doctorate; the simple addition of departmental ratings for the overall ratings, so that a good institution with few departments is disadvantaged; and so on. But when the professional contribution is taken into account, or the number of departments, the ranking hardly changes. For my purposes, the time lag is not important, since the particular year is not. Academic quality across an institution does not change abruptly anyway. Most graduate deans told me that the Keniston survey was reasonably good in their judgment, even though each of them could point out a few places where it "went wrong" in his institution—which is to say, where his judgment differed from the pooled judgment of the disciplinary specialists.

In the end, the critics have to face the fact that the rating was done by those supposed to know. Their judgments are "subjective" to be sure, but so is the concept itself. When you get right down to it, quality is largely a matter of what the field recognizes as such. Surely there is a good deal of prestige mixed up with "quality"—in my personal judgment, the Harvard halo shows through the ratings a little—but the two are after all not unrelated.

So in my view, if the results are taken by clusters of institutions (as used here) and the individual ranks not taken too seriously, then the Keniston survey is a valid classification. Meeting the typical objections would result in moving an institution only one or two places in the ranking at most, and when the universities are grouped, that makes little, if any, difference. Whether, for example, Chicago should be ranked ahead of Michigan, or Minnesota ahead of Pennsylvania, is immaterial in the clusters that result. If it makes some people more comfortable to think of this distinction as entirely one of prestige, they are of course free to do so. All I want to claim here is that institutions do differ by quality and that the Keniston rating can be used as a basis for distinguishing them.*

At the same time, it is important to recognize just what is being classified by such a rating. Because the top institutions have more distinguished faculties and apparently turn out better products, it does not necessarily follow that they have better training programs. Are the products better because the training is better, or because the students were better in the first place? That is an important question because of the implications it carries for the expansion of training. If other institutions give as good training and only need more good students, that is one thing. If their training is inferior as well as their students, that is quite another.

Certainly the better schools attract the better students (who then get to associate with a better group of students, for the stimulation and instruction that in itself provides) so their products should be better by that fact alone, even if their training were equivalent. At least this much can be said, I think: the better institutions get better students to start with, so that they are that far ahead in turning out a superior product. Whether they train them better, too, is much less clear. On that score, some of the top universities are subject to a good deal of criticism, both within themselves and from the outside, in that they do not give sufficient personal attention to their doctoral candidates. The very fact that their faculties are more distinguished and prestigious also means that they are more in demand for committees, consultantships, and other posts that take them away from the campus and their graduate students. The president of the, Woodrow Wilson Foundation, himself the long-time graduate dean at one of the top 12 and a former president of the AGS, recently remarked that "the advantages that come from a close and intimate contact between student and professor, possible in a small unit of graduate study, should

---

* At that, graduate schools probably do not vary as greatly as colleges. According to the dean of education at Harvard, "recent studies suggest that the least able student in one college maintains a higher standard of academic performance than the best of another college." That is probably not the case at the doctoral level (though I am told it probably is true for medical schools).

be emphasized. These opportunities do not exist for the student who is a cipher in a seminar conducted in even a 'prestige' institution by a nationally famous professor, too frequently away from home territory, advising and consulting in problems of industry and state." This is an extremely difficult thing to get at: the recent recipients of the doctorate from the top institutions feel a little less satisfied with the apprenticeship relation than those from the lesser institutions, but at the same time they feel less exploited as research assistants. But the differences here are small, and on similar items non-existent. For whatever it is worth, on the basis of my talks with graduate deans and leading representatives in the major disciplines, I have personally concluded that some departments in some of the lesser schools do at least as good a job of training as their counterparts in the prestigious institutions.

Given that much clarification, then, here are the institutions in the classification I use: the top 12 universities are the top 10 in Keniston—Harvard, California (Berkeley), Columbia, Yale, Michigan, Chicago, Princeton, Wisconsin, Cornell, Illinois—plus MIT and Cal Tech which I arbitrarily added since the Keniston report did not deal with technological institutions. That group awarded 34% of all doctorates in 1957–1958. The next 10, with 20% of the total, are the next 10 in Keniston: Pennsylvania, Minnesota, Stanford, UCLA, Indiana, Johns Hopkins, Northwestern, Ohio State, NYU, and Washington (Seattle). The third group, also with 20%, includes the remaining AAU-AGS institutions—

Brown	North Carolina
Catholic	Pennsylvania State
Clark	Purdue
Duke	Rochester
Iowa	Texas
Iowa State	Tulane
Kansas	Virginia
Missouri	Vanderbilt
Nebraska	Washington (St. Louis)

plus nine universities that received accomplishment awards from the Ford Foundation a few years ago: Baylor, Emory, Fordham, Georgetown, Louisville, Notre Dame, Rice, St. Louis, and Syracuse. All other universities are in the fourth group, with 26% of the doctorates. For most purposes, I combine the second and third groups.

Similarly, I have classified liberal arts colleges into three groups. The "best" colleges, 48 in number, are those that received accomplishment awards under the Ford program, scored high on the Knapp-Greenbaum list, and have high salary scales (which has independently been shown to correlate with institutional quality). This group includes such colleges as Wesleyan, Grinnell, Bowdoin, Amherst, Smith, Williams, Antioch, Kenyon, Reed, Oberlin, Haverford, Swarthmore, and Lawrence. The "better" colleges (70) were judged by the same criteria, but did not stand as high on them; this list includes such institutions as Birmingham-

Southern, Redlands, Whittier, Oglethorpe, Rockford, Centre, Colby, Drew, Bard, Dickinson, Fisk, Middlebury, and Whitman. The remaining colleges are in the third group. In some cases I have combined the first two groups.

Toward the validation of such classifications, I can present the following data that emerged from this study.

As for contributions to science and scholarship, I have data from an analysis made of the authorship of articles in the major learned journals in 1958 (as reported in the Appendix). The number of authors per 100 faculty members was as follows:

The top 12 universities	12.0
The next 10 universities	5.5
Other AGS universities, plus	5.2
Other universities	2.5
"Best" colleges	2.6
"Better" colleges	0.7
Other colleges	0.3

Thus the "top" universities are clearly top on this score of contributing to knowledge. They have less than 10% of the total faculty, but account for almost 40% of the authors in the leading learned journals.* As fur-

* If doctoral work should consist primarily of research training, such an analysis of contributions to the learned journals provides an opportunity to gauge the goodness of the programs. The rationale is that a university that gives many doctoral degrees should also contribute many articles to the journals, as an index of the research productivity that is itself the base of research training. In fact, there is a strong relationship by individual institutions but a few are out of line one way or the other. Here are the ranks for the 15 largest producers of doctorates in 1957–1958:

	Rank in production of doctorates	Rank in contributions to learned journals
Columbia	1	4
Harvard	2	2
Illinois	3	8
California (Berkeley)	4	1
Wisconsin	5	3
NYU	6	21
Michigan	7	5
Ohio State	8	15.5
Chicago	9	7
Minnesota	10	9
Purdue	11	10
Indiana	12	27
Cornell	13	6
Stanford	14	12
Yale	15	13

The only institutions more than five ranks out of line are Cornell in one direction and NYU, Ohio State, and Indiana in the other. I should caution that these ranks probably ought to be based on a larger sample than a single year, and to be done by field in order to represent a university's efforts more directly. But with these caveats, I present the data as an illustration of one objective basis of determining the quality of an institution's doctoral program, and as a way to measure changes in it over time.

ther corroboration, 62% of the graduate faculty in the top 12 institutions published 6 or more scholarly articles in the last five years as against 52% in the other AGS institutions and 36% in the remaining ones.

Similarly, the 1947–1948 recipients of the doctorate from the better institutions had published more by the late 1950's:

	Percentage of recipients who published	Average number of publications per recipient
Doctorates from top 12 institutions	77	4.8
Doctorates from next 10 institutions	73	4.3
Doctorates from remaining institutions	66	3.5

The difference may not seem large, perhaps, but it is there. On the average, the recipients from the best universities contributed a third more publications than those from institutions at the other end of the range. Here are a few more differences among the universities:

	Top 12	Other AGS, plus	Other
Ph.D.'s on graduate faculty	92%	91%	90%
Arts & science students in total graduate enrollment	46%	42%	29%
Doctoral students in total graduate enrollment	45%	23%	14%
Graduate students taking half or more of normal load	72%	43%	37%
Graduate faculty whose teaching load is at least half graduate	69%	64%	53%

Differences of the same kind are found among the colleges (here classified, for sampling reasons, into three groups—the "best" and "better" together, the other colleges, and the teachers colleges):

	Top colleges	Other colleges	Teachers colleges
Doctorates on faculty (medians)	55–60%	30–35%	30–35%
Normal teaching load (hours per week)	12	14	14
Teaching done outside discipline of instructor (averages)	5%	7%	9%
Providing "more research opportunities and facilities for faculty"	60%	35%	25%
Go on to: graduate school	16–20%	11–15%	11–15%
professional school	16–20%	6–10%	5%

THE STUDENTS

In 1920 Dean Woodbridge of Columbia told the AAU that "interest in the students (rather than the subjects) is the great temptation which tries the graduate school and the great obstacle to its success." If the temptation was "great" in 1920, there are hardly words to suggest its magnitude today. Almost everyone connected with graduate education these days is concerned with how many students there are, where they come from, who and why they are, how good they are, who supports them, and how they can get more of them.

Their Numbers

First as to order of magnitude, the figures on the number of graduate students, while not always precise or complete because of definitional and reporting difficulties, are nevertheless satisfactory for our purposes here. During the 1950's the figure has ranged around 250,000 plus or minus about 10%.* This seems like a static situation, but it probably is not. At the start of the 1950's, the figures were still somewhat "inflated" by the backlog of World War II veterans, and a little later by the veterans of the Korean conflict, so that the residual "normal" trend has probably been on the way up, certainly since 1953. The latest figure was about 278,000.

This figure includes all graduate students—Master's candidates as well as doctoral, part-time as well as full-time. Only about a third of the graduate students are "advanced" (i.e., beyond the first year) and only half are "full-time." Not all the "advanced" students are working for the doctorate—some are finishing up their Master's work—but most of them are. If a quarter to a third of the first-year students are also after the doctorate, then nearly half of all graduate students are doctoral candidates. The recent NORC sample split almost equally between Master's and doctoral candidates, but it was limited to the arts and sciences where the proportion of Master's students is low compared to the professional fields. Actually, the figure for Master's candidates is on the low side because the base figure does not include graduate students in the summer session, who are mostly in education and mostly seeking the Master's.

Although these figures are not as clear or hard as crystal, they are sufficient to indicate the size of the enterprise with respect to such prob-

---

* That figure refers to resident fall enrollment. Total resident enrollment for the academic year might be about 10% higher.

lems as recruitment and support. Roughly, there are something like 125,000 doctoral students today, of whom half are "full-time." (That term is itself quite ambiguous: it might be fair, as a quick summary, to say that "full-time" means half-time or more.)

Their Origins

Where do graduate students come from? I have already indicated the major channeling from baccalaureate to doctoral institution. Here I wish to raise a few additional considerations.

If the general impression is that they are regionally home-grown, that impression needs some qualification. Only about a quarter of recent doctorates took their degree in the same state in which they received their high school diploma, and about 40% in the same region. The figures for the Doctor's-Bachelor's relation are slightly higher: 35% and 47%. Thus, a solid majority of doctoral recipients, though probably somewhat fewer doctoral candidates, leave their home territory to seek the degree—far more, of course, than with the baccalaureate (80% in home state). Here is the start of the graduate school's role in social mobility.*

As nearly as I can tell, this situation has remained fairly stable over the past twenty-five to thirty years, though with a slight upward trend in mobility. In the depression period of the mid-thirties, more doctoral recipients stayed at home—but only about 7% more. The greater number, visibility, and attractiveness of the national universities and especially the easier financial situation and the pull of the large national fellowship programs have moved doctoral students farther out into the world. When I asked the graduate deans how, if at all, their graduate student bodies had changed over the past twenty years or so, the answer typically referred to the wider geographical origins of the students. Even the institutions below the top are now attracting students over a broader range.

Institutionally, the graduate universities get only about 15 to 20% of their doctoral students from their own undergraduate colleges. Where, then, do they come from?

* Incidentally, Lindsay Harmon of the National Research Council sets forth an interesting relationship between region and the subject of graduate study: "One might expect that a serious study of any phenomenon will be undertaken by a proportion of people that is directly related to the prominence of that phenomenon in their lives during their early years. In the less urbanized areas, contact with plant and animal life is much more frequent than in the large cities, but interpersonal contacts and cultural conflicts are more rare. Hence, the study of biological science is more frequent, and the behavioral sciences are of less concern. In the congested cities, human contacts of various kinds are a prominent element of life, and contact with infra-human forms is more rare. Hence, the emphasis on the study of behavioral sciences and de-emphasis of biology. . . . In all regions the presence of the physical world is constant; hence, no marked regional variations are found."

In the first place, most graduate students come from a relatively few institutions. In their well-known study, *The Younger American Scholar*, Robert Knapp and Joseph Greenbaum remark on "the concentration of scholarly creativity among a surprisingly small group of institutions" (roughly 50 out of 800), and they conclude that this leaves "undeveloped and unproductive large segments of the American system of higher education. We strongly suspect that under proper circumstances, effective recruitment of younger scholars could be accomplished from many institutions now virtually barren of productivity." The median undergraduate college sends 10 to 15% of its graduates on to graduate school in the arts and sciences, but the range is from less than 5% to well over 40%.

Now Knapp and Greenbaum, and these college figures, deal with rates. But rates do not staff graduate schools; gross numbers do. So far as numbers are concerned, especially of doctoral students, it is the universities that mainly supply the graduate schools. Even in Knapp and Greenbaum's figures, for example, about two-thirds of the "young scholars" (recipients of the doctorate or certain fellowships) took their baccalaureate degrees at universities. According to the NRC study of the baccalaureate origins of all doctorates conferred from 1936 to 1956, concentration at that level is even greater than at the doctoral level itself: less than 10% of the institutions produced nearly 75% of those who went on to the doctorate.

What are the leading producers of baccalaureates who complete their doctorates? With the exceptions of CCNY and Brooklyn (both high because of their attendance by bright Jewish students of New York), all of the top 20 institutions are large universities. Oberlin is the first liberal arts college, and it is 25th; Dartmouth is next, and it is 40th; then Swarthmore (54th), Hunter (59th, again New York City), Amherst (71st), Wesleyan (80th), Reed (81st), and College of Wooster (84th)—and that is all in the top 95 institutions responsible for 74% of all baccalaureates who achieved the doctorate from 1936 to 1956. These eight liberal arts colleges, the top producers in their class, account for less than 4% of the students who went on to the doctorate in that period. Similarly, according to the Kille study of the undergraduate origins of the faculties of undergraduate colleges, well over half of such faculty members received their baccalaureates from universities, as against only a third from liberal arts colleges. The only college in the top 25 baccalaureate producers of such faculties was Oberlin. This picture of the undergraduate origins of graduate students is summarized in the table on the next page.

Hence the majority of doctoral candidates, and even more of recipients, come from the universities. In *rate* of production, the liberal arts colleges may be equally high, but in *numbers* of students they are not.

Where they got their baccalaureate	Doctorates, 1936–1956	Doctorates, 1957	Graduate students, arts & sciences only, 1958 (from NORC)	Doctoral students, arts & sciences, 1958 (from NORC)	Woodrow Wilson fellows, 1945–1959	Nat'l Science Foundation fellows (1st year), 1954–1959
Top universities	18%	14%	15%	18%	21%	53%
Middle universities	22	19	19	20	23	24
Other universities	20	25	18	16	16	14
Top colleges	12	12	6	10	24	5
Other colleges	28	30	42	36	16	4
Total no. of cases (= 100%)	89,528	2,331	2,586	1,264	3,134	4,163

This disparity is likely only to increase in the next years, as the public universities grow more rapidly than the private colleges.

Furthermore, as the origins of graduate students relative to doctoral recipients suggest, and as the origins of fellowship holders partly confirm, the universities are now supplying at least their share of the *better* students.* This conclusion is further reinforced by an analysis done by NRC of certain test scores for the NSF fellowship candidates for 1954: the candidates from large Ph.D.-granting universities did best and those from baccalaureate institutions least well. Some people associated with national fellowship programs believe that they have observed this difference directly. For example, Frank Bowles, after returning recently "to the selection committee of a national fellowship program after an absence of eight years, was immediately struck by the extent to which the proportion of superior candidates of smaller colleges had shrunk, while the candidates from the university colleges had increased in both number and quality." Here again, this does not necessarily mean that the universities are giving better training—it is more likely, I think, that they are attracting abler students among their large numbers. Knapp wrote:

> I think the major single factor determining the scholarly output of a college (or university) is its selection of students, either through repu-

* There are three reasons, I think, for the sharp differences between the baccalaureate origins of Wilson and NSF fellows: (1) NSF is limited to the sciences, where the colleges are by all accounts inferior as a group to the universities in the training they give; (2) the Wilson program operates through institutional nominations, particularly from the colleges, whereas NSF accepts applications directly from the candidates; but mainly (3) Wilson is more interested in college teaching and NSF in scientific research, and this is reflected in the standards for judgment and in the selection of the personnel who do the judging (i.e., college as against university people).

tation or design, and *not* the quality of the instruction and the curriculum offered. The latter are important without question, but the first is of overwhelming significance. The inequalities in the caliber of students attracted to different colleges is far more striking than one might suppose. Learned and Wood in the 1930's give dramatic evidence of this. I am sure the separation now is even more striking.

David Riesman recently remarked that "the big cosmopolitan universities are no longer channeling their best students largely into law, medicine, business, the diplomatic service, and so on, but are increasingly serving also to recruit scholars. This is in part because their student bodies have become less 'social,' and include many relatively poor boys who would once have gone to local and often to denominational colleges." The general prosperity of the country, the ease of travel, and particularly the strong scholarship support now available have all contributed to this situation.

Their Social Background

That raises the question of what graduate students are like these days. As we have seen, the early history of graduate education is full of complaints and observations about the changing—usually the deteriorating—character of the student body: Hughes' plea for better social and religious training, Flexner's criticism of the "prudential" motives of graduate students, Bowman's concern with the "heterogeneous mass."

Certainly, graduate students have become more heterogeneous in background and social origin. That was almost a natural accompaniment of the increase in numbers—there simply were too few of the "elite" variety to support such a growth. Now, the recipients of the doctorates come from a range of social backgrounds:

Father's occupation

Professional and executive	27%
Small business and technical	21
Clerical, sales, service	21
Agricultural	11
Skilled	14
Unskilled	6

Father's education

More than college graduate	13%
College graduate	13
Some college	12
High school graduate	17
Some high school	9
Less than high school	32
Foreign and other	4

The background is pretty much the same by field, though the recipients from the top universities cluster somewhat more at the upper end of this social ladder—partly because they come from better-educated homes to begin with, partly because their families can afford a more costly level of education.

Here again we see the importance of the graduate school as a giant step in the career mobility of young people from what can fairly be described as lower-middle-class homes. Well over half the recent recipients come from families where the father had only a high school education or less—and more often less—or held a job low in the occupational hierarchy. Thus Sartre's cynical comment that the Ph.D. was given in America as a reward for having a wealthy father and no opinions is at least half wrong (in fact, that is much more likely to be true abroad, I am told). By comparison, students of law and medicine come more from the top occupational groups: two-thirds to three-fourths come from professional, managerial, or proprietary families as against less than half the doctoral recipients.* Thus scholarship has come to be more the preserve of less-than-upper-class people, as against professional practice, and the criterion of intellectual capability has made a social selection as well as the one it was directly intended for.

It pleases some observers to see in this, as the jargon puts it, a dangerous tendency toward the alienation of the intelligentsia from the managers of the society, but on the whole I find them more nearly in tune now—partly because of what I earlier referred to as the professionalization of doctoral training. In any case, it is hard to overstate the importance of the graduate school to students of high talent but low origin—and especially to those from an ethnic minority traditionally devoted to learning, like the Jews, who are strongly over-represented in the graduate population—or its contribution in this respect to the American dream.

Another important change in the student body has changed the whole environment of graduate study. Graduate students these days are usually married. Of the 1957 recipients of the doctorate, over half were married when they began doctoral study and three-fourths when they finished. Of those married, over half had children when they started, and almost three-fourths when they finished.

* Actually, lawyers and doctors may be better recruiters for their professions than college and university teachers are for theirs. The three groups are roughly the same size, yet about 15% of law and medical students have fathers in the same profession as against only about 6% for the academics. Does that fact indicate greater morale in the professions, more nepotism in getting sons and nephews into the professional school in the first place, the prospect of more help in getting set up in practice, the lower salaries of academic people, or perhaps their broader interests?

This makes a difference to graduate work in several ways. One is financial: families must be supported, not just the student. This has required the graduate schools or national fellowship programs to add dependency allowances to their stipends. (Graduate students with wives but no children are in the optimal position: they are supported by the working wives. As the saying goes, they get through graduate school by the sweat of their fraus.) Another is social: graduate students live a more normal social life—the wives are even organized on some campuses—and institutions now have the problem of providing housing for married students along with the usual dormitory space.* Another is intellectual: the monastic dedication to graduate study is lessened or gone. Graduate students have families to be dedicated to as well as their studies, and some deans feel that this has had a big and undesirable effect on graduate work in distracting the students' attention from what should be intensive devotion to a subject.

So much is being said these days about the possibility of solving the "college teacher shortage" with women Ph.D.'s that it is perhaps worth noting that they constituted 10% of the doctorates in 1910 and not quite 11% last year. Except for the war years, they have never accounted for a much larger segment than that. Furthermore, as the NORC study shows, only about 15% of women graduate students prefer a full-time professional career for the first five years after completing their work. When these facts are combined with the reluctance of academic employers, not to mention the rules against joint husband-wife employment, they do not leave much room, in my judgment, for reliance on this "solution." It may be, as a foundation officer put it, that "we are losing half our brains" in this way, but it is hard to see much that can be done about it.

Their Motivation

As a result of the professionalization of graduate study, it is not surprising to find, now as earlier, that people are concerned about the "prudential" motivation of doctoral students—the students themselves, along with the faculty and deans:

* The traditional impression, incidentally, is that the living arrangements and social life of the graduate students make for malaise, unhappiness, psychological disturbance, etc. That was not particularly true for the recent recipients; on the whole, they were quite satisfied with their social life as graduate students. But, of course, they are the doctoral candidates who made the grade. The others probably have more social and psychological difficulties with graduate study and the university, as suggested by Edgar Friedenberg and J. S. Roth, *Self-Perception in the University: A Study of Successful and Unsuccessful Graduate Students*, University of Chicago Press, 1954.

> The quality of doctoral work is limited these days by the fact that most students are motivated by the practical objective of getting a job rather than the objective of becoming a research scholar.

	Agree	Disagree	Can't say
Graduate deans	41%	42	17
Graduate faculty	51%	30	19
Recent recipients	45%	29	26

The major differences by field and by institution give a hint as to certain changes in graduate education in recent decades. For both the faculty and the recent students, it is the humanists and those from lesser institutions who are most critical on this score, i.e., those groups most deprived, or feeling most deprived, in the entire system. The criticism is hardly accepted by the scientists in the top universities: they are now ruling the roost, and hence are least likely to think their particular roost is deficient, in this or other regards. Actually, this concern has been expressed so constantly over the years that there is a question as to whether it is any more of a problem now—or, perhaps more precisely, whether it seems more of a problem now than it has ever seemed.

How students feel about the matter is revealed in the answers of the recent recipients to another query along the same lines:

> People have different motives for seeking the doctorate—e.g., the academic objective of becoming a scholar and teacher and the practical objective of getting a job for which a degree is necessary or desirable. Recognizing that such motives are usually mixed, how would you describe why you and most of the students in your department were after the doctorate?

	Myself	Fellow students
More academic	38%	23%
Equally important	33	34
More practical	29	43

I am more academically inclined, and *they* are more practically inclined.* Here the sharp differences appear between the arts and sciences on the one hand and the professional fields on the other—after all, it is more

---

* This reaction is matched by that given in response to a question about "the morale of yourself and your fellow students as you worked toward the doctorate." *Mine* was "consistently high" for 31% of the respondents but *theirs* was that for only 17%. At least, the eventual recipients of the doctorate consider that they got along a little better than their fellows—as, indeed, they probably did since some of their fellows did not finish.

appropriate to be practical in the latter—and among the types of institutions:

	Myself		Fellow students	
	More academic	More practical	More academic	More practical
Top 12 universities	44%	25	32%	34
Other AGS universities, plus	38%	29	22%	45
Other universities	33%	33	15%	53

Once more, the situation in the top institutions is more "academic"; at any rate, the recent recipients think so.

In any case, the practical motivation for graduate study is certainly strong. Whether stronger than before, or too strong, is another matter. The facts are that just under half the students are thought to be primarily motivated by practical considerations and that about half the judges think that is too much. Actually, there has always been a certain amount of external pressure pushing people into graduate school—the degree required for the job—and thus contaminating the purity of the student's motivation. Much as we should like to think so, "love of learning" never was the exclusive motive, probably not the dominant one. In today's society, given the numbers involved and needed, it cannot be. This seems to me a fact not so much to be sadly regretted or angrily exclaimed over, as simply to be accepted as part of the situation.

Their Quality

The motivation of the student leads directly to the central question about today's graduate students, namely, their intellectual quality. How good are they? Are they getting better or worse? What's wrong with them? Frank Keppel has argued,

Recruitment and selection of personnel for the professions are major responsibilities of a university in American life. . . . By the success or failure of their programs of recruitment and selection, they tend for a generation to influence the activity and the standing of the profession they serve. . . . One can even argue that the policies and programs which bring such future leaders to the profession may be more important than the academic training programs themselves.*

* Decades ago, another Harvard man, President Lowell, put the point in vivid terms: "While, therefore, the instruction in our Graduate Schools is admirable, our success in recruiting for them students of the strongest intellectual fibre is by no means so great. This is the vital point, for although eaglets are raised best in an eagle's nest, yet there is a better chance of producing them by setting eagle's eggs under a hen, than hen's eggs under an eagle."

Here again is the point that the students make the university just as—perhaps, just as much as—the university makes the students. Certainly the quality of the students is critical to the whole graduate enterprise.

There are two common complaints about today's doctoral students. One is that under the impact of numbers the quality of graduate students is falling off. If it is, the people most concerned have not noticed it. Is "the quality of the students in doctorate programs declining under the impact of numbers?" No, say two-thirds of the faculty in a position to judge and over four-fifths of the deans. How do they compare with graduate students before the war? A little better, says the graduate faculty (about 3 to 2); a lot better, say the deans.

But beyond the comparison with the trend, what about the comparison with the standard? When I asked the graduate faculty what they thought of "the quality of the student group now coming into graduate study, considering what the doctorate program should attract," only 14% said that the quality was "inferior to proper requirements for the doctorate" as against about the same proportion who thought it was "very good" and another 46% "moderately good." So again on this measure the students come out well—well above the residual "adequate." As a more refined measure, aimed at getting at another complaint about today's students, I asked the graduate faculty how many of "the graduate students these days are not genuinely dedicated to their studies or deeply interested in them—i.e., not really willing to work hard, take pains in their work, have the pride of craftsmanship." Their estimate, on the average, was about 25%. There are no comparable data available, either by time or by vocation, but it would seem, given the human condition, that three out of four with such qualities must be close to par.

On all these measures, then, the graduate faculty acknowledges the merit of today's students—and that despite the growth in numbers. Since this would mean that the *average* student is better, it probably also means that there are more of the outstanding or brilliant or exceptionally able, too.*

---

* This is an appropriate place to report that the people involved do not at all agree with two related legends about doctoral work:

	Proportion agreeing		
	Graduate deans	Graduate faculty	Recent recipients
The doctoral program is designed too much for the students of average competence rather than for the few brilliant students	21%	27%	17%
The rigors of doctoral study tend to discourage the brightest, most imaginative students in favor of the conscientious plodders	9%	15%	19%

The other common complaint is that post-baccalaureate students in the graduate school are not as able as those in the major professional schools of law and medicine. In the historical section, I noted an early concern with this theme. Recently, Dean Keniston remarked on the "widely held impression that the average quality . . . is below that of those who embark on the other learned professions," and Howard Mumford Jones put the point more dramatically:

> Because medical education is under constant pressure to improve the quality of its graduates, students are selected with increasing rigor. In comparison with the haphazard selection (or rather lack of selection) of students by the graduate schools of arts and sciences, among them candidates for the delicate art of teaching college youth, medical education is a thousand miles nearer perfection.

But the evidence does not support this notion that the grass is greener elsewhere. Put most briefly, here are the median AGCT (IQ) scores, from Wolfle:

Medical school students	127
Law school graduates	124
Natural sciences:	
Graduate students	128
Ph.D.'s	133
Psychology:	
Graduate students	132
Ph.D.'s	137
Social sciences:	
Graduate students	124
Humanities (adapted):	
Graduate students	128

Thus in the native intelligence it attracts to the arts and sciences core, the graduate school compares favorably with law and medicine.*

In short, the quality of students seems to be holding up reasonably well, despite their sharp growth in numbers. But in academic life, however good they are, they are never good enough. All my disciplinary consultants claimed that what their discipline needed was more good students—so much so that I began to wonder where they all were. (An economist observed, in this connection, that "there is little point in deploring the fact that there aren't more cases four standard deviations above the mean!") Given the likelihood that the present crop will do, however, there is still the certainty that they have some deficiencies.

* Another legend is strongly disavowed by those involved. Nearly two-thirds of the deans, the faculty, and the recent recipients disagree with the statement: "Students aren't made to work hard enough at graduate school, especially as compared with the major professional schools," and less than one-fifth of them agree. The disavowal is particularly strong in the sciences.

Their Preparation

The next question, then, is: what is wrong with them? This is primarily a question about their undergraduate preparation: what is right and wrong with it? Here are the answers given by the graduate deans and graduate faculty to the question: "By and large, how good is each of the following aspects of the undergraduate preparation of graduate students?" *

| | Percentage "satisfactory" (can't say's omitted) | |
	Graduate deans	Graduate faculty
Foreign languages	12%	21%
Writing and organizing ability	20	22
General background of liberal education	42	46
Ability to work on their own	50	49
Preparation in related fields	78	56
Preparation in major subject fields	96	84

The judgments are sharp and clear, and general to all fields: two aspects of undergraduate preparation are ranked low, one high, and the others are in between.

Now, the foreign language matter is an old irritant, and perhaps to be expected—though not for that reason necessarily dismissed; I return to it later. But the other two extreme judgments are perhaps more nearly basic to the situation.

Over and over in my disciplinary interviews I was told that graduate students today simply cannot express themselves with clarity, accuracy, and economy, to say nothing of grace or style. The complaint is made across the board, in the sciences as well as in the humanities and certainly in the professional fields. The situation has prompted some professors and departments, even at this late stage, to try to do something about this basic deficiency. As a matter of fact, the newly proposed entrance examination for graduate students has as one of its three pieces a test of the candidate's ability to express himself in English. If they could have only one language, I'm convinced, the graduate faculty would choose facility in the native language over that in the foreign.

* As for the recent recipients, they feel that their undergraduate preparation was satisfactory on nearly all counts. There is a bare majority for their training in foreign languages, and a large majority (80% or more) for everything else.

The other extreme judgment is more consequential still. That is the belief that the student's preparation in his major subject field is the most satisfactory aspect of his undergraduate work. (It should be, since that is often what he is selected for.) This conviction is equally strong in all fields, the sciences as well as the others. When I went on to ask, "Would you prefer graduate students in your discipline to have more undergraduate preparation in your own discipline than they now do, or not?," less than a quarter of the graduate faculty wanted more in their own discipline, and almost all the rest did not. The arts and sciences are on the high side, 40% of the humanists and 30% of the physical scientists wanting more, but even there the sentiment is strongly against more undergraduate work in one's own field. "What undergraduate preparation would you prefer?" About half said "broad general education" and the rest mentioned subjects that were at the heart of it, notably, mathematics, chemistry, languages, and English.

This seems to me a highly important twofold vote: for more liberal education as the appropriate preparation for graduate work, against more and more preparation in one's own field. Certainly the climate of opinion in academic life is assumed to be the contrary, namely, that everybody, and especially the scientists, wants a stronger major in his own subject at the undergraduate level as preparation for the minority who will go on to graduate study in the field—a kind of pre-professional training in an academic discipline. Indeed, that very issue is close to, or at, the heart of the debate over the undergraduate curriculum: how to accommodate the majors and non-majors, the vertical and horizontal interests, in the same program of study?

Also in my interviews with the disciplinary consultants, I was struck with the number who did not want more undergraduate training in their own fields for potential graduate students. The motivation is mixed. In some fields, there is currently something of a split in the way the subject is taught at the undergraduate and the graduate levels. For example, undergraduate economics is likely to be descriptive and institutional in the colleges, but heavily statistical, even mathematical in graduate school. Similarly, biology is descriptive below, chemical above; the recent evolution in the field has not yet been fully incorporated at the undergraduate level. In a few cases, I was frankly told that there simply was not enough matter in a discipline to cover both levels, and that it seemed more appropriately reserved for graduate specialization. Laid over much of this, I am sure, is the feeling of the graduate faculties that only they can teach a subject correctly.*

The response of the graduate faculty to another proposition locates

* Certainly the graduate faculties do hold some such opinion. I asked them, "How would you compare the quality of instruction at the undergraduate and graduate levels

the trouble in the relation of graduate and undergraduate programs. The proposition was this: "Graduate work isn't well articulated with undergraduate work, making for waste, repetition, poor sequence in learning, etc." Leaving aside the few "can't say's," here are the proportions who agree in different fields:

Humanities	56%
Social sciences	56
Education	51
Biological sciences	38
Physical sciences	33
Engineering	32

Again the break falls between the "word disciplines" and the "data disciplines." Some unkind critics of the former would argue, as everyone in university life knows, that this lack of articulation is a euphemism for the tendency to review the same ground in graduate school. Throughout all this, however, the recent recipients are better satisfied than the faculty or the deans or even the college presidents: they believe that the relation of their graduate and undergraduate training was, on the whole, all right.

The recent popularity of advanced standing in college has raised questions about advanced standing in graduate school. There are a few experiments along this line, mostly providing an opportunity for individual cases and sometimes allowing credit for graduate courses taken as an undergraduate. But the practice is still quite limited. It is used as a recruiting device, and so is the recent development of research opportunities for undergraduates (2,000 in summer 1959 supported by NSF alone). There is one of the rubs: "better articulation" may have to take place on the graduate school's terms, i.e., more research, moving farther away from what most collegiate advocates of articulation really want, i.e., more liberal or general education. There undoubtedly is an opportunity here to plan the doctoral program from a point in the undergraduate program in order to save time for the better students through compression, as is now being carried forward on a small scale in medicine and, for example, in chemistry at Columbia. However, because of all the personal and institutional obstacles in the way, this practice is unlikely to become general, desirable though it is from several standpoints.

---

at your institution" and "in your discipline generally, across the national scene?" They thought a better job was done in graduate school, even though, in almost all cases, they themselves taught at both levels.

	Institution	Discipline
Better at graduate level	34%	41%
Better at undergraduate level	14	16
About the same	46	23
Can't say	6	20

Even so, however, the picture as given above seems quite clear, and at the least provides a basis for a better rapprochement between the college and the graduate school. If the former can give a solid training in the basic intellectual subjects, the latter will be more than satisfied. If in addition it can move in a research direction in the junior-senior years—a small project, an honors thesis, or the like—the graduate school would be delighted.

Their Recruitment

Perhaps the most significant fact about the decision to go on to the doctorate has to do with when it is made. It is made late: only 35% by the end of college, 65% after that (and most of them only after the Master's). It is made especially late in the humanities and the professional fields.

This is one of the sharp differences between recruitment for graduate work and recruitment for medicine and law. Potential doctors and lawyers know much earlier that they want to go ahead for professional training in their field: almost half the former know by the beginning of college and nearly all of both groups by the end. *By* college for medicine, *during* college for law, but only *after* college for doctoral work—that is a sloganized but not over-simplified version of the facts. Partly this is attributable to the greater day-to-day visibility of the doctor and lawyer to the highschool student and his family; partly to the fact, or the impression, that the professional student must get on the right curricular track early in the game; partly to the fact or impression of greater economic returns in the professions. Whatever the cause, the effect is the same: going ahead for the doctorate seems to be much less the result of a *decision* and much more the result of drift.*

This is confirmed by other data as well. The recent recipients say that no one "particularly influenced you to go to graduate school;" about two-thirds claim they decided "pretty much on their own." The strongest other influence was exerted by the person supposed to be at the center of the process, the undergraduate teacher, but he was influential in only about 15% of the cases—at least in the judgment of the recipients of the influence. Half of the recent recipients "seriously considered some other career choice" but doctoral training was "in any sense the second choice" for only 10% or so. As they now think back on it, they decided on the institution they attended for three main reasons—one intrinsic (its reputation, or that of the department or a particular professor or two) and two more contingent (its location and its financial help).

How can it be that the very profession that is on the inside of so

---

* This is the same conclusion that others have recently reached, e.g., John Stecklein and Ruth Eckert for Minnesota and John Gustad for the South.

much career choice cannot, or at least does not, push its own wares? Half the colleges say they have "special programs or arrangements to encourage your students to go on to graduate work," and half the graduate schools say they have "an active program for recruiting graduate students." But upon scrutiny the former largely come down to informal advising and encouraging, plus financial aid in fewer cases, and the latter to departmental brochures and announcements. Almost half the graduate schools claim they have "some established means of regular contact with the independent liberal arts colleges in your area" and a third of the colleges, mainly the better ones, say they have "some established means of regular contact with the graduate schools in your area." Again, this mainly amounts to personal contact both ways, though in a few cases it does represent a systematic visiting plan by which a graduate school covers its territory. Only about a quarter of the colleges report that "any graduate schools actually recruit for students on your campus." The upshot seems to be that with the institutions no less than with the individuals—or rather, with the institutions and *therefore* with the individuals—entry into doctoral study is left to circumstance.

One consequence is that under the pressure of the competition for graduate students, everybody who wants to get into graduate school does get in. Those graduate deans responding to that question reported that a total of about 74,000 applications for admission were received in 1958–1959, of which about 51,000 were accepted. About 35,000 new students actually registered in these institutions. That is, about half the applicants anywhere showed up somewhere. But, of course, students apply to more than one school, partly as insurance and partly as "shopping around" for the best offer. As a matter of fact, as the NORC data indicate, the average applicant applies to over two schools, or enough to show that every applicant gets admitted and registered. Hence, if more students are wanted in the system as a whole, the answer is not to lower the admission bars and let more of the applicants in. They are already in, all of them.

This makes for some dissatisfaction with the selection and admission policies of the graduate school, particularly in the dean's office where the problem turns up most frequently and sharply. The deans acknowledge that "the graduate schools aren't doing a good job of initial selection of candidates for the doctorate at the time of admission" more than the graduate faculty—48% of the deans agreeing, as against 36% of the faculty. Among the latter, once more it is the humanists and the social scientists who are dissatisfied with the current crop of students, and the faculty in the lesser universities that have to take what they can get.

The "solution" provided by raising admission requirements is no solution for the system, though it may be for a particular institution: there are not enough doctoral candidates as it is. Similarly, the solution of improving the selection devices is at best doubtful. At one time, high hopes were held for the Graduate Record Examination, but now the consensus is, I think, that it is useful only for the candidate from the unknown college, and then only marginally so. A new kind of essay examination is being considered by the AGS and though it may be tried out, it does not seem likely to solve the problem in a satisfactory way, let alone an economic one. In the end, any added discrimination would result in more of the better students going to the better schools.

How can graduate education get more good students? To my mind, the main answer, if not the only one, is to get more applicants.* The more there are, the more good ones there will be. There may be some limits to this pathway—for example, Frank Bowles points out that the top liberal arts colleges are already sending a maximum percentage of their students to graduate schools and John Darley points out that there are only so many people with sufficiently high IQ's—but the limits are by no means insurmountable. On these specifics, for example, the liberal arts colleges are supplying relatively few of those who go on to the doctorate anyway; and according to Wolfle's data, of all male college graduates with the IQ of the average Ph.D. (i.e., an AGCT score of 130 or higher) only about 5% now get the doctorate. In this respect, it appears that the "wastage" of talent not going from high school to college is exceeded by that not going from college to graduate school—especially in view of the social investment already made in it.

The situation differs considerably by field. The number of doctorates in the physical and biological sciences is 12 to 14% of the number of B.A.'s in those fields four years earlier, as against only 4 to 5% in the social sciences and humanities and less than 3% in the professions. But still, in all fields, there is an ample reservoir of potential candidates if the system can find ways to tap it more effectively.

Getting more students is tied to financial factors, as a graduate dean succinctly pointed out:

> We do not select properly because we have too few applicants. We do not pick out the time wasters early enough because we need teaching assistants, or because a professor wants the prestige of directing a dissertation, or more likely seeks the accompanying reduction of undergraduate teaching. This is a vicious process, and I see it in daily operation, doubtless in most cases without conscious analysis or intent. With increased incentives we would have increased applicants and would select far better students. . . . Then, with more students, the professors would not be so

* In this respect, the recruiting power of the NSF programs has probably had a long enough time to take effect, but not so for the augmented Woodrow Wilson program.

inclined to "carry" a student along. Frankly, we merely need more competition to get in and stay in our graduate schools.

And that brings us to a, perhaps the, central question.

Their Support

How is graduate education to be paid for? To begin with, of course, it costs the university much more to train a student at this level than he pays in tuition; but that is what universities are for. Who supports the student while he takes the necessary years to get his degree? The quick answer is that the system supports him in a variety of ways, some of them requiring service from him.

The economics of higher education is such that doctoral students expect "to be supported." This expectation, now assumed to be natural, has placed the burden of providing support on the administrators of graduate study; has forced universities to compete for graduate students through the attractiveness of stipends; and has influenced if not determined important characteristics of doctoral study, like its duration or level of attrition or part-time character.*

There has been so much attention to this matter of support in recent years that the picture is reasonably clear, with regard to both the national system and the individual student. Before proceeding to the details, I sketch in the broad outline.

Besides private support from one's family or spouse or savings or nonacademic earnings or loans—i.e., the out-of-pocket expenditures of the student and his family—there are three major types of support available to the graduate student: fellowships, teaching assistantships, and research assistantships. They are the main sources of support. Unlike the case in medicine and, less so, in law, doctoral candidates do not rely heavily on their own private resources in getting through the additional period of academic training.

The fellowship typically allows the student to spend full time, or virtually that, on his studies (and for that reason, governmental support of veterans can be included in this category). The assistantship requires some service from the students, but in varying amounts and kinds. The teaching assistantship is partly rationalized as contribution to the graduate student's training, but, as I said above, it is also frankly considered

---

* How many graduate deans feel about this is revealed in this quotation from one of them: "Since World War II graduate students have come to expect someone (the government, the graduate school, society) to pick up not only the bill for their graduate education but also the bill for the maintenance of themselves and their dependents. Free education with a subsidy to raise a family is a great deal to expect, and I think that something will have to change. Certainly, the private schools could educate more graduate students if the schools could use more of their money for education and less for the support of the students while they are being educated."

a means of economic survival for both student and institution. The research assistantship, though sometimes exploited, often feeds directly into the student's program by supporting the doing of the dissertation. The fellowship is most to the student's advantage from the standpoint of completing the degree, the teaching assistantship least, and the research assistantship in between (though sometimes it is even more advantageous than the fellowship, in that research expenses are provided as well as time). At the same time, the holders of assistantships do appreciate their value as training opportunities: almost three-fourths believe that the opportunity is "good" or "unusual" and only a very few think it "irrelevant," according to the NORC survey.

Only a few decades ago, graduate fellowships were provided primarily by the universities. Today, they come in large numbers from the great national programs that have arisen in the past decade, after the GI Bill ran its course: the fellowship programs of the Federal government, via the National Science Foundation (2,100 a year), the Public Health Service (about 675 a year with three-year duration, or about 2,000 in any given year), and the National Defense Education Act (1,500 a year with three-year duration, or 4,500 in any given year); and the Woodrow Wilson program financed by foundations (1,000 a year, but with approximately an equal number provided by funds directly to the universities attended by the fellows). In addition, there are smaller governmental programs, e.g., New York State or the Federal foreign language program under the National Defense Education Act; several hundred graduate fellowships provided by business and industry,* and a smaller number supported directly by foundations. In total, then, there probably now are about 15,000 national fellowships available to graduate students, almost entirely for doctoral students. Beyond that, there is PL550 (the GI Bill for the Korean conflict) that is still providing some support for perhaps 10,000 graduate students. And finally, of course, there are the universities' own funds that a few years ago provided for nearly 25,000 fellowships. They are typically small, as compared to the national awards, and it is increasingly common for a few to be combined into a single award, for competitive purposes. However, even at a figure equivalent to the national awards, the universities grant nearly 10,000 graduate fellowships.

For teaching assistantships, we can probably come close to the correct figures simply by using the number of "junior instructional staff (such as assistant instructors, teaching fellows, teaching assistants, and labora-

---

* One problem here is that the industrial sponsors are increasingly distressed that their fellowships, which are made available for local allocation, take a back seat to the national programs. The universities typically encourage their better students to apply nationally and then reserve funds under local control for those not winning out in the broader competition.

tory assistants)" in the Office of Education's survey of faculty in institutions of higher education. In 1955, that figure was about 30,000. Not all of them are doctoral candidates, but probably a sizable majority are.

A figure for research assistantships is harder to get because of all the complications involved, but an approximation can be made by working from the total amount of research support available in the university proper. That total is now of the magnitude of $250 to $300 million annually, and if we assume (as there is reason to) that one research assistant is supported on the average by every $10,000–12,000 of research grants, then that means from 20,000 to 25,000 assistants. Again, not all of them are doctoral candidates; but again, most of them are.

What this adds up to is a total number of stipends roughly equivalent to the estimated number of full-time doctoral students in residence, or about half the estimated total of all doctoral students. The three types of support are of sizable magnitude across the system as a whole, though as we shall see in a moment they are not equally distributed by field or by type of institution. Thanks to the recent governmental programs of support, there are now roughly as many fellowships available as each type of assistantship.

This suggests that almost all doctoral students get some form of support, and that is the fact. The recent NORC survey of graduate students in the arts and sciences found that over three-fourths currently had a stipend. For the sample of recent recipients, the details on support can be presented in summary fashion (see table on p. 149). Here are the main points: (1) At one time or another, almost everyone who gets the doctorate has some support; only 12% had received no stipends while pursuing the degree, and only 8% in the arts and sciences.* (2) Except for education and certain other professions, fellowships are quite evenly distributed across fields to about half the eventual doctors: the NSF and PHS fellowships are limited to the sciences covered by those agencies, but they are balanced by the Woodrow Wilson program and by the allocation of fellowships under local control to other fields. (3) Similarly with teaching assistantships, at a somewhat higher rate; there are undergraduate students to be taught in all academic fields. (4) Research assistantships are largely limited to the sciences and engineering, where

---

* *Plus ça change* . . . A speaker at the AAU in 1917 reported the results of an inquiry sent to all the 630 Ph.D. recipients of 1915–1916. Of the 530 who replied, only 49 had not had a scholarship, fellowship, or assistantship, and most of them had pursued graduate work on a part-time basis which made them ineligible for aid. Said George Barnett of Johns Hopkins: "I think you may say we have almost reached the point when every person who received the Ph.D. degree in the United States has held an appointment (i.e., a scholarship or an assistantship or a fellowship) every year of his work as a graduate student."

Support, by type and field

	Support, outside my own family, requiring no work from me, e.g., a fellowship	Support requiring work that contributed greatly to my degree, e.g., a research assistantship used for dissertation	Support requiring work that did not contribute directly to the degree, e.g., a teaching assistantship	Any of these
Physical sciences	51%	53%	75%	97%
Biological sciences	45	47	62	97
Social sciences	45	28	64	87
Humanities	53	7	63	83
Engineering	48	52	62	95
Education	28	13	48	72
Total Arts & sciences	48	37	67	92
Total Professional fields	35	27	51	80
Grand total	44	33	61	88

research funds are of course concentrated. As a result, the sciences, including engineering, are at a clear advantage over the other fields.

For those who receive these forms of support, the duration in different fields is roughly the same. The average fellowship support runs two years, the average research assistantship nearly two and a half, the average teaching assistantship nearly three. When all forms of support are summated, students in the natural sciences and engineering receive stipends over an average of four years, those in the social sciences and humanities for about three and a half, and those in education for about two and a half. When these figures are compared with the duration of doctoral study, in elapsed time from start to finish, it turns out that the sciences and engineering have such support for virtually the entire time, the social sciences and humanities for about 60% of the time, and education for about half the time.

As for class of institution, there is only one real difference in support: over 50% of the students in the top 12 institutions had fellowships as against about 40% in the other AGS institutions and 35% in the others. This is where local wealth has an effect as well as the national programs that channel students to the top.

Since most doctoral students are supported by such stipends, few of them borrow funds with which to complete their degree: only 13% of the recent recipients took out loans during their period of study, and fewer than 20% of them owed as much as $1,000 as a result of getting the doctorate. According to the NORC data, only a fifth of today's doctoral students receive any financial support from their parents, mainly because they say they do not need it. Almost half the graduate students consider "graduate study expensive (but) in the long run an excellent economic investment." About 70% either are "not worried about your immediate financial situation" or are actually pleased with it. Since "they first began graduate study" (except for those just starting), their financial situation has changed for the better in 45% of the cases and for the worse in only 21%. Over a quarter of today's doctoral students in the arts and sciences have a total income of over $5,400 for the academic year, and a similar proportion have from $3,600 to $5,400. As the crowning irony to an earlier generation, two-thirds own cars.

Under the pressure of the need for trained intelligence, the competition for graduate students, the high proportion of married students, and the general inflation, fellowship rates have gone up. The large programs of the Federal government provide fellowships of from $1,800 to $2,400, plus tuition and dependency allowances, and industrial fellowships are of similar magnitude. As a result, the universities have had to increase their own fellowships or take what was left. Since local fellowships at the private universities often come from old endowments and hence are now limited in size, this problem has been all the harder. Some private universities are being outbid by up-and-coming public institutions as graduate students shop around for the best offer.

The financial situation has improved markedly in the very recent past, primarily with the large post-war expenditures of the Federal government for both fellowships and research. Though mainly for the sciences, that source has enabled universities and private foundations to adjust their support in order to achieve better balance. (Still, the situation is not so easy as it would be if the recommendations of the President's Commission on Higher Education in the late 1940's had been followed: a rise to 30,000 fellowships in the early 1950's, with a maximum of four years to any student, or about as many fellowships as there were doctoral students altogether. There was thus little financial reason for the Commission to have recommended a system of national competitive examinations.)

The present situation does raise certain questions about the effects of support upon the character of graduate study.

The first question is of long standing. A former president of Harvard University made no bones about it. Said Abbott Lawrence Lowell in 1909:

> The graduate schools in American universities . . . pride themselves upon the number of their students, and in order to attract them they compete with one another all over the country by offering many scholarships. It is universally believed that generous aid given too freely at theological seminaries lessened the calibre of the ministry in the last cen-

tury, and there is grave danger that a similar policy in our graduate schools may have the same disastrous effect upon college professors.

The question may be interesting but in view of the present realities it is also academic, in the other sense of the term. More and not less support is the cry—though there is sharp controversy over who is to get it, and in what form.

That leads to the second question, namely, the effect of the national fellowship programs in concentrating graduate students at a relatively few institutions. I discussed this matter in the section on the institutional distribution of graduate students, where it seemed more properly to belong, and I shall return to it in the final section. It is sufficient to repeat here only that the issue has been, and is, highly controversial.

That, in turn, raises a third question, the more general one of what national fellowship programs actually do. By lowering the costs of entry to the academic profession, they have the effect of recruiting talent into graduate study. It may be that only a small minority are recruited directly and that what recruitment does occur is indirect, through the displacement of other funds that can then be used for other students, and so on down a whole line of institutions. Most of the recipients of national awards would probably be in graduate school anyway. But there are other things that fellowships do, too. They provide the opportunity for full-time study, thus lessening the time needed to get the degree and lowering the attrition rate (as noted later in connection with the duration of the doctoral program and as implied in the favorable situation of the sciences). Moreover, they enable the recipients to go to the institutions they prefer instead of those they can afford; though even here, we do not really know how many are moved from one class of institutions to another, rather than simply from one institution to an equivalent one of the same class. Finally, of course, such fellowships are a badge of honor, a built-in reference that is useful far beyond the period of doctoral training.

The fourth question has to do with tug-of-war between different types of support. Fellowships are fine, but if there are "too many" then the universities have some difficulty in finding teaching assistants and even research assistants. Fellowship stipends are good and they allow full-time work on one's studies, but they tend to draw off the better students from the teaching posts. Similarly, the research assistantship on outside funds has typically paid better than the teaching assistantship, and since it often has the advantage of contributing to the dissertation, it too has placed the teaching post in an unfavorable situation. In counteraction, as noted above, some universities are now up-grading the teaching assistantship in both salary and rank ("teaching associateship"). As for source of funds, the public universities will expand more than the private ones in the next years; will need more teaching assistants; will need more graduate students and will have more assistantships for them; and will, therefore, in the fears of some graduate deans of the private schools, have an advantage in the competition for graduate students.

This brings me to the fifth question associated with the funding of graduate students, and one of considerable controversy on the scientific side of the campus. That has to do with the propriety of supporting doctoral dissertations on contract research funds granted to senior professors. This practice is not new, though it is more visible now with the greater support available: it was an established practice in graduate training well before World War II.

The practice is alleged to reduce the student's independence and, as a noted biologist said, to reduce his "freedom to flunk" as well. Under this system, the critics say, the doctoral student becomes a cog in the senior professor's wheel, and does his dissertation more or less to order, after which it is incorporated into a report published under joint authorship. In order to show results on his grant, the sponsoring professor encourages the selection of "safe" projects, and as a consequence creativity is built out instead of in. The vice-president for research of a leading American business firm that employs large numbers of Ph.D.'s in chemistry told me that his company still had to train them because they had not learned how to do independent work while doing their dissertations on contract funds. At least one scientific division in a great institution will not accept a dissertation done in this way, or, indeed, allow a doctoral candidate to be employed on such contract funds, in order to avoid the problem altogether. But that is a small and relatively well-to-do institution; its larger and poorer counterparts simply could not carry on their present graduate programs in some fields without such support.

To judge from the responses of those directly involved, the problem is a real one. Over 60% of the graduate faculty and recent recipients who have an opinion on the matter agree that "too much of what the graduate school does, and how it does it, is adversely affected by the sources of funds, e.g., contract grants supporting dissertation research in the sciences"—and nearly as many of the graduate deans. Even the graduate faculty in the physical and biological sciences, the fields in which the problem exists, tend to agree, and so do the recent recipients in the sciences. In fact, the only group that disagrees is the faculty of the top 12 institutions, precisely where the practice is most likely to be found. Whether this is due to the fuller experience or the greater defensiveness of those faculties, or perhaps the envy of the others, I shall not attempt to guess.

What is more, the recent recipients in the sciences complain in substantial numbers (46% agree to 34% disagree) that "major professors often exploit doctoral candidates by keeping them as research assistants too long, by subordinating their interests to departmental or the professor's interests in research programs, etc." The complaint is made far less frequently in the other fields (or by the faculty itself), and it is strongest in the biological sciences and in universities below the top. With so much smoke, there must be a fire.

Finally, this leads to the effect of "the new support" upon the relations between professors and their students. It has reflected, and perhaps expedited, the growth of "team research," though that is more directly due to the expansion and complexity of the fields themselves, the need for large and costly equipment, etc. It may have promoted the selection of "sure fire" research problems, in order to minimize the uncertainties of support. Perhaps more tangibly, it has drawn some professors away from the graduate students by putting them to work in research centers off the main campus, and it has made of others part-time administrators of big research programs. Someone remarked that a senior professor in the sciences at a major university has more administrative work today than the departmental chairman did before the war. According to the graduate faculty, the load of work not directly involved in teaching or research has markedly increased in recent years for over three-fourths of them.

The upshot is indicated in a substantial affirmation of one of the stock complaints of graduate students. About half the faculty and recent recipients agree that "one basic trouble with graduate school is that faculty members do not consider the students as their main responsibility (as compared to their own research, consultation and service jobs, administration, etc.)" And it is not among the scientists that the complaint is most frequently made, but among the social scientists. As a sociologist said to me, "the problems of the graduate school won't be solved until we decide whether the faculty is there for the benefit of the students or the students for the benefit of the faculty!"

The moral in all these questions is, I suppose, that everything has its costs, including money.

Summary: Comparison with Law and Medicine

In summary, let me draw a comparison with the two other main groups in advanced training, the professional students of law and medicine. It is an instructive one: *

* These figures may not be correct to the last percentage or dollar, but they are, I think, substantially accurate in relative order of magnitude.

	Doctoral students	Law students	Medical students
Personal characteristics			
From professional, managerial, proprietary families	50%	75%	67%
Married	50–75%		60%
with children	50–75%		55%
IQ scores	128	124	127
Admission			
Career decision: median age	22	19–20	18
Applicants admitted	100%		50%
Completion of program			
Full-time study	50%	66%	close to 100%
Duration in years	8	3	4
Attrition	40%	40%	under 10%
Financial support			
Family & spouse	10–15%	55%	55%
Fellowships †	50%	25%	10%
Loans	15%		15–20%
Debt over $1,000 at graduation	15–20%		40–45%
Financial expectations: median income	$7–9,000	$10–12,000	$18–20,000

† Such comparisons, of course, can cut both ways. Some medical groups are now strongly urging that the Federal government provide "educational grants-in-aid for medical students on the basis of merit and need, similar in value and proportionate in number of grants now made to graduate students in other fields of specialization," to quote from the recent report of the Surgeon General's Consultant Group.

Briefly, the picture looks like this: compared with law and medical students, the doctoral students come from families of lower social status, decide much later on going ahead for the degree, get into graduate school more easily and drop out more frequently, are less frequently full-time students * and hence take much longer to get the degree, are supported less by their families and more by fellowships and their own work, borrow less because their prospects of future earnings are less.

This last is an important factor in the situation: "Why should I borrow when I won't make enough later to pay it back, and when I can always get a fellowship or assistantship to see me through?" That is a

* Note the consistent relationship between the prestige of a profession, field, or institution and the incidence of full-time preparation: here in the rank of medical, legal, and doctoral training; and within the latter in the rank of the sciences over the humanities and social sciences and the latter over education, as well as in the lower ranking of certain urban, "streetcar" universities with few full-time doctoral students. Presumably the prestige, and its associated rewards, is the causal factor, and the amount of application the effect.

popular position, and I shall return to the matter in the final section. Another factor is the higher position of the professional student's family, as well as the status attaching to law and medicine, and the sense of family pride in achieving it that warrants greater sacrifices. It is somehow "in the air" that the family's responsibility for advanced *academic* training is nil—that is society's business—whereas its responsibility for advanced *professional* training is accepted. And there the financial return is again crucial: the family gets its money back later, directly or indirectly. A former graduate dean thinks that "the time will come eventually when graduate study will be accepted as a charge against the family budget, just as parents now expect to pay for medical or legal education. But that time is not yet."

Recruitment to a profession depends both on subsequent return (or anticipated return) and on initial cost of entry. Academic salaries are generally considered low as compared with those of similarly trained groups. But so are the costs of entry. As a matter of fact, it may cost society less to subsidize the Ph.D. training program at a relatively low rate and for a relatively short period than to provide the salaries necessary to attract the numbers needed to staff a mass educational system if most candidates had to pay most of their own way, as in the professions. In this sense, it might be said that the subsidies in graduate school have contributed to low salaries in academic life. But the situation is changing: Ph.D.'s in some fields can and do make large salaries outside academic life, and the salaries inside the academy are getting better.

Still, the solution of several of the graduate school's pressing problems —like duration and attrition and recruitment—rests largely upon a solution of the support problem. The real question is to what extent society will pay the bill, whether directly or indirectly, and how it will be paid, i.e., by whom.

THE PROGRAMS

This section takes up a number of programmatic matters now at issue in graduate education. For the obvious reasons, I stay clear of the actual content of training programs in particular disciplines and deal only with those general problems that crosscut the various fields. As discussed here, they are: the duration of doctoral study, the dissertation, the Master's degree, post-doctoral work, the foreign language requirement, and the final examination. Then, summing up: the evaluation of graduate work.

The Duration of Doctoral Study

If the preparation of college teachers and the national distribution of graduate study are the two major issues in graduate education today, then the duration of doctoral study is probably the third. The critics who fear that the system is going to turn out too few doctorates in the years ahead, those who believe that the whole emphasis on research is wrong, those who think that the degree has fallen off from traditional standards, even those who want things added—all of them are concerned about the lengthy period of doctoral study. There is hardly a recent discussion of graduate education in which this note is not played loud and strong.

Considering that so many people hold such strong convictions on the matter, one would think that at least the facts on how long it *does* take to get the doctorate would be readily available and generally accepted. Yet that is not the case. The trustees of the Carnegie Foundation for the Advancement of Teaching, after remarking that "one of the most familiar criticisms is that graduate education takes too long," added in the next sentence that "unfortunately there does not exist any wholly satisfactory data on how long it does take." And Benjamin Wright, then President of Smith College, in his lively indictment of "The Ph.D. Stretch-Out" as one of the *Vital Issues of Education* in 1957, had to rely on some indirect data from a biased sample of doctoral recipients of fifteen to thirty years ago as "the most helpful and most reliable I have been able to discover." Others have found it useful for their purposes to use such phrases as "up to . . ." or "as much as . . ."—in which case, of course, almost any number short of twenty-five years or so would be technically correct but not very enlightening. The general impression is summed up in George Stigler's phrase: the "most protracted period of preparation in any profession."

THE THREE KINDS OF "DURATION"

How long is "too long"? The figures on "how long the doctorate takes" do not always agree if only because there are three ways to measure it:

1. The elapsed time between receiving the Bachelor's degree and receiving the doctorate

2. The elapsed time between entering upon graduate study and receiving the doctorate

3. The actual time spent in doing the work for the degree

Each of these, of course, gives a smaller number than the preceding one. Each is a reasonable and useful measure, depending on the question for which it is the answer. The important thing is not to confuse them and, as has been done, for example, to prescribe a shorter actual program (full-time equivalent) on the basis of figures referring to total elapsed time.

How long *does* it take, then? Let me start at the top and work down.

The best data on the first measure, the elapsed time from baccalaureate to doctorate, are those available from the National Research Council roster of recipients of the doctorate since 1936. That is a nearly complete list and clearly the best available, especially over a period of time. The answer to the first way of asking how long it takes, the way that yields the largest figure, is this: it now takes a median period of eight years.*

Duration in years between Bachelor's and Doctor's degrees

(Medians, from NRC data)

	Doctor's degree granted *in*	
	1936	*1957*
Physical sciences	6	6
Biological sciences	6	7
Social sciences	8	8
Humanities	10	10
Arts & sciences	8	7
Professional fields	11	10
Total group	8	8

These data make two other important points: (1) the duration differs substantially by field—low in the sciences, medium in the social sciences and the humanities, high in the professional fields; and (2) the duration has remained essentially constant in the past twenty years, over the period of the war, for the total group of doctorates.†

* The mean is always larger than the median in these data because of the effect of a few recipients who take a very long time to get their degrees. For this reason, I think the median is the more appropriate measure and I use it in the following tabulations. Incidentally, because of the great variety of patterns of study while earning the doctorate, it is extremely difficult to measure the actual time devoted to one or another activity with full precision. However, I believe the following data are essentially correct, certainly in order of magnitude. The median years from Bachelor's to doctorate for the sample are identical with those for the total NRC roster.

† 1936 may have been a "long" year because of the effect of the depression, but 1940 shows essentially the same results as 1936. Stigler has shown that from 1900 to

The major lengthening, then, has by no means occurred "recently," as some critics claim. A study of doctorates from 16 universities in the period 1883 to 1904 yielded a median of five years and a mean of about five and a half. Doctoral study was then an elite rather than a mass operation and very few of the candidates were married. Although the available data for subsequent periods are not fully comparable, my best estimate is that the current situation has essentially obtained since about 1930. It took less elapsed time before then, when the system was much smaller and less professionalized, and it has taken substantially the same time since then. The differences by field were pretty well established by then too. So over the past thirty years or so these figures have been reasonably stable—despite increased numbers of recipients and of institutions.

The second measure of how-long-it-takes, namely, elapsed time from entry upon graduate study to receiving the doctorate, is harder to get mainly because it is not available from two dates of record but partly because it involves an additional definition of "entry" for certain marginal cases (e.g., someone who gets a Master's in one field and then takes doctoral work in another, or someone who makes up some deficiencies while registered but before being "admitted" to graduate study). A few years ago the Committee on Policies of Graduate Education of the AGS reported that in 30 member institutions these figures were 4.75 years in the physical and biological sciences and 5.5 years in the social sciences and humanities (though there was some question as to whether all the reporting deans answered the question in the same way). The questionnaires to recipients of the doctorate in 1957 collected detailed data on the course of their doctoral study, with the following results for the "number of elapsed years between your start on graduate work toward the doctorate and the award of the degree": *

	Median years, start to finish
Physical sciences	4.5
Biological sciences	4.2
Social sciences	6.0
Humanities	6.0
Engineering	4.3
Education	5.2
Arts & sciences	5.0
Professional fields	5.0
Total group	5.0

1940, for doctorates at Columbia and Harvard, the duration increased to about 175% and 125% respectively—much less in the sciences, more in the social sciences and humanities. The Columbia figures are substantially higher, in part, because the requirement to publish the dissertation was still in effect there in 1940.

* In these and the following data, I consider that the figures refer to calendar years, not academic years.

"Duration" by this measure is considerably less than by the other, more commonly used one. In fact, it is only about two-thirds as long for the arts and sciences and half for the professional fields. Furthermore, the range of duration by fields is considerably less by this measure. In fact the professional fields take no longer than the arts and sciences as a whole, and even less than the social sciences and the humanities.

What this means is that candidates do some other things between getting the Bachelor's and starting on their graduate studies toward the doctorate; and that candidates in some fields, notably education, do a great deal of it. Actually, about half the recipients in the arts and sciences went right on after receiving their Bachelor's but only about 35% in the professional fields. What do the others do? On the average, doctoral recipients spend about 3½ years—under 3 in the arts and sciences—in various kinds of employment, of which about half is academic in character. Such employment varies by field, from an average low of about two years for the physical sciences to a high of about seven years for education. The range directly reflects the availability of subsidies for graduate training: the more subsidy, the less discontinuity.

Now for the third measure: how long does it take in actual time spent working on the degree itself? Here, too, there are difficult problems of measurement, as anyone knows who has tried to define "full-time" in this connection. When how-long-it-takes is limited to the "number of years, in *full-time equivalent*, spent in work *directly* involved in securing the degree (including work on the dissertation)—that is, how long it *really* took you to get the degree if you had been doing nothing else," then the answer takes this form:

	Median years, full-time equivalent
Physical sciences	3.5
Biological sciences	3.3
Social sciences	3.7
Humanities	3.3
Engineering	3.1
Education	2.8
Arts & sciences	3.5
Professional fields	2.9
Total group	3.2

This measure is even more of an equalizer than the other: it takes 3½ years of full-time work in the arts and sciences, a little less in the professions and least in education.* By this measure, no longer are the profes-

* It takes over half a year longer to get the Ph.D. in education than the Ed.D. Both groups are included in this figure.

sions high and the physical sciences low: they have now reversed positions.* There are no differences by class of institution: it takes the same length of time in all of them.

How long, then, does it take to get the doctorate? The answer depends on what the question really means, and for whom:

	Arts & sciences (years)	Professional fields (years)
From Bachelor's to Doctor's	7	10
From start to finish	5	5
In actual time at work	3½	3

It takes the professional fields longer in total elapsed time (and even more so if engineering is excluded), but once they begin they spend about the same time and in actual work, less time. The actual time spent is less than half the elapsed time since the baccalaureate for the arts and sciences, and about a quarter for the professions. In all likelihood, this picture has not changed a great deal over the last twenty-five years or so.

WHO CARES?

As is the case with other aspects of graduate study, the people most directly involved are not the most strongly concerned. It is not the recent recipients who are most critical of the present situation—it is the graduate deans:

	Elapsed time			Actual time		
	Graduate deans	Graduate faculty	Recent recipients	Graduate deans	Graduate faculty	Recent recipients
Too long	68%	34%	48%	23%	14%	16%
About right	26	59	51	74	72	80
Other	6	7	1	3	14	4

---

* It is possible to construct a roughly comparable figure from NRC data on the total group of recent recipients. NRC has information not only on the number of years from baccalaureate to doctorate but also on the "total years of professional work experience (full-time or full-time equivalent)." Subtracting the latter from the former yields a residual figure that could be considered roughly the full-time equivalent of the time spent working for the doctorate. The medians by field:

Physical sciences	4 years
Biological sciences	4
Social sciences	4
Humanities	5
Professional fields	3

While the data are comparable to those in the text, they are only roughly so. Incidentally, this method of computation yields a number of cases in which the subtraction results in a minus number, recording the handicap under which some people labor in doing their degree "on the side."

When the recommendation to expedite the degree is put most directly, it is the deans who are eager—victims of their own propaganda?—and the faculty and the recent recipients who together are resistant:

Doctoral candidates should be required to get
through their programs more quickly

	Graduate deans	Graduate faculty	Recent recipients
Agree	74%	31%	28%
Disagree	14	51	51
Can't say	12	18	21

Actually, the faculty and recent recipients are split on the question by fields, and identically so: the social sciences and humanities somewhat more for expediting, the others less. The natural scientists and engineers see no particular need for a speed-up in *their* fields, and the other professionals are perhaps afraid that such a requirement would work to their disadvantage vis-à-vis the arts and sciences. (There is the possibility that the deans were answering for *elapsed* time and the others for *actual* time.)

As a matter of fact, several observers are cautioning against the current stress on expediting the degree if it means less actual time spent in doctoral work. They point out that as the amount of material to cover increases, there is more to master. Furthermore, they claim that with the increase in numbers, the students come to graduate school less prepared, less devoted to learning, and more interested in a job; so there are deficiencies to be made up as well as less ability and motivation in general. Indeed, they go on, time itself does something: scholars do not mature quickly, any more than wine does. A distinguished scholar of literature said, "It would be a serious error to debase the Ph.D. in the interest of reducing its time," and there are many deans and professors, and even students, who agree.

In recent years, as part of the concern with the "Ph.D. stretch-out," there have been several calls, notably by the 1957 committee of AGS deans, to set a clear norm for how long it should take to get the doctoral degree. The norm proposed is usually three or four years, and on this point everyone seems to agree. When the graduate deans and the graduate faculties were asked "about how long it should take a qualified student" (in full-time equivalent of actual work on the degree), these were their replies:

	Median (years)	Mean (years)
Graduate deans	3.1	3.5
Graduate faculty:		
Arts & sciences	3.0	3.4
Professional fields	2.7	3.0

In short, the norm proposed is almost exactly what it now *does take,* in full-time equivalence. Hence, when people call for the establishment of a norm for the duration of doctoral work for the full-time qualified student, they should know that it is here: it is agreed upon, probably as well as anything in academic life, and it is being realized in practice. The problem is not how much time a student should spend in working on his degree, but rather over how long a period of time he should do it— which is quite a different matter.

THE REASONS BEHIND DURATION

Then why don't doctoral candidates finish sooner? Some don't want to, like those perennial, "professional" doctoral candidates, especially at the better universities, who prefer a Bohemian existence on Fifty-seventh Street or Morningside Heights or around Harvard Square to what they consider exile in some institution down the line, to them the Siberia of Academia. Though picturesque, they are few.

Some can't, simply because they have difficulty meeting the requirements for the degree; a little more difficulty and they become a part of the attrition, as we shall soon see.

Some aren't encouraged or even allowed to finish because they are needed as teaching assistants for the department or research assistants for the professor.* It is manifestly difficult to know just how serious this is; not many recent recipients mention it as a cause of a too-long program, but over a third—more in the sciences—agreed with the proposition that "major professors often exploit doctoral candidates by keeping them as research assistants too long, by subordinating their interest to departmental or the professor's interest in research programs, etc." Nearly a third of the graduate faculty agree and 40% of the graduate deans, in whose office the complaints end up. No doubt there is something that needs correcting here.

Some have trouble with the dissertation; that is one of the two major reasons given for a too lengthy period of doctoral study by the recent recipients. About a third of the recent recipients believe that "doctoral candidates get too little direct attention, supervision, and guidance on their dissertations from their major professors, and that makes for un-necessary prolonging of the period of doctoral study"—and nearly a quarter of the professors agree with them. This is more of a problem outside the natural sciences; there the laboratory makes for a regular and intimate contact between student and professor that is lacking on the other side of the campus. Moreover, the sheer task of writing down a

---

* In the humanities, according to Dean Elder of Harvard, himself a classicist, "there is still a touch of the genteel tradition, a feeling that there is something inelegant and ill-bred about hurrying a man along."

"word" dissertation of several hundred pages takes longer than a "data" dissertation only a third as long.

Finally—and probably the major reason—some cannot afford to finish sooner, i.e., they cannot spend full-time on their studies because of lack of support. This is far and away the major reason given for the delay in completing the degree by the recent recipients themselves. Doctoral candidates who must support themselves—and as often as not these days, support a family as well—cannot complete the requirements in one period of uninterrupted work and have to do the best they can while serving as a teaching assistant, research assistant, tutor, and after the comprehensive examination, a full-time teacher. The more support a field has, in the form of fellowships or research assistantships that contribute to the dissertation, the faster its students complete their degrees.* In this regard, the natural sciences and engineering are the best off, the social sciences next, then the humanities, and last, education and the other professional fields—exactly the order of elapsed time needed to complete the degree.

Nor is other evidence lacking for the same point. Hans Rosenhaupt has shown for Columbia that veterans with government support finished up faster than the non-veterans, especially in the social sciences and humanities where other funds were less available. Perhaps the best evidence comes from a careful study by Lindsay Harmon of the Office of Scientific Personnel of the NRC, in which government fellowship holders in the sciences were carefully matched with a group of non-fellows on ability and academic attainment. The holders of fellowships who finished their doctorates did so more than a year earlier than the non-fellows—and more of them finished, too. If this occurs in a field where other support is available, such differences would probably be greater in the social sciences, humanities, and professional fields.

Money also works indirectly to shorten the period of doctoral study in those fields where high salaries are available outside academic life. As Sir Hugh Taylor has said, "The financial rewards of a Ph.D. degree in industrial and governmental research in the last decade have provided a potent incentive to the rapid completion of the degree requirements." The uncompleted degree is perhaps more negotiable *inside* the academy than outside.

WHAT DIFFERENCE DOES IT MAKE?

What difference does the attenuation of doctoral study make? One result is, allegedly, that people are ready to enter upon their careers at

---

* The more support the individual has, the faster he finishes too; but that relation needs to be qualified by the fact that the better students (who would finish sooner anyway) get more support.

too late an age—although most doctoral recipients are at work long before they receive the degree. In 1903 William James was complaining about candidates who "prolonged the process into middle life." In point of fact, here are the median ages of the recipients of the doctorate a few years ago (from NRC data):

Physical sciences	29
Biological sciences	30
Social sciences	33
Humanities	35
Arts & sciences	31
Professional fields	36
Total group	32

Other consequences have to do with the character of the interruptions and their effect. Some fields, like education, prefer that their doctoral candidates have some practical experience before continuing their studies —and there are many people in the humanities and social sciences who think that would be desirable for their students as well, as a matter of maturation. But once students are in the process, most people think they should have a continuous period of study, if not a full-time one. As the above figures reveal, though, doctoral candidates, unlike baccalaureate candidates on the one hand and law and medical students on the other, do not work straight through on their degree programs, and still less do they work full-time on their studies. The course to the degree is not continuous for nearly half of them—that is, it is interrupted by a time away from the campus—and it is particularly discontinuous in the social sciences, humanities, and education (about 60%) as compared with the sciences and engineering (about 30 to 35%). Here is another effect of greater support for the latter.

Most doctoral candidates are part-time students in one or the other sense. What else do they do while working for the degree? They work to support themselves, and primarily in academic employment: an average of nearly a year at the doctoral institution, well over a year in other academic employment, and about two-thirds of a year in non-academic jobs, or a total of almost three years. Again, the sciences and engineering are low (under 2 years), the other fields high (over 3½).

Here is another irony in the debate over doctoral study. The critics of the length of doctoral study want the candidates turned out faster, in part, so that they will be available for academic employment. But that is precisely what they *are* engaged in, many of them full-time. Even if the candidate did finish in a shorter period of *elapsed* time but with the same *actual* time spent on the degree, there would be little gain for the system—only a redistribution of academic talent institutionally and at a higher rate of pay.

There are still other reasons advanced to get people through faster. One is so that they will leave room for others, thus enabling the graduate school to turn out more degree-holders with the same staff and facilities. This is a possible benefit but by no means a clear one nor, I think, so large a one as its advocates believe. To the extent that the doctoral candidate is using up additional faculty and institutional time, equipment, and space as he works his way through, yes; but if he "consumes" the same *amount* only over a longer period, no. The actual situation in this regard is probably mixed, so that some saving of faculty and institutional resources could be made for investment in other students, but probably not a great deal.

Some observers, like former President Wright, believe that "The duration of the present system does subject the young men and young women who enter graduate school to physical and nervous strains, many of them unnecessary, the total effect of which is an accumulated fatigue and a kind of nervous insecurity." There is probably something in that, especially when one remembers that many doctoral candidates work long hours and under great pressure, both personally and academically, at this critical point in their careers. At any rate, half the recent recipients agreed that "as it operates, the doctoral program produces too much anxiety in many students, and unnecessarily so," and only a third disagreed. The proportions were reversed for graduate deans and graduate faculty—as one observer put it, "America is becoming too anxious about the prevalence of anxiety."

Others, again quoting President Wright, think that "The lengthening of the process has made the doctorate somewhat easier for those whom we may call capable routineers, while discouraging a good many young people who would be much more stimulating teachers." Whether this is true or not, certainly those involved do not agree with a related argument: two-thirds of the graduate faculty and recent recipients and over four-fifths of the deans dissent from the proposition: "The rigors of doctoral study tend to discourage the brightest, most imaginative students in favor of the conscientious plodders."

Of course, there still remains the possibility that a substantial number of the "brightest, most imaginative" students who *were* discouraged, were not tapped by this survey. However, other evidence suggests that this is not the case. The fact is that the ablest students finish earlier: they get most support and probably most attention. For example, the graduate faculty members who took a shorter time to complete their degrees are now more productive than those who took longer. This holds true consistently in every field.

Proportion publishing over five scholarly articles in the past five years

Elapsed time, Bachelor's to doctorate	Physical sciences	Biological sciences	Social sciences	Humanities	Professional fields
5 years or less	66%	78%	57%	46%	60%
6 to 9 years	53%	62%	41%	32%	52%
10 years and more	40%	51%	39%	27%	32%

Now this may mean, as some say, that the protracted character of doctoral study burns out one's scholarly interests. Perhaps the explanation is simpler: the better people tend to finish sooner and the better people are more productive.*

Involved in this whole matter of duration is, again, a question of one's conception of the doctorate. Specifically, how far down the scholarly road is the doctoral signpost to be located? Is it a guarantee of scholarly achievement or only a promissory note? Over the years and with the growth in numbers, it is probably fair to say that the prevalent opinion has shifted toward the notion of the doctorate as only the beginning of the scholarly career. For recent examples, take Dean Keniston: "We must give up the idea that the graduate student should emerge from his studies a fully formed scholar." Or President Wright: "The conception of the Ph.D. that I have tried to present is not that of the degree as a final achievement, or of the Ph.D. thesis as a life work, a *magnum opus*. It is a degree which, like the LL.B. or the M.D., is an introduction to a learned profession, a profession which requires preliminary study and training, but a profession which can never be mastered in graduate school, no matter how long the period of study." President Wright recognizes that what is involved here is the sensitive question of standards: how

---

* Another indication along this line is provided by the duration data for the graduate faculty. The actual time they spent on the doctorate is only a little less than for the recent recipients but the elapsed time is quite a bit less. Some of the difference may be due to the earlier period in which the faculty got their degrees, but at the same time the people who end up in graduate faculties tend to be the abler recipients, and they get through the program faster.

This can be extended even further: the faster the graduate faculty people got through their doctoral programs, the higher in the institutional hierarchy they now are. Here are the average elapsed times in years, Bachelor's to doctorate, for the various groups:

Are now at	Received doctorate from		
	Top 12 universities	Other AGS universities, plus	Other universities
Top 12 universities	7.1	7.2	8.2
Other AGS universities, plus	7.4	8.7	8.7
Other universities	8.7	9.0	11.0

preparatory can the degree become before it no longer stands for high (the highest) academic achievement?

To sum up: the problem of how-long-the-doctorate-takes is not a problem of actual time but of elapsed time. Despite the ever-growing needs of the subject matter, it is hardly realistic to expect that much more actual time can be taken. If nothing else, the prospects for economic returns place restrictions on the size of the investment. Actually, the tendency is to shorten rather than to lengthen.

As for elapsed time, that is partly a problem of the dissertation but even more a problem of support. Changing the program will make some difference, to be sure, but finding a way to support full-time doctoral study will make a much bigger difference. It would probably be desirable for more doctoral candidates to finish their degrees in one continuous period of full-time work, like students in medicine and in the better law schools. Everyone would benefit: the student, in both psychological and career returns; his professors, in being able to demand intensive work and in not having the stragglers in view or in conscience; the institution, in being able to apply standards more directly, and the same for the stragglers; the employer, in getting a more nearly finished product at an earlier age. Certainly a good deal of the tension and trauma in the present system would be dissipated under such an arrangement.

ATTRITION IN DOCTORAL STUDY

Does the length of the training period unduly discourage the candidates, deplete their finances, wear them out? Is attrition a major problem of doctoral study, wasting human and institutional resources?

There are certainly those who think so. President Wright speaks of the "inordinately high" attrition rate in graduate school and concludes that "we can save a very considerable number of those who now drop out of graduate school and could save them for the teaching profession." While graduate dean at Columbia, Jacques Barzun deplored "the appalling waste on both sides—of student energy, hope, and money, and of faculty time and effort"; and while graduate dean at Princeton, Sir Hugh Taylor waged a private war on the problem. Said he recently:

If the graduate schools of the country would solve this problem of attrition, if we could determine whether (and if so, how) the proportion of successful candidates can be increased, we could raise substantially the output of the graduate schools of the country without increased enrollment or additional expenditures for faculty and facilities. The schools owe it to themselves and to those who provide for their support, financially so expensive, to make a thorough examination of conscience in this matter. . . .

Let us begin the examination.

The first and obvious question is: how much attrition is there? Given the complexities of graduate education, the term itself is exceedingly difficult to define, but here are the estimates of the deans:

Median institution

About what percentage of the students who entered graduate school in fall 1950 have received degrees since then?	60–65%
About what percentage of those who entered in fall 1950 and sought the doctorate have now received it?	50–55%
Of the students who start work toward a doctorate at your institution, about what percentage never finish?	35–40%

According to these estimates, then, attrition at the doctoral level is about 40%.*

Is that high? Yes, when compared with medical school, where the figure is under 10%, and with the better law schools. For *all* law schools the figure is about the same (40%) but almost all the drop-out in law school occurs in the first year whereas in graduate school it comes later. Is that disadvantageous to graduate study or not—more "wastage" or more training? The professional schools typically screen their students more intensively before admission and the graduate school after—what has been described as the differing policies of birth control and infanticide. The medical or law student seeks to be graduated "with his class"; the doctoral student has no class to be graduated with.

The "wasteful" consequences of attrition are more serious for the professional student than for the doctoral candidate. The degree is an absolute necessity to the career of the lawyer or doctor; he simply cannot practice his profession without it. But not so for the doctoral candidate; he gets something negotiable in his training short of the degree, so there is less compulsion to finish it. On the average, he cannot do as well, to be sure, but he can follow an academic or research career in the sense that the professional candidate cannot follow a medical or legal one. As a matter of fact, this situation, as Sir Hugh Taylor has pointed out, "has tended to cause colleges, due to meager resources, to recruit personnel before the thesis has been written. A larger salary differential

---

* I asked essentially the same question of the graduate faculty and got an answer only half as large: an average just over 20%. I assume that there is more selective perception on the part of the faculty than the deans, and that the latter are more nearly correct, having in their possession the official records and the job of follow-up. In any case, here is a point where one side needs to educate the other. If the estimates of the graduate faculty are more nearly right, then there is not much to the problem of attrition at all. According to the faculty, incidentally, attrition is lower in the biological sciences, higher in the social sciences, and higher in the "lesser" institutions—but not by a great deal in any case.

between instructors with and without dissertations completed might help correct this situation, providing thus a stimulus to completion of dissertation requirements while in residence."

The attrition rate in graduate school is not high when compared with the undergraduate levels where it is also about 40% (measured similarly, as those starting who do not get the baccalaureate degree). But the matter is perhaps more serious for the graduate school because its selection is supposed to be better; its type of education is much more expensive; and, as with law, its drop-outs stay around longer than the undergraduate drop-outs, half of whom leave in the first year.

Actually, the attrition in doctoral study is accepted as more or less natural by the faculty. Since they believe that the figure is only about 20%, they also believe, quite consistently, that that amount is acceptable (85% of those with opinions on the matter) and that the problem is not an important one in graduate study (70%). Graduate deans, being closer to the situation administratively, are more concerned. Half of them consider it an important problem for their institutions, though only two deans mentioned it spontaneously when asked to name "the single most important problem of graduate study today."

Finally, what causes the attrition? When I asked the deans and graduate faculty whether it was more a problem of selection or of program, they replied, in effect, that it was both. But their listing of what they consider the "most important" reasons for attrition at the doctoral level reveals more than that. (I asked the same question of the recent recipients, referring to their colleagues who did not finish, and I add their replies for the comparison.)

	Graduate deans	Graduate faculty	Recent recipients
Lack financial resources	69%	29%	25%
Lack intellectual ability to do the work	50	64	52
Lack proper motivation	38	45	47
Lack necessary physical or emotional stamina	33	33	49
Found the degree wasn't necessary for what they wanted to do	19	10	12
Disappointed in graduate study and quit	1	12	21

Now several points are made or suggested by these data.*

First, they show why the graduate deans and the faculty do not take the problem more seriously: they do not consider it the fault of the graduate school. It is mainly a matter either of money or of the stu-

---

* Incidentally, in a recent study of attrition at the undergraduate level, Robert Iffert found that the major reasons there were essentially the same: money, lack of interest, and discouragement because of low grades.

dent's capability. The heavy stress by the deans on money is probably due to the fact that that is how the matter gets presented to them, that is, in the form of a request by a marginal student for more funds to stay in school.

Second, the recent recipients are probably closer to the mark than either the deans or the faculty in their estimate of the disappointment of the doctoral candidates who leave. (If *they* were included, the figure would be higher still.) The farther from the dean's authority, the more the inclination to blame the graduate school. What is critical frankness between doctoral candidates becomes in the dean's office lack of funds or a personal change of plans.

Third, the recent recipients are also probably closer to the truth, being closer to the persons involved, in stressing the matter of stamina more than the deans or the faculty—even if we discount their tendency to feel a little superior upon attaining the degree and thus demonstrating their own supply of stamina.

Finally, all three groups agree that a lack of intellectual ability to carry through on doctoral work characterizes the drop-out. Even if, again, we discount the institutional "patriotism" of the deans and faculty and the "superiority" of the recent recipients, the point probably remains. It conforms to the earlier evidence that the candidate's ability is directly related to his speed in finishing: on the average, the best students complete their degrees first, the less able take longer to do so— and the least able do not finish at all.

In sum, then, the issue of attrition does not seem to be quite as important as it is often made out to be. It is large compared with medicine and perhaps with law, but it is not clear that it is *too* large, considering (1) the need for graduate students and graduate assistants, (2) the lower economic returns of the degree, (3) the negotiability of partial training (so that not everything is "wasted"), (4) the difficulties of selecting the proper students, (5) the desirability of giving some students the opportunity to try themselves in the program, and (6) the imponderables of the doctoral program (no research training or dissertation required in law and medicine). According to the interested parties, money is partly responsible, but intelligence and motivation more so. It would of course be useful to hear directly from the other interested party himself, but we can assume, I think, that he would place more blame at the door of the graduate school than that institution is apparently willing to take on itself.

At the least, all parties would probably agree that it would be better if there were less attrition in doctoral study—*with* the same number of students and the same standards of performance—but they would similarly agree that some attrition is necessary. More than that: a number of realistic-minded deans would prefer the present rate of attrition if a much lower rate meant fewer students, and almost everyone would prefer the present rate to a lowering of standards. In the end, attrition may be one of the costs of a rapidly expanding system.

THE ABD'S

But there is a special kind of attrition, or extended duration, that requires special attention. I refer to those doctoral candidates who have completed everything for the degree except the dissertation and who are away from the campus on a full-time job. They are so numerous and so visible that they have been given a "degree" of their own. They are the ABD's—"All But Dissertation."

Every graduate university has some of them, often in large numbers. Sixty-three graduate deans reported a total of about 7,400, or an average of over a hundred per institution. A few large universities, especially those urban institutions with sizable proportions of part-time students, have several hundred. Nearly three-fourths of them "are still actively after the degree" according to the deans, and their estimate corresponds to that of the graduate faculty on the number of ABD's for whom they are the major thesis advisers. The average faculty member has nearly two ABD's under sponsorship: the range is from five in education to nearly three in the social sciences and humanities and down to less than one in the sciences and engineering—still another indication of the effect of support. As a result the problem is a "serious" one to about 40% of the faculty in the social science and humanities departments but to only 15% in the science and engineering ones.

Almost all the liberal arts colleges, all but 3–4%, have some ABD's on the faculty. The college presidents reported an average of six or seven an institution. Taking account of the sampling returns, I estimate that in the entire system there are upwards of 10,000 ABD's with the serious intention of completing their dissertation and getting the degree.

The situation is uncomfortable and undesirable to all concerned. The uncompleted dissertation hangs over the candidate like a black cloud, interfering with his career, his domestic life, even his peace of mind. The employing institution wants him to finish and often uses salary or promotion as pressure for completion, so that another Ph.D. can be added to the rolls; too often the situation is a source of continuous tension between the young faculty member and his employing department or administration. The doctoral institution has the problem of keeping track of the candidate and the worry of another potential case of attrition so near the end of the line, the department feels it must pass an inferior product for neatness' sake, and the major professor is faced with another case of thesis supervision at long distance and in bits and pieces.

As with duration generally, the deans consider the ABD's more serious a problem (40%) than the graduate faculty. Only a few years ago the Conference of Western Graduate Deans resolved "that serious study be given to ways and means of providing financial assistance to those young men and women of demonstrated worth, now teaching in colleges and universities, who have not quite attained the Ph.D., to permit them to return to complete the degree requirements."

But it is the college presidents who are most concerned. When asked, "Do you consider it highly desirable for most of them to complete their degrees, or do you think it doesn't matter so much, now that they're in active teaching?" over 95% of them responded that it was "highly desirable." Without doubt, such near unanimity is partly due to the increment in prestige rather than substance to be gained from conferral of the degree (William James again), but there it is. What is more, when the presidents were asked, "Would you welcome a program that would enable most of them to complete their work for the degree, even if that would take them away from campus for six months to a year?," 90% said "yes."

Again the problem is primarily one of dollars. Most of the ABD's are in the humanities and the social sciences, i.e., in those fields where subsidies are less available to support students to completion. Some fellowship programs are now being aimed at the terminal year—i.e., the year of the dissertation—precisely in order to hold down the number of ABD's. But the battle may be a losing one over the next years: the pressures and opportunities for college teaching, coupled with the natural pressure for married students to get into earning jobs as quickly as possible, will certainly intensify the problem.

The Dissertation

Near the center of many issues in doctoral study—its purpose, program, quality, and duration—stands the doctoral dissertation. Sooner or later the debate gets to it, and any decisions made about it are likely to affect most other areas of graduate education.

Professor Cowley has noted that historically the thesis has been dropped as a requirement in higher education under the impact of numbers—first at the Bachelor's level, then the Master's, and even for some professional doctorates. However there is no prospect that it will be dropped as a central requirement for the Ph.D.; almost everything else would have to yield before it would. Given its importance and durability, let us see what the dissertation is supposed to be, how useful it is, what problems it presents, and what might be done about them.

THE PURPOSE OF THE DISSERTATION

The traditional conception of the dissertation is clear. It was supposed to be an original and significant contribution to knowledge. Now that, of course, is only a statement of intent. The decision as to what was sufficiently original and significant, what was contributory, and indeed, what was knowledge, was left to the departments, as no doubt it had to be.

Over the years, however, questions have arisen not only about realizing that aim but even about the appropriateness of the aim itself. As for originality, for example, quite often these days the author of a dissertation in the natural sciences is not really considered as an independent investigator, but rather a member of a research team. When I asked a distinguished biologist what happens to the "original contribution to knowledge" under this system, he first thought I was pulling his leg, then replied: "It's that by definition!" Another well-placed observer of the biological sciences told me that "the old classical tradition of the thesis, that is, the large dissertation with a full review of the literature, is being queried. There is a tendency now to do the dissertation so that the student learns how to do articles for the scientific journals."

The originality of the contribution is also being rationalized away, especially on the humanistic side of the campus. Dean DeVane of Yale told the ACE Conference of 1958 that "Thomas Carlyle has a word for it. . . . He says that the essence of originality is not that a thing be new but that it be a man's own." A recent committee of the College English Association "called attention to the danger of interpreting too narrowly the requirement that the thesis should constitute 'an original contribution to knowledge.' . . . Significance and relevance as well as originality should also [sic] be criteria in judging a thesis."

The notion of "significant contribution of knowledge" has come in for some hard questioning too, as by Meredith Wilson, then President of the University of Oregon, Chairman of the ACE Conference of 1958 and of its Committee on College Teaching, and President of the Council in 1959:

> To assure "contribution" a premium is placed on novelty when the problem is set, with the result that the dissertation is more frequently peripheral than central; more often incidental than fundamental. . . . Insofar as the thesis problem is recondite, or has permitted sacrifice of significance to gain novelty or originality, the thesis process is bad education. . . . At any rate, it would be worth our time to examine, in graduate schools, whether the allegations are correct that (1) the thesis diverts attention from the significant central problems of the discipline toward the novel and peripheral, thus sacrificing the prospects of wisdom and understanding in the false hope of guaranteeing a contribution to knowl-

edge; and that (2) the thesis as presently required may burn over more creative minds than it awakens to continuing creativity.

And the Committee of Fifteen distinguished sharply between the honorific term "contribution to knowledge" (though they added the qualifier "real" and put forward the forbidding example of Bryce's *American Commonwealth*) and "a merely arithmetical addition." They went on to argue that too many dissertations, at least in the humanities and social sciences, were of the arithmetical kind.

If the dissertation is not to be judged by these traditional terms, then what is the alternative? It is to consider the dissertation an instrument of research training. In the words of the Trustees of the Carnegie Foundation, "It would be a trial run in scholarship and not a monumental achievement." The primary test would be, in other words, whether it contributed to the student's knowledge, not the world's.

Over the years, this notion has probably gained supporters, so that at the present time the parties concerned are split quite evenly on the matter. "Should the doctoral dissertation be regarded more as a training instrument than as an 'original contribution to knowledge'?" Yes, say about 55% of the deans, 45% of the graduate faculty, and 40% of the recent recipients. Nor is this simply a semantic distinction: the dissertation used as a vehicle of training could be quite different from the dissertation held up to the original criterion. For example, this difference is involved in the issue over "team research" and indeed in the very conceptions of the end of doctoral study itself—that it should complete scholarly training or that it should initiate it: the guarantee versus the promissory note.

Which way is the tide running? The increase in the body of knowledge itself implies an answer: the more there is to master, the more the training period will become the start rather than the finish. More directly, we can get an idea from a similar question asked of the graduate faculty and the recent recipients about "most dissertations in your department" and "your dissertation," respectively:

Regardless of what the formal requirements are, do you think that the value of the dissertation is primarily as an original contribution to knowledge or primarily as an exercise in research training? In your view, which should it be?

	Graduate faculty		Recent recipients	
	Is	*Should be*	*Is*	*Should be*
Primarily contribution to knowledge	15%	25%	26%	25%
Primarily research training	57	31	31	18
Both equally	26	42	42	56
Can't say	2	2	1	1

In the first place, the recent recipients think better of the contribution to knowledge made by their dissertations than their sponsors do. And—the new members of the club upholding its standards—they are quicker to stand by the traditional idea as the requirement. But more importantly, both groups, and especially the faculty, believe that training *is* the outcome more often than it should be. In this case, where *is* and *should be* differ, it is probably more likely that standards will be brought into line with reality than the other way round. Faculties are likely to temper ideal requirements with practical considerations, especially when there is ample rhetoric to rationalize the shift. Over the long-run, faculty sentiment is probably moving toward "training instrument" and away from "contribution" as the *raison d'être* of the dissertation.

In the humanities, this "revisionist" movement is bold enough to call into question the very notion of research, in the narrower sense, as being applicable to such fields. For example, in his recent review of the present state of the humanities, Howard Mumford Jones says:

> At the end of the nineteenth century it was commonly held that the doctoral dissertation must represent a contribution to knowledge in the sense of bringing something undiscovered into the world of learning. Although this concept of the dissertation still lingers, the dissertation is now more commonly regarded (in the humanities, at least) as a test of maturity of mind and of professional competence. . . . It is a problem of mature interpretation rather than of originality in the sense of the "unique thing."

A chairman of a leading department of English said that the better departments were now encouraging criticism and interpretation, and were aiming not at training researchers but at providing a "valuable educational experience" via the dissertation, whereas the poorer departments were still insisting on "research." He added with a smile: "Another instance of cultural lag."

This movement is of course consistent with the long-run trend against the positivistic or scientific approach to humanistic studies as noted earlier: a trend away from research and toward scholarship, if one may use the terms in that way.* This development points up an important difference in the dissertation as conceived on the scientific and the hu-

---

* It is no secret that many people outside the humanities, and not a few inside, believe that part of the drive in this direction is due to the lack of good thesis topics in the field, so that by now students have to "research" the nth rate writers. The current trend is, I think, in a part a reaction against that practice. In addition, many would agree with one outside observer who pointed out the "it is easier for the sciences to call for a contribution in the dissertation because most of the creative scientists are in the universities, whereas most of the creative people in the humanities are probably outside the universities—writers, artists, musicians, publishers, some lawyers, and so on."

manistic sides of the campus, between the data disciplines and the word disciplines. In the language of Carlyle, cited above, the scientific dissertation may not be the student's own but it does produce something new, whereas the humanistic dissertation may not be new but it is the student's own.

ITS VALUE

Despite all the jokes about the doctoral dissertation—jokes that usually consist of selected titles or of such definitions as Laski's "island of words in a sea of references"—despite them, the supervisors and the subjects of doctoral study both consider it the most valuable part of the training.* When asked to evaluate eight major aspects of the doctoral program—course work, preparation for the general examination, the assistantships, and so on—both the graduate faculty and the recent recipients put the work for the dissertation at the top of the list of those "particularly valuable": three-fourths of the former and even more of the latter.

Both sponsors and candidates are quite satisfied with the product as well as the process itself:

How do you feel about the dissertation—as you think of the return on the investment of time and energy?

	Graduate faculty (replying for "most of the dissertations done in this department")	Recent recipients (replying for "your dissertation as a piece of work, not as a requirement for the degree")
Very satisfied	10%	29%
Fairly satisfied	66	52
Rather dissatisfied	17	15
Very dissatisfied	1	3
Can't say	6	1

Despite the legendry about the tediousness and flatness of dissertations, at least the writers themselves feel pretty good about them two years later. Only about a fifth of each group is dissatisfied, and in a human

---

* I leave out of consideration here one valuable aspect of dissertation work that many people disapprove, I think wrongly, as illegitimate and exploitative, namely, the dissertation's contribution to the research program of a senior professor. According to a graduate dean, himself a chemist and speaking for the sciences, "in the case of many a professor in distinguished institutions, the major scholarly work of the professor is simply the summation of the original work which graduate students have done in collaboration with him. Only occasionally does a professor of chemistry write an article which is not in collaboration with a graduate student."

enterprise of this complexity and career importance it is unlikely that dissatisfaction would ever be much less than that, no matter what changes were made. I must add, however, that faculty dissatisfaction is twice as high in the humanities, social sciences, and education (about 25%) as in the natural sciences and engineering (12%). The word-data break is the watershed for many matters connected with the degree, and with virtually all involving the dissertation.

This general state of affairs is supported by other data too. About 75% of the graduate faculties say that the present character of the dissertation in their field is "about right," again with the same differences by field. As the recent recipients look back on their experience with the dissertation, about half of them acknowledge that some drudgery was involved in the dissertation along with the excitement, but fewer than 10% think it was mainly "tedious, pedantic drudgery; not worth the effort in itself, but necessary for the degree" as against 35% who now, two years later, call it an "exciting, enlightening intellectual experience."

As for the quality of the dissertation, the major check on that has disappeared. Not so long ago, the dissertation had to be published by university requirement. But numbers and costs have taken care of that (except for the microfilming solution). Now, with no compulsion, only a minority of the recipients of the doctorate in 1947–1948 published some or all of their dissertations in the following decade: 50 to 60% in chemistry and biology, 30 to 40% in physics, psychology, and mathematics, 20% in history, 10 to 15% in English, philosophy, and education. If something could be done to reinstate the publishing requirement, it might have an important effect on the merit of doctoral dissertations. At any rate, everyone thinks so: the proposal, "if at all possible, require publication of the dissertation in some form, as a way to maintain standards of doctoral study," was agreed to by about two-thirds of the respondents, though by many fewer in the social sciences and humanities (where the problem is supposed to be most acute).

THE MAJOR PROBLEMS

From this general discussion of conception and value, I turn now to the major specifics under criticism in the debate over the dissertation. They are three: the amount of independence given the student in selecting the topic and doing the research, the time it takes to do the dissertation, and its length.

INDEPENDENCE. Part of the "original" work involved in the dissertation is supposed to be the student's selection of his own dissertation topic. What actually happens? The answer depends on which party to the transaction you ask:

How is the dissertation topic really selected?

	Graduate faculty (replying for "most" topics)	Recent recipients (replying for "your" topic)
Student selects it independently	8%	46%
Student and sponsor jointly select it	68	39
Sponsor really selects it	21	15
Can't say	3	1

The student thinks he chooses it, but the sponsor thinks otherwise. What actually happens, probably, is that the typical student picks up several ideas for dissertations from his professors and then settles on one. To him, *he* selected it; to the professor who suggested it, it was at least a joint selection.

Here again, there is an important difference by field. According to the faculty, the student selects his own topic in this many cases:

Physical sciences *	2%
Biological sciences	4
Engineering	7
Humanities	9
Social sciences	12
Education	19

By this definition, "originality" is inversely related to prestige.

On the whole, then, the faculty cannot escape direct responsibility for poor dissertation topics—for what someone has called "the choice between thinness and minutiae." To the extent that the topics are badly chosen, the faculty is responsible not only for approving them but, by its own claim, for selecting them in the first place. In the current discussion about the dissertation, many people are urging that the student be guided to his topic more directly in order to save him from "floundering around trying to select a problem" (as the Yale report on economics puts it). But there is already a great deal of such guidance in the eyes of the graduate faculty, even though, so far as the students are concerned, it is apparently done with nice discretion.

In the doing of the dissertation, too, the faculty has to walk a fine line between two critical camps: too little independence for the student (especially in the sciences), too little supervision of him (especially out-

* A physicist at a major university told me that "the practice these days, especially with so much sponsored research, is to give the student a dissertation topic not really at the frontier of knowledge but in the area just this side of it. A topic at the frontier would be both too difficult and too uncertain."

side them). The other side of the coin of independence appears to be neglect.

Among the reasons often given for the length of the doctorate, as well as for the insufficient merit of many doctoral dissertations, is the insufficient supervision given by the thesis advisor.* Again, however, the parties involved do not think so:

How closely does the thesis advisor work on doctoral dissertations, i.e., how much attention, direction, supervision, etc.?

	Graduate faculty (replying for themselves as major sponsors)	Recent recipients (replying for their own case)
Close and continuing supervision	32%	27%
Less, but sufficient for the purpose	50	58
Hardly any or not enough	5	13
Can't say	13	2

The same is the case for a more general question as to the value of the apprenticeship relation, a basic rationale underlying graduate training and one thought by many to be undermined by the numbers of candidates now presenting themselves for attention. Again, about 80% of each group is satisfied, the students even more so than the faculty.

Even so, there is another aspect of the "original" dissertation in the sciences that requires some attention. Its true originality is perhaps best revealed by what happens to it. The fact is that of all the dissertations (or parts thereof) published by recipients of the doctorate in 1947–1948, only about half in physics and biology and fewer than a fifth in chemistry were published under sole authorship, as compared with 100% or close to it in all other fields. What is more, over a third in chemistry and a tenth in physics and biology were published with the doctorate recipient as the junior author. As my consultant said, the dissertation is original by definition. But note that the judgment of this practice depends on the conception of the dissertation: if it is a training instrument, then there is nothing necessarily wrong with this arrangement.

TIME. The dissertation certainly contributes to the "undue length" of doctoral study. As I noted above, it is second only to money as the cause of too much elapsed time (nearly 30% of the cases) and it is also

---

* It is of course impossible to say how many doctoral dissertations under supervision are too many—that depends on the field, on how closely they are tied in with the professor's own research program, on what else he has to do, etc. But the figures on how many now are under supervision do not seem particularly high. About a third of the graduate faculty were now major sponsors of none, and another 40 to 50% were sponsors of from 1–3. The average was about 2½ (though over twice that in education).

important in the case of too much actual time (nearly 50%). How long did it take "in total time spent working directly on it?"

	Median years
Physical sciences	1.7
Biological sciences	1.6
Social sciences	1.1
Humanities	1.3
Engineering	1.2
Education	0.9
Arts & sciences	1.5
Professional fields	1.0

The mean is nearly half a year longer. Even the graduate faculty, presumably the pick of the Ph.D. crop, took nearly as long to do their dissertations.

There is some discrepancy between this reality, especially in the sciences, and the norm of one year now being proposed by those who seek to expedite the training program. As it is, the dissertation now takes more than that: less than a third in the arts and sciences complete it within a year and only half in the professional fields.

Why does it take that long—leaving aside the reason obvious to any Ph.D., namely, that it is a lot of work. Part of the problem is a faulty start: a third of the recent recipients actually started more than one dissertation topic. Partly it is a late start: over half did not begin work on the dissertation until after taking the qualifying examinations—about two-thirds outside the sciences. Partly it is the ABD problem: a third did "all or the major part" of the dissertation away from the campus— a half outside the sciences—and half of them admittedly "not in close contact with" the thesis sponsor.* Partly it is the wrong topic: the common complaint that "doctoral candidates are too often allowed or encouraged to attempt a major contribution as their dissertation rather than take on a manageable topic that can be finished in a reasonable time" gets assent from a majority of the deans but from only a third of the faculty or the recent recipients.

But these reasons don't seem to carry us very far. The very fields where they least apply, in the sciences, take the longest to do the dissertation—and they have less to write as well. And that is where the dissertations are most satisfactory to the faculty. (It is also there where the topics are most clear-cut, the methods most highly developed, and the

---

* On the record, however, these factors make no difference in the sciences and not much in the social sciences and humanities; the most important delaying influence (in actual time) is doing the dissertation away from the campus—that adds about four to six months (another reason to finish the degree before leaving the university).

results most reliably judged.) Does quality have something inevitable to do with the time spent? Can the time for the dissertation be shortened without cutting standards by roughly the same amount?

LENGTH. The major cry about the Ph.D. dissertation—aside from its occasional pedantry or sheer silliness—is its length (outside the sciences). All three groups agree that "doctoral dissertations, at least outside the sciences, are too long," but here again the faculty and the recent recipients are not nearly so sure as the deans: 86% of the latter to only about 60% of the former (though considerably more in the top institutions, where more dissertations have to be read).

It is always possible to cite extreme cases in which it took a great deal of space to say not very much. Once more let us look at the record. How long are doctoral dissertations these days? Those accepted in American universities in 1957–1958 were this long:

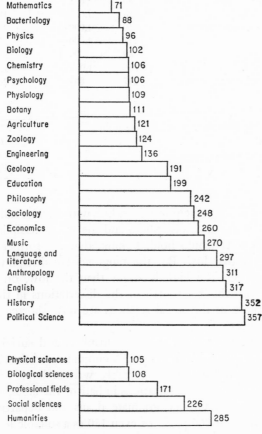

FIG. 11. Length of dissertations by field (median number of pages).

Disciplines	Range Low	Range High	Middle half of the cases fall between
Mathematics	18	379	48–105
Bacteriology	28	237	70–122
Physics	24	419	71–128
Biology	22	459	66–137
Chemistry	27	403	85–141
Psychology	17	492	75–143
Physiology	38	298	81–132
Botany	39	577	80–160
Agriculture	44	498	92–155
Zoology	62	694	85–180
Engineering	31	617	102–185
Geology	52	668	128–272
Education	24	1,000+	147–281
Philosophy	87	525	192–325
Sociology	61	989	178–352
Economics	60	811	192–339
Music	58	1,000+	186–417
Language and literature	60	1,000+	225–393
English	112	1,000+	227–401
Anthropology	89	800	237–393
History	145	1,000+	379–452
Political science	147	863	268–443

Divisions			
Physical sciences			82–151
Biological sciences			64–146
Professional fields			117–241
Social sciences			123–342
Humanities			207–384

The great range among disciplines is in line with the prevailing academic assumptions about the data disciplines and the word disciplines—although the same assumptions would hold, I think, that the former are not that high or the latter that low. But the range *within* disciplines is, if anything, more striking: the high is larger than the low, on the average, by a factor of 16. About a fourth of the dissertations in the humanities and a half of those in the social sciences are now shorter than the top 10% in the sciences.

The length of dissertations in the humanities and social sciences are high enough to concern many people. A committee of the AGS recently proposed "a well-ordered and respectably written book of 250 pages," which would mean shorter dissertations in half of the cases, as the median became the maximum. Others, graduate deans and departmental chairmen, have talked about 200 pages or even 150 as a suitable length: "There are very few candidates who could not marshall their evidence and say what they have to say in 200 pages at the outside."

Beyond that, however, there are a growing number of advocates of a shorter dissertation still—say, from 50 to 100 pages. The advocates usually feel quite strongly about the matter. As a departmental chairman in social science said to me: "The article-length dissertation is just common sense and is long overdue. The scholar typically gives only 50 pages or less to the profession, short of the finished book which we can't expect from the Ph.D. candidate. Why should he give more to his professors?" Similarly a graduate dean at a top university: "The dissertation now is neither fish nor fowl so far as scholarship is concerned—neither a book nor an article, the two products scholars produce. We cannot require the first, so why not the second?" Or in the words of Dean Keniston, a humanist: "If quality, not quantity, is the desideratum, then [that] can be as well demonstrated in a brief monograph, or even an article of journal length, as in a vast compilation, *monstrum informe, ingens*, which often is largely made up of a rehash of what others have written."

The first reaction to the proposal of so short a dissertation in the word disciplines is, typically, that it would mean a lowering of standards. But subsequent reactions qualify that. As a matter of fact, more than one leader in the humanities objected that an excessively severe demand would be made of the candidate by the short dissertation: "That is asking too much."

Indeed, a major advantage argued for the innovation is precisely the improvement of the training and the product.* An economist who is in the forefront of introducing a short dissertation in that discipline is sure that it "improves quality rather than deteriorates it. The idea is to go from a bad book to a good article." Students cannot pile up pedestrian material as a way of overpowering their sponsors or simply reproduce

---

* One way to have the best of both worlds, which may or may not work in other fields, was experimented with in the department of biology at the University of Rochester in recent years. There the doctoral dissertation was divided into two parts: (1) "a monograph comprehensively and critically dealing with the subject matter of some biological or other scientific field related to the research problem that the candidate intends to investigate"; this part has to be done *prior* to the qualifying examination, and indeed was a requirement for taking the examination, and (2) "the original research work of the candidate" which had to be prepared "as a manuscript in final form for submission to a scientific journal." In the words of its advocate, Dr. Kenneth Cooper (now at the Dartmouth Medical School), the idea was to "have the student do early what he ordinarily does later or not at all, namely, professionally master an area of knowledge, largely by himself, that is generally much broader than his immediate research interest and effort and present this in essay form, in precise language and with skillful reasoning and logic, as a critical and scholarly monograph. . . . The degree of mastery shown by the monograph provides good evidence and test of scholarly capacities *before* the qualifying examination."

in extenso the work of others. Departments would not be faced with the poignant problem of the diligent student who spends a long time assembling a great deal that in the end is not really enough for a good piece of work—but is enough, human feelings being what they are, to get the degree.

Mainly, however, the argument is simply that "such a short thesis, of publishable quality, could be examined or criticized in greater detail by the faculty, and, if needed, revised more often and more basically by the student" (Yale report on economics). Along the same lines, from a different discipline: "Better a thesis of limited scope, written and rewritten until economy and even grace of expression have been achieved, than a tome too diffuse in organization and language to be readable" (the committee of the College English Association). The shorter dissertation might be easier because of greater focus—though that would seem to be an advantage in many fields—but it would be harder because the faculty could demand higher standards.

The central fact is that the typical dissertation of 250 pages and up can be carefully read by only one or two faculty members and can hardly be redone in its entirety, out of considerations both of time and humanitarianism. The dissertation of 50 or 100 or even 150 pages could be read and criticized by four or five faculty members and could be redone until it was right. The result can be better training for the student and better scholarship for the field, plus the by-products of improved writing and more likely and quicker publication. For the word disciplines there may be some gain in time as well, although the example of the sciences suggests that that will not be very large.

Can it be done? A few dissertations in the word disciplines are now as short as 100 pages but, to be sure, not very many. How willing are people to consider shortening the traditional dissertation? I asked the question in progressively demanding terms:

Proportion agreeing ("can't say's" omitted)

		Graduate faculty			Recent recipients		
	Graduate deans	Social sciences	Humanities	Education	Social sciences	Humanities	Education
Allow, or even encourage, shorter dissertations	82%	68%	75%	62%	73%	68%	63%
Allow dissertations of 50-100 pages	69%	61%	56%	61%	63%	38%	57%

The proportion of "can't say's" increases from the first, general prescription to the second, specific one—from about 20% to 35% for the faculty and the students, but much less than that for the deans, who have been forced by their responsibilities to think the matter through.

The groups most concerned, then, favor a shorter dissertation by two or three to one—even more in the top universities. Except for the humanists who have just written one, they favor a much shorter dissertation, though not so strongly.

The Master's Degree

Like the doctoral degree, the Master's has a long history of concern over the same problems raised in the same terms. As early as 1902 the AAU was debating whether it was a terminal degree or a steppingstone to the doctorate. In 1910 Calvin Thomas of Columbia described it to the AAU as slightly a cultural degree, partly a research degree, but everywhere a teaching degree, mainly (even then) for secondary schools. In 1932, an AAUP committee concluded that the "widespread dissatisfaction is justified"—a conclusion, incidentally, agreed to in a 1945 AAU report. In 1934, an ACE committee noted the confusion between the academic and the professional uses of the degree, and in effect threw up its hands. In the same year, the John report from the Office of Education suggested that the place of the degree "doubtless never will be answered finally." Never is a long time, but certainly the past quarter century bears out this judgment of the Master's situation. In its most recent full-dress review of the degree, the AAU concludes that "the situation . . . has not improved."

The trouble appears to be twofold.

The first, strangely enough, stems from one of the alleged glories of American higher education, namely its diversity. The very diversity of the Master's degree troubles those people who want a degree to mean one thing only, or at most a very few. The recommendations of the 1945 AAU committee were based on a desire for "uniformity" of standards and requirements—recommendations that were apparently as quickly forgotten as they were adopted, if one may judge by subsequent practice. A graduate dean, after a recent tour of graduate schools, remarked on "this confusion of inconsistency" and pointed to "an urgent present need for more nearly standardizing" the degree. It remained for the graduate dean at Harvard to characterize the situation in a striking figure: "The Master's degree," he wrote last year in *The Journal of Higher Education*, "is, at present, a bit like a streetwalker—all things to all men (and at different prices)."

That the Master's is many different things is certainly true. As Howard Mumford Jones put it a few years ago, it started as a "social distinction, became a post-graduate degree, . . . and is today alternately a consolation prize, an insurance policy, or a sop to public education." It is given in a large number of forms in addition to the traditional MA and MS, probably on the order of 100—MBA, MSW, MPA, MFA, M.Ed, MLS, MAT, MSE, et al. It is given for a wide range of work: another year of course work with no general examination, no thesis or "essay," and no foreign language; a two-year professional program as in business; even a three-year program in the history of fine arts, where it is a strong degree and recognized as such. In several universities, standards for the degree vary within a single department, as with the many optional plans for the Master's (usually with or without thesis); some have so varied for decades, as at Minnesota. The very proliferation of titles for the degree indicates how varied it is.

Whether the Master's is academic or professional in character makes a big difference in what it "means." In many academic fields, the Master's is given to a candidate on the road to the doctorate almost automatically, and certainly with little detour or cost of time. In many professional fields or parts of them, the Master's is, or may be on the way to becoming, the first professional degree, e.g., in engineering, business, education, social work, library science. In such fields, it is the capstone to the final year of what is essentially a five-year program of study. In many academic fields, it is the terminal degree mainly in cases of discouragement and consolation; in most professional fields it is terminal by design.

Much of the early rationale for the degree has been attenuated, or lost. If, as the 1910 quotation says, it had a cultural purpose at an early stage, it hardly does any more; few students these days take a Master's degree simply to become "better educated." More importantly, it has lost some of its earlier point as a testing device for the doctorate, except in its featherbed position for those falling from doctoral grace. Indeed, if "true graduate work" requires orientation to research and the advancement of knowledge, as well as independent work in the form of a thesis and a comprehensive examination, then it is fair to say that much Master's work today is not graduate in character but more nearly on the order of a fifth year of undergraduate work. Almost 600 institutions now award the Master's in this country. Over a quarter are given by liberal arts or teachers colleges (as against only about 3% of the doctorates), and the universities themselves now award the Master's in as many fields as they do baccalaureates. The attitude of industrial employers indicates the current situation in the sciences: the major distinction they make in their employing policy is between the Master's and the Doctor's, not between the Master's and the Bachelor's.

The second trouble is that under the demands of diversity and the stress of numbers, the degree has been weakened, at least in prestige. It is generally assumed in academic circles that the Master's "does not mean as much as it used to." Almost all the disciplinary consultants said so for their own fields, and nearly two-thirds of the graduate faculty and half the graduate deans acknowledged that "the Master's degree has become easier to get at your institution as compared with 20 years ago." In a few more cases, the deans admitted that it was easy enough then.

This weakening of the degree's prestige, if not its merit, is in turn made up of two strands. The first is that the degree has become associated with professional practice rather than academic scholarship: only 29% of the Master's degrees in 1957–1958 were in the arts and sciences, down about 10 percentage points in the past decade. The well-known pressure toward Master's work that is exerted by state requirements for appointment and promotion has meant that the Master's is now largely a degree in education, for service in the secondary schools. In 1940, about a third of all Master's degrees were conferred in education; today nearly half are. Of the doctoral recipients in 1957, 98% of those in education had Master's degrees as against only 79% in the arts and sciences (only 64% in the physical sciences; it is the humanities that pulls the figure up, with 94%).

The second is that the degree has weakened most in the better institutions. In the first years of the century, we may recall, it was pointed out that the Master's was stronger in departments that did not give the doctorate. It now tends to be stronger in universities that do not concentrate at the doctoral level. When the graduate faculty was asked whether "the Master's degree in your department has come to be neglected relative to the doctorate," here were their replies:

	No	Yes, but not matter of regret
Top 12 universities	40%	40%
Other AGS universities, plus	59	22
Other universities	70	11

The higher degree tends to crowd out the lower one: if nothing else, there are simply too many theses to supervise, and the doctoral load takes precedence.

This has meant a decline both relatively and absolutely. For example, the top 12 universities award fewer Master's degrees now than they did a decade ago (and only about 15% of the total). As noted earlier, the strong emphasis on education has meant that most of the Master's are given at institutions with heavy education faculties, at state universities, and at urban universities. The attitude of "the great private universities" may perhaps be summed up in the recommendation of the recent Committee on the Educational Future of Columbia University:

The emphasis in graduate work at Columbia should be on the training of Ph.D. candidates. Some departments, indeed, may wish to receive only students who state their intentions to proceed to the Ph.D., although some may intend to take the Master of Arts degree as an incident (!) in the process . . . The shift is consonant with the University's proper emphasis, especially in view of educational developments in the New York metropolitan area, which have already made available additional M.A. programs.

Or, again, the graduate dean at Harvard at the 1958 ACE meeting: "In this connection, we might just as well say openly—I point a finger at some areas in my own Cantabrigian backyard—that universities should either improve their weak or easy or consolatory Master's programs or should stop awarding that degree in those fields. Gresham's law works too surely." On the same occasion, the graduate dean of a Southern institution summed up the situation: "Most of the damage has been done east of the Hudson on the M.A. . . ." This development has undoubtedly hurt the degree: if the prestige institutions neglect it, the others can maintain it only with great difficulty, if at all.*

What should, what can be done about the degree? As anyone knows who glances at the literature on higher education these days or walks through an educational meeting, there is a great deal of talk about reviving, restoring, resuscitating, renovating, or otherwise strengthening the Master's as a degree for college teachers in the "crisis" ahead—and most of the talk is favorable. Should we "restore the standards of the Master's degree as a way to get more college teachers?" On the producing end, almost two-thirds of the graduate deans think so and over half the graduate faculty (though, again, many fewer in the top places.) On the consuming end, two-thirds of the college presidents think so too, even though, as we have seen, they much prefer the doctorate. Dean Elder of Harvard expressed the common sentiment on the *should* and *can* in a recent article on "Reviving the Master's Degree for the Pro-

---

* These twin developments are reflected in the opinions of the graduate faculty on the present situation. They were presented with a double-barreled proposition: "The graduate schools have wrongly allowed the Master's degree to deteriorate in quality"— Did it deteriorate? Was it wrong? Here are the proportions agreeing (omitting about a quarter of "can't say's," evenly distributed):

Arts & sciences	60%
Professional fields	42
Top 12 universities	50
Other AGS universities, plus	56
Other universities	58

In the first case, the professional fields do not feel that the degree has deteriorated, not in *their* field (and especially so in engineering). In the second case, the faculties in the better institutions are less inclined to think the deterioration was *wrong*.

spective College Teacher": "The most pressing question that now faces us is not, in my opinion, the academic one of whether it would be good or wise to revive—perhaps I should say exhume—the Master's degree for college teachers, but how in the world we can revive it and what the specific program should be."

As to the *should*, I have already indicated my doubt that the "crisis" is a solid justification for a maximum effort to revive the Master's— certainly not as the central teaching degree. But beyond that, there is a real question as to whether it *can* be revived. The historical fact is, I think, that degrees are not strengthened as a matter of requirements and standards. In this respect, if they move at all, they move down-hill rather than up. Given the pressure of numbers, the tendency is to relax requirements, not to stiffen them, and to look to the next level to take up whatever slack is thus created. Occasionally, an island of merit can be maintained or developed under special circumstances, as indeed now obtains with the Master's in some fields and some institutions.*

The prospects of making the Master's a highly respected, research-oriented, 1½- or 2-year degree for college teachers on a national scale are, I think, not bright. There is too much going against it: the historical decline, the lowered prestige, the diversity of meaning, the numbers of claimants relative to the numbers of faculty available for sponsorship and guidance, the competitive disadvantage relative to the doctorate, the coolness of the better colleges, the reluctance of the better students, the poorer career prospects, the low return on investment. I conclude that this clock cannot be turned back.

At the same time, I hasten to add, the degree is by no means on its way out. If it were going to die in our generation or the next, it would have died long ago! Instead, it is flourishing: an average in the 1950's of well over 60,000 a year. The reason is simply that it is needed for many of the tasks noted above—for certifying, for testing, for consoling (and thus protecting the faculty and the doctorate against the inevitable mistakes in the selection of candidates), for ensuring the student against eventualities. It is worth something on the consuming end, too. After all, a Master's does mean more than "some graduate work." If anything, it is becoming more important in the secondary schools, especially in the growing attractiveness of the Master's with subject matter emphasis, as in the Master of Arts in Teaching programs now developing. Ac-

* For example, there is now considerable interest in developing solid Master's programs in a few good liberal arts colleges, as a contribution to the "crisis." They would probably be good programs, but they would cost the college something beyond money, and they would confer so few degrees as not really to affect the national picture. In any case, when asked what they would like as college teachers, college presidents placed such a Master's sixth on a list of six, below a Master's from a university.

cording to a well-placed biologist, "therein lies the method for avoiding rote work and copybook teaching in secondary schools, which is usually a direct consequence of the teacher's trying to stay one jump ahead of his students" on the subject matter.

The Master's carries its weight in the academic procession, but it cannot carry a great deal more. It is a necessary degree today, but it cannot be made into a prestigious one today or tomorrow.

Post-Doctoral Work

In 1901 Henry Pratt Judson of the University of Chicago called for more post-doctoral fellowships, at the expense of the pre-doctoral variety, in order to give impetus to "research for its own sake." In 1930 Abraham Flexner noted the need for more post-doctoral work and participated in founding the Institute for Advanced Study at Princeton in order to facilitate it. Today there is so much post-doctoral training that many people are becoming perplexed or even alarmed at where it is all going to end, or rather, are becoming concerned lest it not end anywhere!

Certainly there is a good deal of post-doctoral training today, though it is not of such recent origin as is commonly believed. Of the graduate faculty, 23% of those under thirty-five had "a post-doctoral fellowship for study with a senior person at any stage in your career"—but so did 17% of those over fifty. Most of this, of course, is in the sciences:

	Had post-doctoral fellowship	
	Graduate faculty	Recent recipients
Physical sciences	29%	16%
Biological sciences	27	23
Social sciences	13	9
Humanities	13	6
Professional fields	9	3

The recent recipients are lower simply because they are only two years beyond the doctorate; several of them will still have this experience. As a matter of fact, many more 1957 recipients of the doctorate in the physical and biological sciences have had post-doctoral training than have gone into liberal arts college teaching—half again as many.*

* All these figures refer to post-doctoral training in a formalized manner. However, the actual practice of "post-doctoral training" in the sciences may be even greater, in this sense: in about a third of their publications from three to ten years after receiving their degrees, the doctorates of 1947–1948 were the junior authors. Incidentally, there is also a certain amount of post-doctoral training that now goes on outside the universities, in industrial and governmental installations and in both the natural and the social sciences (e.g., tax economics or international economic development).

One reason for the disparity by fields is, clearly, the disparity in available funds. The National Science Foundation awarded a total of about 425 post-doctoral fellowships in 1959 and the Public Health Service another 300 or so, nearly all in the sciences. Actually, about a third of the recent recipients in the arts and sciences *plan* to have post-doctoral work, but those in the sciences *do*. As some humanists and social scientists told me, "We'd have post-doctoral fellows too, if we could afford them."

An associated reason for the incidence of post-doctoral work is the sheer requirement imposed by the subject itself—its growth and its specialization, particularly in fields where the break between graduate and undergraduate programs is most sharp. "In your field, is post-doctoral training becoming necessary or highly desirable for proper advancement?" Here are the proportions who think so:

	Graduate faculty	Recent recipients
Physical sciences	62%	30%
Biological sciences	65	40
Social sciences	48	27
Humanities	33	17
Engineering	32	9
Education	33	14

The differences by field are clear—and so is the difference between the faculty and the new doctorates. Whether the latter difference is due to the faculty's tendency to up-grade the claims of their field or to the recipients' not yet appreciating the facts of life, I cannot say; probably it is a little of both.

But the rank order is the same, and it reflects again the basic differences between the two sides of the campus. A leading physiologist, speaking of the "explosion" in his subject, said that post-doctoral programs would grow because the nature of the field was forcing change in that direction. A leading mathematician also used the "explosion" figure, added that in his field the student must master the earlier material as well as the new, and concluded that "the Ph.D. has, in effect, a general education in mathematics; he needs more specialization and that is where the post-doctoral program comes in." The 1959 report on *Graduate Education in Psychology* notes that there are now 151 post-doctoral programs in 40 universities. Just as some subjects begin in the graduate school and move down to the college level—for example, sociology a few decades ago, biochemistry now—so the training for a few technical specialties now exists mainly at the post-doctoral level.

Post-doctoral work confers not only new knowledge on the trainee but also new prestige. The National Research Council post-doctoral fellows of a few decades ago are generally acknowledged to have been "outstandingly successful," whether because of selection or training. The current fellows, too, get a quick start on their careers, partly because they have survived a further screening on the national scale and hence are tagged as particularly promising. Moreover, they typically serve as post-doctoral fellows in precisely those American institutions that are at the top—so that even if they took their doctorate lower down, they now can step off the career ladder from one of the highest rungs. Actually, most of them go from one top-ranking university to another, to work with a distinguished professor, so the present system does less than it might in serving as a channel by which talent from one class of institution can move to another class, instead of from one institution to another of the same class. For example, of the 1958 and 1959 regular post-doctoral NSF fellows moving between American institutions, about 65% came from the top 12 universities and 80% went to them to study.

Just as doctoral work was once highly concentrated in the universities at or near the top, so is post-doctoral work today. Almost every graduate university today has some post-doctoral fellows in residence. A total of 1,790 "post-doctoral students or fellows in residence" was reported by 66 universities, and almost all the graduate deans expect more in the next three to five years. But the leading universities average 75 to 100 each, compared with 40 to 45 in the next group, 20 in the next, and 10 in the others. Indeed, there are now so many that several of the top universities are becoming concerned about the allocation of so much space, equipment, and faculty time to a group that provides no tuition. Historically there were so few post-doctoral fellows that universities were glad to provide the courtesy of their facilities. Now the very growth of the practice is raising serious financial problems.

But the universities get something in return. Many top professors prefer post-doctoral fellows because they are better research assistants. This is also a useful device to test out and recruit new faculty members without the commitment of even the initial term appointment. That is a practical and realistic consideration to put alongside the idealistic one that a few promising young men need more intensive training in their specialties, and usually in a new setting—very much like the residency in medicine.

As for the new-ness of the setting, that appears to be of such importance that of all levels of education post-doctoral work is the most international. Nearly half of the post-doctoral students and fellows in residence at American universities are foreigners. Of all the regular post-doctoral fellows supported by the NSF in 1959, over half planned to do their work abroad: more in Cambridge, England, than in Cambridge, Massachusetts; more at Copenhagen than at Columbia.

Post-doctoral work gains prestige for a university today just as doctoral work did fifty years ago, before so many institutions were involved in it. As a well-known economist told me:

> We need more organization of post-doctoral work, more leadership and structure to it. Training doesn't really end at the Ph.D. any more. The graduate institution now depends on post-doctoral work, just as the undergraduate depends on graduate students. The university that has it has something to offer the faculty, and it will be able to get good faculty members just as in the old days the graduate school performed that function.

Indeed, so many Ph.D.'s are coming to the leading universities for further research training, especially in the sciences, that the institutions are starting to make special arrangements for them. Appropriately enough, MIT and Cal Tech are in the vanguard. MIT has established a School for Advanced Study for post-doctoral work, with a Director, Institute Professors, and Fellows. Cal Tech has a School for Advanced Research with over 100 research fellows in residence. "It should have encouragement and support," said President DuBridge in a recent annual report; "it is becoming more and more important for many young research workers in both pure and applied science to continue research experience beyond the Ph.D. before seeking a permanent position." There are further stirrings in this direction: Illinois has recently set up a Center for Advanced Studies; Michigan has proposed an Institute for Science and Technology that would be post-doctorate in part; Chicago has a plan for a Center for Advanced Study in Mathematics; a panel at Columbia suggested that serious consideration be given to setting up a small Institute of Advanced Study there, in a Memorandum on the Graduate Faculties prepared for the study of the Educational Future of the University.

Most of this activity is in the sciences, but similar developments now exist in the social sciences too: the National Bureau of Economic Research, the Bureau of Applied Social Research at Columbia, the Russian Research Center at Harvard. Indeed, major facilities for the post-doctoral level—some of it training, some independent work—are now nationally available in mathematics and physics at the Institute of Advanced Study at Princeton, in the biological and medical fields at the Rockefeller Institute in New York, and in the social sciences at the Center for Advanced Study in the Behavioral Sciences in California. Only the humanities lack such an institution.

To many people, this whole development is a sad one. On the institutional side, it suggests that the universities have not been able to meet the need for continuing study and training for their staffs. A large university today is so bureaucratized, so pressured, and so busy that the old image of the "ivory tower" of study and reflection could hardly be less appropriate. Traditionally, the university was meant to provide time and atmosphere for contemplation and thought. To find these conditions today, the faculty finds it increasingly necessary to leave the university or to escape into an isolated part of it, such as an institute.

Nor is the growth of post-doctoral study viewed as an undiluted gain on the personnel side. Those concerned about the duration of doctoral work are horrified at the extension of training under another label; to the trustees of the Carnegie Foundation it would have "the great disadvantage of lengthening a process that has already grown unbearably long." Those concerned with independent and creative work are horrified at an extension of the period of "dependence and immaturity"; to one dean, that would be the "ultimate tragedy." Those concerned with the quality of doctoral study are horrified at the relaxation of standards that could be justified; as another dean put it:

> The present rapid growth of the post-doctoral fellowship idea is, at least in part, a direct result of many of our Ph.D.'s having been trained in too-large groups, in over-extended graduate departments, and under "team research" circumstances. Having sought properly to achieve the purposes of a doctor's degree in gaining the understanding and maturity to undertake independent research, they are compelled to return to an academic setting to learn what they should have learned before their degrees were granted.

Those concerned with the numbers problem often see it as a necessary evil, as, for example, a well-known American historian:

> The pressure to increase the number of qualified teachers—that is, of such as can wave a degree of some sort—will very likely prove irresistible and threatens to stifle scholarship, not to say intellectuality. . . . I am inclined to believe that what is most necessary is a genuine post-doctoral program that will rescue men of ability lost in hasty or ill-directed graduate work.

In the large, then, the development of post-doctoral work is directly tied to two of the major long-run trends in graduate education: the constant increase in numbers of students, the constant increase in the amount of material to be mastered. For the visible future, both trends will continue to operate. The rationalizers, if not necessarily the advocates, of the present trend put the argument this way:

> Whenever a massive enrollment has hit a level of education in this country, two things seem to happen. First, there is at least a diversification in the educational program and perhaps a watering-down as well; and secondly, to the extent that there is some deterioration, that level passes on to the next higher level the problem of repairing its deficiencies. Thus the high school has to take things slower because the elementary

school has not taught students how to read properly, the colleges have to teach elementary mathematics because the high schools have not done the job, and the graduate school has to worry about foreign languages and even about training the student in how to organize his thoughts and write intelligible English. The Master's program has already been brushed aside in many places in favor of the next higher level, namely, the doctoral program. But where is *it* to turn? The sign on President Truman's desk used to say, "The buck stops here." But not quite. Whatever deficiencies remain there, partly the result of those with which people came to the graduate school and partly because of the developments of the fields themselves, can be remedied for a select few at the next higher level. The training for the doctoral degree, which used to be all there was and clearly enough, is now insufficient for some people with genuine research potential and ambition in fields of increasing specialization. They need to be given "real doctoral training"—at the post-doctoral level.

The same rationale was recently put in comparative terms by Ralph Gerard of the University of Michigan:

An increase in the level of education for the many is necessarily accompanied by a deterioration in the quality of education for the previous elite. Again in compensation, a new level is added; and, again, it is eventually overwhelmed. Thus, the A.B. was once a mark of scholarship, then the M.A. was superposed, and later the Ph.D. Today, even this is often a "commercial degree" and various types of more advanced doctorates are in the offing—degrees comparable to the British D.Sc., which has been maintained at high standard in the Empire by allowing the Ph.D. to slide under it. Actually, such piling up of degrees and levels is an inevitable consequence of sheer size. As an army gets larger, it is necessary to create ever new top grades, of generals and super-generals, in order to satisfy the hierarchical needs of the organization. Similarly, as the base of education is widened, there must be an ever increasing number of levels up to the apex.

I doubt that a new super-degree is in the offing—the post-doctoral fellowship is still distinctive enough to carry its own prestige—but certainly post-doctoral training is here to stay.

On the whole, using the post-doctoral route as a way to solve some problems of graduate education is disapproved by all the interested parties—except one. The respondents were asked for their opinion of this suggested reform: "Make the Ph.D. readily available for fulfillment of three years of acceptable work, and give additional training at the post-doctoral level for the few really able researchers." The graduate deans, the graduate faculties, and recent recipients all disagreed by at least two to one—even more in the sciences and the top institutions, where it would be most appropriate—but college presidents had just the opposite reaction. The former groups see the proposal as a threat to the maintenance of Ph.D. standards and prestige; the latter group sees it as a way to get college teachers faster and with less intensive research training. Such a plan could relieve several of the graduate school's problems, and I shall return to it in the final chapter.

The Foreign Language Requirement

Somewhere in this country today, any day, another faculty committee is drawing up another report on the foreign language requirement for the doctorate.

In the early decades of the century, the requirement was settled: two languages—first only French and German, then *usually* French and German. But since the 1930's, little by little, the requirement has been eroded, so that now, while two languages are still required at the majority of institutions, (1) they do not have to be French and German; (2) the examinations are increasingly given by the subject matter departments rather than the language departments, thus making the requirement somewhat easier to fulfill; (3) one of the languages can increasingly be replaced by another "tool" such as mathematics or statistics—on the ingenious ground that they too are languages foreign to most students—or by additional work in a related discipline; (4) the requirement is satisfied in some universities by a thorough knowledge of one language rather than two poorly mastered, and in others by one language, period; and (5) notably in education, but also in some other professional fields, the doctorate can now be secured with no foreign language at all. As for the language requirement at the Master's level, that was typically discarded some time ago.

Despite this tendency—or rather *because* of it—the topic has constantly been under discussion in faculty meetings and never resolved. In part, this is due to the fact that some humanists feel they have a guardian's responsibility for the language requirement, not to mention the more selfish interests involved on the part of some of them. But mainly it is due to the fact that the reason for the language requirement is still very much in debate. Is it to assure that the highest-earned degree goes only to "educated men"? Or is it to provide scholars with a scholarly instrument?

The deans and graduate faculty were asked: "Two justifications are usually given for the foreign language requirement for the doctorate: (1) the cultural justification that foreign languages are needed as a mark of the educated man; and (2) the professional justification that the languages are needed as a tool for research in the discipline. Which justification seems more important to you?"

	Professional	Cultural	Both equally	Can't say
Graduate deans	31%	14	51	4
Graduate faculty	43%	17	35	5
Physical sciences	58%	6	34	2
Biological sciences	50%	6	42	2
Social sciences	37%	24	31	8
Humanities	30%	17	51	2
Engineering	52%	13	29	6
Education	29%	29	25	17
Top 12 universities	51%	14	30	5
Other AGS universities, plus	43%	16	37	4
Other universities	36%	20	36	8

Thus a basis of controversy exists in the division of sentiment among fields, and to a lesser extent, institutions. The professional reason is probably gaining strength—that accounts for many of the inroads on the traditional requirement—but there is still a large proportion of faculty members who believe that there is something important in the cultural basis of the requirement too.

Regardless of what the requirement is supposed to be, there is much more agreement on what it has come in reality to mean. It is no secret in academic circles that it has become something of a farce. One scholar told me that he was "willing to participate in the deception" and most graduate deans, graduate faculty, and recent recipients know what he meant. About three-fourths of each group agreed with the proposition: "The foreign language requirement at the doctoral level has come to be a form without much substance in a sizable proportion of cases," and more agreed "strongly" on this statement than on any other in a list of over 40. And this near-unanimity extends across classes of universities and fields: humanists agree even more than scientists.

Aside from the corner-cutting tolerated on the matter—this is the prohibition amendment of graduate training—the basis for this feeling is twofold: doctoral candidates are alleged by the critics of the requirements not to know the languages of which they have a "reading knowledge" and not to use them. Now the first assumption is quite true, according to the recent recipients themselves: only a fourth of them "feel you really know the language(s) in which you passed the necessary examinations." But the second needs considerable qualification. Almost half the recipients said that they had "actually used the language(s) in your graduate training or in preparing your dissertation" or that they had used them in their professional work subsequently.

But the range is considerable. Here are the reports on how many recent recipients claim to have used the foreign language(s) in graduate training, in preparing the dissertation, or in subsequent professional work:

	Proportion of cases
Chemistry	85%
Zoology	84
Biology	77
Mathematics & statistics	75
Religion	75
Music	74
Botany	71
English	63
Philosophy	63
Physics	62
History	62
Geology	57
Engineering	54
Political science	52
Sociology	33
Agriculture	29
Economics	19
Psychology	17
Education	10

With such a range, it is no wonder that the matter is so frequently in debate within the faculty.

What can be done? One of the troubles, everyone agrees, is that the student's undergraduate preparation is weakest in this respect. Less than a fifth of the graduate faculty considers it "satisfactory," and even fewer of the deans. About half the recent recipients think *their* preparation was all right, but even with them, it scores lower than any other aspect of undergraduate work. Here, then, the graduate school is pinning some blame for the relaxation of this particular standard on the college and the high school. Doctoral students cannot be held for much, it says in effect, because they come with deficiencies in language training too great realistically to be overcome. The proposal to require one or two languages for admission to graduate school would cut the number of students sooner than it would improve the colleges and high schools; moreover, it would work to the disadvantage of the weaker institutions.

Partly in consequence, there is a split in faculty opinion between let's-end-the-sham and let's-really-require-knowledge-of-the-language, a split that sometimes compromises on solid knowledge of *one* language in preference to shaky knowledge of two. The split is sharply revealed in the graduate faculty's answer to this question: "Where would you change the present requirements for doctoral training in your field?" A third think the language requirement is "OK as is"—the fewest for any aspect of the training. Another third would relax the requirement—the most support for any relaxation. The other third would demand more knowledge. So there is little satisfaction with the present situation but sharp disagreement on which remedy to apply, the easy one or the hard one.

Among the "reforms or changes" presented to my respondents were two dealing with the foreign language requirement. One was to "cut down," and only a quarter of the arts and sciences faculty agreed, and even fewer of the deans (12%). The other was to "leave the requirement up to each department rather than the graduate school as a whole" and that was more acceptable: half the faculty, a quarter of the deans. In both cases, it is the social sciences and education who tend to agree. It is clear that if the requirement is left to the departments, it will be cut there: those who favor departmental decision are six to one more inclined to cut it down than those who want the decision kept in the graduate school as a whole.

So the lines are drawn. In the sharp disagreement between different sides of the campus—the natural sciences and the humanities ranged against the social sciences and most professional fields—that is as close to a "solution" as the situation apparently will allow. I put the term in quotation marks because it is not agreeable to those who support the traditional standards of doctoral study. Yet the trend is probably running against such standards, if for no other reason than because erosion will beget erosion: the graduate faculty is somewhat reluctant to impose requirements on current students that they could not meet themselves, hence their "participation in the deception."

There are several other problems of graduate education more substantial than this one, but its specificity, its tradition, and its symbol as a measure of the quality of the doctoral program make it a constant source of tension within the graduate faculty.

The Final Examination

The last stage in the doctoral candidate's course toward the degree is the final examination, the defense of the dissertation. At one time, this was a genuine examination and a genuine defense. Today it tends to be neither.*

As the number of candidates increased and the university became more bureaucratic, the final examination changed from *the* comprehensive examination—it was moved up in time—and became something of a routine that both faculty and students have to get through, though neither quite

---

* In this respect it is very different from the qualifying, comprehensive examination, which is not only a real examination in substance and importance but one that contributes, through his preparation for it, to the candidate's breadth within his own discipline.

knows why. As the graduate dean at Harvard said recently, "the final oral has been variously modified, heaven knows, from its European model, but generally this modification has been more or less *ad hoc*. It is generally kept because it is in the pattern. But why kept is rarely asked!"

At that point, at most though not all universities, it is extremely rare for a candidate to fail—not, as academic agreement has it, that many may not deserve to fail, but (1) because it is then too late for a faculty to assert itself "in all fairness to the candidate" and (2) because even though it may be feasible to fail the candidate, it is difficult or highly embarrassing at that point for a department to fail his sponsor, his committee, or even itself in the process. In the course of my interviews, I collected many of the stock phrases used to justify and rationalize the dubious pass:

> He may not be one of our strongest candidates, but he isn't as weak as so-and-so last year.

> He may not be one of our strongest candidates, but he will do a creditable job of teaching where he is going.

> Perhaps he shouldn't have been allowed to go on, but since we did not discourage him sooner we have to assume some of the responsibility now.

> This may not be a good topic for a dissertation, but after all, we let him go ahead on it so we have to take some of the responsibility now.

> True, he didn't acquit himself well on the examination, but he is really better than that.

—not to mention the statements including note of the candidate's personal situation.

In short, the system is moving away from the original intent for the occasion, as Leonard Beach, graduate dean at Vanderbilt and a past president of the AGS, was frank enough to say recently:

> What was originally a day of glory, the emergence of the butterfly from its chrysalis, has deteriorated into a perfunctory hearing, at which the well rehearsed resume and the planted questions relieve the candidate (and the director) from any possibility of embarrassment, and the occasion from any quality of climax or distinction. In the family of scholars, this moment of arrival should be a rite of jubilation and of deep intellectual significance. Insofar as it is a meaningless relic of the Continental system, it might better be abandoned.

Actually, most of the deans disagree with him, and the graduate faculty and recent recipients are split evenly on the matter. "Is the final oral examination, or defense of the dissertation, only a ritual now, without a useful function?" Yes, say about half of the faculty, a little fewer of the recent recipients, and about a third of the deans. Similarly, when the graduate faculty was given a list of doctoral requirements and asked to say where they would relax the standards and where demand more, the respondents again split evenly on the final defense. The arts and science people, except in the biological sciences, are more likely to consider the examination an empty ritual than the faculty in professional fields; and the faculty in the top places a little more likely than the others.

What difference does it make—to the student, the faculty, or the institution? Strange as it may seem to anyone who has watched doctoral candidates go through the trauma of anticipating the examination, the students probably want an occasion to symbolize their winning of the prize so long sought. The collective commencement is too anonymous to fill the bill. The present examination, even though perfunctory, *can* become a hurdle; and even though safe (or perhaps *because* safe), it is supposedly the moment of achievement and the definite point in time when the student becomes the scholar. But only, I'm afraid, supposedly and romantically so: when asked, "about when, on the way to the doctorate, did you come to think of yourself as a scholar or scientist rather than a student?", only 14% of the recent recipients said it was when they passed the dissertation defense. (The rest, incidentally, were strung out all along the route to the doctorate; most, about 30%, connected the feeling with the dissertation and 15 to 20% said "not yet"!)

From the standpoint of the faculty, the occasion provides an opportunity for an exchange of views on academic standards, research methods, theoretical positions, and the like. True, this can and does go on in the normal course of disciplinary activity and departmental meetings. The advantage here—perhaps not great but sometimes, in a badly divided department, critically important—lies in the very indirectness of the exchange: the faculty can speak frankly to one another through the candidate. This is not a happy solution to the problems of faculty communication, but it is often an effective and even necessary one, though it does not seem to justify the whole practice of the final oral.

From the standpoint of the institution, the question arises as to whether the form is worth the price, considering what it has become and what it costs. For a university awarding 300 doctorates a year, the examinations themselves require something like 3,000 to 4,800 faculty man-hours (assuming two-hour examinations and five to eight faculty members in attendance), not counting the hours that go into reading the dissertation. At a university with 200 doctorates, the cost is from 2,000 to over 3,000 faculty hours. The direct result, in numbers of students failed (who are, in any case, students at the margin), does not appear to justify that expenditure of time by busy professors. Is it justified by the ritualistic function and the by-products—e.g., occasional revisions of dissertations? Can a more economic substitute be found?

The Evaluation of Graduate Work

The big question about graduate education is the one on which it is most difficult to get solid evidence: how good is it? The ultimate answer to that question must be found in one of two directions, both closed to me by the nature of this study. One is an inquiry into the content of the programs; that must be done by representatives of the disciplines themselves. The other is an objective investigation into the quality of the product; that is an extremely large and complicated matter in itself. Either of these, or both together, would give a more nearly final answer to the persistent question of quality.

Although I cannot deal with this question directly, I can deal with the next best question, namely, how good people *think* it is. That is, after all, not far from the original question; indeed, it is more often than not taken as its equivalent in educational circles.

For is the academic discussion of the rights and wrongs of graduate work not usually an exchange of opinions, viewpoints, convictions . . . about the matter? Given the nature of the situation, is not the value of graduate training often gauged by what people think it is? How, usually, do we decide how good it is in general or in a specific institution or discipline, except by asking the people in a position to know? If the judgments of such people are not to be given serious consideration, then whose are?

So the following data are in my view more than simply a collection of information bearing on quality. They actually tell a good deal about quality itself, however that slippery concept is defined.*

GENERAL SATISFACTION

To start with the broadest question: how satisfied are people with graduate work and what comes out of it? † Almost everyone can say how satisfied he is, and almost everyone, except those most directly in charge, is satisfied or better. The students who recently emerged from

---

* In judging quality, it is important to note one important difference between the graduate school and the professional schools of law and medicine. The latter are more likely to judge quality on the basis of what *all* their graduates do. The graduate school is more likely to judge on the basis of what their *best* graduates do, largely because of the importance of the criterion of contributing to knowledge.

† The questions are slightly different, but similar enough to warrant this comparison. Here are the actual phrasings:

Graduate faculty: "By and large, how would you say you feel about the state of graduate training in your field at your institution?"

Recent recipients: "Taking everything into account, how do you feel about the graduate work leading to your doctorate—what you got out of it compared with what it cost in time and energy and money?"

College presidents: "By and large, how satisfied are you with the products of the graduate schools that are available to you as college teachers?"

Industrial representatives: "On the whole, how satisfied are you with recent products of the graduate schools that are available to you as industrial researchers?"

the program are satisfied, and so are the employers in industry and, let it be especially noted, in the colleges. Those who take the training and those who take the product are at ease, but not those who *give* the training—certainly a better state of affairs than the other way round.

	Graduate faculty	Recent recipients	College presidents	Industrial representatives
Very satisfied	8%	35%	24%	37%
Satisfied	53	53	69	58
Dissatisfied	33	9	4	0
Very dissatisfied	5	1		
Can't say	1	2	3	5

The recent recipients are so well satisfied that no differences appear either by field or by institution. Nor do they when the recipients judge, "as nearly as you can now tell, how good your doctoral program was in training you for the position you now hold?" They had been in the field for about two years when questioned, long enough to have checked their training against their first job experience. This is how it measures up, in their view:

Very good	51%
Fairly good	39
Just adequate	7
Unsatisfactory	2
Quite poor	1

No one knows what par is for an educational venture, but so far as the satisfaction of the product goes, this must be well over it. Furthermore, the satisfaction is slightly greater precisely where graduate training is alleged by the majority of critics to be most deficient, namely, in preparing college teachers. The recent recipients now in college employment think their training was "very good" for their present positions (56%) even more than those in universities (51%) or in non-academic jobs (46%).

In general, the satisfaction with graduate training is least where the recipients are least satisfied with their jobs, as follows:

How well pleased are you with your present position?		Proportion of each group dissatisfied with graduate training
Thoroughly satisfied	33%	5%
Satisfied	56	10%
Somewhat dissatisfied	9	20%
Thoroughly dissatisfied	2	23%

Thus the recent doctorates who don't like their training tend to be in jobs they don't like (the poorer students?). Over-all, about 90% like their jobs, and 90% approve of the training they got to prepare for them.

Only the graduate faculty is inclined to be very critical: partly because they are protecting "standards," partly because they tend to be self-critical perfectionists, and partly, I think, because they feel it is expected of them.* For example, the faculty was also asked how they thought their colleagues felt about graduate training. Throughout the sample, the respondents' colleagues were reported to feel better about the situation than they themselves, by 10 percentage points or more. The respondent always "holds higher standards" and "is more critical" than his associates.

But satisfaction is by no means evenly distributed across the campus or the system. As for the campus, the social sciences and the humanities are more dissatisfied than the sciences and the professions, but not by a great deal (45% to 35%). And this difference, which will appear throughout this section on evaluation,† is quite consistent across the major disciplines, as indicated in the table to be found on the next page. Such a range, of course, can reflect either adherence to higher standards as the proportions of dissatisfaction increase or recognition of lower performance.

As for the system, the dissatisfaction increases regularly from less than a third in the top institutions down to nearly half in the universities, and hence this subjective measure appears to have a base in reality.‡

But there is one group more critical than the graduate faculty. That is the graduate deans. They are the most critical of all. They have the administrative responsibility for improving the system, and they are more likely than the graduate faculty to have criticisms brought home to them from the outside. They go to more meetings where these mat-

---

* This was also the case, I think, when the graduate faculty was asked: "Considering what you think a Ph.D. in your field ought to know, how satisfied are you with what the current crop of Ph.D.'s actually do know?" Over 40% said that they "know less than a Ph.D. should"—and nearly a third of the recent recipients agreed for themselves. Now if a third or more of Ph.D.'s know "less than a doctorate should," then (1) something is seriously wrong with the norm, or (2) something is seriously wrong with the students and/or the programs, or (3) this response has to be taken as part of the academic man's loyalty to ever higher standards to which "no one" ever measures up. I think (3) is more nearly the correct interpretation. Incidentally, here again the difference by field appears: only about 35% of the faculty in the professions think their doctorates know less than they should as against about 40% in the sciences and 50% in the social sciences and humanities. The differences by class of institution are negligible.

† For example, it is the social scientist and the humanists among both the faculty and the recent doctorates who are more likely to think that numbers are jeopardizing standards, or that graduate training sometimes has the effect "of dampening the student's enthusiasms for learning and scholarship."

‡ At the same time, there is a tendency to upgrade one's own department in a comparative ranking with other departments. Only 25% of the faculty (arts and sciences only) agree with the Keniston rating of their own department, and even fewer of the recent recipients for the department in which they took their doctorate. Both groups put their department on the high side in most of the remaining cases.

Proportion of graduate faculty dissatisfied with
graduate training

Arts & sciences

Geology	14%
Mathematics & statistics	32
Biology	33
Zoology	34
Physics	34
Botany	35
Chemistry	36
Psychology	37
Modern languages	43
History	44
English	46
Sociology	48
Political science	48
Economics	50

Professional fields

Education	30
Engineering	34
Agriculture	35
Business	44

ters are discussed, they read more of the literature, they ponder the
questions more. I am not suggesting that they are for those reasons more
likely to be right, but am only trying to explain why they are more
inclined to be critical.

For that they are. An index of criticism of the graduate school was
based on 10 of the 40 propositions contained, in identical form, in the
questionnaires sent to the deans, the graduate faculty, and the recent recipients (as reproduced in the Appendix). Those 10 criticized the graduate schools on the following issues: too little independent work, not
enough training in teaching, poor selection of students, too casual handling of the foreign language requirement, standards being jeopardized
by numbers, deterioration of the Master's degree, trivial dissertations,
period of study too long, undue stress on research, undue specialization.
The deans accept a balance of five or more of the criticisms twice as
frequently as the faculty or the recent recipients (27 to 14%).

WHAT IS RIGHT AND WRONG

As a kind of summary of the specifics involved, it is worth reviewing,
first, what the faculty and the recent recipients consider the most and
least valuable aspects of doctoral training; and second, what changes the
faculty would make in the present requirements.

With regard to the first, there is strong agreement in all fields and in all classes of institutions on what counts most and least in doctoral training:

	Proportion naming the item as among the	
	Most valuable	Particularly valuable
	Graduate faculty	*Recent recipients*
Dissertation work	75%	82%
Independent reading	57	79
Course work	53	78
Relation to major professor(s)	52	72
Teaching assistantship	27	32
Preparation for general examination	25	46
Research assistantship	23	34
Relation to fellow students	19	59

On the whole, the faculty and the students agree on what stands at the top of the list; after that, however, they disagree. The faculty considers the last four aspects of training as more or less of a piece, but the recent recipients distinguish quite sharply: their fellow students are far more important than the faculty thinks (or is willing to acknowledge?) and the assistantships rank at the bottom of the list. Over-all, of course, the recipients mention more things as "particularly valuable" because, as we have just seen, they think better of the training they receive than the faculty does of the training it gives.

The next question to the faculty asked what they would change, "as you consider the situation realistically—where would you favor relaxing requirements somewhat and where would you make them still more demanding?" Here are their answers:

	OK as is	*Would relax*	*Would demand more*	*Can't say*
Dissertation	69%	6	23	2
Residence requirements	67%	24	4	5
Comprehensive examination	63%	13	21	3
Final defense	63%	16	17	4
Course requirements	59%	26	13	2
Qualifications for admission	51%	3	43	3
General quality	47%	*	48	5
Training in teaching	41%	6	40	13
Independent work	37%	*	58	5
Foreign languages	33%	28	35	4

* Less than 1%.

The minor differences by field and by institution only go to reinforce the relative dissatisfaction of the social sciences and the humanities on the one hand and the lesser universities on the other. Over-all, the faculty is undecided on very little indeed—only in the vexing question of training in teaching is there more than a trace, and even then not much.

On balance, the faculty would take less of hardly anything: relaxing residence or course requirements is involved in promoting more independent work, and the foreign language requirement is highly controversial. The faculty wants more of nearly everything: better students, better dissertations, more independent work, better training in teaching, better quality in general. This demand for more, while giving up little, reinforces my feeling that the relatively high dissatisfaction of the faculty tends to be stereotyped perfectionism.

A number of these issues, like those referring to the foreign language requirement, training in teaching, the dissertation, and the students, have already been discussed in detail. But one residual matter is of sufficient importance to require separate treatment here. That is the issue on which the faculty and deans both feel quite strongly, and the recent recipients too—namely, more independent work. There is hardly another matter that solicited as firm an expression of opinion by all three groups, especially in the reverse variant that "doctoral programs should be 'tightened' and regularized, more like the training programs in medical and law schools." The same sentiment is apparent in the list just above: the faculty would relax residence and course requirements and most of all would demand more independent work.

Now a good deal depends, of course, on what is meant by the term. To the extent that it means something like the European system of placing the student very much on his own, to that extent its value can, I think, be called into question in the American system. Certainly independent work is one of the attractive watchwords of graduate study; it is a central plank in the platform. Just as with the quality of the students, you can never get enough of it. It is a way to get more breadth into graduate study—a president told me that "graduate students want to roam but the system won't let them"—as well as to distinguish sharply between graduate study and undergraduate. It is a way, as another president nicely put it, "to return to first things: to focus on objectives, not requirements." As a result, from time to time efforts are made here and there to bring more independent work into doctoral study, as currently at Northwestern (more independent study after the first year) and Harvard (reduction of certain course requirements). Despite the general disposition to favor independence, however, not all graduate schools move in that direction, nor do all graduate departments when given the opportunity (as currently at Northwestern and Harvard). Here as elsewhere, this elementary fact—widespread approval of the idea but not widespread action on it—suggests that there is more to the matter. Is the desire real or is the term more of a symbol to which allegiance is auto-matic, in principle and almost by definition?

In the first place, one of the major reasons advanced for the student's independence in doctoral study is his need to be independent subse-quently, as a scholar. Dean Keniston puts the point well:

> Almost without exception the graduate schools proclaim that their purpose is to train men for independent work. Yet in many institutions the course requirements occupy almost the entire program. Why should the mature graduate student not be given the freedom and responsibility of practicing that independence which he must display throughout his subsequent career?

But it is by no means clear that independent study is necessarily related to subsequent independence. To the contrary, there are some indications, or at least suggestions, against it. The importance attached to the ap-prenticeship experience is one of them. The relative lack of such inde-pendence in medical and legal programs of study is another—or, if that is not an acceptable analogy, the fact that the doctoral programs con-sidered most satisfactory on the campus, those in the sciences, are prob-ably least independent, i.e., most prescribed by those in control. The later productivity of post-doctoral fellows is another case in point; true, they tend to be the more productive to start with, but their "prolonged dependence" does not appear to diminish their creativity. In short, it is not immediately clear that independent work is automatically valuable, from this standpoint.*

There are still other considerations to be taken into account. As it is, doctoral recipients reported that "there were times when you felt you did not know where you stood with your major professor or depart-ment"—10 to 15% "often," 40% "occasionally." As for the prime evil of "too many courses," the deans are convinced (70%) but not the graduate faculty (30%) and still less the alleged victims, the recent re-cipients (17%). Moreover, the symbolic role of "independent work" is suggested by the further fact that it was approved about equally by those who think the students are now neglected by the faculty and those who do not think so (68 to 62%). As I mentioned earlier, there is a narrow line between more independence for the students and less con-

---

* I must quote here a most distinguished scientist to the contrary. Albert Einstein said in his *Autobiographical Notes* (in P. A. Schilpp, ed., *Albert Einstein: Philosopher-Scientist*. Tudor, 1951): "It is, in fact, nothing short of a miracle that the modern methods of instruction have not yet entirely strangled the holy curiosity of inquiry; for this delicate little plant, aside from stimulation, stands mainly in need of freedom; without this it goes to wrack and ruin without fail. It is a very grave mistake to think that the enjoyment of seeing and searching can be promoted by means of coercion and a sense of duty." In the balance between stimulation and freedom, perhaps most graduate students need more of the former and most Einsteins the latter.

cern for them—between independent work on the one hand and faculty neglect on the other. In any case, independent study is a value not without its costs, and it is not altogether clear just how valuable it really is.

Finally, there is the basic point that high independence in study presumes high quality in the students. As Dean Beach has put it, "the freedom which we hope to give to advanced graduate students must be withheld unless they are ready for it. . . . Carefully selected first-year graduate students, full-time study without financial worries or the distraction of an assistantship, dedicated instructors, and constant advisers: some or all of these conditions might be difficult or impossible for many of our graduate schools to meet." Many students are, no doubt, not ready for the challenge on objective grounds, and many do not welcome it either. It is easy to say that in that case they should not be in graduate school, but the numbers problem probably makes that an unacceptable answer. In short, if the graduate schools must handle large numbers of candidates, there is a limit on how many can manage or profit from the kind of independent work so widely approved. However desirable as a symbol of true graduate work, independent work is probably most efficient when applied selectively.

EVALUATION THROUGH COMPARISON

To return to the general theme: the effort at evaluation through comparison can be carried four steps further.

First, there is the comparison with an earlier time, for those who were around or remember the situation then. The respondents were asked to compare the quality of the programs or products today with those before World War II, with these results: *

	Graduate deans	Graduate faculty		College presidents	Industrial representatives
		Discipline	Institution		
Better then	8%	11%	9%	10%	27%
Better now	80	67	74	40	35
About the same	12	22	17	50	38

* Again the questions differ slightly, as follows:

Graduate deans: "On the whole, how do you think the quality of the doctoral program at your institution now compares with that before World War II?"

Graduate faculty: "On the whole, how do you think graduate work for the doctorate degree in your discipline and at your institution compares in quality with that before World War II?"

College presidents: "How do you think their quality (the products of the graduate schools that are available now as college teachers) compares with that before World War II, at your institution?"

Industrial representatives: "How do you think their quality now compares with that before World War II?"

In academic life the improvement, or rather the judgment that things have improved, is marked—even though that is tantamount to saying that the situation is better today than it was "in our day"! Only in industry is the situation equivocal; but business and industrial firms are now taking so many more people with advanced training than they did before the war that some have had to go down a step or two in quality in order to get enough. Among the faculty, incidentally, the sense of improvement is strongest in the professions and the lesser institutions, with the post-war expansions of both. Over-all, considering the natural tendency of academic people to be self-critical, I take this to be a fact: doctoral study is getting better.

Second, there is the comparison by the recent recipients of "the quality of teaching and training that you received at different levels of education. That is, compare how the high school did its job with how the college did its job and how the graduate school did its job. How would you rank them?" Here is their reply:

	Graduate school	College	High school
First choice	54%	27%	19%
Second choice	28	51	21
Third choice	18	22	60

This does not necessarily mean that the college and the high school do a poorer job than the graduate school. But it does mean that they do so for those students who later work their way to the highest earned degree—or, more precisely, that they do so in the judgment of such people (though it must be added that this result may be affected somewhat by a tendency to regard the most recent experience as the most favorable). Similarly, as reported earlier, the graduate faculty thinks that the quality of graduate instruction, in both institutions and disciplines, is substantially better than at the undergraduate level. By this test too, graduate programs come off well.

Third, there is the comparison of the American version of graduate study with its equivalent abroad, in the opinion of the graduate faculty (and including only those who felt they had sufficient knowledge to judge):

	Comparison with			
	Great Britain	West Germany	U.S.S.R.	France
Better in U.S.	43%	64%	70%	78%
Better in foreign country	19	13	12	10
About the same	38	23	18	12

The same question was asked of the graduate deans, with essentially the same results. Only in a few specifics does graduate study abroad compare favorably with that in this country, in the judgment of the faculty: the physical sciences in the U.S.S.R. and the humanistic studies and biology in Britain. Moreover, it is the faculty in the top institutions who feel surest of American superiority. It may be, of course, that the Americans are prejudiced in their own favor, but time and again this judgment has been confirmed by reports from abroad. For example, an American administrator wrote, after a tour of inspection in Europe, that

> . . . the people I talked with there seemed to think that our graduate students, or rather our Ph.D. holders, compare quite favorably with what they call Ph.D.'s. It is at the Bachelor's level particularly, and to some extent at the Master's level, that the training of our people is not regarded as comparable. I suppose I could put it all more simply by saying that the American specialist in his field of specialization is regarded as a strong competitor whereas the supposedly general educated fellow is not.

Or again, a scientist trained in Britain believed that the advanced training in England was too narrowly focused on "research and only research. . . . That develops too narrow a man. The English B.A. is better educated than the B.A. in this country but the Ph.D. here has it over theirs, and mainly because of the systematic course work to which students are exposed here."

Fourth, there is an implicit comparison between the present state of graduate training and the present state of the disciplines, as judged by the graduate faculty and the recent recipients. Both groups were asked: "How would you characterize the current state of health of your discipline—its intellectual vigor, development, progress, etc.?" Here are their answers:

	Graduate faculty	Recent recipients
Very satisfactory	30%	32%
Quite satisfactory	37	37
Adequate	24	24
Unsatisfactory	9	7

For the recent recipients, graduate training and their discipline get roughly equivalent approval. But for the graduate faculty, the discipline is in better shape than the graduate school, at least as judged in this way.

Again in both groups, there are sharp differences in satisfaction among the broad divisions of knowledge:

Proportion describing the present state of their discipline as "very satisfactory"

	Graduate faculty	Recent recipients
Physical sciences	49%	46%
Biological sciences	35	41
Social sciences	23	23
Humanities	14	22
Engineering	38	29
Education	18	25

Once more the break between the data fields and the word fields is apparent; it corresponds to the break in the appraisal of graduate training itself. But the gap between them is less with the recent recipients than with the faculty, so perhaps it is being closed somewhat.

As a matter of interest, here are the results for each of the major fields (including all those for which there are at least 40 respondents):

Proportion describing the present state of their discipline as "very satisfactory"

	Graduate faculty	Recent recipients
Arts & science disciplines:		
Physics	64%	58%
Mathematics & statistics	59	61
Biology	49	46
Chemistry	48	42
Psychology	40	28
Zoology	29	33
Botany	25	38
Sociology	21	13
Modern languages	20	23
History	19	20
Economics	17	21
Geology	16	30
English	10	21
Political science	6	13
Professional fields:		
Engineering	38	29
Agriculture	26	29
Business	18	21
Education	18	25

The great range is itself instructive, but perhaps of even more significance for the future is the fact that on the whole the recent recipients are less extreme in their appraisal than the graduate faculty: they are not so optimistic at the top of the range, nor so pessimistic at the bottom—less impressed on the one hand, less depressed on the other. If this were reversed, I suppose we would say that the faculty is more judicious than the newcomers.

But as related to the prevalence of graduate training, perhaps the most important fact about the appraisal of the disciplines is its close association with the appraisal of graduate study itself. The two go hand in hand. As suggested in the historical section, many critics of graduate study have really been discontented with their own fields and have found that criticizing the graduate program was a handy tool to use on the discipline, and perhaps an effective one as well. Many of the critics of graduate education these days are humanists and social scientists, who are as a group less happy with their fields.* In the graduate faculty generally, dissatisfaction with one's discipline is closely tied to dissatisfaction with the graduate training offered in it:

	State of discipline			
State of graduate training	Very satisfactory	Quite satisfactory	Adequate	Unsatisfactory
Very satisfactory	15%	6%	3%	2%
Satisfactory	60	58	48	31
Unsatisfactory	25	36	49	67

The same finding appears in the case of the recent recipients as well.

Which leads to the other would be hard to disentangle: no doubt there is an interplay between the two so that this relationship really reflects a single state of feeling about one's profession. But it is well to remember this association when appraising the criticisms of graduate study: they typically contain an element of unhappiness about one's own field. The critics seek to change their disciplines, not just the training given in it —or rather, to change their disciplines by changing the training. Nor is this an unrealistic or illegitimate expectation: in a real sense, the graduate school "owns" the discipline. But the fact remains that just as the

* There is an important problem here, that I cannot go into, of the attraction of talent to various fields of knowledge. Said a judicious foundation official (a scientist): "We need better people in the social sciences and the humanities, but we get into a spiral where the better people go into the sciences and thus attract the better people of the next generation. With the great emphasis on scientific education and the glamour of the field, this disparity may even increase." And a young social scientist agrees: "The physical sciences outdraw biology in recruitment, money, etc., and biology outdraws the sciences of human behavior. Yet the problems ahead are largely biological (e.g., overpopulation) and human (e.g., social problems of various kinds). Thus there is a misallocation of resources precisely because the successful fields have already paid off, leaving the major problems in those that have not. Yet the talent gets attracted the other way around."

critics among the recent recipients do not like their jobs, so the critics among the faculty tend not to like the present character of their fields.

As a conclusion to this section on the evaluation of graduate study, the second-to-last word is given to the 1957 recipients of the doctorate and the last word to a graduate dean. With all the problems, anxieties, hard work, disappointments, deficiencies, and the rest, would the recipients still go through it again? "Yes," say over 90%—and most of the rest aren't sure: only 3% definitely say "no." Would they take essentially the same program? "Yes," say three-fourths. Would they go to the same institution? "Yes," say two-thirds. And as an unfair, yet revealing, question, that was intended to get at the motives of the recent doctorate more than his appraisal of graduate study: "Would you be willing to undertake the same program if there were no degree, or its equivalent, awarded at the end—just for the learning involved?" A third say they would,* and less than half say "no"; the rest can't say. So all in all, the critics of graduate education must recognize that even though the recent recipients do indicate a number of things wrong with the training program as now conducted, by and large they give it a strong vote of approval.

The graduate dean provides some perspective on the broad picture of graduate work in this country, and does so with eloquence:

> Around 1900, American universities were incapable of providing adequate training for scholars in many areas of learning. To become scholars, Americans felt they had to go to European universities. Within a half a century, American universities developed to such an extent that they acquired the capacity to train scholars at the highest level in every branch of modern learning, and their faculties were making contributions to learning that have given them world prominence. Moreover, it is not only in one or two centers of learning that this is the case. I do not believe there is any record in the history of education that is any more impressive and remarkable. This elementary datum is completely ignored or at least unmentioned in our present re-evaluation of education in America, yet not to recognize this fact or take it into account in any review of our graduate institutions is almost irresponsible . . .
>
> This does not mean to imply that all is necessarily well. Many undesirable practices have crept in, many new demands and pressures have exerted their influence, so that problems and dilemmas confront us today which we must seriously consider. Nevertheless, to represent graduate education today as a shocking, discreditable, shabby, disorganized affair is simply wrong. To present this picture publicly as the true state of graduate study in America is naive and it is unscholarly . . .

---

* Those who consider this proportion a disappointing vote for the life of scholarship might consider what the proportion would be if the graduate faculty were asked if they would continue at three-fourths the salary.

It is an error to alter the character of the Ph.D. degree in order to meet the objections, trivial as well as serious, to the current failings of the degree programs, or to adjust the degree to meet the necessity of solving immediate problems for government and industry, satisfy the ambitions of foundation directors, upgrade certain professions, turn out vastly greater numbers of teachers, or provide training in wisdom. . . . If we do force the Ph.D. to serve as primary or essential ends anything other than the training of scholars and the advancement of learning, we will to that extent weaken the essential character of our universities and go a long way toward repudiating a great accomplishment.

PART THREE

Conclusions, Commentary, and Recommendations

After the quick trip through the history of graduate education and the extended stop on the present situation, we come to the threshhold of the future: what should it be?

In the preceding sections I have tried to present the issues, review the arguments, and bring the facts to bear. In doing so, I have intruded my own views only on occasion, and as little as possible. In this section, I try to put the results of that analysis back together again and then to add how, in my judgment, the present situation might be changed for the better. Accordingly, it is only fair to note explicitly that my own views enter quite fully here. At the same time, to repeat what I said at the start, the preceding material still remains to be taken into account regardless of one's reaction to the following comments.

CONCLUSIONS AND COMMENTARY

Here are what seem to me the major facts that must be taken into account in current appraisals or proposed reforms, together with a running commentary on their meaning and significance. Since the ground has been covered so recently, I state the important generalizations in summary form and hope that they will recall and be supported by what has appeared above.

THE HISTORY

1. From nearly the beginning, the system of graduate education has had to accommodate itself to the double pressures of numbers of students and expansion of knowledge.

2. The consequence has been diversification: in students, in institutions, in fields of study, in objectives.

3. Most of the central characteristics of graduate study were established early in its development: the place of the Ph.D. degree, the organization and administration of graduate work within the university, the dominance of research and research training, the utilitarian purposes, the status of science.

4. Through the years, there has been a great deal of self-scrutiny and controversy over the nature of graduate study (though perhaps not more than for any other part of American education); from one academic generation to the next, the debate has been substantially the same; and the debaters have more often been humanists and social scientists than natural scientists.

5. In the nature of the case, there is an inherent clash of interests between service and standards, teaching and research, the university and the college, academic and professional objectives, different classes of institutions, different fields.

6. As far as the paper standards are concerned, they have gone down: the Master's thesis is less frequently required; the publication requirement on the doctoral dissertation is out; the general examination has been moved to an earlier, less culminating point; the minor is on the way down; the foreign language requirement is being eroded.

To my mind, the history of graduate education strongly suggests a few morals. One is that since the typical criticisms, typically made, have never really taken hold, there must be good and sufficient reasons why they have not and will not (assuming that the graduate school is not really the devil its critics sometimes claim). Accordingly, whatever reforms are indicated, they must take place within the present guide-lines.

It is clear that the mere presence of criticism is not enough to warrant serious changes. Criticism is endemic in the educational world and will be as long as clear measures of the quality of the product are not available—and after too, for that matter. My point is the simple one that in an enterprise of this complexity, there is, and indeed ought to be, a minimal dissatisfaction, say of the order of 20 to 25%. No changes will reduce it by very much. Anything below that suggests to me that people think things are going very well indeed; anything much above requires looking into.

For certainly the debate itself is the thing. The debate is highly important simply in keeping different parts of the system aware of one another and hence in maintaining the necessary or desirable equilibrium among the contesting elements. As an experienced educator told me: "What this means for action is that the tension between polarities should be clearly recognized by the leaders and they should not allow external circumstances to settle the question or run the show. For example, they should do what they can to bring the 'service realities' into 'pure fields' like history and English, and vice versa."

Now and earlier, what is currently being done in one's own field and institution always seems "natural." Alternative proposals, being untried, usually have had to face the nearly insurmountable hurdle of "lowering standards." As I have tried to suggest, the alternatives themselves would seem just as natural today had the system started that way, as for example with the intermingling of graduate and undergraduate students or even the separation of graduate and undergraduate faculties. This implies that the system has more leeway for innovation without deterioration than its defenders typically believe. Perhaps more here than in other professions, present practice is perpetuated precisely because the judges of the product are themselves earlier products and present producers, so there is a closed system at work.

Now and before, the critics have typically been dissatisfied with their own fields of study or with American education in general, and have sought to use the graduate school to reform one or the other. This effort seems to me quite legitimate, but it also seems worth noting. One consequence, or at least corollary, has been that the scientists have made changes in the program of doctoral study (e.g., what they have done with the dissertation) while the others have been exhorting the system without a feasible program (e.g., in the case of preparing college teachers). A university administrator, himself a scientist, told me that there were no innovations or experiments in graduate study in his field because "there are so many interesting problems to think about or work on that the creative individuals are fully occupied in this way and have no time to spend trying to think up ways to invert the curriculum just for the hell of it."

Finally, it is important to keep in mind the diversity and complexity of the total system of graduate education if appropriate changes are to be made. Too often in the past, the debate has called into action an ambiguous "we"—"we" must clarify our ends, "we" must uphold standards, "we" must reform our procedures, "we" must redefine the doctor's degree, and so on. The point is that if "we" could do any of these things, there would be no problem. But "we" do not agree, in all conscience and sincerity, on what is now going on, let alone what should be done.

To most people, the diversity of higher education is one of its glories: there is no centralized "we" that can affect the system once it decides what it wants to do. Instead, it is a matter of persuading or activating a large and varied number of "we's"—chemists who are satisfied with their programs and humanists who are not; a few top institutions that are satisfied with their position and the several lesser institutions that are trying to better theirs; the graduate professors whose only concern is to train a brilliant researcher and the college deans whose only concern is to find a brilliant teacher; the older professors who worry about what is happening to the traditional values and the candidates who want to get the "union badge" and then get a good job; the great universities that cannot be bothered with the Master's degree and the good, small institutions that still take it seriously because it is their top job; the graduate dean and the president who are ambitious for their institution and want to grow in size and the department head who is concerned about standards. "We" are all of these, and more.

GROWTH

7. The system of graduate education is growing and will continue to grow in the next years—in students, degrees, faculty, departments, institutions, support.

8. The body of knowledge to be handled by the graduate school is growing and will continue to grow, thus adding problems of complexity and specialization.

9. The demand for products of the graduate school is substantial and will grow in the next period of years. "Everyone" wants doctorates—the universities, the colleges, government, industry, the junior colleges, the top of the secondary school system.

10. On a long-term basis, the doctoral product is increasingly going into non-academic work, not only in the physical sciences where such employment is traditional but also in the biological and social sciences. This trend will continue, though probably not accelerate a great deal.

The system of graduate education is a dynamic one and will be for the visible future. Two factors that account for the dynamism are prominent, but one gets more attention than the other.

The one is the growth in numbers. That pressure will continue because the total demand for highly trained personnel, i.e., for people with the doctorate, is growing. Non-academic agencies want more, and inside the academy not only are the normal university and college employers in the market, but others too: the Bayne-Jones committee on medical education wants more Ph.D.'s in medically related sciences for the medical research program of 1970, a representative of junior colleges at the ACE Conference served notice that the junior colleges wanted more, Hans Rosenhaupt quotes Professor I. I. Rabi as saying that in physics even high school teachers "must have a training at least of the scope and intensity of the Ph.D." Throughout a society like ours, the call for specialized talent is strong and growing. That is the kind of society it is. As the Rockefeller Brothers Fund report put it: "It is the constant pressure of an ever-more complex society against the total creative capacity of its people. . . . We must prepare ourselves for a constant and growing demand for talents of all varieties, and must attempt to meet the specific needs of the future by elevating the quality and quantity of talented individuals of all kinds."

The other factor is the body of knowledge itself—its uneven and uncontrollable growth, its changing character from field to field and from time to time within the same field. It deserves more credit for present achievements and more blame for some of the continuing problems. It is perhaps not too much to say that the subject matter is the master of graduate education: the latter prospers with the former.

The subject matter has been responsible for differential support within the graduate school, with all the problems associated with disparity of income; for differential morale; for periods of spurt and lags; for slow shifts in conception; for kudos or ridicule from the larger society. It is at the bottom of the most deeply felt complaints by the graduate school's severest critics: the humanists who feel themselves strangers and afraid in a world they never made—and, as *their* critics allege, have never really caught up with.

Growth over the next years, and pressure for growth, will confront the graduate school with at least as many problems as in the past. The problems will particularly mount up in the late 1960's as the "bulge" of students works its way into the graduate school—problems of finance, of space, of institutional load, of faculty and, inevitably, of standards.

CONCEPTION

11. Training in scientific research and for humanistic scholarship is at the center of the graduate school's program at the doctoral level: it is the essential element for a strong majority in the arts and sciences and it is good for most of the rest.

12. In the arts and sciences, experiments to change the character of the traditional program for the Ph.D. by making it broader have usually failed and have rarely achieved the respect and status of the traditional program, especially at the better universities. No viable substitute for major disciplines has emerged.

13. There has been a mutual infiltration of academic and professional work at the graduate level: the growth of professional fields has meant a growing demand for professional training at the graduate level and at the same time the development of applications in academic disciplines has meant the growth of professional work within them.

14. Professional fields (other than medicine and law) have constantly increased their programs at the doctoral level and in general have coveted the Ph.D. in preference to setting up their own doctoral degrees, even if that meant conforming to the general standards for the Ph.D. set up by the graduate school for the entire university.

It appears to me that two basic propositions are central here and I state them as my own convictions: (1) training in research and scholarship should be the primary purpose of doctoral study and (2) training at the doctoral level must be specialized.

The first seems to me to be warranted not only by the market argument detailed above, but also by the topical importance of the matter in the modern complex society and above all by the timeless objective of furthering man's knowledge. A large and growing number of people with such training are needed, and the graduate school is the only place where they can get it. It is its *raison d'être*.

The second seems warranted because of the need for soundness and depth in knowledge. In a way, it seems strange that a few words must be said in academic circles on behalf of specialization at the close of a formal educational career, specialization as the handmaiden of excellence, specialization to keep up with the advance of knowledge—in short, on behalf of training people who know what they are talking about. As noted above, few people ever complain about specialization in graduate study as such—it is always "narrow" specialization or "undue" specialization or "over-" specialization that is criticized. Obviously, it is hard to be for *them*. But it is easy to be for that degree or kind of specialization necessary for depth in knowing and understanding.

Some people "solve" the problem by defining it away. To be operationally clear, I would suggest that as things stand in scholarship today, specialization cannot normally extend beyond the normal discipline—its concepts, its methods of inquiry, its substance. Indeed, though the disciplines are still the units of graduate study, it is a rare discipline that can turn out a specialist in the field as a whole. The Ph.D. today is more likely to be a *specialist* in American history or social psychology or Italian literature of the Renaissance or high energy physics or Greek drama or biostatistics or topology or genetics or econometrics. In the course of becoming that, he comes to know something of the rest of his discipline, and that is about the best that can be done.* That is

---

* I do not mean to suggest that the present disciplines need to be taken as given, or that they are necessarily just the right divisions of knowledge, or that they will not change. What I do believe is that the changes should emerge from the requirements of the subject matter and its proper investigation, rather than from curricular requirements, and that the rough scope of a discipline is by and large the most appropriate unit for graduate training. There is always room for some specialists in the interdisciplines that may themselves grow into autonomous fields, as they have in the past.

A young social scientist, who himself is an interdisciplinary man though rooted in his own specialty, remarks: "Any university obviously has to break up the world's knowledge into disciplines, but it is a good thing to keep these divisions in constant flux . . . The three or four fields, humanities, natural science (biology and physical together or separate) and the social sciences represent the state of intellectual activity of the 1920s. It would have made no sense in the 1820s, for example, when there was no full grown social science but only some branches of humanities. It is making decreasing sense today. In the 1920s the social sciences were asserting their independence of the dominant humanities, but they had few points of contact as yet with the natural sciences. . . . Today the humanities are dying. Shutting them off in a division

enough, though, and that is what should be done—should, that is, in preference to the alternative of seeking to produce a "specialist" in Western thought or the philosophy of history or the social sciences or the liberal arts. That way lies journalism—which, however high, is not scholarship. No amount of interdepartmental reshuffling of graduate training will make a sick discipline well. If the graduate school has to choose between breadth and thinness or specialization and depth—in view of the time and talent available, it often does have to—it should choose the latter.

In short, the graduate school should aim at training the skilled specialist—not, if I may say so without being misunderstood, at producing the "educated man," the "cultured man," the "wise man," (nor, for that matter the "mere technician," either). Liberal education is the task of the college and if it is not done well there, then it is not the best solution to push the demand up on to the graduate school, which has another spirit to serve. To the argument that the college cannot do the job because the graduate school sends it the wrong kind of teachers, my reply is that as part of his undergraduate education the student should learn a lot about something important (plus, if possible, something of how it came to be learned), that the best liberal education is a sound one in the basic disciplines, and that the best teachers for that program are the specialists in the fields.

Where then will come the men of breadth and wisdom, the leaders outside the disciplines? They will come, some of them from a sound liberal education, a sound graduate education—and the experience of life. As far as the graduate school is concerned, wisdom and leadership are best approached, like happiness, indirectly. Perhaps it is too much to say that "wise leaders" cannot be trained, but it is probably not too much to say that we cannot do it directly now. Certainly wisdom is not the equivalent of breadth, if the term is taken to mean more than expert judgment about a subject. As for leadership, the fact is that many leaders outside the disciplines do emerge from graduate programs, even many in broad public affairs outside education itself.

If "wisdom" and "leadership" are limited to a few, the graduate school has too many students to make them workable objectives for everyone anyway. Years ago, the sociologist Charles Cooley made an appropriate observation:

> It is strange that we have so few men of genius on our faculties; we are always trying to get them. Of course, they must have undergone the regular academic training and be gentlemanly, dependable, pleasant to live with, and not apt to make trouble by urging eccentric ideas. Institutions and genius are in the nature of things antithetical, and

of their own is not doing them a favor, but is rather isolating them from the major sources of strength in the universities."

if a man of genius is found living contentedly in the university, it is peculiarly creditable to both. As a rule professors, like successful lawyers or doctors, are just hard-working men of some talent.

One further point: it is often alleged that we suffer because trained specialists cannot communicate with one another. But that too is over-drawn: they communicate as citizens, as faculty colleagues, as friends, as interdisciplinary collaborators. Certainly the common problems of gradu-ate education have drawn communication across fields—not always agree-ment, but that is quite another matter. Actually, my impression is that those who decry the lack of communication more often than not are really concerned about the lack of agreement—with themselves.

In short, it would seem enough if the graduate school takes as its pri-mary and central task the turning out of men well trained in their sub-jects—"hard-working men of some talent" in the main, with more than their share of "wisdom" and "leadership." If the Ph.D. is not also an "educated man," perhaps the fault is the college's, not the graduate school's. If two or three decades ago, the critics had had their way and the graduate school had turned primarily to the production of under-graduate teachers of greater breadth, then I am confident we would be worse off today with respect to scholarship and knowledge, both pure and applied. To say the least, I am not sure we would be better off with respect to college teaching; personally, I think we would be worse off there too.

As for the conception of graduate study as "academic" or "profes-sional," I do not fear the latter so long as its meaning is clearly under-stood, i.e., that it does not necessarily mean the automatic acceptance or automatic rejection of proposals or practices in medicine, law, or ed-ucation. After all, the products of the graduate school do practice a learned profession. Indeed, the graduate school is in the midst of a long movement in the professional direction that is not necessarily to be deplored but to be appreciated and exploited. The very increase in non-academic jobs for graduate school products has meant a decline in the exclusively *academic* character of the institution. Nor do I deplore the mutual infiltration of academic and professional fields as described above: I believe that each has something to learn from the other and that close relations between them are much better than mutual insulation and isola-tion.

COLLEGE TEACHING

15. The central divergence in opinion on the purposes of graduate study hinges on the teacher-researcher issue, though most people think that the single track in advanced study is the preferred or only practical one.

16. Only a minority of the recent recipients of the doctorate go into undergraduate teaching exclusively or mainly, with the familiar differences by field.

17. Most of the groups involved believe that training in teaching in graduate school is valuable and needed; and further, that the present practice is faulty in high degree. At the same time:

(a) College presidents place even more value on instruction in the problems, history, and philosophy of the liberal arts college in America.

(b) Given the economics of the situation, the other pressures on the student's time, and the arts and science faculty's attitude toward formal course work in teaching methods, the graduate school's action in this regard will mainly have to be tied to the teaching assistantship or its equivalent.

(c) The responsibility of the college for interning the new Ph.D. in the practical problems of teaching has not been met.

18. As an employer of the doctoral product, the liberal arts colleges, except for a few at the top, are at a serious disadvantage, but the fault lies partly with themselves: low salaries, poor libraries and other facilities, high teaching load, little research opportunity, poorer students, poorer colleagues, extra-curricular demands and restrictive atmosphere, dead-end career line, etc. Under such conditions, they cannot expect to attract the top doctoral product.

19. The crisis over having enough college and university teachers in 1970 is generally overstated: the prospects do not constitute a "dire threat" to the present level of higher education. Good salaries is one key to the situation.

(a) The employment of more women, people from industry, or retired military men as a way to "solve" the "crisis" will not account for much, probably not enough to justify special campaigns and programs.

The argument over the graduate school and college teaching is clarified by the arithmetic of the situation: the graduate school is increasingly producing for the university as employer—the research-oriented university—rather than for the college. Hence its research-oriented program of training is increasingly appropriate. The tide in American higher education is probably running toward the universities, not toward the colleges. If the case presented for more attention to the college's needs was not strong enough to carry the day three or four decades ago, it is weaker still today.

As the doctoral enterprise has grown in prestige and in demand, the smaller and poorer colleges (poorer at least financially and probably in quality as well) have found it hard to staff their institutions with top-grade academic talent. It is customary in some circles to put the blame for this state of affairs on the graduate school. But if blame must be fixed, the colleges must take some of it on themselves. In their situations, they cannot expect to get the better products of the graduate schools, nor should they. The graduate schools are not producing for that market, nor should they. The deficiencies in the large number of weak colleges in this country should not be laid at the door of the graduate school nor should the graduate school be expected to turn from its task to accommodate itself to such deficiencies. It is not at all unlikely that there are simply too many such colleges. These are perhaps harsh judgments, but they are, I fear, necessary ones lest the graduate school be diverted from its own and the society's best interests.

In two other respects, the colleges are at fault in the situation, in my view. The first has to do with their recruiting for advanced training and academic life: it could be stronger and more systematic, not only directly but indirectly through exemplification of the attractions of academic life (including salaries). As an historian pointed out, "Many potential scholars are never introduced to the concept of scholarship in the colleges and hence are lost at the start." The second has to do with their own responsibility for training in teaching: they do not now accept it sufficiently. This is the internship idea for the teaching profession: the graduate school to train in *what* to teach, the first employing institution in *how*. That seems to be a good arrangement in principle, each side doing what it can do better than the other and thus gaining the elementary advantages of the division of labor. As between the graduate school and the liberal arts college, it seems to me a sensible solution to the perennial problem. Even within the university, it has its points.

But the general question remains of training in teaching as a part of the graduate program and it faces all the old hurdles: *whether* there is anything to teach, *what* it is, *when* should it come (i.e., in competition with everything else in the student's program), *how* it is to be done, and *who* will do it. At the least, it may be fair to say that training in *what* to teach may not be sufficient for a college or university teacher but it is necessary, whereas training in *how* is neither.

Here I must confess my own prejudice, since it is in opposition to the general run of opinion of those concerned: until some hard evidence is in, I remain skeptical that formal training in teaching is a more effective way to get a good undergraduate teacher than simply selecting those doctoral students who are seriously interested in that kind of work. But the college presidents say it matters, and so do the recent recipients, and I defer to them—though not without some reservations. I am much more willing to agree with the presidents that attention to the history and problems of the liberal arts college is of clear importance.

As for numbers, the problem there does not seem to me in itself to justify a change in the basic character of the doctoral program. The numbers question may be more important for what it will do to the stratification of higher education in America. A "shortage" is avoided or short-lived if the factors involved are adjustable, and in this case, in large measure, they are, as in the acceptance of students or the size of classes. (Do twice as many students need twice as many teachers?)

If the indefinite expansion of higher education is given, then something else will (and should) give too. As larger and larger proportions of the age group go into college, the average quality of each successive increment of students will probably go down. Unless the society supports higher education in a substantially larger degree and unless our selection methods substantially improve—both unlikely—then it is inevitable and, what is more, appropriate that the quality of instructional programs go down too: appropriate, that is, in the sense that each additional increment will have on the average less capacity for schooling and hence should not, simply as a matter of the allocation of scarce intellectual resources, be given the same quality of education. The bottom 20%, in short, should neither expect nor get the schooling of the top 20%. That too may seem harsh, but the alternative is harsher.

Here is another of the costs of mass higher education, and the system of higher education, and the society, will have to decide how much of it to pay. That is important enough to be underlined: the numbers question cannot be discussed apart from such considerations. If we want mass education at the higher levels, we shall have to pay for it—in various ways, not just in dollars.

THE INSTITUTIONS

20. There has been a constant increase in the number of graduate universities but a high degree of stability at the top (in judged quality).

21. Most institutions have expanded their programs in kind or in number, can expand them, and will continue to expand them over the next years. But the newer, lesser, and public universities will probably expand somewhat faster than the established, top, and private ones.

22. The stratification of American higher education is a fact: where graduate students come from and where they go is determined in large part by the institutions through which they pass. Given the stratification of both undergraduate and graduate institutions and the differing quality of students, something like a rough matching goes on of students to graduate training institutions (out and up) and products to employing institutions (out and down).

23. The graduate school is the society's central channel not only for the training of scholarly talent but also for its recognition and selection. As such, the graduate school serves as the career ladder for able students in all academic fields.

24. The graduate enterprise in American universities is characterized by a weak administrative position: locally with little authority over appointments or budget; nationally with little coordination, organization, spokesmanship, etc.

The difference between a university and a leading university is the strength of its doctoral program. As a result, institutions compete for faculty, students, fellowships, research grants, and the other ingredients that measure their standing in this major league of academic prowess.

The stratification by institutions means, in effect, that there are a number of subsystems of graduate education that touch one another at several points, that give verbal allegiance to the same sets of standards, but that are truly competitive for faculty and students only at the margins. Most of the competition goes on *within* the layers, as faculty members move from one institution to another of the same class and as students are drawn by stipends from one to another. On the average, the top institutions have the first pick of talent, by their own standards, and the choice then filters down the hierarchy, imperfectly to be sure, but still effectively.

The consequences, and implications, are several. For the doctoral student, the importance for his career of starting at the highest possible point of the institutional pyramid is hard to exaggerate. In this connection, the value of national fellowship programs is precisely in moving able students *up* the ladder—precisely, that is, what they are under attack for doing. For the lesser but ambitious institutions, the instrumental implication is to attract (via stipends) the ablest possible set of doctoral students, even in preference to the ablest possible faculty, as the quickest way to achieve a position of excellence in graduate study.

The graduate school stands at the center of a vast screening mechanism that makes it one of the society's major devices for selecting intellectual talent. How much more paradoxical, then, that it operates on a weak organizational base, both locally and nationally.

THE STUDENTS

25. Across the system as a whole, just about everyone who applies to a graduate school gets into one.

26. The only way to get more good people trained at the doctoral level for industrial employment or university research or college teaching or professional practice, or any other specific outcome, is to get more good people trained. The only way to get more good people trained is to get more good applicants. The only way to get more good applicants is to get more applicants.

27. The students for doctoral work come largely from the undergraduate colleges in the graduate universities, and they will do so even more in the next decade.

28. The quality of doctoral students appears to be holding up, despite the prevalence of practical motives.

29. The undergraduate preparation preferred by the graduate faculty is a sound training in the basic disciplines, and not necessarily in the

discipline to be studied in graduate school. Undergraduate preparation in the major discipline is already its most satisfactory aspect.

30. Almost all doctoral students receive support from the universities, or through them from the large national fellowship programs. Most students, that is, "are supported" through graduate school.

I wish here only to underline two major points. The first is that the graduate faculty apparently does *not* seek to transform the undergraduate program into a kind of pre-professional training in their various disciplines—that, on the contrary, it thinks that a solid and sound liberal education is the most suitable preparation for graduate study. The second is that what the graduate school needs, perhaps more than anything else (including money), is more good applicants. More of them at the input end will solve a lot of problems at the output end—and in between too, for that matter. How to get them is the central problem of the next years. The solution involves not only recruiting practices in the narrow sense (the *before*), but also continuity and appropriateness of graduate programs (the *during*), and subsequent status and economic position (the *after*).

DEGREES

31. The Master's degree has lost status in the arts and sciences; has become largely a professional degree, especially one in education; is no longer under the control of the top institutions; and cannot be recovered as the acceptable degree for college teachers.

32. Post-doctoral work is growing, especially in fields that can support it and at the top institutions; and it will continue to provide further specialization for a favored few who are particularly interested or competent in research. However, the occasional suggestions for a new super-degree have not taken hold.

33. In the arts and sciences, efforts to supplant the Ph.D. with an equivalent, but different, doctoral degree have never succeeded.

34. The best chance for revising the traditional graduate program to produce an undergraduate teacher for the smaller liberal arts colleges lies in introducing a new intermediate degree with a (not *the*) doctoral title.

The symbolism of graduate degrees cannot be dismissed as either trivial or degrading—too much depends on it. The image and the prestige of the Ph.D. are in the center of the stage and cannot be moved away, not in the visible future. Any proposal for reform must come to terms with that hard fact. Blame it on the misguided ambitions of the colleges, the pride of the universities, the false assigning of priority to a mere symbol over a preferred reality, the improper standards of the accrediting agencies, the arrogance of the holders—but there it is. Some reforms would be easier to introduce if they could involve only the substance of trained intelligence, but as it is, the package comes complete with label.

Not only do institutions and people want the label, but fields too. In a way, it would be cleaner and in some ways perhaps preferable if professional fields had established their own doctorates and the system had restricted the Ph.D. to the arts and sciences. The professions would have been freer in setting their own standards and governing their own programs—but they would not have had the coveted symbol. It is only when doctoral training is aimed at secondary education and below, as with the Ed.D., that the alternative doctorate is accepted and even preferred. For higher education, it is the Ph.D. that is wanted.

As for the "meaning" of the degree, I am not inclined to agree with those who deplore the present range by both field and institution. Any number of distinctions are made among Ph.D.'s and after all, ambiguity has some functions in so large and complicated a system. In any case, hardly anyone is fooled by the tag who doesn't want to be.

Under the impact of numbers and of institutional diversification, something had to give way in the degree structure and since the Ph.D. would not, the Master's did. Graduate education is now so large and so diversified that many feel there is room for a new degree—either an intermediate one between the Master's and the doctorate, or one that goes beyond the present doctorate. Things being what they are, the name to be given the new degree is by no means the least controversial issue involved in the matter. My own view is that a post-doctoral degree is not needed—the very fact of post-doctoral work is still enough recommendation in itself. The possibility of introducing an intermediate degree, while backed by an attractive rationale, is probably stymied by the realities of the situation—that it would be looked upon as a poor second to the genuine article. In a small way, engineering already has such an intermediate degree—Mechanical Engineer, Electrical Engineer, etc.—but it has not caught on, it is not highly prized, and it is considered, as perhaps any intermediate degree would be, as a token given students who started for a doctorate but did not quite make the grade.

THE PROGRAMS

35. The critical problem in compressing the duration of doctoral study is that of supporting large numbers of doctoral students in full-time work.

(a) Compression would enable the system to handle more students at the doctoral level, but not a great deal; it will do more for the quality of training, since it will make for more continuity in the program.

36. The actual time needed to get a doctorate is only from a half to a third the elapsed time, depending on field, and it has not changed a great deal in the past thirty years or so. The elapsed time could be drastically shortened; the actual time is already close to the norm that is highly accepted as the minimum time necessary.

(*a*) The difference between elapsed and actual time mainly goes into academic work of the same kind the candidate does after formally receiving the degree.

37. Attrition at the doctoral level, while sizable, is not so serious a problem as is commonly assumed. Given the conditions likely over the next years, it will inevitably be of the order of a quarter or so of entering students, under the best realizable circumstances.

38. It would be desirable for all concerned if the present ABD's were cut in numbers, though that end must be justified on psychological and institutional grounds as well as on scholarly ones.

39. The justification for the doctoral dissertation is shifting from its traditional conception as an "original and significant contribution to knowledge" to that of a training instrument.

(*a*) The dissertation is most satisfactory today where it least conforms to the initial conception, i.e., in the sciences—but where it also takes most time to do.

40. The foreign language requirement is a constant irritant as a symbol of standards because of disagreement within the faculty on its proper justification and because of differences among fields. In any case, most people agree that the requirement actually is more form than substance today.

41. Similarly, the final oral examination has taken on more of a ritualistic function than the ostensible one of testing the student.

Here again only a few points need underlining.

The key to a continuous "normal length" doctoral program, to less attrition, and to fewer ABD's is full-time work by the students, and the key to that is financial support.

That the doctorate takes "too long" may be true for the elapsed time measures, but not for actual time; and the latter is closely related to the quality of the program. Proposing less actual time as a solution to a long elapsed time misses the point.

The figures on elapsed time are often misused as horrible examples; the fact is that most of the time, most candidates are doing the same kind of work they would be doing if they had the degree. Elapsed time is "waste" or "procrastination" in only a small fraction of the cases.

The dissertation is, and should remain, the heart of true doctoral work. It should be considered as the major instrument in training for research and scholarship.

The comparison with post-baccalaureate programs in law and medicine is justifiable only selectively, but so are some rationalizations used by the graduate school. For example, to justify a loose doctoral program in graduate school by citing the "over-tightness" of law and medical programs designed for non-research practitioners is, in my judgment, inadmissible.

The foreign language requirement and the final defense of the dissertation have both lost, or are losing, their original functions, and both have a ritualistic residue. Their substance is now less important, by and large, than their form—and that is maintained through another paradox of doctoral study. In the whole battery of varied and ambiguous requirements across the graduate school, these at least are concrete, specific, and visible, so that "maintaining standards" is often linked symbolically with the least productive of the graduate school's requirements. For example, the intermingling of graduate and undergraduate students is, to my mind, a much more serious matter.

In the present situation, keeping in mind both the numbers of students and the increases in knowledge, graduate training should be rationalized more as a *sampling* of the material and methods to be covered, just as the degree should be considered as the *start* of the scholarly or scientific career. Life and learning will continue.

EVALUATION

42. The present doctoral program is considered quite satisfactory by the students and the employers, but least satisfactory by those who give the training and administer the program.

(*a*) It is approved most in the top institutions, where the leadership resides.

(*b*) It is considered more satisfactory in the sciences and the related professional fields of engineering and agriculture; less satisfactory in the social sciences and humanities.

(*c*) Those directly concerned, and self-qualified, consider the state of graduate training more satisfactory than it was twenty years ago, than it is at lower educational levels, or than it is in the same fields abroad.

(*d*) Among the recent recipients, dissatisfaction with graduate training is greatest among those who do not like their present jobs. Among the graduate faculty, dissatisfaction is greatest among those who do not like the present state of their discipline.

43. Despite the coming growth of the middle-level institutions (middle in both size and quality), a substantial proportion of doctoral degrees are given and will continue to be given over the next years by the top institutions. The correlation between quantity and quality will continue to hold.

44. On the whole, the quality of doctoral students is holding up within classes of institutions, but since the lesser institutions are growing faster than the traditional leaders, the *average* quality may be going down (only *may be*, because of the relatively thin slice of talent involved).

45. The doctoral program in the arts and sciences differs from comparable programs in law and medicine in certain important respects: the students are more capable of self-support in the latter, partly because of higher income of the parental family and partly out of consideration of

anticipated earnings; the program, being directed more at practice and very little at training for research, is tighter and more prescriptive; the outcome is less negotiable short of completion; and as a result, the duration of the program is normalized.

46. The range in quality of doctoral work from the worst to the best institutions is probably less, and considerably less, than the range in the colleges or the secondary schools, or the professional schools of law and medicine.

By and large, the graduate school is doing a reasonably good job or better, as judged by both the students and the employers. As for the trainers themselves, even they think that things are better today than they were in "the good old days" when *they* were being trained.

Two other points about evaluation are worth stressing. The first is the comparative one about graduate training here and abroad. Not only does the faculty give the United States version a strong vote of confidence—and, I think, not simply out of self-interest—but that appraisal is confirmed by the judgment of most disinterested observers. The major differences are worth noting. The American version can be characterized as follows, compared to most graduate study in Europe:

Many more students, relatively
More concern for average students
More decentralized
More course training (the European university is more of a lecturing and examining institution)
Less separation among fields
Faster recognition of young merit; more opportunities
Less a research degree (i.e., the doctorate)
No super-doctorate
Less prestige for products (related to numbers?)

Note that a big difference derives largely from an aspect of doctoral training often derogated in favor of "independent work," namely, the course and seminar work. That is what is often missing abroad, and it is at the base of preference for the American version.

The other point is that the present graduate program is most highly approved at the head of the procession—that is, in both the most prestigious institutions and the most prestigious fields. With regard to the former, the point is simply that they are the leaders. With regard to the latter, the sciences, the point is that in many respects their training program is least like the traditional image, as in its regularized character or the dissertation. Indeed, in some fields, the program is quite "professional" in conception and in operation, and the dissertation, in the words of the Committee of Fifteen, makes an "arithmetic addition" to knowledge as against a "real contribution." However, as a graduate dean points out (a chemist),

> As knowledge becomes more and more extensive, it is not likely that an individual student is going to produce relatively as large a contribution as he did fifty or a hundred years ago. (What he does) is likely to turn out to be a rather small cog on a rather small wheel in a very important mechanism. After all, this is what most of us do in society during most of our lives.

The roots of the present situation are, of course, intertwined in the history of higher education in this country. Note how much of the picture is accounted for by these five factors:

> The rise of mass higher education and its attendant diversification
> The expansion of the body of scientific and scholarly knowledge
> The demand for the Ph.D. as product and the prestige of the Ph.D. as symbol
> The ambitions of particular universities
> The system of student support

All of these, I take it, are given for today and tomorrow and all of them place certain limits on what can be done. They exact a price from the system. If the society wants "everyone" to have a college education, the society will have to pay for it not only in dollars but in relative quality as well. If we want knowledge, we shall have to pay in specialization. If we consider diversity a value, we shall have to pay in diversification of standards too. If student support on a large scale is not forthcoming from some source, then the problems of duration, attrition, and interrupted study will remain with us.

RECOMMENDATIONS

What is to be done? As a friend cautions, "criticism is easy compared to suggesting solutions. Suggesting solutions is easy compared to suggesting workable ones. And suggesting workable solutions is easy compared to putting them into practice."

At this point, in such reports, it is customary to close with the rhetoric of calls to action—actions that are to be bold, yet sound; imaginative, yet considered; preserving the best of the past while reaching for the best of the future; and so on. As such a call concluded some years ago: "The present may well be the appropriate time for individual graduate schools to review their respective aims, inquire into their own conditions, and seize upon the principles and the implements that most promise improvement."

Now everyone is in favor of bold, yet sound proposals. It would be easier, and certainly safer, to close in a similar way. Questions only arise when proposals are specified. For example, who would disagree, to cite a few recent proposals, that "meaningless requirements should be eliminated" or that "the dissertation should be freed of pretentious scholarship" or that "programs should be clarified," "goals courageously reexamined," and "problems realistically faced" or that "the basic principles of the field should be grasped." The disagreement appears when someone says *which* requirements are meaningless or *whose* scholarship is pretentious or *when* purposes are clarified, or *how* to re-examine courageously, or *what* are the basic principles.

Rather than rest the case in that way, I shall undertake to submit a set of proposals that seem to derive from the preceding analysis and to fit the conclusions reached. If they were put into effect, I believe they would make a genuine improvement in the state of graduate education. In that sense, I shall claim they are bold; naturally, I think they are sound.

In addition to being specific, proposals have to be possible; that is, they should be actions that particular people or groups of people could put into effect if they wished to do so. This implies that they cannot be global recommendations directed, in effect, at having the system remodel the system. That has not worked before, nor will it now. My theme here is: "Better to kindle a little light than to chide the darkness."

As I have said, recommendations, to be useful, must start from here, from where the system is. My reading of the history of graduate education convinces me that it is idle to repeat once more the old songs; both words and music are wearing out. If we were starting anew to devise a system of graduate education for this country, we could go in several directions that are now closed to us by the history, the commitments, the experience, and the interests involved in the present system. In a word, any recommendations must be realistic, a term that in this context has a favorable connotation to my mind. Following, then, are my recommendations, based on the earlier material and analysis.

WITH REGARD TO PROGRAM

1. *The norm of a four-year doctorate should be enforced by the universities.*

The norm of four academic years plus a summer or two, or a little over three calendar years in actual study, is now the general practice and should remain so: less would lower standards, more is beyond the market for the totality of candidates and can be handled selectively. But the period has spread out too far, is discontinuous for too large a proportion of students, and is filled out with off-campus study for too many. It is better for all concerned if the work is done more speedily (in elapsed time), more consecutively, and more locally. In addition to better academic work, this should make for less attrition and less anxiety, for larger numbers of completed products in the decade ahead, for less premature employment of ABD's in the colleges, for longer careers, for more natural enthusiasm and energy on the first jobs. It will also mean support at a lower per capita cost since the ABD's and similar "over-age" candidates will be fewer: the lower the age of training, the less the average cost.

This problem is largely an economic one, and I shall come to that later. The proposal would also benefit from certain administrative arrangements, e.g., graduate deans can keep the pressure on both students and departments by withholding fellowship consideration for students in process until certain hurdles are taken, as at Princeton.* But beyond that, it involves expectations and customs and "understandings" and it is to such matters that I particularly refer here. The universities should let it be understood that this is what they expect, that this is their norm, that they mean it. At present, the understanding is close to the opposite.

The simple determination by the universities to turn doctoral work into more of a full-time, coherent, definite occupation would not do the whole job but it would do a great deal in itself as soon as the students saw that it was seriously meant. In this respect, I think the graduate school can learn from the better law and medical schools. The argument that doctoral work is too uncertain, because of the creative requirements of research training and the dissertation, can apply in individual exceptions, but not across the board: we know about how long the dissertation takes for the group as a whole. Indeed, it would probably do a great deal for doctoral work to institute the notion that a student should finish "with his class"—four years after he starts. There will always be exceptions but the idea is to make them a small minority, not the sizable number they now are.

Aside from the usual reasons for doing this, there is an additional reason for doing it now; namely, to prepare for the graduate school bulge of the middle and late 1960's.

2. *The program for doctoral training should be "tightened."*

By "tightening" I mean a clearer, more compact, more specified program of study *including* more supervision and direction by the faculty. I recognize that this is an unpopular proposal since it goes directly against the formidable symbol of "independent work" to which everyone in graduate school gives such strong allegiance.

* One dean even suggests that the universities "increase tuition after three years of study toward the doctorate. The sympathy of the professor would lead him to closer counseling." Another suggests that the colleges should differentiate even more sharply between young instructors with and without degrees, in order to add that pressure for completion.

I have come to believe that that allegiance is based upon two faulty assumptions: first, that it is necessary or desirable to distinguish graduate and undergraduate work as sharply as possible, almost on the ground that anything characterizing undergraduate work should be reversed in graduate school; and second, that "independent work" in graduate school is the best possible preparation for independent work later. The first seems to me properly irrelevant, and the second, as I argued above, dubious. Furthermore, I think the present situation does not really allow for "independent work" on a large scale; the students as a group are not ready for it (and probably never were, for that matter). Properly administered, "independent work" does not save faculty time; if anything, it costs more of it. Finally, the more "independent work" we have, the farther we go from a major strength of the American system of doctoral education as compared with most foreign versions, namely, course and seminar work.

I believe that from the sheer standpoint of learning the subject, there is a certain wastage in the system that is now disguised as "independent work," and that the symbol is probably not worth its cost. After all, the graduate faculty is (or should be) the source of doctoral training. The faculty knows (or should know) what training is best for students of different interests, specialties, and capabilities. Some independent work may be profitable at some stage, typically on the dissertation, though even there, as most thesis advisors know, it is not characteristic of most students to demand or want a completely free hand. (I asked the recent recipients whether they had perhaps received "too much supervision" from their thesis advisors, and 1.2% said they had.) In short, I believe that the danger lies in giving too much independent work to too many students rather than too little to too few.

In a way, the present system is a compromise between "loose" and "tight" programs, between independent work and directed work, between objectives and requirements. I believe it is both impossible as well as undesirable to move toward the former and that the system should move toward the latter.* If it were done, it would represent a net gain in training, it would be an economic gain for all concerned (the unusually gifted could always be handled specially), and it would soon seem as "natural" as today's arrangements.

(a) As part of this development, departments locally and disciplines nationally should work out more clearly and explicitly than is now typically the case just what they expect their doctoral candidates to know or be able to do, in three concentric circles: (1) the core material that every Ph.D. in the subject should know; (2) the particular

* Medical education is probably in process of moving toward the graduate school model. Perhaps both moves are desirable.

material that every Ph.D. specializing in a sub-area of the subject should know; and (3) the preferred optionals. The last should be thought of as a sample of the remaining material—the best possible sample for students of different kinds.* Such an arrangement of the desired curriculum would not be easy to come by—part of the attractiveness of "independent work" is precisely to mask the faculty's inability or unwillingness to work this out—and it would have to take account of local conditions. Despite these difficulties, the clarity in curriculum would be valuable for the faculty and for the students, reducing for the latter the "unnecessary anxiety" to which they now testify.

(*b*) Also as part of this development, disciplines should review some of the innovations in the programming of doctoral work that are currently in the picture. The normal pattern of course work may turn out to be the right way to do things, but it may not. For example, two recent experiments at Chicago are worth considering and there may well be others in different disciplines elsewhere.

In geography, under the leadership of Gilbert White, the experiment is to take the new doctoral candidates through intensive work in a number of the major areas of the field, *seriatim*, in his first period in residence, with each faculty member taking the group for a few weeks at a time, full-time. The student sees the field and the faculty in overview, and the faculty sees him. The student begins with two weeks of field work and then moves into problems requiring a variety of bibliographic, statistical, and cartographic analyses for solution. By the end of that period, a student is likely to know his field of interest and the faculty to know his capabilities (the doubtful cases are told then to withdraw or settle for a Master's). In any case, better educational planning by both is then possible. The faculty develops an individual program for each student on the basis of the first quarter's performance and the student's sharpened interests. Furthermore, the students get a good deal of attention early, when they need it, rather than later when they are close to a professor and to other students and generally know the ropes. It also capitalizes on their early enthusiasm and energy. This is a small department, but there seems no reason why such a plan would not be adaptable to larger departments (i.e., they are larger in faculty members, too).

In economics, under the leadership of Milton Friedman, there have developed a number of "workshops" in the major areas of the field, each with one or two major professors in charge, one or two junior faculty

---

* It is such a sampling notion that keeps me from getting very concerned about "too many" graduate courses. If every graduate professor, in addition to the basic material in (1) and (2), were to have one or two seminars or courses with broad titles but shifting content to reflect his current research interests, there would be many fewer "courses" but the actual situation would be pretty much the same. A large diversity of course titles can, and usually does, represent the same sampling of the total discipline or the total material to be mastered.

in attendance, and four or more doctoral candidates at work. After some course work, the candidate spends a great deal of his time in workshops he selects, usually one at a time, and develops a thesis topic early and collectively in connection with his work. In a way, this invention is the equivalent in the social sciences of the natural science laboratory. With good full-time students and real research interest in the faculty, it seems to work well.

Similarly, for example, a humanistic equivalent of the laboratory—that important locus for good graduate training in the sciences—might be the editing by the doctoral candidates of a small literary review of high standards, like the law review that provides so much training on that side of the campus. Still another idea for those doctoral candidates specifically interested in a career of college teaching is to combine course work and examinations at the university with some seminars, supervision in teaching, and guidance on the dissertation at a nearby college. Once the graduate faculty starts down the programmatic road, other devices (in the same sense that a course is a device) should become visible. But guidance in course selection and direction of the student in course work is the thing.

(c) As another, minor part of the same development—and this will be even harder to take, being most reminiscent of what should have been outgrown—doctoral students might be graded on a more differentiated basis. The tradition at most places (though not all) is to use only A's and B's in marking graduate students, aside from the many symbols for auditing ("independent work" in compromise form). While it is not of great importance because of the supremacy of the comprehensive or qualifying examinations, a more differentiated system would alleviate one real problem—the anxiety of students who do not know where they really stand or how well they are doing. It would also contribute to the clearer recognition of excellence without aggravating any problem except the symbolic one of sharpening the difference with undergraduate work. As for that, the grading system would be less detrimental to the student than the use of undergraduate courses for graduate credit.

Along the same line, it might even be worth considering some differentiation in the degree itself, especially in view of the numbers here and coming. President Lowell reminded the system years ago, long before it had grown to the present size let alone the imminent one, that

In our graduate schools, where it is most important to attract and stimulate excellence, the element of competition is absent. They confer only degrees without distinction of quality. In Germany this is not so, for the doctorate is given in four different grades, plain, cum laude, magna, and summa. . . . We may well ask why, when this degree was imported, the distinction in grades that counts for much there was not brought with it.

In effect, of course, the distinction *is* there, only not publicly so. It is an open question whether the gain in clarity and the spur of competition would be worth the cost in invidiousness and competitiveness.

3. *The dissertation should be shorter.*

The argument for the shorter dissertation as detailed previously seems to me compelling, even in (especially in) the most wordy of the word disciplines. I believe, for the reasons cited, that quality would not suffer but improve: the less demanding and less worthy parts of the dissertation would fall away and the rest would be better through criticism and revision. The time spent in rehashing the literature once more and in the very task of writing so many pages could be better spent in attending to the actual substance. Few doctoral candidates have upwards of 250 or more pages worth saying and they should not be required by custom to say it at that length. Nor are the by-products unimportant —clearer exposition, more considered expression, prompter publication.

No fixed number of pages can be set for the dissertation, considering the range in fields and topics. But to give a sense of order of magnitude, I suggest aiming at a median of 100 pages or so in the fields where that is not now the practice. Some dissertations will still be 250 pages long or more, but they should be the justified exceptions rather than, as now, the other way around.

4. *Post-doctoral work should be regularized.*

As I have tried to show, the system and the bodies of knowledge have grown to the place where something had to change. What is changing slowly and reluctantly is the idea that the Ph.D. is the absolute top of the mountain. The development of post-doctoral work is here and it ought to be better rationalized and programmed within the present system.

The first step is to accept it, if not as desirable, then as inevitable. Beyond that, two things should be done.

First, instead of pushing for the highest standards for the Ph.D. for *all* candidates who will present themselves to the graduate school in the next years, and for whom jobs of various kinds are waiting—instead of that, we should settle for a solid, adequate doctorate as has been outlined. Then the 20 to 25%, or so, who would benefit from further advanced training should get it without imposing the requirement on the total group. This is a way to reward "only competence" yet handle the gifted student as well, and it is again aimed at compressing and limiting the regular doctoral program. It seems to me the natural and economic way to handle the double problem of growing numbers of students and expanding bodies of knowledge.

The problem will only be aggravated by the graduate school bulge of the middle and late 1960's. But the deans, the graduate faculties, and the recent recipients all disapprove of the idea to "make the Ph.D. readily available for fulfillment of three years of acceptable work, and give additional training at the post-doctoral level for the few really able researchers"—and they disapprove all the more in the places where post-doctoral work is heavy, as in the sciences and at the top universities. Here is a situation, I think, in which the symbol of the Ph.D. gets in the way of a rational training system, and in the way of matching a short supply of training talent to a short supply of trainee talent.*

The other point is that post-doctoral work now makes possible an inter-institutional equalization of opportunity for the ablest students that used to be provided by doctoral work itself. Thirty years ago, an able student would be encouraged by his baccalaureate institution to go to the top graduate universities for the Ph.D.—the feeder system previously noted. Now the feeders are themselves producers and they seek to keep their able students at home.

One result is to handicap such students in their climb up the career ladder. Post-doctoral training could now fulfill the same function for the few ablest students, and again it could be good for everyone: the student (in both training and career), the university that sent him on (pride in the achievement of *their* student), and the university that gets him (discovered talent). As it is, however, the system does not work that way. The post-doctoral fellows are passed around largely *within* the top group. A greater effort should be made to locate post-doctoral students *from* the lesser institutions and place them *at* the top ones. The normal channels of faculty communication could serve the purpose if both sides saw the desirability and took it seriously.

5. *The foreign language requirement should be left to the departments.*

I believe that the cultural argument for the foreign language requirement is inappropriate in the first place and wrong in the second. It is inappropriate because, as I have argued, the "cultured man" should not be the primary object of graduate training. It is wrong because meeting the requirement is typically not a matter of cultural growth at all: the tests are often weak, the performance is something of an academic joke, and, as Dean Keniston rightly says, "Certainly we cannot expect that the

---

* A doctoral candidate said to me: "At places like Columbia, Chicago, Harvard, etc., faculty attention is a priceless asset that we do not treat as such. A great professor's time and talents are certainly as valuable as, say, those of the president of a large corporation. But we tend to throw him away indiscriminately to any student who can pay the tuition necessary to be a perennial member of the class. These priceless assets should be reserved, except for lecture presences, for the really advanced students. Let such advanced training be self-selected beyond the extraneous reasons, that is, the prudential ones for getting a Ph.D."

kind of 'cramming' which students undergo in preparation for the language examination will result in any real understanding of linguistic values or cultural content." The present arrangement is not worth the cynicism and deception it fosters.

If, as I believe, the professional argument is the proper one, then it is clear that *how much* language and *which* ones differ from field to field. There is, of course, no magic to French and German as scholarly languages. Hence, the requirement should be set by each field—to the extent that knowledge of foreign languages is necessary for the conduct of research or scholarship in the field.

I make this recommendation in full recognition that, if adopted, it would result in an over-all lowering of the foreign language requirement. In making it, I do not use the argument, incidentally, that it should be lessened because of the failure of the college and the high school to provide such training—an argument I consider spurious.

6. *The final oral examination as a defense of the dissertation should be eliminated in those institutions where it is now mainly a form, and a substitute ceremonial event put in its place.*

If only a rare student fails this final "examination" then it is not a real examination.* But its ritualistic function needs to be taken care of. Can something be done that will meet the ceremonial needs inherent in the occasion, not cost so much in faculty time, and perhaps contribute more to the candidate's training? Perhaps it can. For example, suppose doctoral candidates were required, toward the end of the semester or quarter in which they would receive the degree, to offer a public lecture: a review or evaluation of their field, a summary of their own dissertation research, a statement of their own research or scholarly plans for the next few years, a presentation of some important theses to be defended (in the old style), perhaps (for those going into college teaching) a prototype of a classroom lecture or an outline of an organized course. At that point, the candidates would be doctors in everything but title and this series of talks could be established and symbolized as their first formal offering as scholars. Even in the large universities, the numbers would not be prohibitive, field by field. This kind of thing is institutionalized abroad; in this country there is always the risk of poor audiences.

Or, to take a quite different example: suppose that at the end of each academic period, all the doctorates-designate would meet in an evening

---

* To the argument that, after all, a few students do fail at this stage I reply in two ways: (1) discarding the final oral would locate more responsibility directly on the dissertation committee and that body would be less inclined to pass the buck to an occasion not designed for a real decision; and (2) the failing students are marginal in any case, or they would not have got that far, and it is hard to argue that fine distinctions can be made at the margin.

session with the departmental faculty and perhaps an outside visitor or two for a discussion of some problems of their discipline, the agenda to be planned by the students. Recently the University of Cincinnati has transformed the final oral into an open seminar—though this version does not save much faculty time. A few such devices could serve the over-all purposes of the present "examination" and in a deeper sense could actually be more of a formal introduction to scholarly life.

I do not consider this a matter of first importance, but I would think something could be done to improve the present situation. If nothing else, putting the same time into an oral examination at the *start* of the dissertation might be more helpful.

WITH REGARD TO SUPPORT AND COMPLETION

7. *The support of doctoral students should be regularized and they should be expected to pay more of their own way.*

In order to normalize the doctoral program, the system somehow has to solve the problem of student support. The total amount of support now available is moving toward the magnitude of a solution, especially if it continues along the trend of recent years. But it has not really reached the point of "total support" and there is no reason to think it will, particularly with the present proportion of married students with children.

To my mind, there is only one further source of support that will make possible the realization of the normal program just described, with all its benefits. That is the student himself and his family. For reasons linked with low academic pay, graduate study has never been considered a proper charge against the family or one's own resources, as are legal or medical training. But academic salaries are getting better, especially for doctoral holders, and especially for the growing number of people going into non-academic work. On the whole, doctoral study today is probably profitable, simply as a private investment. Accordingly, the candidate should be expected, and in view of the related benefits required, to pay more of his own way and get through faster.

This would require two innovations. Both, I think, are proper and feasible. The first is the introduction of a needs test for applicants to national fellowship programs, like those at the undergraduate level. This would probably not save a large proportion of the fellowships, but even if it meant a 20 to 25% difference, the total funds available would go a good deal farther. In addition, the practice would tend to lessen the present competition in which universities are forced to "buy" good graduate students away from one another, thus driving up the price and limiting the distribution of funds even more. To the argument that "everyone *needs* support," there is the counter-argument that, as in Parkinson's law about work expanding to fill the time available, so "need" expands to fit the amount of fellowship funds available. The result would be of clear benefit to the normalized program.

The second innovation is the greater use by students of loan funds, especially toward the end of their period of training. It is true that students typically do not use the funds available today but that is partly because of indulgent universities who let them drag along (and sometimes, sadly, because it is to the institution's interest to retain a valued teaching or research assistant), and partly because of the student's ignorance of his own financial advantage. As for the first, once the institution told doctoral students it expected them to work full-time on their studies and to finish "with their class," plus or minus a brief period for exceptions both ways, the students would be much more receptive to the idea. As for the second, it is usually to the student's own monetary advantage to borrow the funds needed to finish in one year in preference to spending two or three years on an assistantship or other part-time work, or even on a regular appointment as an ABD, because he can command a higher-paying job with the degree than without it. In addition, the student gets a year or two start toward tenure and professional recognition. It is usually poor economics for a doctoral candidate to drag out the completion of the degree. Even if he has to borrow money to finish, it is better to get the degree out of the way.

So the advantages seem clear to both the system and the student, but the graduate schools have to enforce the normal program and protect the candidates from institutional, departmental, or professorial exploitation. Given the other sources of support, and the other needs in the system of training, I suggest a model of a four-year program along these lines (a program that has been in effect at Tulane University under Graduate Dean Robert Lumiansky for the past few years, and successfully so): a fellowship the first year, research and teaching assistantships the second and third years, a loan the fourth. Whenever students can be supported otherwise, without cutting into their time for study (e.g., by family, spouse, additional fellowships, etc.), so much the better for themselves and indirectly, by freeing resources, for others. If students could have both teaching and research assistantships in the middle years, so much the better for their training: given the realities, however, there will be more teaching assistantships in the humanities, more research assistantships in the sciences (but that does have the virtue of matching subsequent activities).

The Federal government has provided sizable loan funds that can be used for this purpose—repayment at 3% interest, starting a year after the student concludes full-time study and running over a ten-year period with some forgiveness for public school teaching—but the use of these funds is being hampered by the controversy over the "affidavit of belief" provision. A useful alternative or supplement would be a privately operated, foundation-supported loan fund with eligibility limited to doctoral candidates. The administrative costs could be taken over by the foundation, and the repayment in both time and amount would be linked to the borrower's subsequent economic status, perhaps with certain forgiveness features for college and university teaching.* Under such a scheme, those who benefit would pay, and those who benefit most would pay most. In order to encourage private support and thus share the burden and the fellowship wealth, terminal year fellowships could be linked to loans on, say, a half-and-half basis so that the beneficiaries bear more of a load and so that there can be more beneficiaries in toto.

Whatever the particulars, these are the essentials: it is highly desirable that doctoral programs be full-time, continuous, and expeditious, similar to those of medicine and law; the only way for that to happen is to put more of the burden for financing the program on the student (and that is just, since he will directly benefit). The major channel is through loans of one kind or another and the basic requirement is that the universities insist on full-time study in the four-year norm, informing and encouraging the graduate students to that end. I say "the universities" because a large number, at least a large number of the same class, would have to move in this direction simultaneously or some would fear the competition from the others—even though, I am convinced, they could demonstrate the economic value of the arrangement to most of their candidates. This type of doctoral program will be better in both respects—educationally and financially—and in a short time, it too would become "natural."

8. *A sizable proportion of the present crop of ABD's should be encouraged to complete their degrees.*

This should be done for the reasons indicated before in the section on this topic. The only questions are *how many* and *how*.

No one can say how many of the more than 10,000 ABD's are seriously interested in completing their degrees, would definitely benefit from the completion, would be able to do so in the next few years, and are worth helping toward completion. Suppose the figure is half the total: it probably is not higher than that. A combination of support can do the job: part from a special fund for the purpose; part from loans, as mentioned above; part, perhaps, from the current employers (with the understanding that the candidate would return to his job for a specified period after receiving the degree). Preference might be given to ABD's

---

* The general rationale has been convincingly argued by Milton Friedman in his article, "The Role of Government in Education" (in Robert Solo, ed., *Economics and the Public Interest.* Rutgers University Press, 1955).

in academic life, and the employing institution should have a voice in the selection of candidates as well as the training institution. Here again it would be profitable for the ABD to borrow part of the necessary funds from a source such as the one outlined above since possession of the degree will almost automatically bring him a higher salary and often a promotion in rank.

The idea is to work off the present backlog of ABD's before the graduate school gets immersed in the numbers of the late 1960's, and, through the arrangements described, make it impossible for such numbers to accumulate again. If nothing else, it is simply a matter of economy: it costs much more to complete a year of an ABD—older, more family responsibilities, higher salary and living standards, travel—than the terminal year of a student in process.

9. *Industry should provide more support for graduate schools, and more free support.*

The graduate enterprise is costly and the bill must be paid. I have already recommended that the direct beneficiaries, the candidates themselves, pay more of their own way, but even so, they will bear only a fraction of the true cost of their training. Industry is another beneficiary of the graduate enterprise, both directly and indirectly, and it has begun to contribute to its support (about $6.5 million a year from 43 industrial firms reporting in the questionnaire, including most of the large ones). It should contribute more: the large majority of the industrial representatives themselves agreed in their replies (53 out of 63). Furthermore, in recognition of the indirect benefits it receives, industry should provide more funds for local allocation. As it is now, their support comes mainly in the form of fellowships and research grants, i.e., the form from which they feel they will benefit most directly.

But even if industry were to increase its contribution substantially, the main costs of graduate study over the next years will, I think, have to be borne by the Federal government—in both public and private institutions, directly and indirectly.

WITH REGARD TO STUDENTS

10. *Recruiting for doctoral study should be conducted more systematically and more energetically.*

The graduate schools need more good applicants for doctoral study more than they need anything else. They are not likely to get more qualified applicants unless they make a determined recruiting effort. They should do so. The effort should be conducted by all graduate schools in behalf of all—not simply for one's own graduate school, but for graduate study as such. It has to proceed in two ways, one for the undergraduate college in the university and one for the independent liberal arts college. Both programs should be run by the graduate dean's office as one of its most important tasks.

Inside the university, it is not enough simply to say that the departments and the individual faculty members are or should be on the lookout for promising graduate students. The job is too critical to be left to such unorganized good intentions. It should be done along the lines used by Dean Lumiansky of Tulane. At his university, every junior with a satisfactory grade average is seen by the graduate dean or a faculty member appointed for the purpose, who invites him to consider graduate work, explains what would be involved, outlines plans for financial assistance, indicates the career opportunities in his field, and—at Tulane —offers registration in a graduate course during his senior year which can later count as graduate credit.*

Tulane is a relatively small graduate institution but there seems no reason why this plan could not work in larger places simply through delegation of the interviews. The point is a very simple one: more students will apply if they come to know more about graduate work, and particularly if they feel that someone cares. A systematic campaign of this sort could produce a sizable number of good applicants who would not otherwise be attracted to graduate study—with all that would mean for better selection, less attrition, and better work generally. The program of recruitment in the universities is particularly important because, as we have seen, the undergraduate college in the universities is now the major source of numbers.

In the liberal arts colleges, the recruiting program provides an opportunity for closer and better university-college relations. What is required again is not simply the good will and interest of the college faculty—though that is important and can be improved upon, as the Woodrow Wilson Program has shown—but the active collaboration of distinguished members of the graduate faculty. On a regional basis, universities and colleges should work out plans to have members of a nearby graduate faculty visit the college campus for a lecture or honors seminar or the like and for an informal talk with the abler upper-classmen in his field. The visit would be followed up by the college faculty itself. If the college had a small fellowship fund, to help send its own graduates on to graduate school, so much the better: such local encouragement is often enough to tip the balance. It would be an easy matter for the dean of the college and the graduate dean to work out such arrangements, and since a few universities are normally available to any liberal arts college, it would not mean an undue strain on any of them. Again,

---

* In both universities and colleges, incidentally, the use of the senior as assistant in either teaching or research is useful for educational as well as recruitment purposes. Recent experiences along this line have on the whole been quite happy.

the plan would be good for educational as well as recruiting purposes.

Let me emphasize that recruitment in both the university and the college, for best success, requires (1) recruiting not for one's own school but for graduate work generally, (2) an efficient training program, i.e., a compressed one in time, and (3) good academic salaries afterwards.*

11. *The writing deficiencies at the graduate level should be attacked directly.*

This is a highly specific item within the entire system of graduate education, but it is of great importance. The graduate school can push responsibility off onto the colleges and the high schools but nothing more can come from those sources, given their own realities. The graduate school must either do something or make do. I favor the former.

Poor writing and the associated bad organization of research and scholarly reports is so general across the fields, so indicative of unclear thinking and analysis, and so costly of the time and resources of others that some intensive efforts at improving the situation seem to be required. If justification for highlighting the problem is needed, it lies in the rationale, as the Yale report on economics put it, that "writing itself is a tool, and is part of the basic methodology of the profession," analogous to problem drilling in mathematics, briefs in law, or laboratory work in the sciences.

There is no easy solution. The graduate faculty can be admonished and they can pass on the admonition to their graduate students, but that will not lead far; it has not in the past. The department of bacteriology at Wisconsin considers the matter so important that it has set up an experimental course in oral and written reports that is required of its graduate students. The Yale report on economics states that "the members of the panels believe that the solution of the problem of training students to write coherently lies in the direction of more writing practice early in the graduate training program and reliance on a larger number of shorter papers."

Some new institutional form is needed to give full attention to the matter. My colleague Paul Lazarsfeld of Columbia University suggests a scheme such as the following. Suppose, for example, that a large university took on three or four young men or women skilled in clarity of expression, trained in the practice of scholarly editing, and interested in and knowledgeable about broad fields of knowledge—people with the qualities of good editors in serious publishing. Those doctoral students who need the training would be required to submit their regular papers

* Not only an increase in faculty salaries but an increase in range is important for recruiting purposes. The better young people are attracted more by a profession's top salaries than by its average, for the obvious reason. The striking uniformity in academic pay relative to other professions (as documented by George Stigler) has no doubt served as a deterrent in the past.

to such readers, and a number of extra ones as well, and to revise and rewrite until their style had sufficiently improved. Doing several short papers under such supervision should be instructive.

I make no large claims for this particular device, though I think it would make a measurable difference in perhaps half the cases. I do believe that whatever is done must be institutionalized in order to amount to anything. Even in disciplines such as English and history, where good writing is in itself a part of the job, professors are too busy with their own work to do much more than complain about the students' inability to write.

12. *Informal social centers for graduate students should be set up on the campuses where they do not now exist.*

I think of such centers not primarily as providing for the social life of graduate students and reducing the anxieties of graduate study, though they would help in both respects, but rather as an informal means of enriching and broadening the life of the graduate school. Where they now exist, the common rooms for doctoral students do contribute substantially to the common enterprise. Dean Keniston has recommended such a development for each of the broad divisions of knowledge; it might be even more useful to bring together students of literature and biology, of chemistry and history, of philosophy and psychology. Such centers, whether residential or not, would not "solve the problem of breadth" but they would do some good in effecting better communication across the university campus.

Once more, I do not consider this a central recommendation but I do believe it would do some good if implemented.

WITH REGARD TO COLLEGE TEACHING

13. *Training in teaching should be handled differently within the doctoral program.*

If for no other reason, the recurring controversy over this matter would seem to indicate that something different should be tried. The differences, I suggest, should be these:

(*a*) *All* doctoral candidates should have some actual teaching experience as part of their doctoral requirements, not less than half time for half a year. I suggest this although I recognize that many holders of the doctorate do not go into teaching and although I am personally not convinced of the value of the training as preparation for college teaching. But I make the recommendation for these reasons:

1. Most people involved believe the assistantships are useful.

2. The teaching assistantship, whatever it may do for training in teaching, is a useful device for training in the subject itself: "You never know a subject until you can teach it."

3. It is economically necessary for the students under the plan of support outlined above.

4. It is thought to be economically necessary for the university to have a large supply of teaching assistants. (Actually, if it takes three teaching assistants to equal one full-time instructor, it is not economic for the institution.) This requirement would provide assistants, by spreading the load more thinly over a larger number.

5. As a minor fiscal reason: if the assistantship is made an educational requirement for all candidates, the stipends become tax exempt (and almost two-thirds of the recipients have them as it is).

6. The assistantship provides an early opportunity for the candidate to test his interest in teaching, and capability for it. Furthermore, the practice in teaching itself makes for a psychological commitment to academic work.

(*b*) Teaching assistantships at the university should be supervised, department by department—not simply in name, but in the deliberate assignment of responsibility and time to an interested senior man who would advise and consult. Among other benefits, this should be of value to the undergraduate being taught.

(*c*) Teaching assistantships should be limited in time, preferably to half time for a year, certainly not more than twice that. This would compress the period of study for the doctorate, as indicated above. As a training device, no more time can be justified.

(*d*) Teaching assistantships should not be limited, as they are now, to the more menial parts of college teaching—freshman composition, chemistry lab sections—but should be systematically varied like a true educational experience and for the effect on interest and enthusiasm. However, the more menial parts should not be excluded: they are part of the job too.

(*e*) The graduate school should set up a course or seminar (without credit) on the character of the liberal arts college and its problems, for those doctoral candidates interested in college teaching. It should be staffed partly by visiting lecturers from nearby colleges. Among other things, it would have the advantage of bringing together, probably for the first time, doctoral candidates from all sides of the campus in a common educational venture related to their future work on a college campus. One of its tasks would be the exploration of the place of the candidate's discipline in the undergraduate curriculum. President Butterfield of Wesleyan, at the Lake Mohonk Conference, suggested some summer seminars for young college instructors on the questions of liberal education that involve their own discipline and its philosophy. In a way, here is an equivalent at this level of the pedagogical component below: analysis of goals rather than training in methods.

(*f*) The college itself should take more responsibility for training in teaching—the internship in *how*, conducted on the spot by people who know and care. Thus some of the load would be taken off the graduate school where it has never been carried to the college's satisfaction and placed on the college where, in my view, it more appropriately belongs.

Beyond those developments, two things more. The first is that if the colleges really do want something more or something different still, they should get together, work out a clear bill of particulars and a feasible program, and present it to the graduate school. The graduate faculty says it is willing to consider any workable plan that does not undercut its own spirit and mission as it sees it—and under the circumstances, it certainly has the right to set that condition.

The second is that if the liberal arts college wants more and better Ph.D.'s, they will have to be prepared to pay for them—not only in dollars, but in facilities, intellectual atmosphere, work load, and all the rest. Without that, it cannot, will not, and should not get the better products of the graduate schools. Here, incidentally, we are close to a weak link in American higher education—the many small and poor colleges. What should happen is least likely to happen, given the realities of the situation, namely, the consolidation of weak colleges into fewer, stronger institutions. The analogue is the district high school. As Beardsley Ruml and Donald Morrison say, "If we take the college of below average size —below the simple statistical average—the outlook is not good. Major and heroic labors will be required in reorganizing, re-financing and consolidation to preserve these many colleges, their services and their traditions."

14. *The new intermediate degree might be tried.*

I described earlier the conception and characteristics of this two-year "Doctor's" degree designed for undergraduate teaching. It would fill the bill at a large number of liberal arts colleges, and perhaps in the undergraduate college of some universities, and there are advantages in saving time on the production end. This seems a more feasible means to meet the alleged problem than recovering the Master's degree although, all things considered, it remains a poor second to the present doctorate.

Part of "all things considered" is the symbolic problem. Will good students and the colleges take such a degree—a degree that, no matter what, will be considered second-class in comparison to the "true doctorate"? I am more doubtful of the colleges' and students' acceptance than I am of the graduate school's ability to produce such degree-holders. Considering the benefits that *could* result, the experiment might be justified—but only if the colleges (in a single region, at first) say they really want such a program in preference to what they would otherwise get and if a few good universities put their backs into the venture, in at least a few fields. The top faculties at the top universities should probably not be engaged in such a program any more than their top students would sign up for it. Foundation funds are, of course, needed.

An easier alternative is being proposed, namely, to give everyone some sort of diploma or license when he passes his comprehensive examination for the Ph.D. This would stamp an official "degree" on the ABD and it might be a little more negotiable than nothing. In my view, this would not do much harm, but it would not do much good either. It does make the degree symbolism more blatant and we do not need that.

On the whole, I am not particularly hopeful about the new intermediate degree—I would personally rather go in the direction of the compressed doctorate and subsequent work for the few ablest men—but the new degree may be worth a careful trial.

WITH REGARD TO INSTITUTIONS

15. *The relations between the liberal arts colleges and the graduate schools should be improved.*

The gulf between the colleges and the universities is growing and is likely to grow, I fear, over the next years. Getting the two together will be beneficial for the system of higher education, and for the elementary and secondary levels as well.

Meetings among top administrative personnel, presently the typical mode of collaboration, are good but not enough. A bridge needs to be built between the two groups of faculty members. As it happens, there are at least four important ways this can be done.

The first I have mentioned: visits by graduate faculty members to college campuses for recruiting purposes. On such trips, it would be natural for the graduate faculty people to hold one or two meetings with the college faculty in their subject and related ones, in which the faculty would be brought up to date on recent developments in the universities and the visitor would learn something more of the college's problems in the field.

The second has to do with the graduate school's offering of more systematic work in the history, philosophy, problems of the liberal arts colleges for intended college teachers, also mentioned above. Here it is natural and desirable to bring college faculty members to the university campus for their participation, even leadership. The by-product here would be the opportunity it afforded the college faculty for recruitment in reverse—recruitment of young faculty members either for their own colleges or for college teaching in general.

The third is a plan to provide refresher work for college faculty members on the university campus, ranging from a few seminars a year for several people to lengthier periods for a few, so that the college faculty could work more extensively on the latest developments in their subjects, do some research and writing, talk with their university counterparts, and recharge their intellectual batteries in general. This obviously ties in with the ABD matter, but it would be unfortunate if it were restricted to ABD's; it is really meant for somewhat older people who have been in college teaching for six to ten years.

The fourth is the reverse side of the third: while a few college people are at the university, their places on the college campus could be taken by doctoral candidates interested in college teaching—a supervised teaching assistantship on the college campus itself—or by young faculty members who would like to try themselves in a different environment. This would not only be desirable for the people and institutions involved, in actual experience and testing of interest, but it would ease the financial burdens of the two-way plan.

All of these would best be done on a regional basis, partly for economic reasons. The distribution of colleges and universities is now such that there would be little difficulty in matching up institutions. Naturally, a single college or university could have such arrangements with a number of other places. The net effect, I think, would be a better understanding of the college's and the university's problems by major representatives of the other side. Such a series of arrangements has all the advantages of local determination of activities and at the same time, by widening and deepening membership in what Frank Bowles calls "the university community," helps to fulfill the graduate school's position of responsibility and leadership in the national system of higher education.

16. *Over the visible future, the national load of doctoral study should be carried mainly by the presently established institutions of top and middle-level prestige.*

Leaving aside an occasional exception, such as a cooperative program among institutions, it makes less sense as a national policy, economically and educationally, to set up new doctoral programs than to expand those already set up and operating. They should be encouraged to grow with the national need and the available resources should be put to their use.

The trouble is that there is no "national policy" and under present circumstances, cannot be.* This really comes down, then, to advice to three sources:

---

* This needs to be qualified a little. We have the makings of a national policy in the "new or expanded" provision of the National Defense Education Act, but it is not, in my judgment, the wisest policy.

To the small and less prepared institutions, to remember how hard and how costly it is to become a successful institution at the doctoral level; and accordingly to exercise restraint over its ambitions.

To the foundations and government grant-making agencies, to build on present and clearly potential strength.

To the doctoral student, to attend an institution as high in the prestige scale as he can.

This last is desirable not only to fill graduate schools from the top down over the next years—important in every way from a national standpoint —but it is also crucial for the student's own career. If the students could be brought to further their self-interests in this way, the problems of institutional distribution would be on the way to their best possible solution. Incidentally, such a development would take care not only of the short run, but of the middle run too, by encouraging the moderately prestigious institutions. It would also guard against what may possibly become a problem a decade hence, namely an *over*expanded training system at the doctoral level once the famous "bulge" becomes the natural order of events.

If it is technically feasible, a systematic study should be made of the effect of initial selection as against actual training, as contributing to institutional differences in the doctoral product. Such a study would go a long way toward answering some of the questions now involved in institutional quality and it could lead to a sounder national solution of the problem of institutional load.

(*a*) The great universities at the top should become "super" graduate schools, in two respects.

One has to do with the spread of post-doctoral work, as described above, which will and should be located primarily in the top universities. The other has to do with the trend toward their concentration on the doctorate at the expense of the Master's: that trend should be continued and even accelerated. In the present situation, it is more important for such institutions to put their valuable and scarce resources to work at the highest points of advanced training.

WITH REGARD TO ADMINISTRATION AND ORGANIZATION

17. *The office of the graduate dean should be strengthened.*

The graduate enterprise is too important to be left to the ambiguities of the present situation. The dean's office should be strengthened in four ways: by giving the dean more authority over questions of appointments, promotions, space, and academic policy as they affect the graduate enterprise at the university; by increasing his budgetary powers, especially over the research funds of the university (which will increasingly come from outside the institution just as the educational budget will come from inside); by providing for associate deans from the major subject fields as needed; and by appointing only strong men to the office.

The dean should lead the university's efforts at recruitment of graduate students, as outlined above. He should also head up the program of college-university relations. He should be the fund-raiser for the graduate enterprise and the leader of such innovations as the compressed doctoral program. There are several high university officials who think that the graduate dean should also exercise authority on admissions, requirements, standards, and the like over the departments but I see no way for this to be effected in practice, and I am not sure it is desirable anyway. The departments certainly have their faults, but so do any realistic substitutes.

It is idle to try to specify the matter much further because of the great administrative variety in American universities. I happen to believe that the Chicago divisional organization is a good one for a large graduate institution, in effect with four graduate deans. But that is both controversial and impractical at institutions with other traditions and histories, so the objective is about all that can be set down in view of adjustments that have to be made to local conditions and personalities.

However, the responsibility for realizing the objectives can be clearly allocated: it is the president's. He should take the graduate school as seriously as he takes the medical and law schools—it is at least equally important—and he should take the graduate dean as seriously as the law and medical deans. Both the position and the person must be built up, and the president is the only one in a position to start or accelerate a spiral in that direction.

18. *The national organization of graduate schools should be strengthened.*

Here I agree with the minority of graduate deans that a more centralized and somewhat more inclusive national organization, with a secretariat, is needed for the purposes indicated above. It ought to include, say, every graduate school offering as many as 20 to 25 doctorates a year for three consecutive years. That would not quite double the present membership of the AGS but would in about five years. Such an organization, properly run, could do a great deal in guiding the direction of the national graduate enterprise, representing it in Washington and elsewhere, finding the important facts, and in general rationalizing it even more. The importance of the enterprise warrants the move.

WITH REGARD TO CONCEPTION AND EVALUATION

19. *The graduate faculty, by discipline and by institution, might systematically review a range of questions involved in their graduate programs.*

The attitudes toward the graduate enterprise held by faculty members and deans are characterized by both inconsistencies and disagreements. It is perhaps possible to reduce the latter by uncovering the former.

The only way to do that is to engage in a systematic discussion of the important issues. The discussion might center particularly on three kinds of programmatic questions: those on which faculty opinion is split as evenly as 60/40 or so, those on which faculty opinion is now undecided as much as 25 to 30%, and those on which the recent recipients of the doctorate are critical of present practice in the amount of 40% or more. Taken together, these issues come down to the following:

> Conception and purpose of the doctorate: research/teaching, independence/direction, "academic"/"professional," specialization/breadth, skills/wisdom
> Undergraduate preparation, and the articulation of graduate and undergraduate work
> Training in teaching, broadly conceived
> The duration of the doctorate and the problem of attrition
> The character and length of the dissertation
> The intermingling of graduate and undergraduate students
> The exploitation of students as research or teaching assistants
> The degree structure: the Master's and post-doctoral training
> The foreign language requirement
> The final oral
> The size of the enterprise and its institutional distribution

Their importance will range from place to place and from field to field. No one should expect full agreement to result; but there might come some narrowing and specification of the disagreements.

Not all these recommendations are, to my mind, of equal standing. Half of them are more important than the rest and would be particularly consequential for the next years of graduate education in the United States:

> The normal program
> The tightened program
> The shorter dissertation
> The regularized post-doctoral program
> The rationalized support
> The systematic program of recruitment
> The revised program for training in teaching
> The improved relations between university and college
> The distribution of the institutional load

All the recommendations to this point, those and the others, deal with one or another aspect of the present program. They are internal to the present system of graduate education. In addition, there are two further suggestions to be made that deal with matters outside the current set of arrangements and, indeed, refer to the entire enterprise. Whereas the earlier recommendations have to do with continuing processes within the present framework, these suggestions each involve a single institutional effort to improve the state of affairs in higher education. One calls for the establishment of a center for advanced study in the humanities and the other for a new graduate university.

Part of the current dissatisfaction with graduate study derives directly from the fact that the traditional center of academic scholarship, the humanities, has been bypassed by rapid changes in the mass technological society and by developments in the sciences. The humanities may not be as badly off intellectually as it is fashionable to think, but even the humanists themselves are unhappy with their academic status and their intellectual progress relative to other fields. Their morale is lower; so are their self-confidence and their respect for their own disciplines. Some are able to rationalize the situation by blaming it on the heavy support now given to the sciences and even to the social sciences, but such martyrdom is hard to wear constantly and has worn a little thin in spots.

In any case, whether the humanities are down because they are out or out because they are down is an unproductive question of the chicken-egg variety. The question is what can be done about it. Something might be done through a center for advanced study in the humanities. Every other set of disciplines now has such a center for advanced work for the faculty members. The return to the humanities should, if anything, be greater than to the others, precisely because they are word disciplines and hence can profit more from talk and discussion.

The center should bring together not only academic humanists but also social scientists involved with problems of philosophy and human values, men of affairs who are faced with important decisions involving ethical concerns, working humanists in the writing and publishing field, men of the law, and so on (with some of the objectives noted in the footnote on page 81). As I write, for example, there is an important public question to which such a center could give a valuable intellectual and moral lead, namely the role of mass media in our society. Efforts should be made to broaden the concern of the center beyond the narrower ranges of humanistic scholarship, though they should by all means be included.

Within the humanities, such a center could help to improve morale and develop a sense of tone now lacking at what should be the core of the university.* It could re-examine the basis of learning in the humanities: research or scholarship. It could contribute to graduate study in the best way, by improving the disciplines themselves. Outside the humanities, it could contribute to the social sciences themselves, to the clarification of moral and philosophical questions in the present age, and perhaps to the development of a few more of the "gifted generalists—men with enough intellectual and technical competence to deal with the specialists and with enough breadth to play more versatile roles—whether as managers, teachers, interpreters, and critics" for which the report on education of the Rockefeller Brothers Fund pleads.

In a country as large, as varied, and as rich as this one, a great new university should be founded about every fifty years as an influence, a model, a standard-setter. The last great university was the University of Chicago, which was certainly a pioneering institution in its own right, a national leader of graduate education in every sense, and an important contributor to the strength of the public universities in the Middle West. Since then, seventy years ago, no great new institution has been established, and one is overdue.

In reviewing the history of graduate education, I tried to show how encrusted such a system inevitably becomes, and how difficult it is to move it from within. The sources of important innovation in higher education are four: individual leadership, sharp social change, money—and new institutions. A dramatic experimental model starting *de novo* without the restrictions of established traditions, established practices, or established personnel would be free to do what operating institutions cannot now try. I shall not suggest what it ought to do, since that would be determined by the men who would run it. But I shall say only that there are enough things it could do to warrant the effort. Even if it became nothing but a great graduate university run roughly along the present model, that would in itself be desirable both in process and as outcome.

The graduate enterprise is now so large and so important that a university restricted to it alone is warranted: a super-graduate school for the doctoral and post-doctoral level. Such an institution has failed in the past, but given proper support it could now succeed. Two earlier points against such a project are now inoperative, I think: lack of students in the absence of an undergraduate college to feed them in, and lack of service opportunities to the community. The former should be no prob-

* Efforts in this direction are under way under the sponsorship of the American Council of Learned Societies, e.g., the recent publication of *One Great Society* by Howard Mumford Jones; and in the current study of the humanities at Princeton.

lem these years, certainly not if the institution began with the prestige of a distinguished faculty. The latter would be taken care of in its location.

That is an important part of the idea. The new university should be located in Washington. The United States is perhaps the only major country in the world without a first-rate university in the nation's capital. Such an institution there would lend tone to the intellectual life of the capital and to the nation as a whole. Its faculty could be available to the government as expert consultants, and government personnel could take refresher courses at the university. In any number of ways, such a faculty could serve the national community. The location in Washington could have one important by-product: the further upgrading of higher education in the South, for which it could serve as supplier and trainer of talent, special consultant, and educational leader in general.

Establishing such an institution would probably be strongly opposed by the institutions now at or near the top. Their arguments might be similar to those used against establishing graduate education eighty years ago, e.g., "Why start something new when we cannot support what is already under way." Most likely such an institution would have to recruit its faculty from several of the top institutions, but on the other hand the "raiding" point can be put affirmatively, namely, the task of staffing the new university would tend to raise academic salaries and to "loosen" other places by bringing in new talent there. Thus the new graduate university could have positive effects by its very establishment— even before it had made its own contribution to learning.

A new university of this character could hardly fail: top-grade people rarely fail. The question is whether it could be a great success or only a moderate one.

There is something to do for everyone connected with graduate education—the university president, the graduate dean, the faculty, the students, the colleges, industry, the government, the foundations. That is as it should be: graduate training belongs to all of them.

It belongs to the society as well. On the whole, over the years, the graduate school has done a great deal for the society:

> It has grown from a few fields training a few students in a few institutions to a large and impressive national system of advanced training.
> It has trained a large body of professional teachers for American higher education and trained them in subject matter.

It has increasingly trained staff for the secondary and elementary school system, especially at the level of leadership.

It is increasingly training personnel for administrative as well as research posts in industry and government.

In addition to providing personnel for enriched undergraduate work on its own campus, it has led a number of educational experiments at the collegiate level and it produces a number of the leading texts used throughout the system of higher education.

It is now taking the lead in reconstructing parts of the curriculum at the high school level and in the further training of high school teachers.

In all these ways it has served as the source in which a large part of the educational system renews and refreshes itself.

In both educational and non-educational spheres, the graduate school's stamp is accepted as a qualifying mark of competence, often *the* qualifying mark, so that the graduate school has become the chief screen of scientific and scholarly talent in the society.

Its leading personnel have increasingly served as advisors and consultants on the largest issues of our national life—foreign relations, economic affairs, scientific policy, civil rights and liberties, health and welfare.

In one of its spheres it has become a key to the national security, and in others it has made direct contributions to the good life through the application of learning.

In a relatively brief period of years, it developed an American brand of advanced training that surpassed the models abroad and not only held American students but attracted more and more foreign ones.

And overlaying and underpinning it all, it has brought American research and scholarship to a position of world leadership and it has systematically furthered man's knowledge of himself and his world.

To anyone who sees life steadily and sees it whole, this is quite an accomplishment for a relatively few decades.

What is most needed now is threefold. The first need is some perspective on the chronic criticisms of graduate study. There is almost as much complaint about graduate education as about the human condition, and for the same reasons. Those who take part in it are talking about themselves: their lives rich or wasted; for graduate students, the crucial step in their careers; for faculty and presidents, the world most closely around them. But life is often disappointing and always imperfect. Some of the complaint is professional, coming more from social scientists than biologists. Some of it is situational, coming from those toward the bottom of the academic totem pole. Some of it is endemic, coming from a highly articulate and self-critical sector of the American intelligentsia, the humanists. Some of it is misshapen: the image at variance with the fact. Some of it is suspect, the easy repetition of the cliché: specialization is always "undue," the doctorate always "takes too long," students are never "good enough," standards always "need strengthening," programs always need "more breadth." Somehow the rhetoric of the discussion has got stuck and needs oiling.

The second need of the times, in my view, is to make graduate training more efficient: more purposeful, more directed, more compressed, less beholden to the Ph.D. symbol and more dedicated to the actual task of training men of skill and knowledge. That seems in a way a prosaic prescription. But it rests on a grander conception that is the third need of the system of graduate training.

That is the sheer recognition of itself as a leader of American education, even of American life, and the acceptance of the responsibility that position implies. Whether it wants it or not, the graduate school now has the responsibility. As the system of higher education becomes more massive, in the next years, and as the society itself becomes more complex, the need for trained intelligence will grow, and so will the importance of the graduate school. As the president of the Carnegie Corporation told the American Council on Education, less than a year ago, "The role of the universities is undergoing a remarkable change. They are being thrust into a position of great responsibility in our society—a position more central, more prominent, more crucial to the life of the society than academic people ever dreamed possible." And this role of the universities—really, these days, the multiversities—is played out predominantly by the graduate school.

What American academic life needs is a sense of pride, of *esprit de corps*, of profession in the best sense. That is what the American graduate school must take the lead in supplying, to itself and its constituency. It holds a critical position in the life of the mind in this country, as the primary home of the American scholar.

Appendix

Acknowledgments

I am indebted to the Carnegie Corporation of New York for the grant that made this study possible, and I am personally grateful to John Gardner, its president, for his friendly encouragement and support over many years. I was of course completely free to conduct the study in my own way and I alone am responsible for this report.

The University of Chicago was good enough to serve as sponsor for the study during my tenure as a member of the faculty of the Graduate School of Business and the Division of the Social Sciences. A group of my colleagues at the University were helpful in advising with me during the early stages of the study: Earl Evans, professor of biochemistry; Herman Fussler, director of libraries; Edward Levi, dean of the Law School; Richard McKeon, professor of philosophy; Leonard Savage, professor of statistics; Edward Shils, professor of sociology and social thought; and Allen Wallis, dean of the Graduate School of Business.

During the course of the study and the final preparation of the manuscript, I received guidance and help from a number of people concerned with graduate study. I am grateful to all of them, and particularly to graduate deans Leonard Beach of Vanderbilt, Henry Bent of Missouri, J. P. Elder of Harvard, Robert Lumiansky of Tulane, Moody Prior of Northwestern, and Ralph Sawyer of Michigan. I am also indebted to my friends William McPeak, John Eberhart, Robert Morison, David Sills, Robert Merton, Paul Lazarsfeld, Gary Steiner, Ralph Tyler, and Herman Fussler for their good advice after reading the manuscript.

While at the University of Chicago, I received assistance in interviewing from Harold Metcalf and in statistical matters from William Kruskal. Mrs. Leonora Thelen was an able research assistant; Fred Meier was, as usual, highly competent in processing large amounts of data; and Mrs. Nan Reiss served as secretary and coordinator far beyond the call of duty.

While in New York, I was aided in any number of ways by my present colleagues at the Bureau of Applied Social Research, Columbia University. Abram Jaffe was helpful in connection with the numbers problem; Clara Shapiro managed fiscal matters with care and economy; Susanne Popper processed the manuscript with notable efficiency; and Albert Gollin, Helmut Guttenberg, Carol Bowman, and Sarina Hirshfeld handled the large amount of questionnaire data, as well as bibliographical and other matters, with such skill and good humor as to make me feel both gratitude and awe.

I am indebted to the following publishers for permission to quote: Harcourt, Brace and Company, Inc., for Howard Mumford Jones, *One Great Society; Behavioral Science* for Ralph W. Gerard, "Problems in the Institutionalization of Higher Education: An Analysis Based on Historical Materials" (vol. 2, no. 2, April, 1957, pp. 134–146); Basic Books, Inc., for Theodore Caplow and Reece J. McGee, *The Academic Marketplace; The Journal of Higher Education,* for Leonard B. Beach, "Freedom and Discipline in Graduate Programs" (vol. 30, no. 3, March, 1959, pp. 120–123) and for J. P. Elder, "Reviving the Master's Degree for the Prospective College Teacher" (vol. 30, no. 3, March, 1959, pp. 133–136); Longmans, Green & Co., Inc., for William James, "The Ph.D. Octopus," in *Memories and Studies;* and Columbia University for *The Educational Future of Columbia University.*

Finally, I want to say how grateful I am to all the respondents who took time out from their busy schedules to tell me what they knew and thought about graduate study in response to a long and sometimes restricting questionnaire.

In short, a large number of people have contributed immeasurably from their experience and wisdom to the preparation of this report. Most of the ideas I got from them; the faults remain my own.

Bernard Berelson

March 10, 1960
Irvington-on-Hudson, New York

Bibliography

Except for the first section, which includes some titles for general background, this bibliography contains titles utilized and referred to in the text. It does not list specific items from such sources as the AAU *Proceedings* that are already sufficiently identified.

General

Richard G. Axt. *Research on Graduate Education. Report of a Conference.* The Brookings Institution, 1959.

Frank H. Bowles. "The Splendid Anachronism." Talk at a meeting of the Middle States Association, November, 1955.

Frank H. Bowles. "Trends and Choices in Higher Education." Address at the meeting of the Association for Higher Education, Chicago, March, 1959.

Committee of Fifteen. *The Graduate School, Today and Tomorrow. Reflections for the Profession's Consideration.* Fund for the Advancement of Education, 1955.

The Educational Future of the University. The Report of the President's Committee. Columbia University, 1957.

Educational Policies Commission. *Higher Education in a Decade of Decision.* National Education Association, 1957.

Walter Crosby Eells. *College Teachers and College Teaching. An Annotated Bibliography.* Southern Regional Education Board, July, 1957. Supplement, June, 1959.

Faculty Supply, Demand, and Recruitment. Proceedings of a Regional Conference, sponsored by the New England Board of Higher Education, 1959.

Graduate Education for Women. The Radcliffe Ph.D. A Report by a Faculty-Trustee Committee. Harvard University Press, 1956.

Graduate Education in Psychology. Report of the Conference. American Psychological Association, 1959.

Graduate Training in Economics. A Report on Panel Discussions at Yale. Yale University, 1956.

Hayward Keniston. *Graduate Study in the Humanities.* The Educational Survey of the University of Pennsylvania, December, 1957.

A. Lawrence Lowell. *At War with Academic Traditions in America.* Harvard University Press, 1934.

Earl J. McGrath. *The Graduate School and the Decline of Liberal Education.* Institute of Higher Education, Teachers College, Columbia University, 1959.

Frederic W. Ness, ed. *A Guide to Graduate Study.* Association of American Colleges, 1957.

President's Commission on Higher Education. *Higher Education for American Democracy.* Vol. 4: *Staffing Higher Education.* December, 1947.

The Production of Doctorates in the Sciences: 1936–1948. American Council on Education, Research Staff on Scientific Personnel, September, 1951.

Report of the President's Committee on Education Beyond the High School, July, 1957.

A Survey of Research Potential and Training in the Mathematical Sciences. Final Report of the Committee on the Survey. University of Chicago, March 15, 1957. (The Albert report.)

Hugh Taylor. "Graduate Education in the National Interest." Address, April, 1959.

John C. Weaver. *Some Dilemmas in Graduate Education. A Report to the Carnegie Corporation of New York on a Travelling Fellowship,* 1957–1958.

History

As I say in the text, this is not intended as an original history of graduate education. I am glad to acknowledge again my reliance upon the prior work of a number of scholars. Incidentally, this particular phasing of graduate education, which seems to me the most serviceable for seeing the developments in broad outline, has also been noted by others, e.g., Hollis.

For the pre-history, the major source is:

Richard J. Storr. *The Beginnings of Graduate Education in America.* University of Chicago Press, 1953.

For the first period of graduate study, there is:

W. Carson Ryan. *Studies in Early Graduate Education. The Johns Hopkins University, Clark University, The University of Chicago.* Bulletin 30 of the Carnegie Foundation for the Advancement of Teaching, 1939.

and the historical sections of:

Walton C. John. *Graduate Study in Universities and Colleges in the United States.* U.S. Office of Education Bulletin 20, 1934.

Ernest V. Hollis. *Toward Improving the Ph.D. Programs.* Prepared for the Commission on Teacher Education, American Council on Education, 1945.

In addition, there is much useful material in the biographies, autobiographies, letters, memoirs, papers, etc., of early figures like Hall, Harper, Eliot, Tappan, Gilman, White, Burgess; in the histories of particular institutions, like Hoxie on the Faculty of Political Science at Columbia, French on Johns Hopkins, Goodspeed on Chicago, Morison on Harvard, Pierson on Yale, Gray on Minnesota; and in some general histories of higher education (e.g., like Brubacher and Rudy, 1958, or Hofstadter and Hardy, 1952).

I am particularly grateful to Professor W. H. Cowley of Stanford both for the use of his unpublished manuscript *An Appraisal of American Higher Education*, which contains a large amount of historical and analytic information; and for the series of dissertations sponsored by him on the topic, particularly

Glenn Reed, *Criticisms of the American Graduate School, 1900–1945;* and
   Robert Wert, *The Impact of Three Nineteenth Century Reorganizations Upon Harvard University.*

Anyone interested in the subject ought not deny himself the pleasure of looking through the proceedings of the Association of American Universities, at least for the early years. As I have tried to indicate, that is an entertaining, sobering, and altogether rewarding experience.

In addition, the following titles are referred to in the text:

American Association of University Professors. *Report of the Committee on College and University Teaching.* The Association, 1933.

American Council on Education. *Report of Committee on Graduate Instruction.* Washington, D.C., April, 1934.

Joseph Axelrod, ed. *Graduate Study for Future College Teachers.* American Council on Education, 1959.

Theodore C. Blegen and Russell M. Cooper, eds. *The Preparation of College Teachers. Report of a Conference.* American Council on Education Studies, July, 1950.

Isaiah Bowman. *The Graduate School in American Democracy.* Bulletin no. 10, U.S. Office of Education, 1939.

Consultation on the Preparation of College Teachers. Lake Mohonk, N.Y., October 31, November 1, 2, 1947. Mimeographed.

Consultation on the Preparation of College Teachers. Poughkeepsie, N.Y., October 17–18, 1948. Mimeographed.

Charles G. Dobbins, ed. *Expanding Resources for College Teaching. A Report of the Conference.* American Council on Education Studies, 1956.

The Education of College Teachers. Summary of a Discussion by the Trustees of the Carnegie Foundation for the Advancement of Teaching. Reprinted from the 1957–1958 annual report.

Marcia Edwards. *Studies in American Graduate Education. A Report to the Carnegie Foundation.* With an introduction by Walter A. Jessup. Carnegie Foundation for the Advancement of Teaching, New York City, 1944.

Laurence Foster. *The Functions of a Graduate School in a Democratic Society.* Huxley House Publishers, 1936.

William S. Gray, ed. *The Training of College Teachers.* Proceedings of the Institute for Administrative Officers of Higher Institutions. University of Chicago Press, 1930.

H. H. Horne. "Study of Education by Prospective College Instructors." *School Review,* March, 1908, pp. 162–170.

Byrne J. Horton. *The Graduate School (Its Origin and Administrative Development).* New York University Bookstore, 1940.

Raymond M. Hughes. *A Study of American Graduate Schools Conferring the Doctorate, 1937–38 to 1941–42.* Ames, Iowa, 1946.

Raymond M. Hughes. *A Study of the Graduate Schools of America.* Miami University, Oxford, Ohio, 1925.

William James. "The Ph.D. Octopus." In his *Memories and Studies,* Longmans, Green & Co., Inc., 1912.

Fred J. Kelly, ed. *Improving College Instruction. Report of a Conference.* American Council on Education Studies, 1951.

Clarence Lindquist, ed. *Staffing the Nation's Colleges and Universities. Report of a Conference.* Office of Education, 1957.

Leon B. Richardson. *A Study of the Liberal College.* A Report to the President of Dartmouth College, 1924.

George F. Zook and Samuel P. Capen. *Opportunities for Study at American Graduate Schools.* U.S. Bureau of Education. Bulletin no. 6, 1921.

Purposes

David Blank and George Stigler. *The Demand and Supply of Scientific Personnel.* National Bureau of Economic Research, 1957. No. 62, General Series.

George H. Chase, "Report of the Dean of the Graduate School of the Arts & Sciences, 1925–1926," in *Reports of the President and Treasurer of Harvard College,* Harvard University Press, 1927, p. 114.

Commission on Human Resources and Advanced Training. *America's Resources of Specialized Talent. A Current Appraisal and a Look Ahead.* Report prepared by Dael Wolfle, Director. Harper & Brothers, 1954. (The Wolfle report.)

Herbert Goldstein. "Recent Trends in and Outlook for College Enrollments." *Monthly Labor Review,* March, 1956, pp. 286–291.

M. E. Haggerty. "Occupational Destination of Ph.D. Recipients." *Educational Record,* 9 (October, 1928), pp. 209–218.

Howard Mumford Jones. *Education and World Tragedy.* Harvard University Press, 1946.

Toby Oxtoby, Robert Mugge, and Dael Wolfle. "Enrollment and Graduation Trends: From Grade School to Ph.D." *School and Society,* 76, 1952, pp. 225–230.

George J. Stigler. *Employment and Compensation in Education.* Occasional Paper #33, National Bureau of Economic Research, 1950.

Teacher Supply and Demand in Universities, Colleges, and Junior Colleges, 1957–58 and 1958–59. Research Division, National Education Association, June, 1959.

Teachers for Tomorrow. Fund for the Advancement of Education, Bulletin no. 2, November, 1955.

R. B. Thompson. *The Impending Tidal Wave of Students.* American Association of Collegiate Registrars and Admission Officers, 1955.

Gregory D. Walcott. "Statistical Study of Doctor of Philosophy Men." *School and Society,* 1, January, 1915, pp. 66–71, 102–107.

J. F. Wellemeyer, Jr. and Pauline A. Lerner. "Higher Education Faculty Requirements in the Humanities and the Social Sciences." *School and Society,* 78, November 14, 1953, pp. 145–151.

Paul Woodring. *New Directions in Teacher Education.* Fund for the Advancement of Education, 1957.

Institutions

Theodore Caplow and Reece J. McGee. *The Academic Marketplace.* Basic Books, Inc., 1958.

Hayward Keniston. *Graduate Study and Research in the Arts & Sciences at the University of Pennsylvania.* The Educational Survey of the University of Pennsylvania. June, 1958.

Frank R. Kille. *A Study of the Baccalaureate Origins of College Faculties.* Association of American Colleges, 1959. Mimeographed.

David Riesman. *Constraint and Variety in American Education.* Doubleday & Company, Inc., 1958.

Beardsley Ruml and Donald H. Morrison. *Memo to a College Trustee.* McGraw-Hill Book Company, Inc., 1959.

Logan Wilson. *The Academic Man. A Study in the Sociology of a Profession.* Oxford University Press, 1942.

Students

The Advancement of Medical Research and Education. Final Report of the Secretary's Consultants on Medical Research and Education. June 27, 1958. (The Bayne-Jones report.)

Graduate Student Enrollment and Support in American Universities and Colleges, 1954. National Science Foundation, 1957.

Charles M. Grigg. *Who Wants to go to Graduate School, and Why?* Research Reports in Social Science, Center for Social Research, Florida State University, February, 1959.

George L. Gropper and Robert Fitzpatrick. *Who Goes to Graduate School?* American Institute for Research, September, 1959.

John W. Gustad. "The Choice of a Career in College Teaching; a Preliminary Report of Research." Address, ACE meeting, 1958.

Robert E. Iffert. *Retention and Withdrawal of College Students.* Office of Education. Bulletin no. 1, 1958.

Charles V. Kidd. *American Universities and Federal Research Funds.* Harvard University Press, 1959.

Robert H. Knapp and H. B. Goodrich. *Origins of American Scientists.* University of Chicago Press, 1952.

Robert H. Knapp and Joseph J. Greenbaum. *The Younger American Scholar: His Collegiate Origins.* University of Chicago Press, 1953.

National Academy of Sciences–National Research Council. *Doctorate Production in United States Universities, 1936–56, with Baccalaureate Origins of Doctorates in Sciences, Arts, and Humanities.* Publication 582, 1958.

Physicians for a Growing America. Report of the Surgeon General's Consultant Group on Medical Education. Public Health Service, October, 1959.

Virginia Bosch Potter, ed. *Fellowships in the Arts and Sciences, 1960–61,* 3d ed. Association of American Colleges, 1959.

Hans Rosenhaupt, with the assistance of Thomas J. Chinlund. *Graduate Students Experience at Columbia University, 1940–56.* Columbia University Press, 1958.

John E. Stecklein and Ruth E. Eckert. *An Exploratory Study of Factors Influencing the Choice of College Teaching as a Career.* Bureau of Institutional Research, University of Minnesota, January, 1958.

Howard E. Tempero. *The Geography of Certain Phases of Graduate Instruction in the United States.* Ph.D. Dissertation, University of Chicago, 1944.

Program

Doctoral Studies in English and Preparation for Teaching. A Committee Report of the College English Association. June, 1957.

R. W. Gerard. "Problems in the Institutionalization of Higher Education: an Analysis Based on Historical Materials." *Behavioral Science,* 1956, pp. 134–146.

A Graduate Program in an Undergraduate College. The Sarah Lawrence Experience. By Members of the Committee on Graduate Studies, Sarah Lawrence College, edited by Charles Trinkaus. Wesleyan University Press, 1956.

Howard Mumford Jones. *One Great Society: Humane Learning in the United States.* Harcourt, Brace and Company, Inc., 1959.

Benjamin Wright. "The Ph.D. Stretch-Out," in *Vital Issues in Education,* 1957.

The Studies

Faculty Origins

I started with the catalogues of the seven classes of institutions—four classes of universities and three of liberal arts colleges. The sampling aimed at securing about 400 names for each class of institutions. In the first two classes, with a total of only 22 cases, all the institutions were sampled; every nth name was taken where n was calculated to yield about 400 of the estimated total (omitting faculties of law and medicine). In the other five classes of institutions, the institutions were sampled first and then names as before. The number of institutions in each of these cases ranged between 24 and 39 and the sampling ratio of faculty members from 20 to 67%. In these classes, not more than 10 names were taken from a single institution.

I was after information on the highest earned degree and its institutional source but that was not equally available from catalogue listings. The data were given in 85% of the cases in the lower classes but only 8% in the top class. Accordingly, the names secured from the catalogues were then searched in the appropriate volume of the standard directories of American scholars and were found in inverse order: 55% of the residual faculty members from the top class and 17% from the lower ones. The total proportion of sample names for whom the needed information was found ranged from 60 to 65% at the top to 85 to 90% at the bottom, with an over-all proportion of 73%.

Authorship in Major Journals

First scholars were consulted in the various fields in order to develop a list of (1) the most important journals in the field that (2) contain signed articles (3) by American scholars and (4) that would be judged representative of the major journals in the field. I selected at least two journals in each discipline or field and not more than seven; the number roughly reflected the total number of doctoral degrees conferred in the field. In all, 80 journals were included, as follows:

SOCIAL SCIENCES
    History
        American Historical Review
        Journal of Modern History
        Journal of the History of Ideas
        Mississippi Historical Review
    Economics
        American Economic Review
        Quarterly Journal of Economics
        Journal of Political Economy
    Psychology
        Psychological Review
        Journal of Applied Psychology
        Journal of Abnormal and Social Psychology
        Journal of Clinical Psychology
        Journal of Experimental Psychology
        Psychological Bulletin
    Sociology
        American Sociological Review
        American Journal of Sociology
    Anthropology
        American Anthropologist
        Human Organization
    Political Science
        American Political Science Review
        Political Science Quarterly
        World Politics

HUMANITIES
    Philosophy
        Journal of Philosophy
        Philosophical Review
    Fine Arts and Music
        Art Bulletin
        Musical Quarterly
        Journal of American Musicological Society
    Language, Literature and Classics
        American Journal of Archeology
        Classical Philology
        American Literature
        Publications of Modern Language Association (PMLA)
        Studies in Philology
        Modern Philology
        Romanic Review
        Germanic Review

PHYSICAL SCIENCES
Mathematics
American Mathematics Monthly
American Journal of Mathematics
Annals of Mathematics
Geology and Geography
Geographical Review
Economic Geology
Astronomy
Astronomical Journal
Astrophysical Journal
Physics
Journal of Chemical Physics
Physical Review
Review of Modern Physics
Journal of Applied Physics
Optical Society of America Journal
Chemistry
Analytical Chemistry
Journal of Biological Chemistry
Journal of Physical Chemistry
Journal of Organic Chemistry
Journal of American Chemical Society
Industrial and Engineering Chemistry
Statistics
Journal of American Statistical Association
Annals of Mathematical Statistics

BIOLOGICAL SCIENCES
Biology
Biological Bulletin
Journal of Morphology
Anatomical Record
Genetics
Journal of Bacteriology
Journal of Parasitology
American Journal of Physiology
Zoology
Journal of Experimental Zoology
Physiological Zoology
Botany
American Journal of Botany
Plant Physiology

PROFESSIONAL FIELDS
Business
Journal of Business
Harvard Business Review
Education
Educational Record

Harvard Educational Review
Journal of General Education
Association of American Colleges Bulletin
Journal of Higher Education
Engineering
　　Institute of Radio Engineers Proceedings
　　Mechanical Engineering
　　Electrical Engineering
　　Civil Engineering
　　Mining Engineering
　　Chemical Engineering Progress
Agriculture
　　Journal of Animal Science
　　Agronomy Journal
　　Ecology

The analysis of the institutional identification of each author, for major articles only, was then done for each journal for the latest available volume, usually that for 1957–1958. Where there were more than 800 articles per field or discipline, every nth article was taken to yield approximately that number. The number of articles ranged from 44 in fine arts and music, 65 in history, 67 in anthropology, 74 in political science, and 75 in economics, to about 800 each in chemistry and biology, 750 in physics, 635 in engineering, and 560 in psychology.

Length of Dissertations

The data were collected in two stages. First, I gathered all the figures on length of dissertation that were available in *Dissertation Abstracts* from August, 1957 to July, 1958. However, some institutions do not list their dissertations in that source and others are represented only partially. For such institutions, I wrote to the librarian and asked him to provide me with the necessary data. All major institutions were thus included and most minor ones. The number of dissertations included is 7,317, or over 80% of the estimated total for that period.

Amount of Publication

The first step was to construct a sample of 1947–1948 recipients of the doctorate, by name, from the list of *Doctoral Dissertations Accepted by American Universities*. The sampling took every nth name from each of the disciplines listed in order to yield between 120 and 240 names per discipline, depending on its size. The names were then checked in the appropriate scholarly bibliographies or abstracts (e.g., *Chemical Abstracts, Psychological Abstracts, PMLA Bibliography, Education Index*, etc.) for every year, up to 1956 (except for English, which was checked only through 1955 because the PMLA listing changed form at that point).

The data are, if anything, a little on the low side since it was impossible to be sure of authorship for common names with initials only or for women who secured the degree under their maiden names but published under their married names.

The Questionnaires

The questionnaires were sent to five groups: graduate deans, graduate faculty, recent recipients of the doctorate, college presidents, and representatives of industrial firms employing large numbers of holders of the doctorate.

Graduate deans. The questionnaire was sent on June 21–22, 1959 to 92 deans in the United States members of the Association of Graduate Schools (39) and in all other universities granting at least ten doctorates annually (53). A total of 79 questionnaires were received, or 86%. The 92 institutions are listed at the end of this section.

Graduate faculty. The questionnaire was sent on June 23–25, 1959 to a total of 4,440 members of the graduate faculties in the same 92 institutions. Names were taken from the institutional catalogue, usually that for the graduate school or its equivalent, but occasionally from the general university catalogue. (The questionnaire asked whether the respondent was a member of the graduate faculty and a very few "no's" were discarded.) Every eighth name was included in the sample (except for law and medicine, professors emeriti, and full-time administrators). Omitting a number of replies from people no longer in the indicated positions (about 8% of those sent), a total of 1,821 questionnaires were received, or 41%.

Recent recipients. The questionnaire was sent on June 11–12, 1959 to a total of 3,843 recipients of the doctorate in 1957. The recipients are recent enough to recollect their experience readily and for the most part to refer to the current system, yet out long enough to test their training against the requirements of their jobs. The names were taken from the virtually complete roster maintained by the National Research Council and the questionnaires were sent to the "permanent address" listed there. The sample included every other recipient in the arts and sciences and every third one in the professional fields (but again not law or medicine). Wherever a proportion is reported in the text for the recent recipients as a whole, the figure has been adjusted for the difference in sampling ratios used for academic and professional doctorates. Foreign recipients were eliminated. A total of 2,331 questionnaires were received, or 61%.

College presidents. The questionnaire was sent on June 21–22, 1959 to

856 presidents of all independent liberal arts colleges and teachers colleges (four-year degree-granting institutions), according to the Office of Education classification. A total of 609 questionnaires were received, or 71%. About half of them were filled out by the presidents themselves and half by the academic deans, deans of the college, and holders of similar positions.

Industrial employers. The questionnaire was sent on July 10, 1959 to 191 companies selected from the publication *Industrial Research Laboratories of the United States,* issued by the National Research Council-National Academy of Sciences. Every company listed there as employing over 100 people on its scientific research staff was included, although it turned out that this over-sampled the field considerably. The questionnaires were sent to the president of the firm with the request that he pass them on to the appropriate person. A total of 70 questionnaires were received, or 37%.

To all but the industrial sample, a second wave of questionnaires was sent out in the last week of September, 1959. The first wave had been sent out at a bad time, just when the school year was closing, so another set went out to the non-respondents just after the beginning of the fall term. Actually about 125 more questionnaires were received than indicated above, but too late for inclusion in the tabulations.

Accordingly, unless otherwise specified in the text, the following are the numbers of cases on which the standard tabulations are based (except for a few "no answers" on most questions:)

	Graduate deans	Graduate faculty	Recent recipients	College presidents	Industrial employers
Total	79	1,821	2,331	609	70
Top 12 universities	12	474	773		
Next 10 universities	8	287	473		
Other AGS universities	23	407	474		
Other universities	36	653	539		
Best liberal arts colleges				31	
Better liberal arts colleges				42	
Other liberal arts colleges				402	
Teachers colleges				134	
Physical sciences		340	559		
Biological sciences		237	355		
Social sciences		386	520		
Humanities		253	280		
Education		142	294		
Engineering		215	133		
Total arts & sciences		1,216	1,714		
Total professional fields		559	600		

I make no particular claims for the representativeness of the industrial sample, though I did receive replies from nearly all the major industrial employers. Their response accounts for far more of the scientific personnel working in industry than the indicated proportion of returns. However, I do believe that the returns are reasonably representative for the academic samples.

Graduate deans. In this case, virtually complete returns were received. Only two of the top 22 institutions did not reply; those not responding gave only 747 of the doctorates in 1957–1958, or less than 10%.

Graduate faculty. Following are proportions of questionnaires returned by different groups (in percentages):

Top 12 universities	43%
Next 10 universities	43
Other AGS universities, plus	41
Other universities	39
Physical sciences	43
Biological sciences	52
Social sciences	46
Humanities	32
Professional fields	38

Thus the humanities are underrepresented by an amount that in most cases will make a difference of not more than five percentage points in the figure for the arts and sciences as a whole.

There are only small differences among those who responded early or late; the first wave was split at about the point of median return. This again suggests that the non-respondents are unlikely to be substantially different from the respondents. Here are a few illustrations:

	When Questionnaire Returned		
	Early in first wave	*Late in first wave*	*Second wave*
Percentage "satisfied" with "state of graduate training in your field at your institution"	58	59	59
Percentage "very satisfied" with "current state of health of your discipline nationally"	29	30	29
Percentage associate professors	34	29	29
Percentage full professors	47	51	54
Median number of articles published in last five years	4.8	4.6	4.7

	Early in first wave	Late in first wave	Second wave
Percentage "more preparation for research than for teaching" in doctoral study: is now	62	62	59
should be	37	36	33
Percentage agreeing that "graduate schools unduly stress research . . . at the cost of properly preparing college teachers"	33	35	34

Recent recipients. Following are the proportions of questionnaires returned by different groups:

Top 12 universities	57%
Next 10 universities	60
Other AGS universities, plus	61
Other universities	63
Physical sciences	58
Biological sciences	63
Social sciences	63
Humanities	58
Professional fields	62

Again the differences between early and late responders are small:

	Early in first wave	Late in first wave	Second wave
Percentage "very satisfied" with "graduate work leading to your doctorate"	36	34	34
Percentage who think doctoral program was "very good in training you for the post you now hold"	52	48	48
Percentage "very satisfied" with dissertation	29	28	29
Percentage "willing to undertake the same program if there were no degree, or its equivalent, awarded at the end"	33	32	33
Age at time of Ph.D.	31	31	32
Duration, Bachelor's to Doctor's: median years	9	8	9
Percentage in university employment	34	35	30

	Early in first wave	Late in first wave	Second wave
Percentage assistant professors, of academically employed	44	44	42
Percentage agreeing that "graduate schools unduly stress research . . . at the cost of properly preparing college teachers"	31	32	30

These data also suggest that the non-respondents do not differ substantially from the respondents. In addition, there are the following comparisons with the total NRC roster:

	NRC roster	This sample
Bachelor's to Doctor's (median number of years)		
Physical sciences	6	6
Biological sciences	7	7
Social sciences	8	8
Humanities	10	10
Total arts & sciences	7	7
Total professional fields	10	10
Total group	8	8
Age at time of doctorate		
Physical sciences	29	28
Biological sciences	30	30
Social sciences	33	32
Humanities	35	34
Total arts & sciences	31	31
Total professional fields	36	35
Total group	32	32

College presidents. Following are the proportions of questionnaires returned by different groups (in percentages):

Top liberal arts colleges	74
Other liberal arts colleges	69
Teachers colleges	78

Here again the differences between early and late respondents are small:

	Early in first wave	Late in first wave	Second wave
Percentage with enrollment of 1,000 and over	35	37	39
Percentage of faculty with doctorate (medians)	34	33	35

	Early in first wave	Late in first wave	Second wave
Graduate school is "doing reasonably well in supplying college teachers"	46	45	51
Development of more research facilities on campus "desirable"	59	62	59
Research training at doctoral level necessary	26	23	32

Following are the 92 institutions generally included in the samples of graduate deans and graduate faculties:

Top 12 universities

California (Berkeley)
California Institute of Technology
Chicago
Columbia
Cornell
Harvard
Illinois

Massachusetts Institute of Technology
Michigan
Princeton
Wisconsin
Yale

Next 10 universities

Indiana
Johns Hopkins
Minnesota
New York University
Northwestern

Ohio State
Pennsylvania
Stanford
UCLA
Washington (Seattle)

Other AGS universities, plus

Brown
Catholic
Clark
Duke
*Emory
*Fordham
*Georgetown
Iowa
Iowa State
Kansas
Missouri
Nebraska
North Carolina

*Notre Dame
Pennsylvania State
Purdue
*Rice
Rochester
*St. Louis
*Syracuse
Texas
Tulane
Vanderbilt
Virginia
Washington (St. Louis)

Other universities

Alabama	Louisiana State
American	Loyola
Arkansas	Maryland
Boston	Michigan State
Brooklyn Polytechnic	New Mexico
Buffalo	North Carolina State
Carnegie Institute of Technology	Oklahoma
Case Institute of Technology	Oklahoma State
Cincinnati	Oregon
Colorado	Oregon State
Colorado State College	Pittsburgh
Connecticut	Rensselaer Polytechnic
Delaware	Rutgers
Denver	Southern California
Florida	Temple
Florida State	Tennessee
George Peabody	Texas A & M
George Washington	Utah
Houston	Virginia Polytechnic
Illinois Institute of Technology	Washington State
Kansas State	Wayne State
Kentucky	Western Reserve
Lehigh	

* Ford Foundation accomplishment awards; remaining institutions are in AGS.

Disciplinary Consultants

As indicated in the text, I held some long talks about graduate study in their disciplines with a number of American scientists and scholars. I benefited greatly from their observations and wisdom and I am glad to acknowledge their guidance. These disciplinary consultants were:

In the sciences:
George Beadle, California Institute of Technology, biology
R. W. Burris, Wisconsin, botany
William Cochran, Harvard, statistics
Ralph Gerard, Michigan, physiology
William McElroy, Johns Hopkins, biochemistry
Kenneth Pitzer, California (Berkeley), chemistry
Frederick Seitz, Illinois, physics
Burr Steinbach, Chicago, zoology
A. W. Tucker, Princeton, mathematics
John Tukey, Princeton, statistics
C. B. van Neil, Stanford, bacteriology
Douglas Whitaker, Rockefeller Institute, biology
Perry Wilson, Wisconsin, biology

In the social sciences:
Herbert Blumer, California (Berkeley), sociology
George Graham, then Princeton, political science
Morton Grodzins, Chicago, political science
Ernest Hilgard, Stanford, psychology
Richard Hofstadter, Columbia, history
Carl Hovland, Yale, psychology
Paul Lazarsfeld, Columbia, sociology
Sidney Painter, Johns Hopkins, history
Richard Ruggles, Yale, economics
George Stigler, then Columbia, economics
Sherwood Washburn, then Chicago, anthropology

In the humanities:
  M. H. Abrams, Cornell, English
  Fredson Bowers, Virginia, English
  Roderick Chisholm, Brown, philosophy
  Heinrich Henel, Yale, German
  Paul Henle, Michigan, philosophy
  Rensselaer Lee, Princeton, fine arts
  Whitney Oates, Princeton, classics
  Bernard Weinberg, Chicago, French
In engineering:
  Harold Gotaas, Northwestern
  L. E. Grinter, Florida
  Newman Hall, Yale
  Frederick Lindvall, California Institute of Technology
  Frederick Terman, Stanford
In education:
  Stephen Corey, Teachers College, Columbia
  Francis Keppel, Harvard
  Willard Olson, Michigan
  Ralph Tyler, Center for Advanced Study in the Behavioral Sciences

Following is the common list of questions put to the consultants:

In general, what I would like to learn from you is what has happened, is happening, will happen, and should happen in graduate work in your discipline and closely related areas.

The following list of questions indicates the kind of thing I'm interested in. It probably does not cover all the important matters in your field, and in such cases I'd like to get the relevant questions from you as well as the answers. I am giving the same list to representatives of all the major disciplines, even though some questions may not apply to some fields. I'd be grateful if you would think not only about these questions, but also about any other problems they suggest in the whole field of graduate education as you know it.

I'm after the facts where you know them; your impression of the facts where you don't; and your opinions as representative of the opinions of the abler people in your field. Wherever your judgment may differ from that of a large number of qualified people, I hope you'll point that out to me. Incidentally, if you would like to discuss this with some of your colleagues before replying, please feel free to do so.

A. Questions Dealing with Your Discipline

What have been the major changes or developments in your discipline over the past twenty years, or longer? What have been the effects of such developments on graduate education in the field? What should they be?

Disciplines develop differently, and at uneven rates of growth. At any given time, therefore, disciplines are at different points in the cycle of growth. For example, I have been told that some fields are now at the point of exploiting major break-throughs; others are engaged in mopping-up operations based on earlier advances; some are in process of breaking up into two or more fields; some are in process of integration; etc. In this broad historical way, how would you describe the present state of your discipline?

Some disciplines live largely within themselves while others have important, continuing, stimulating contacts with neighboring fields. What is the situation in this respect for your discipline?

Are there now some sub-fields within your discipline that seem to be growing particularly rapidly? Are they important enough to affect programs of graduate education in the next years?

What are the major divisions within your discipline currently? How has this changed in recent years? Are there sub-fields that are quite different from one another? Do some of them have closer relations outside the department than inside? In other words, is the department or discipline really a unitary whole? What about "schools of thought"?

There probably is such a thing as scholarly morale within fields, that is, the extent to which the members of a discipline feel that their field is making steady or rapid progress. How would you describe the state of such morale in your field?

B. Questions Dealing with Graduate Work in the Field

What do you see as the major problems of graduate education in your discipline? How can they best be handled?

What important changes in graduate training have been made in your field in the past twenty years or so? Have they been for better or for worse, in your judgment?

What is the general quality of graduate training in this field now, as compared with, say, the pre-war years? For the system as a whole? For the better institutions? For the lesser institutions?

In most fields, the numbers of graduate students, and particularly of doctoral students, has gone up sharply in recent years. How has this affected the quality of training? How is it likely to affect it in the years ahead? Can quality be maintained against the impact of numbers? If so, how can this best be done?

Is your discipline generally satisfied with the character of its graduate training programs? What are the reasons for the major blocs of opinion, whatever they are? Have they changed over recent years?

What are the particular aims of graduate education in your field, currently? That is, what are people being trained for, or in? What are the particular competencies, in skills or bodies of knowledge, that a master's or doctor's candidate is expected to have? Has this changed in recent years, and if so, how?

Do graduate students at different universities get essentially the same training, in scope and in quality? How about students in different subfields within the discipline?

I enclose a list of the doctorate-granting institutions in your field, with the numbers of doctorates granted in 1955–56. How does training differ as between the better and the poorer institutions? Is the extension of doctorate training to more institutions a matter to encourage or deplore?

Is a doctoral candidate expected to be as much an "independent worker" now as he was, say, when you took your doctoral training? Should he be made more independent today? Does the system of support, i.e., research and teaching assistantships, militate against this?

Is the duration of the doctorate period a problem in your field? Does it take longer now than, say, before the war? Why? What can be done about it?

Are doctoral programs too "loose"? Too remedial of undergraduate deficiencies? Are there "too many courses" at the graduate or doctorate level?

What, roughly, is the ratio of ordinary classroom instruction to laboratory or field work in your discipline?

Are there currently any undue emphases or even fads in graduate training in the field?

Are there currently any important innovations or experiments in graduate training in your discipline? How do they seem to be working out?

How does your discipline handle the training problems presented by the expansion and proliferation of the fields of knowledge themselves? For example, does such expansion, coupled with the need for specialization, mean that each new generation of doctoral candidates is trained in a narrower portion of the total field? If so, is this bad from the standpoint of the need for generalists?

Is the degree of specialization in your discipline now about right so far as graduate training is concerned? Are there any important efforts at producing generalists? What about inter-departmental programs and requirements?

Graduate schools typically prepare three kinds of products: researchers, college teachers, and practitioners. How does this stand in your field? What are the implications for the training program? Can a single program produce all three kinds of people, or should their training be differentiated? What are the trends in this regard?

What are the ties, if any, between academic training in your field and related practice in professional, business, and governmental fields?

How much is doctoral training in your field "professional" as against "academic"—that is, aimed at doing, rather than learning and teaching? What is the trend in this regard? What is the significance for doctoral training?

As you know, some critics of graduate education feel that it is too narrow and too specialized—that it prepares "mere technicians" rather than "creative scholars." Does this question of depth versus breadth make sense in your field?

Specifically, what about the preparation of researchers as against college teachers? Is this a problem in your field? What can and should be done about it? Is the teaching assistantship helpful in this regard?

Is the present organization of graduate training the best possible one? Are the relations within and between fields optimal? Are the current definitions of "departments" about right? Are they in any way restrictive?

Some people feel that under the impact of numbers, the pressure of the need for preparing college teachers, and the pressure from an expanding subject matter, there will be an increasing number of the "real researchers" prepared at the post-doctorate level in the years ahead. How about this in your field? What do you see as the future of post-doctorate programs over the next decade or so?

C. Questions Dealing with the Doctorate Program and Dissertation

In general, is the discipline satisfied with the present state of the dissertation? How has this feeling changed in recent years?

How and when is the dissertation topic typically chosen? Does the student select it "by himself" or is he more or less given it by the professor?

Is the length of the dissertation a problem in your discipline? What about limiting the dissertation to article length, or, say, fifty pages?

To what extent are some typical criticisms of the doctoral dissertation applicable in your discipline, namely, that it is a chore to every one concerned; that it is based on wrong standards; that it is too often trivial and unimportant; that it is limited and narrow, etc.?

What is and should be the aim of the dissertation? An "original contribution to knowledge"? A "research exercise"? A training instrument?

What is the present state of the language requirement and what is happening to it? What should happen?

Is the typical final oral examination in your field a matter of genuine substance or primarily a matter of form?

D. Questions Dealing with the Master's Degree

What is the present state of the Master's in your discipline? And what is the trend?

Is the discipline generally satisfied with the status of the Master's degree? How is this likely to change in the years ahead? For example, is the degree on the way out?

E. Questions Dealing with the Graduate Students in your Discipline

Are they good? Are they as good as they used to be?

Do you get as many good students as the training institutions can handle? That is, is your field attracting the kinds of students you want, and in sufficient numbers? If not, to whom is it losing them, and why?

Are the students coming, by and large, from the same types of institutions they used to? (For example, I have been told that in the sciences it is unlikely that the liberal arts colleges are now supplying as many good people for graduate work as they used to, relative to the big universities.)

I have been told that A students will take care of themselves, but that B students are the problem, especially since we need so many of them. Does this make any sense in your field?

Do the selection devices for admission work about as well as can be expected? Is the attrition better or worse than it ought to be? Are the students motivated properly?

By and large, is the undergraduate preparation of graduate students satisfactory? How might that be changed for the better? For example, would the change mean more or less undergraduate work in the same discipline?

What about job opportunities for new masters and doctorates? Where do they now go? What are the trends in this respect?

I am considering asking a sample of recent Ph.D.'s, and perhaps current graduate students, about their experiences with and attitudes toward graduate work. Would you encourage or discourage this? If I were to do it, what would be the most important questions for your field?

F. Questions Dealing with the Organization and Support of Graduate Work

By and large, does authority and responsibility in your field rest in departmental autonomy? Should it do so more or less than is currently characteristic of the field?

Are research institutes growing in your field? If so, what relationship do they have to the departments and to the system of graduate education in general? What is their future?

Is the financial support of graduate work a major problem? If so, in what ways?

Have the sources of funds, and particularly governmental sources, influenced the character of graduate study? If so, how, and for good or ill?

Are there certain facilities—like libraries, laboratories, equipment, field research stations, etc.—that are required for adequate doctorate training in your field? Is this an important limiting factor at present?

Finally:

1. If there are any current, recent, or notable studies of graduate education in your field, I'd like to hear about them.

2. If there are some members of your discipline who are particularly knowledgeable about and interested in such matters, I'd like to know about them.

3. If you'd like to sum up—what are the major problems and what should be done about them—I'd like to get that.

4. If you have some observations and opinions about graduate education as a whole, or anyway outside your own field, I'd like to hear them, too.

Responses to
"Criticisms and Reforms"

A common set of "criticisms and reforms" was put to the graduate deans, graduate faculty, and recent recipients in their respective questionnaires. Following are the percentages who agree in each group, arranged in descending order of agreement by the deans.

The graduate faculty and the recent recipients agree with one another more than either group agrees with the graduate deans, as indicated by the following rank-order correlations:

	Criticisms	Reforms
Graduate faculty and recent recipients	.84	.88
Graduate faculty and graduate deans	.76	.70
Recent recipients and graduate deans	.60	.56

The following specific points have been made in the criticisms directed at the graduate schools over the past few years. A few of them may overlap earlier questions but are included here for comparability with other groups. On the whole, how do you feel about each of them?

	Percentage agreeing		
	Graduate deans	Graduate faculty	Recent recipients
Doctoral programs should be "loosened" by placing more responsibility upon the student and encouraging him to do more independent work	86	64	54
Doctoral candidates should be required to get through their programs more quickly	74	32	28
Too many courses are offered at the graduate level by most departments	71	31	17

288

| | *Percentage agreeing* | | |
	Graduate deans	*Graduate faculty*	*Recent recipients*
The foreign language requirement at the doctoral level has come to be a form without much substance in a sizable proportion of cases	71	75	75
Doctoral dissertations, at least outside the sciences, are too long	71	32	27
Doctoral candidates are too often allowed or encouraged to attempt a major contribution as their dissertation rather than to take on a manageable topic that can be finished in a reasonable time	64	32	32
Doctoral candidates preparing for college teaching don't get enough training in teaching while in graduate school	63	53	48
The graduate schools have wrongly allowed the Master's degree to deteriorate in quality	63	41	56
Doctoral candidates preparing for college teaching don't get enough background in the history, problems, and philosophy of the American college	59	40	37
The doctoral dissertation should be regarded more as a training instrument than as an "original contribution to knowledge"	56	45	40
Too much of what the graduate school does, and how it does it, is adversely affected by the sources of funds, e.g., contracts grants supporting dissertation research in the sciences	49	47	39
Doctoral work suffers because many students don't really want to be researchers but have to go through research programs in order to get the "union badge" for college teaching	45	46	49
The practice of having graduate students and undergraduates in the same classes lowers the quality of graduate instruction	44	45	46
Major professors often exploit doctoral candidates by keeping them as research assistants too long, by subordinating their interests to departmental or the professor's interests in research programs, etc.	41	30	36
The quality of doctoral work is limited these days by the fact that most students are motivated by the practical objective of getting a job rather than the objective of becoming a research scholar	41	51	45
The doctoral dissertation is too often a pedantic or trivial exercise rather than an intellectual experience of genuine substance and interest	40	36	37

	Percentage agreeing		
	Graduate deans	Graduate faculty	Recent recipients
Graduate students do not clearly know what they must do to get the doctorate and are not counselled well on the way (i.e., there are ill-defined expectations and inadequate guidance)	38	35	43
Graduate work isn't well articulated with undergraduate work, making for waste, repetition, poor sequence in learning, etc.	37	40	30
The graduate schools aren't doing a good job of initial selection of candidates for the doctorate at the time of admission	35	28	25
Doctoral programs stress techniques and skills too much, at the expense of broad understanding, cultivation, and wisdom	33	36	29
There is too little provision for social contact among graduate students, so that they are isolated and personally unhappy during the course of doctorate study	33	17	17
Doctoral work is conceived too much as professional training, oriented to practice, rather than as academic learning, oriented to scholarship	33	30	25
The graduate schools unduly stress research and research training at the cost of properly preparing college teachers	32	34	32
The final oral examination, or defense of the dissertation, is only a ritual now, without a useful function	32	46	42
As it operates, the doctoral program produces too much anxiety in many students, and unnecessarily so	31	32	49
Doctoral candidates get too little direct attention, supervision, and guidance on their dissertations from their major professors, and that makes for unnecessary prolonging of the period of doctoral study	30	21	30
Under the impact of numbers, the standards of doctoral study are being jeopardized	28	32	37
One basic trouble with graduate school is that faculty members do not consider the students as their main responsibility (as compared to their own research, consultation and service jobs, administration, etc.)	27	40	44
The first year of graduate study toward the doctorate is often repetitive of the undergraduate program	23	23	19
Doctoral programs are too specialized and narrow	23	26	24

	Percentage agreeing		
	Graduate deans	Graduate faculty	Recent recipients
Graduate training too often has the unfortunate effect of dampening the student's enthusiasm for learning and scholarship	23	21	29
The doctoral program is designed too much for the students of average competence rather than for the few brilliant students	21	27	17
The atmosphere in graduate schools tends to lessen people's interest in and respect for undergraduate teaching	21	37	27
Students aren't made to work hard enough in graduate school, especially as compared to the major professional schools	19	22	14
With the numbers of students now involved in doctoral study, it has become almost impossible to provide the basic necessity of research training, namely, proper apprenticeship relations	17	23	30
Doctoral training for research is inefficient and wasteful because so few recipients of the degree become productive researchers in the field	14	14	16
Graduate work would be done better if the graduate faculty did not also have to handle undergraduate work	12	22	36
Under the impact of numbers, the quality of the students in doctoral programs is declining	12	24	25
Doctoral programs of training for research are so onerous and distasteful that they repel almost as many people from research work as they attract	9	11	15
The rigors of doctoral study tend to discourage the brightest, most imaginative students in favor of the conscientious plodders	9	15	19
Doctoral programs are insufficiently specialized	3	6	8
Doctoral programs should be "tightened" and regularized, more like the training programs in medical and law schools	1	10	15

Here are some suggested reforms or changes in graduate education that have been advocated in recent years. What do you think of each of them?

Allow, or even encourage, shorter dissertations	80	48	49
Develop more interdepartmental and similar programs, as a way of broadening doctoral study	72	69	76

	Percentage agreeing		
	Graduate deans	*Graduate faculty*	*Recent recipients*
If at all possible, require publication of the dissertation in some form, as a way to maintain standards of doctoral study	67	62	60
Restore the standards of the Master's degree, as a way to get more college teachers	64	52	62
Require all doctoral candidates to do some undergraduate teaching, under supervision	58	58	53
Allow dissertations of 50–100 pages (in fields where that is not common now)	55	44	43
Introduce a new intermediary, 2-year degree between the Master's and the Ph.D., specially designed for college teachers; somewhat broader than the Ph.D. program, and with less research emphasis	47	33	32
Set up two degree programs at the Ph.D. level —one for researchers, one for college teachers	24	25	35
Leave the foreign language requirement up to each department rather than the graduate school as a whole	23	52	63
Make the Ph.D. readily available for fulfillment of three years of acceptable work, and give additional training at the post-doctoral level for the few really able researchers	21	30	30
Cut down on the foreign language requirement	12	31	39

Summary of Comparisons by Field

Following is a capsule indication of the modal response of the graduate faculty and the recent recipients to a number of questions discussed in the text. Where no differentiation is given (GF, RR), the responses of the two groups were similar.

Purpose	Physical sciences	Biological sciences	Social sciences	Humanities	Engineering	Education
Research emphasis proper?	Yes, strongly	Yes, strongly	Yes	Yes, but less	Yes	No
More stress on training in teaching desirable?	Yes, somewhat	Yes	Yes, somewhat	Yes	No	Yes, strongly
Competing demands a problem?	No	No	Yes	Yes	No	No
Single training program for all?	Yes	Yes	Yes	Yes	Yes	No
Doctoral training now narrower than pre-World War II?	Yes	Yes	Yes	No	No	No
Present level of specialization about right?	Yes	Yes	Yes	Yes	Yes	Yes
Want more interdepartmental programs?	Yes	Yes	Yes	Yes	Yes	Yes
General conception is	Professional	Professional	Professional	Academic	Professional	Professional
General conception should be	Academic	Academic	Academic	Academic	Academic	Academic
Major task of graduate school in your field (ranked first)	Training research scholars	Training research scholars	Training research scholars	Training college teachers	Training research scholars	Training college teachers

Institutions	Physical sciences	Biological sciences	Social sciences	Humanities	Engineering	Education
Expansion jeopardizing standards?	No	Yes, somewhat	Yes	Yes	Yes, somewhat	Yes, strongly
Better to limit institutional expansion?	Yes	Yes	Yes	Yes	Yes	Yes
Variation in standards across institutions a serious problem?	No	No	Yes, somewhat	Yes	No	Yes
Can faculty handle graduate and undergraduate work in same department?	Yes	Yes	Yes	Yes	Yes	Yes
Will this reduce quality of instruction?	No	No	GF: No RR: Yes	Yes	No, not much	Yes
Is admissions policy OK as it is?	Yes	Yes	Yes, but could be tougher	Yes, but could be tougher	Yes	Yes
Are requirements clearly stated, students adequately counselled?	Yes	Yes	No	No	GF: Yes RR: No	GF: Yes RR: No
Is increased non-academic work of faculty detrimental to students?	Yes, somewhat	No	Yes	Yes	No	Yes
But are students still seen by faculty as their main responsibility?	Yes	GF: Yes RR: No	No	GF: Split RR: No	GF: Yes RR: No	GF: No RR: Yes
Too many courses?	No	No	Yes	No	No	Yes, somewhat
Impact of numbers jeopardizing standards, serious problem?	No	No	No	No	No	No

Students	Physical sciences	Biological sciences	Social sciences	Humanities	Engineering	Education
Quality of students same (or better) than pre-World War II?	Yes	Yes	Yes	Yes	Yes	Yes
Quality of students as good as program should attract?	Yes	Yes	Yes	Yes	Yes	Yes
Motives are primarily:	Mixed	Academic	Mixed	Mixed	Practical	Practical
Does practical emphasis make doctoral work suffer?	No	No	Yes, somewhat	Yes	No	Yes
Percentage unwilling to work hard enough	10–25	10–25	10–25	10–25	10–25	Less than 10%
Students work hard enough?	Yes	Yes	Yes	Yes	Yes	Yes
Though morale fluctuates, is it generally OK?	Yes	Yes	Yes	Yes	Yes	Yes
Many students socially isolated and unhappy?	No	No	No	No	No	No
Does doctoral program create unnecessary anxiety?	GF: No RR: Yes, somewhat	GF: No RR: Yes, somewhat	GF: No RR: Yes	GF: No RR: Yes	No	Yes
Supervision of students adequate?	Yes	Yes	No	No	Yes	GF: Yes RR: No
Brighter students discouraged in favor of plodders?	No	No	No	Yes, somewhat	No	No
Undergraduate preparation:						
adequate?	Yes	Yes	No	No	Yes	No
well-articulated with graduate?	Yes	Yes	No	No	Yes	No
repetitive?	No	No	No	No	No	No
Percentage who made decision to get doctorate after college	50	60	60	67	67	85
Support for training:						
percentage receiving none	4	2	13	20	5	25
limits direction of research, or quality of training?	Yes, somewhat	Yes, somewhat	Yes, a little	Can't say	Yes	Can't say

295

Students	Physical sciences	Biological sciences	Social sciences	Humanities	Engineering	Education
How much attrition of doctoral students in your department?	20–25%	10–15%	20–25%	15–20%	15–20%	20–25%
Attrition figure too high?	No	No!	No	No	No!	No
Attrition important problem?	No	No	No, not much	No	No	No
Program						
Should program be loosened to allow for more independent work?	No	Yes	Yes	Yes	No	Yes
Requirement for comprehensive examination OK as is?	Yes	Yes	Yes	Yes	Yes	Yes
Training for research: repels students from doing further research?	No!	No!	No	No	No!	No
inefficient because few become researchers?	No!	No!	No	No	No!	No
dampens enthusiasm for learning and scholarship?	No!	No!	No	No	No!	No
Is dissertation too long?	No	No	Yes	Yes, somewhat	No	Yes
Should it be limited to 50–100 pages?	Yes!		Yes	No		Yes
Should it be published, to maintain standards?		Yes!	Yes	Yes	Yes!	Yes
Selection of topic: often by student alone?	No	Yes	Yes	Yes	Yes	Yes
Supervision adequate?	Yes	Yes	Yes	Yes	Yes	Yes
More than ⅓ begin more than 1 dissertation?	Yes	No	Yes	No	No	No
Defense of thesis a ritual?	No	No	GF: Yes RR: No	No	No	No

296

Program	Physical sciences	Biological sciences	Social sciences	Humanities	Engineering	Education
Dissertation should be primarily research training instrument?	No	No	Yes	No	No	Yes
Is dissertation often trivial or pedantic?	No	No	Yes	Yes	No	No
Generally satisfied with quality of dissertation?	Yes	Yes	Yes	Yes	Yes	Yes
Quality of discipline and institution—better than pre-World War II?	Yes	Yes	Yes	Yes	Yes	Yes
Was doctoral training worth the effort?	Yes	Yes	Yes	Yes	Yes	Yes
Would you demand more for general quality of the doctorate?	No	Yes, a little	Yes	Yes	No	Yes, somewhat
Do Ph.D.'s know as much as they should?	Yes	Yes	GF: No RR: Yes	GF: No RR: Yes	Yes	Yes
Duration (elapsed time) too long?	No	No	Yes	Yes	No	No
Should students be required to get through program faster?	No	No	Yes	GF: Yes RR: No	No	No
Is duration extended by exploitation of students by major professors?	Yes	Yes	No	No	Yes	No
Are part-time students a major problem in duration?	No	No	Yes	Yes	No	Yes
Are ABD's a problem?	No	No	Yes	Yes	No	Yes, somewhat
Percentage doing dissertation at the university:	84	84	54	49	81	44
Foreign language requirement—form without substance?	Yes	Yes	Yes	Yes	Yes	Yes
Should it be cut down—left up to department?	Yes	Yes, perhaps	Yes	GF: No RR: Yes	Yes	Yes

Program	Physical sciences	Biological sciences	Social sciences	Humanities	Engineering	Education
Is the justification for the requirement cultural or professional?	Professional	Professional	Professional	Both	Professional	Cultural
Was language used in graduate training or professional work?	Yes	Yes	No	Yes	Yes, somewhat	No
Feel need for post-doctoral work?	Yes, somewhat	Yes	Yes, somewhat	No	No	No
Is post-doctoral work necessary or highly desirable in your field?	Yes	Yes	Yes, somewhat	No	No	No
Has the Master's degree deteriorated?	Yes	Yes	Yes	Yes	No	No
Is it easier to get?	Yes	Yes	Yes	Yes	Yes	Yes
Often given as a consolation prize?	Probably not	Yes	Yes	Yes	No	No
Require all doctoral candidates to do some undergraduate teaching under supervision?	Yes	Yes!	Yes	Yes	GF: Yes RR: No	Yes
Atmosphere in graduate school tends to lessen people's interest in and respect for undergraduate teaching?	No	No	GF: Yes RR: No	No	No	No

The Questionnaires

1. QUESTIONNAIRE TO GRADUATE DEANS

• 1 •

BACKGROUND DATA

13—

1. a) Your name ....

14—
15—

   b) Official position .... Institution ....

   c) Your department or field .... d) Year you became graduate dean ....

16—
17—

2. In how many departments or fields does your institution now award the Bachelor's degree? The Master's? The Doctor's?

Bachelor's degree .... 18—

Master's degree .... 21—

Doctor's degree .... 24—

Which ones does you institution award, besides the Ph.D.?

.... 27—

   a) In about how many of the fields offering the doctorate do you have ten or more doctoral candidates now in residence? .... 28—

   b) In the regular faculty of the university as a whole, roughly how many holders of the doctorate are now employed (not including medicine or law)? 31/x

3. Please provide the following figures for new graduate students for the academic year of 1958-59:

Applied for admission to graduate school ....

Accepted for admission ....

Actually registered ....

   a) Is the problem of multiple applications a serious one at your institution?

   Yes ☐ 0   No ☐ 1   32—

   b) About what percentage of the doctorate students at your institution come from your own undergraduate college(s)?

Less than 10% .... ☐ 0

10% - 25% .... ☐ 1   33—

25% - 50% .... ☐ 2

50% - 75% .... ☐ 3

Over 75% .... ☐ 4

4. I would like to get enrollment figures at your institution for the following categories of students. I know that such figures are often difficult to get precisely, but I'll be satisfied with approximations if the exact figures aren't readily available.

	Total undergrad. enrollmt.	Total grad. enrollmt. in residence (not incl. law and med.)	Grad. enrollmt. in arts and sciences, in residence	Enrollmt. of grad. sts. seeking doctorate	Enrollmt. of grad. sts. taking ½ normal load or more
Fall 1950					
Fall 1952					
Fall 1954					
Fall 1956					
Fall 1958					

   a) What is your current estimate of the same figures for Fall 1959?

Fall 1959					

299

· 2 ·

5. As a rough estimate, about how many doctoral candidates at your institution have completed everything for the degree except the dissertation **and** are now on a job away from the campus?

About ....

a) About how many of them would you estimate are still actively after the degree?

....

b) About how many of them hold teaching positions in colleges and universities?

....

c) In what departments or fields are they most and least frequent?

Most ....

Least ....

d) Is this problem of uncompleted dissertations, after completion of all other requirements for the doctorate, a serious one at your institution?

Yes ☐ 3   No ☐ 4   34—

6. Thinking only of those students seeking the doctorate, about how much could your institution expand that enrollment within your present facilities and without lowering standards—assuming you could get qualified students? In your view, how much should you?

	Could	Should
None	☐ 0	☐ 0	35—
Up to 10%	☐ 1	☐ 1
10% - 25%	☐ 2	☐ 2	36—
25% - 50%	☐ 3	☐ 3
50% - 100%	☐ 4	☐ 4
Over 100%	☐ 5	☐ 5
Can't say	☐ 6	☐ 6

a) If the expansion wouldn't be general across the graduate school, where would it mainly fall?   37—
38—

Major fields that **could** expand ....

Major fields that **could not** expand ....   39—
40—

7. About how much expansion in undergraduate, graduate, and doctoral enrollments at your institution do you expect over the next five years?

	Undergrad. enrollment	Graduate enrollment	Doctoral enrollment
None	☐ 0	☐ 0	☐ 0	41—
Up to 10%	☐ 1	☐ 1	☐ 1
10% - 25%	☐ 2	☐ 2	☐ 2	42—
25% - 40%	☐ 3	☐ 3	☐ 3
40% - 65%	☐ 4	☐ 4	☐ 4
Over 65%	☐ 5	☐ 5	☐ 5	43—

8. Has your institution prepared a plan for the development of the graduate school over the next years—its growth, operation, programs, etc.?

Yes ☐ 6   No ☐ 7   44—

If Yes: I would like very much to see a copy of the plan. If it is not restricted to local use, please send it under separate cover.

9. Now to the difficult problem of attrition in graduate study: As you know, the graduate school is being criticized these days on the ground that too few of those who start on graduate programs ever get degrees. I'm interested in the situation at your institution. Here again, I know that such figures are hard to get and I'll be satisfied with your approximations.

a) About what percentage of the students who entered graduate school in Fall 1950 have received degrees since then?

.... %   45—

• 3 •

b) About what percentage of those who entered in Fall 1950 and sought the doctorate have now received it?

.... %   46—

c) Of the students who start work toward a doctorate at your institution, about what percentage never finish?

.... %   47—

d) For the group that does not finish, which of these reasons are involved, as far as you know?
(*Check as many as apply*)

	Most important	Least important
Lack intellectual ability to do the work	☐ 0	☐ 0
Lack necessary physical or emotional stamina	☐ 1	☐ 1	48—
Lack financial resources	☐ 2	☐ 2
Found the degree wasn't necessary for what they wanted to do	☐ 3	☐ 3
Disappointed in graduate study and quit	☐ 4	☐ 4	49—
Lack proper motivation	☐ 5	☐ 5
Other reasons (*specify below*)	☐ 6	☐ 6

e) Do you consider such attrition an important problem of graduate education at your institution?

Yes ☐   No ☐ 0   50—

If Yes: Is the problem primarily one of admission policy and initial selection or primarily one of what happens during the degree program?

Primarily at admission .... ☐ 1

Primarily during program .... ☐ 2

Substantially both .... ☐ 3

Can't say .... ☐ 4

10. Roughly what percentage of the recipients of the Ph.D. **in the arts and science disciplines** at your institution get some teaching experience while graduate students?

.... %   51—

a) About how long, on the average? .... months   52—
53—

b) On the whole, how well would you say they were supervised and guided?

Very well ☐ 0   Somewhat ☐ 1   Not much at all ☐ 2   54—

11. Does you institution have an active program for recruiting graduate students?

Yes ☐ 4   No ☐ 5   55—

If Yes: What does it consist of?

12. Does your institution have some established means of regular contacts with the independent liberal arts colleges in your area?

Yes ☐ 7   No ☐ 8   56—

If Yes: What is it?

How well does it work?

· 4 ·

13. Has the Master's degree become easier to get at your institution as compared with 20 years ago, in respect to such requirements as the thesis, general examinations, foreign language, etc.?

Yes, in most or all fields .... □ 0

Yes, in some fields .... □ 1

Yes, as an option .... □ 2

No; such requirements not imposed even

then .... □ 3   57—

No; such requirements still generally in

force .... □ 4

Can't say .... □ 5

a) Would you say that the Master's degree in the arts and sciences at your university has come to be neglected relative to the doctorate?

No .... □ 6

Yes, but not matter of regret .... □ 7   58—

Yes, but regrettable .... □ 8

Can't say .... □ 9

14. About how many post-doctorate students or fellows were in residence at your institution this academic year (1958-59)? ....

59/x

a) Roughly what percentage were foreign students? .... %   60—

b) Do you anticipate having more post-doctorate students or fellows in the next three to five years?

Yes □   No □ 1   Can't say □ 6

If Yes: Do you favor this development or not?

Yes □ 2   No □ 3   Can't say □ 4   61—

c) Do you now have, or plan to have, some special office or central agency for post-doctoral students?

Yes □ 0   No □ 1   62—

If Yes: What is it?

15. At your institution, do you have any arrangements for giving advanced standing in graduate programs to qualified holders of the Bachelor's degree—e.g., outstanding people from an honors course in a good college?

Yes □ 3   No □ 4   63—

If Yes: Please describe the arrangements briefly.

16. Over the past 20 years or so, has there been a shift in the institutions from which your graduate students come—in type, geographical location, etc.?

Yes □ 6   No □ 7   Can't say □ 8   64—

If Yes: Of what kind?

17. What special pressures, if any, are put on doctoral candidates at your institution to finish up?

None, particularly .... □ 0   65—

These: ....

• 5 •

18. In your view, has the load of work **not** directly involved in teaching or research increased markedly for the graduate faculty in recent years—i.e., administration, consultation, conferences, committee work, service jobs, etc.?

Yes, generally .... ☐ 0   If so: Which ones ....   66—

Yes, in some fields .... ☐ 1

No .... ☐ 9

Can't say .... ☐ x   67—

If Yes: Is this development seriously interfering with graduate training, in your judgment, by taking major professors away from direct work with graduate students?

Yes ☐ 0   No ☐ 1   Can't say ☐ 2   68—

19. Have there been any important innovations or experiments in graduate education at your institution in the past five years or so?

Yes ☐ 5   No ☐ 6   69—

If Yes: Please describe briefly what they were.

a) Have any earlier attempts at innovation been given up in the past five years or so?

Yes ☐ 8   No ☐ 9   70—

If Yes: What were they?

20. In your judgment, does the office of Graduate Dean at your institution have enough authority to do the job properly?

Yes ☐ 0   No ☐ 1   Can't say ☐ 2   71—

a) Would it be better for graduate study at your institution if the office were strengthened?

Yes ☐ 4   No ☐ 5   Can't say ☐ 6   72—

21. Regardless of formal regulations, where are the following policies or practices actually determined at your institution—at the level of the graduate school or the department? *(If both, check each column)*

	Graduate school	Department
Foreign language requirement	☐ 0	☐ 0
Student admission	☐ 1	☐ 1
Residence requirement	☐ 2	☐ 2
Character of doctoral dissertation	☐ 3	☐ 3
Amount of course work	☐ 4	☐ 4
Master's degree requirements	☐ 5	☐ 5
Type of general or qualifying examination on the subject field (e.g., oral or written, when given, etc.)	☐ 6	☐ 6
Membership in graduate faculty	☐ 7	☐ 7

73—

74—

1/29
2—
3—
4—
5—
6—
7—
8—

22. On your campus, which of the major fields in the arts and sciences do you consider in a particularly good state of health as disciplines (i.e., vigorous, making progress, high morale, etc.) and which are in relatively poor condition? (Name three of each)

Good condition   Poor condition

....

....

....

· 6 ·

CONCEPTION AND EVALUATION OF GRADUATE WORK
(Answer primarily with your own institution in mind, unless otherwise stated)   9/x

23. How would you rank the major tasks of the graduate school, in order of their importance?
(Rate for each column, 1 to 5)

	In the phys. sci.	In the biol. sci.	In the soc. sci.	In the humanities	In professional programs
Training research scholars					
Training college teachers					
Training professional practitioners (e.g., clinical psychologists, industrial chemists, etc.)					
Doing basic research					
Doing applied research, consulting, etc.					

35/x

24. How would you say the graduate faculty, as a whole, feels about the state of graduate training at your institution?

Well satisfied ☐ 0   Dissatisfied ☐ 2   36—
Satisfied ☐ 1   Quite dissatisfied ☐ 3
          Can't say ☐ 4

25. On the whole, how do you think the quality of the doctoral program at your institution now compares with that before World War II?

Better then ☐ 6   About same ☐ 7   37—
Better now ☐ 8   Can't say ☐ 9

a) How about the quality of the Master's program?

Better then ☐ 0   About same ☐ 1   38—
Better now ☐ 2   Can't say ☐ 3

b) In general, how about graduate work at most other institutions you know?

Better then ☐ 5   About same ☐ 6   39—
Better now ☐ 7   Can't say ☐ 8

26. In the current debate over graduate education, there are two points of view about what graduate study is for—what its major aim or purpose is or ought to be. Put oversimply for sharpness, they are represented by these terms:

Professional Conception		*Academic Conception*
Training	as against	Education
Development of skills	as against	Development of wisdom
Development of depth	as against	Development of breadth
Specialist	as against	Cultivated man
Technical expert	as against	Scholar-Teacher

Where do you think the emphasis is at your institution, and where should it be?

	Is	*Should be*
More with professional conception	☐ 0	☐ 4
More with academic conception	☐ 1	☐ 5
Can't say	☐ 2	☐ 6

40—

10-	15-	20-	25-	30-
11-	16-	21-	26-	31-
12-	17-	22-	27-	32-
13-	18-	23-	28-	33-
14-	19-	24-	29-	34-

• 7 •

27. As you know, there has been a good deal of criticism of graduate education in the past few years (e.g., the Committee of Fifteen, the report of the AGS Committee, the report of the Carnegie Foundation, etc.). On the whole, how do you feel about such criticism?

On the whole, justified .... ☐ 0   On the whole, not justified ... ☐ 2

Justified in part .... ☐ 1   Can't say .... ☐ 3   41—

28. Another criticism of the graduate school is that within departments it usually offers the same program of doctoral study for three different kinds of people—those who will become researchers, those who will become college teachers, and those who will become professional practitioners (e.g., clinical psychologists, industrial chemists, etc.). What is your view on this matter?

Single program is best for all .... ☐ 5

Single program may not be best, but it's the only practicable one .... ☐ 6

Single program is seriously deficient and should be changed .... ☐ 7   42—

Other (specify) .... ☐ 8

....

29. There is currently a good deal of controversy over the appropriate national distribution of the doctoral load in the next few years—that is, whether it should be carried primarily by the institutions already well established in the field or spread out to the newer graduate schools. What are your views?

Would be desirable to limit doctoral training to the major established institutions, if possible .... ☐ 0

Established institutions should be filled first, then other institutions should expand as necessary .... ☐ 1   43—

Newer entrants into doctoral training should be encouraged to expand right now .... ☐ 2

Can't say .... ☐ 3

a) Do you think that some institutions not really qualified for doctoral work are jeopardizing standards by expanding too rapidly?

Yes ☐ 5   No ☐ 6   Can't say ☐ 7   44—

30. As you know, many people are concerned about where the college teachers are going to come from to meet the expected bulge in college enrollments, and they are critical of the graduate school for not "facing up to this problem." What do you think?

The graduate school is now doing a good job on this score, and the criticism is unjustified .... ☐ 0

The graduate school would be willing to do more, if a realistic program were put forward .... ☐ 1   45—

Whether it should do something or not, the graduate school can't really do much more than it is now about preparing college teachers without changing character, lowering standards, etc. .... ☐ 2

The graduate school is not really facing up to the problem, and should do much more .... ☐ 3

Can't say .... ☐ 4

If should do more: What should be done, in your view?

a) Where are the college teachers going to come from, in your view?

b) What can or should the graduate school do about the problem?

• 8 •

31. Some people believe that under the pressures of the years ahead, the independent liberal arts colleges will be able to attract only the less able Ph.D.'s, on the average, in competition with the major universities and industry. What is the experience of your institution in this regard?   46—

         Already happening .... □ 1 } If only in certain
         Probably will happen .... □ 2 } fields, which ones: 47—
         No sign now, and no likeli-
         hood .... □ 0 ....
         Can't say .... □ x ....

  a) Do you have any serious question about the quality of some of the academic institutions to which doctorates from your university go—in terms of what they can offer in intellectual opportunities, academic atmosphere, etc.?

         Yes, in many cases .... □ 0   No, or only in a few .... □ 2   48—
         Yes, in some cases .... □ 1   Can't say .... □ 3

32. By and large, would you say that the quality of the graduate students at your institution is as good now as it was, say, just before World War II, despite the increase in numbers?

     Better now □ 5   Worse now □ 6   About the same □ 7   Can't say □ 8   49—

33. By and large, how good is each of the following aspects of the undergraduate preparation of the students you admit to graduate study?

	Satisfactory	Unsatisfactory	Can't say	
Foreign languages	□ 0	□ 1	□ 2	
Writing and organizing ability	□ 5	□ 6	□ 7	50—
Preparation in major subject field	□ 0	□ 1	□ 2	
Preparation in related fields	□ 5	□ 6	□ 7	51—
General background of liberal education	□ 0	□ 1	□ 2	
Ability to work on their own	□ 5	□ 6	□ 7	52—
Other (..)	□ 0	□ 1	□ 2	53—
				54—

34. As you know, there has been a lot of talk recently about how long the doctorate takes.

  a) Do you consider that the **total elapsed time** (in calendar years) from starting graduate work to getting the degree, is too long or not?

         Too long □ 0   Not too long □ 1   Can't say □ 2   55—

  b) How about the time **actually spent** working on the degree?

     Too long □ 4   Too short □ 5   About right □ 6   Can't say □ 7   56—

  c) About how long **should** it take a qualified student to get the doctorate degree, in your judgment?

         .... years (full-time equivalent of actual work on the degree, to nearest half-year)   57—
         58—

35. Two justifications are usually given for the foreign language requirement for the doctorate: (1) the cultural justification that foreign languages are needed as a mark of the educated man; and (2) the professional justification that the languages are needed as a tool for research in the discipline. Which justification seems more important to you?

         Cultural .... □ 0   Both equally .... □ 2   59—
         Professional .... □ 1   Can't say .... □ 3

36. How does graduate study in this country compare in quality with similar levels of education abroad, so far as you know?

	U.S. better	Foreign country better	About same	Can't say	
With Great Britain	□ 0	□ 1	□ 2	□ 3	
With West Germany	□ 5	□ 6	□ 7	□ 8	60—
With France	□ 0	□ 1	□ 2	□ 3	
With U.S.S.R.	□ 5	□ 6	□ 7	□ 8	61—

• 9 •

37. As you know, there has been considerable discussion in the last few years about the national organization of graduate study. What is your opinion?

The present situation is satisfactory, by and large .... □ 0

There should be a single strong, comprehensive, central organization of graduate schools .... □ 1   62—

If so: About how many schools should be in it? ....   63—

Should it have a full-time secretariat or staff?   64—

Yes □ 3   No □ 4   65—

What briefly, should be its major functions?   66—

• 10 •

CRITICISMS AND REFORMS

38. The following specific points have been made in the criticisms directed at the graduate schools over the past few years. A few of them may overlap earlier questions but are included here for comparability with other groups. On the whole, how do you feel about each of them?

1/39
2—
3—
4—
5/x

	Agree strongly	Agree	Can't say	Disagree	Disagree strongly	
a) Graduate work isn't well articulated with undergraduate work, making for waste, repetition, poor sequence in learning, etc.	☐ 0	☐ 1	☐ 2	☐ 3	☐ 4	6—
b) Doctoral work suffers because many students don't really want to be researchers but have to go through research programs in order to get the "union badge" for college teaching	☐ 6	☐ 7	☐ 8	☐ 9	☐ .x	7—
c) Doctoral programs should be "loosened", by placing more responsibility upon the student and encouraging him to do more independent work	☐ 0	☐ 1	☐ 2	☐ 3	☐ 4	8—
d) Doctoral programs should be "tightened" and regularized, more like the training programs in medical and law schools	☐ 6	☐ 7	☐ 8	☐ 9	☐ x	9—
e) Doctoral candidates preparing for college teaching don't get enough training in teaching while in graduate school	☐ 0	☐ 1	☐ 2	☐ 3	☐ 4	10—
f) Doctoral candidates preparing for college teaching don't get enough background in the history, problems, and philosophy of the American college	☐ 6	☐ 7	☐ 8	☐ 9	☐ x	11—
g) The graduate schools aren't doing a good job of initial selection of candidates for the doctorate at the time of admission	☐ 0	☐ 1	☐ 2	☐ 3	☐ 4	12—
h) Doctoral programs stress techniques and skills too much, at the expense of broad understanding, cultivation, and wisdom	☐ 6	☐ 7	☐ 8	☐ 9	☐ x	13—
i) There is too little provision for social contact among graduate students, so that they are isolated and personally unhappy during the course of doctorate study	☐ 0	☐ 1	☐ 2	☐ 3	☐ 4	14—
j) Too many courses are offered at the graduate level by most departments	☐ 6	☐ 7	☐ 8	☐ 9	☐ x	15—
k) Graduate work would be done better if the graduate faculty did not also have to handle undergraduate work	☐ 0	☐ 1	☐ 2	☐ 3	☐ 4	16—
l) Graduate students do not clearly know what they must do to get the doctorate and are not counselled well on the way (i.e., there are ill-defined expectations and inadequate guidance)	☐ 6	☐ 7	☐ 8	☐ 9	☐ x	17—
m) Major professors often exploit doctoral candidates by keeping them as research assistants too long, by subordinating their interests to departmental or the professor's interests in research programs, etc.	☐ 0	☐ 1	☐ 2	☐ 3	☐ 4	18—

• 11 •

n) The foreign language requirement at the doctoral level has come to be a form without much substance in a sizable proportion of cases .... ☐ 6 ☐ 7 ☐ 8 ☐ 9 ☐ x **19—**

o) Doctoral candidates get too little direct attention, supervision, and guidance on their dissertations from their major professors, and that makes for unnecessary prolonging of the period of doctoral study .... ☐ 0 ☐ 1 ☐ 2 ☐ 3 ☐ 4 **20/x** **21—**

p) Doctoral programs of training for research are so onerous and distasteful that they repel almost as many people from research work as they attract .... ☐ 6 ☐ 7 ☐ 8 ☐ 9 ☐ x **22—**

q) Doctoral training for research is inefficient and wasteful because so few recipients of the degree become productive researchers in the field .... ☐ 0 ☐ 1 ☐ 2 ☐ 3 ☐ 4 **23—**

r) With the numbers of students now involved in doctoral study, it has become almost impossible to provide the basic necessity of research training, namely, proper apprenticeship relations .... ☐ 6 ☐ 7 ☐ 8 ☐ 9 ☐ x **24—**

s) Under the impact of numbers, the standards of doctoral study are being jeopardized .... ☐ 0 ☐ 1 ☐ 2 ☐ 3 ☐ 4 **25—**

t) Under the impact of numbers, the quality of the students in doctoral programs is declining ☐ 6 ☐ 7 ☐ 8 ☐ 9 ☐ x **26—**

u) The quality of doctoral work is limited these days by the fact that most students are motivated by the practical objective of getting a job rather than the objective of becoming a research scholar .... ☐ 0 ☐ 1 ☐ 2 ☐ 3 ☐ 4 **27—**

v) The practice of having graduate students and undergraduates in the same classes lowers the quality of graduate instruction .... ☐ 6 ☐ 7 ☐ 8 ☐ 9 ☐ x **28—**

w) Doctoral candidates are too often allowed or encouraged to attempt a major contribution as their dissertation rather than to take on a manageable topic that can be finished in a reasonable time .... ☐ 0 ☐ 1 ☐ 2 ☐ 3 ☐ 4 **29—**

x) Doctoral dissertations, at least outside the sciences, are too long .... ☐ 6 ☐ 7 ☐ 8 ☐ 9 ☐ x **30—**

y) The doctoral dissertation should be regarded more as a training instrument than as an "original contribution to knowledge" .... ☐ 0 ☐ 1 ☐ 2 ☐ 3 ☐ 4 **31—**

z) The graduate schools have wrongly allowed the Master's degree to deteriorate in quality ☐ 6 ☐ 7 ☐ 8 ☐ 9 ☐ x **32—**

aa) The doctoral dissertation is too often a pedantic or trivial exercise rather than an intellectual experience of genuine substance and interest .... ☐ 0 ☐ 1 ☐ 2 ☐ 3 ☐ 4 **33—**

bb) Doctoral candidates should be required to get through their programs more quickly .... ☐ 6 ☐ 7 ☐ 8 ☐ 9 ☐ x **34—**

cc) The doctoral program is designed too much for the students of average competence rather than for the brilliant students .... ☐ 0 ☐ 1 ☐ 2 ☐ 3 ☐ 4 **35—**

• 12 •

	Agree strongly	Agree	Can't say	Disagree	Disagree strongly	
dd) The first year of graduate study toward the doctorate is often repetitive of the under-graduate program	☐ 6	☐ 7	☐ 8	☐ 9	☐ x	36—
ee) Doctoral work is conceived too much as pro-fessional training, oriented to practice, rather than as academic learning, oriented to schol-arship	☐ 0	☐ 1	☐ 2	☐ 3	☐ 4	37—
ff) The atmosphere in graduate schools tends to lessen people's interest in and respect for undergraduate teaching	☐ 6	☐ 7	☐ 8	☐ 9	☐ x	38—
gg) The graduate schools unduly stress research and research training at the cost of properly preparing college teachers	☐ 0	☐ 1	☐ 2	☐ 3	☐ 4	39/x 40—
hh) Doctoral programs are too specialized and narrow	☐ 6	☐ 7	☐ 8	☐ 9	☐ x	41—
ii) Doctoral programs are insufficiently special-ized	☐ 0	☐ 1	☐ 2	☐ 3	☐ 4	42—
jj) One basic trouble with graduate school is that faculty members do not consider the students as their main responsibility (as com-pared to their own research, consultation and service jobs, administration, etc.)	☐ 6	☐ 7	☐ 8	☐ 9	☐ x	43—
kk) The rigors of doctoral study tend to discour-age the brightest, most imaginative students in favor of the conscientious plodders	☐ 0	☐ 1	☐ 2	☐ 3	☐ 4	44—
ll) Too much of what the graduate school does, and how it does it, is adversely affected by the sources of funds, e.g., contract grants sup-porting dissertation research in the sciences	☐ 6	☐ 7	☐ 8	☐ 9	☐ x	45—
mm) The final oral examination, or defense of the dissertation, is only a ritual now, without a useful function	☐ 0	☐ 1	☐ 2	☐ 3	☐ 4	46—
nn) As it operates, the doctoral program produces too much anxiety in many students, and un-necessarily so	☐ 6	☐ 7	☐ 8	☐ 9	☐ x	47—
oo) Graduate training too often has the unfortu-nate effect of dampening the student's en-thusiasm for learning and scholarship	☐ 0	☐ 1	☐ 2	☐ 3	☐ 4	48—
pp) Students aren't made to work hard enough in graduate school, especially as compared to the major professional schools	☐ 6	☐ 7	☐ 8	☐ 9	☐ x	49—

• 13 •

39. Here are some suggested reforms or changes in graduate education that have been advocated in recent years. What do you think of each of them?

	Agree strongly	Agree	Can't say	Disagree	Disagree strongly	
a) Set up two degree programs at the Ph.D. level —one for researchers, one for college teachers	☐ 0	☐ 1	☐ 2	☐ 3	☐ 4	50—
b) Introduce a new intermediary, 2-year degree between the Master's and the Ph.D., specially designed for college teachers; somewhat broader than the Ph.D. program, and with less research emphasis	☐ 6	☐ 7	☐ 8	☐ 9	☐ x	51—
c) Make the Ph.D. readily available for fulfillment of three years of acceptable work, and give additional training at the post-doctoral level for the few really able researchers	☐ 0	☐ 1	☐ 2	☐ 3	☐ 4	52—
d) Allow, or even encourage, shorter dissertations	☐ 6	☐ 7	☐ 8	☐ 9	☐ x	53—
e) Allow dissertations of 50-100 pages (in fields where that is not common now)	☐ 0	☐ 1	☐ 2	☐ 3	☐ 4	54—
f) Cut down on the foreign language requirement	☐ 6	☐ 7	☐ 8	☐ 9	☐ x	55—
g) Leave the foreign language requirement up to each department rather than the graduate school as a whole	☐ 0	☐ 1	☐ 2	☐ 3	☐ 4	56—
h) If at all possible, require publication of the dissertation in some form, as a way to maintain standards of doctoral study	☐ 6	☐ 7	☐ 8	☐ 9	☐ x	57—
i) Require all doctoral candidates to do some undergraduate teaching, under supervision	☐ 0	☐ 1	☐ 2	☐ 3	☐ 4	58—
j) Develop more interdepartmental and similar programs, as a way of broadening doctoral study	☐ 6	☐ 7	☐ 8	☐ 9	☐ x	59—
k) Restore the standards of the Master's degree, as a way to get more college teachers	☐ 0	☐ 1	☐ 2	☐ 3	☐ 4	60—

40. Finally: What do you consider the **single most important problem** of graduate study today?

61—

b) If you could institute **one change** of policy or practice in graduate study, what would it be?

62—

• 14 •

I'd be glad to get any additional comments you care to make about the state of
graduate education—what's right and wrong in the system, what the problems are, what
ought to be done about them, the points I ought to make and the policies I ought to
recommend in my report, etc. Please add your comments here.

And again, many thanks for your help.

63—

64—

65—

66—

67—

68—

69—

70—

2. QUESTIONNAIRE TO GRADUATE FACULTY MEMBERS

• 1 •

BACKGROUND DATA

1. Name .... a) Year of birth .... b) Sex: M ☐ 1 F ☐ 2   8—

2. Position (rank and department) 9/x

Institution ....

   a) What is considered the normal teaching load in your department? .... hours a week   19/x

   b) Have you ever taught full-time in an independent liberal arts college? Yes ☐ 0   No ☐ 1   20—

   c) Are you a member of the graduate faculty at your institution? .... Yes ☐ 3   No ☐ 4   21—

   d) About how many books or articles of a research or scholarly character have you published in
the past five years? ....   22—

   e) About how many doctoral dissertations are you now supervising as major sponsor? ....   25—

   f) Roughly, what has been the distribution of your teaching load the past few years?

        0 ☐ Only graduate instruction

        1 ☐ Mainly graduate instruction, but some undergraduate

        2 ☐ About equally graduate and undergraduate instruction

        3 ☐ Mainly undergraduate, but some graduate

        ·4 ☐ Only undergraduate instruction   28—

        5 ☐ No teaching (research or administration, mainly)

        6 ☐ Other (specify ....)

3. Earned degrees

	Year	Institution	Field or discipline	
Bachelor's				29/x
Master's				
Doctorate				
If not Ph.D. what was it?				
....				55/x

4. Your father's major occupation ....   56—

Your father's highest level of formal education ....   57—

10-	13-	17-
11-	14-	18-
12-	15-	
	16-	

BA: 30-	MA: 38-	O: 46-
31-	39-	47-
		48-
32-	40-	49-
33-	41-	50-
34-	42-	51-
35-	43-	52-
36-	44-	53-
37-	45-	54-

• 2 •

5. I'd like to get some information on your period of doctorate study. (If you don't have the doctorate, just skip this question.)

a) Amount of **elapsed time** (calendar years) between your start on graduate work toward the doctorate and the award of the degree.

.... years   58—

b) Number of years, in **full-time equivalent,** spent in work directly involved in securing the degree (including work on the dissertation) —that is, how long it **really** took you to get the degree if you had been doing nothing else.

.... years   61—

[If you had a research assistantship and the work was used for your dissertation, count that amount here.]

c) If b) is less than a): What else did you do between starting graduate work toward the doctorate and receiving the doctoral degree? (Give answers in amount of time, to nearest ½-year of full-time equivalent.)

Academic employment at the doctorate institution **not** directed to securing the degree (e.g., teaching assistant) ....   64—

Other academic or educational employment ....   67—

Non-academic employment ....   70—

Other (*specify*) ....   73—

1/2x
2—
6. Now a few other figures related to the duration of your doctoral program.   3—

a) Counting from the time you started graduate work toward the doctorate, how long did you spend in **full-time** work toward the degree (to nearest ½-year)?   4—
5—
.... years   6—

b) For the same period, how long did you spend in **full-time** employment **not** directed toward the degree?

.... years   9—

c) As a rough indication, how long did it take you to do your dissertation in total time spent working on it? (Include any time as a research assistant if the work went directly into your dissertation.)

.... years   12—

d) Did you complete the doctorate in one continuous period or was your work toward it interrupted or seriously delayed by **full-time** work on something else?

Continuous ☐ 0   Interrupted ☐ 1   15—

7. As a rough estimate, about how many doctoral candidates for whom you are **the major** thesis advisor have completed everything for the degree except the dissertation **and** are now on a job away from the campus?

....   16—

a) About how many of them would you estimate are still actively after the degree?   19—
....

b) About how many of them hold teaching positions in colleges and universities?   22—
....

c) Is this problem of uncompleted dissertations, after completion of all other requirements for the doctorate, a serious one in your department?

Yes ☐ 3   No ☐ 4   Can't say ☐ 5   25—

8. Thinking only of those students seeking the doctorate, about how much could your department expand that enrollment within your present facilities and without lowering standards—assuming you could get qualified students? In your view, how much should the department expand?

	Could	Should	
None	☐ 0	☐ 0	26—
Up to 10%	☐ 1	☐ 1	
10% - 25%	☐ 2	☐ 2	
25% - 50%	☐ 3	☐ 3	
50% - 100%	☐ 4	☐ 4	27—
Over 100%	☐ 5	☐ 5	
Can't say	☐ 6	☐ 6	

• 3 •

9. Has the load of work **not** directly involved in teaching or research increased markedly for you or your colleagues in recent years—i.e., administration, consultation, conferences, committee work, service jobs, etc.

Yes ☐   No ☐ 0   Can't say ☐ 5   28—

If Yes: Is this development interfering with graduate training, in your judgment, by taking you or your colleagues away from direct work with graduate students?

Yes ☐ 1   No ☐ 2   Can't say ☐ 3   29/x

10. How would you rank your department among other graduate departments in your field in the U.S.?

First or second .... ☐ 0   Eleventh to twentieth .... ☐ 3
Third to fifth .... ☐ 1   Lower .... ☐ 4   30—
Sixth to tenth .... ☐ 2   Can't say .... ☐ 5

11. On the whole, how would you characterize the current state of health of your discipline nationally—its intellectual vigor, development, progress, etc.?

Very satisfactory .... ☐ 7   Adequate .... ☐ 9   31—
Quite satisfactory .... ☐ 8   Unsatisfactory .... ☐ x

12. a) In your field, is post-doctoral training becoming necessary or highly desirable for proper advancement?

Yes ☐ 0   No ☐ 1   Can't say ☐ 2   32—

b) Did you have a post-doctoral fellowship for study with a senior person at any stage in your career?

Yes ☐ 4   No ☐ 5   33—

13. The expansion and proliferation of the fields of knowledge themselves can make for problems in graduate education by presenting more material for the student to master. In your field, has this meant that doctoral candidates are now trained in a narrower portion of the total field than they were, say, before World War II?

Yes ☐ 7   No ☐ 8   Can't say ☐ 9   34—

14. Have there been any important innovations or experiments or changes in graduate education in your discipline in the past five years or so?

Yes ☐ 0   No ☐ 1   Can't say ☐ 2   35—

If Yes: Please describe briefly what they were.

15. Do doctoral students in your discipline at different universities get essentially the same training, in quality and scope?

Yes ☐ 4   No ☐ 5   Can't say ☐ 6   36—

16. On the whole, considering what the doctorate program should attract, what do you think of the quality of the student group now coming into graduate study?

Quality very good .... ☐ 0   Quality adequate .... ☐ 2   37—
Quality moderately good ...... ☐ 1   Quality inferior to proper requirements for the doctorate ☐ 3
                                                        Can't say .... ☐ 4

a) By and large, would you say that the quality of the graduate students in your department or discipline is as good as it was, say, just before World War II, despite the increase in numbers?

Better now .... ☐ 5   About the same .... ☐ 7   38—
Worse now .... ☐ 6   Can't say .... ☐ 8

b) Some people say that too few graduate students these days are genuinely dedicated to their studies and deeply interested in them—i.e., that students aren't really willing to work hard, that they don't take pains in their work, that they don't have the pride of craftsmanship. How true is this, in your experience?

True of none, or only a very
few .... ☐ 0   True of about 50% .... ☐ 3   39—
True of about 10% .... ☐ 1   True of well over half .... ☐ 4
True of about 25% .... ☐ 2   Can't say .... ☐ 5

• 4 •

17. By and large, what is your judgment of each of the following aspects of the undergraduate preparation of the graduate students in your field?

	Satisfactory	Unsatisfactory	Can't say	
Foreign languages	☐ 0	☐ 1	☐ 2	40—
Writing and organizing ability	☐ 4	☐ 5	☐ 6	41—
Preparation in major subject field	☐ 0	☐ 1	☐ 2	42—
Preparation in related fields	☐ 4	☐ 5	☐ 6	43—
General background of liberal education	☐ 0	☐ 1	☐ 2	44—
Ability to work on their own	☐ 4	☐ 5	☐ 6	45—
Other (specify _____)	☐ 0	☐ 1	☐ 2	46—

47—

a) Would you prefer graduate students in your discipline to have more undergraduate preparation in your own discipline than they now do, or not?

    0 ☐ More in my discipline   48—
    x ☐ Not more
    9 ☐ Can't say

If not: What undergraduate preparation would you prefer?

    2 ☐ Broad general education   49—
    ☐ More work in (name subjects) ....
    ....
    ....

    ☐ Other (specify below)

18. So far as doctoral students in your department are concerned, about how much attrition is there among those entering the training program?

Less than 10% don't finish	☐ 0	
From 10% - 25% don't finish	☐ 1	
From 25% –50% don't finish	☐ 2	50—
Over 50% don't finish	☐ 3	
Can't say	☐ 4	

a) Would you say that figure is too high for the reasonable efficiency of the training system, or is it acceptable considering all the requirements and imponderables of doctoral study?

    Too high ☐ 6   Acceptable ☐ 7   Can't say ☐ 8   51—

b) For the group that does not finish, which of these reasons are primarily involved, as far as you know? (Check as many as apply)

	Most important	Least important	
Lack intellectual ability to do work	☐ 0	☐ 0	52—
Lack necessary physical or emotional stamina	☐ 1	☐ 1	
Lack financial resources	☐ 2	☐ 2	
Found the degree wasn't necessary for what they wanted to do	☐ 3	☐ 3	53—
Disappointed in graduate study and quit	☐ 4	☐ 4	
Lack proper motivation	☐ 5	☐ 5	
Other reasons (specify _____)	☐ 6	☐ 6	

c) Do you consider such attrition an important problem of graduate education in your department?

    Yes ☐ 0   No ☐ 1   Can't say ☐ 2   54—

If Yes: Is the problem primarily one of admission policy and initial selection or primarily one of what happens during the degree program?

Primarily admission	☐ 4	Substantially both	☐ 6	55—
Primarily during program	☐ 5	Can't say	☐ 7	56/y

CONCEPTION AND EVALUATION OF GRADUATE WORK   64/x

19. How would you rank the major tasks of the graduate school in your field, in order of their importance?

	Rank	
Training college teachers	......	65—
Training research scholars	......	66—
Training professional practitioners ...	......	67—
Doing basic research	......	68—
Doing applied research	......	69—

20. By and large, how would you say you and your colleagues feel about the state of graduate training in your field at your institution?

	How you feel	*How most colleagues feel*	
Well satisfied	☐ 0	☐ 6	70—
Satisfied	☐ 1	☐ 7	
Dissatisfied	☐ 2	☐ 8	
Quite dissatisfied	☐ 3	☐ 9	71—
Can't say	☐ 4	☐ x	

a) On the whole, how do you think graduate work for the doctorate degree in your discipline and at your institution compares in quality with that before World War II?

	Your discipline	*Your institution*	
Better then	☐ 0	☐ 0	72—
Better now	☐ 1	☐ 1	
About same	☐ 2	☐ 2	73—
Can't say	☐ 3	☐ 3	

b) How about the Master's degree?

	Your discipline	*Your institution*	
Better then	☐ 5	☐ 5	74—
Better now	☐ 6	☐ 6	
About same	☐ 7	☐ 7	75—
Can't say	☐ 8	☐ 8	

21. What do you consider the most and least valuable parts of doctoral training in your field? *(Check as many as appropriate)*

	Most valuable	*Least valuable*	
Course work	☐ 0	☐ 0	76—
Independent reading	☐ 1	☐ 1	
Relation of student to major professor(s)	☐ 2	☐ 2	
His relation to fellow students	☐ 3	☐ 3	
Teaching assistantship	☐ 4	☐ 4	
Research assistantship	☐ 5	☐ 5	77—
Preparation for general examinations	☐ 6	☐ 6	
Dissertation work	☐ 7	☐ 7	
Other *(specify)*	☐ 8	☐ 8	

• 6 •

22. As you consider the situation realistically, where, if at all, would you change the present requirement for doctoral training in your field—where would you favor relaxing requirements somewhat and where would you make them still more demanding?

	OK as is	Would relax	Would demand more	Can't say
Qualifications for admission	0	1	2	3
Foreign languages	5	6	7	8
Course requirements	0	1	2	3
Dissertation	5	6	7	8
Independent work	0	1	2	3
Comprehensive examination	5	6	7	8
Final defense of dissertation	0	1	2	3
Training in teaching	5	6	7	8
Residence requirements	0	1	2	3
General quality of doctorate	5	6	7	8

23. At your institution, how would you compare the quality of instruction at the undergraduate and graduate levels, on the whole?

Better at undergraduate level ☐ 0　　About the same ☐ 2

Better at graduate level ☐ 1　　Can't say ☐ 3

a) In your discipline generally, across the national scene, how would you compare the quality of instruction?

Better at undergraduate level ☐ 5　　About the same ☐ 7

Better at graduate level ☐ 6　　Can't say ☐ 8

24. Considering what you think a Ph.D. (or other doctorate) in your field **ought** to know, how satisfied are you with what the current crop of Ph.D.'s actually do know?

Know less than a Ph.D. should ☐ 6

Know about as much as a Ph.D. should ☐ 7

Know more than a Ph.D. is expected to ☐ 8

Can't say ☐ 9

25. In your discipline, has the Master's degree generally become easier to get in the past 20 years or so, in respect to such requirements as a thesis, general examinations, foreign language, etc.?

Yes ☐ 0　　No ☐ 1　　Can't say ☐ 2

a) Would you say that the Master's degree in your department has come to be neglected relative to the doctorate?

No ☐ 4

Yes, but not matter of regret ☐ 5

Yes, and regrettable ☐ 6

Can't say ☐ 7

26. Consider the balance in doctoral study in your field, as between preparing for teaching and preparing for research. What is it now and what should it be?

	Is now	Should be
More preparation for research than for teaching	0	5
More preparation for teaching than for research	1	6
About equivalent preparation for both	2	7
Can't say	3	8

• 7 •

27. Many people are concerned about where the college teachers are going to come from to meet the expected bulge in college enrollments, and they are critical of the graduate school for not "facing up to this problem." What do you think, so far as your own field is concerned?

The graduate school is now doing a good job on this score, and the criticism is unjustified .... ☐ 0   **23—**

The graduate school would be willing to do more, if a realistic program were put forward .... ☐ 1

Whether it should do something or not, the graduate school can't really do much more about preparing college teachers without changing character, lowering standards, etc. .... ☐ 2

The graduate school is not really facing up to the problem and should do much more .... ☐ 3

Can't say .... ☐ 4

If should do more: What should be done, in your view?

   24—

   25/x

28. Some people believe that under the pressures of the years ahead, the liberal arts colleges will be able to attract, on the average, only the less able Ph.D.'s in competition with the universities and industry. Is this likely in your field?

Already happening .... ☐ 0   No sign now and no likelihood .... ☐ 2   **26—**

Probably will happen .... ☐ 1

Can't say .... ☐ 3

a) Do you have any serious questions about the quality of some of the academic institutions to which doctorates from your departments go—in terms of what they can offer in intellectual opportunities, academic atmosphere, etc.?

Yes, in many cases .... ☐ 5   No, or only in a few .... ☐ 7   **27—**

Yes, in some cases .... ☐ 6   Can't say .... ☐ 8

29. Do you think the undergraduate teacher in your discipline needs to be a productive research man (i.e., one who publishes papers in the learned journals) in order to be a good teacher?

Yes ☐ 0   No ☐ 1   Can't say ☐ 2   **28—**

a) Do you think the research training experience at the doctoral level, and particularly the dissertation, is necessary or desirable for the undergraduate teacher in your field?

Necessary .... ☐ 4   Not necessary and not desirable .... ☐ 5

Desirable but not really necessary .... ☐ 6   Can't say .... ☐ 7   **29—**

30. In the current debate over graduate education, there are two points of view about what graduate study is for—what its major aim or purpose is or ought to be. Put oversimply for sharpness, they are represented by these terms:

Professional Conception		Academic Conception
Training	as against	Education
Development of skills	as against	Development of wisdom
Development of depth	as against	Development of breadth
Specialist	as against	Cultivated man
Technical expert	as against	Scholar-Teacher

Where do you think the emphasis now lies, in your field, and where should it?

               Does   *Should*

More with professional conception .... ☐ 0   ☐ 4   **30—**

More with academic conception .... ☐ 1   ☐ 5

Can't say .... ☐ 2   ☐ 6   **31—**

• 8 •

31. Another criticism of the graduate school is that within departments it usually offers the same program of doctoral study for three different kinds of people—those who will become researchers, those who will become college teachers, and those who will become professional practitioners (e.g., clinical psychologists, industrial chemists, etc.). What is your view on this matter, in your own field?·

Single program is best for all .... ☐ 0

Single program may not be best, but it's the only practicable one .... ☐ 1   32—

Single program is seriously deficient and should be changed .... ☐ 2

Other *(specify)* .... ☐

....

Can't say .... ☐ 9

32. Do you think the present character of the dissertation in your field—what's required and allowed, how it's done, etc.—is about right or not?

About right ☐ 0   Not right ☐ 1   Can't say ☐ 2

If not right: What's wrong with it?   33—

    34—

a) Frankly, how do you feel about most of the dissertations done in your department—as you think of the return on the total investment of time and energy?

Very satisfied with them .... ☐ 0   Rather dissatisfied with them ☐ 2   35—

Fairly satisfied with them ...... ☐ 1   Very dissatisfied with them ☐ 3

                                       Can't say .... ☐ 4

b) Regardless of what the formal requirements are, do you think that the value of most dissertations in your department is primarily as an original contribution to knowledge or primarily as an exercise in research training for the student? In your view, which should it be?

	Is	*Should be*
Primarily contribution to knowledge	☐ 0	☐ 5 36—
Primarily research training	☐ 1	☐ 6
Both equally	☐ 2	☐ 7 37—
Can't say	☐ 3	☐ 8

c) As you know, there has been a lot of talk recently about how long the doctorate takes.

a) Do you consider that the **total elapsed** time (in calendar years), from starting graduate work to getting the degree, is too long or not?

Too long ☐ 0   Not too long ☐ 1   Can't say ☐ 2   38—

b) How about the time **actually spent** working on the degree?

Too long ☐ 4   Too short ☐ 5   About right ☐ 6   Can't say ☐ 7   39—

c) About how long **should** it take a qualified student to get the doctorate degree, in your judgment?

.... years (full-time equivalent of actual work on the degree, to nearest half-year)   40—

33. There is currently a good deal of controversy over the appropriate national distribution of the doctoral load in the next few years—that is, whether it should be carried primarily by the institutions already well established in the field or spread out to the newer graduate schools. What are your views, so far as your field is concerned?

Would be desirable to limit doctoral training to the major established institutions, if possible .... ☐ 0

Established institutions should be filled first, then other institutions should expand as necessary .... ☐ 1   43—

Newer entrants into doctoral training should be encouraged to expand right now .... ☐ 2

Can't say .... ☐ 3

• 9 •

a) Do you think that some institutions not really qualified for doctoral work in your field are jeopardizing standards by expanding too rapidly?

Yes ☐ 5   No ☐ 6   Can't say ☐ 7   44—

34. Two justifications are usually given for the foreign language requirement for the doctorate: (1) the cultural justification that foreign languages are needed as a mark of the educated man and (2) the professional justification that the languages are needed as a tool for research in the discipline. Which justification seems more important to you?

Cultural .... ☐ 0   Both equally .... ☐ 2   45—

Professional .... ☐ 1   Can't say .... ☐ 3

35. How does graduate study in your field in this country compare in quality with similar levels of education in Europe, so far as you know?

	U.S. better	Foreign country better	About same	Can't say	
With Great Britain	☐ 0	☐ 1	☐ 2	☐ 3	46—
With West Germany	☐ 5	☐ 6	☐ 7	☐ 8	47—
With France	☐ 0	☐ 1	☐ 2	☐ 3	48—
With U.S.S.R.	☐ 5	☐ 6	☐ 7	☐ 8	49—

36. In general, how closely do you, as major sponsor, work with your doctoral candidates on their dissertations; i.e., how much attention, direction, supervision, etc., do you give them?   50/x

Close and continuous supervision .... ☐ 0

Less, but sufficient for their purposes .... ☐ 1   51—

Hardly any; students should work mainly on their own .... ☐ 2

Can't say .... ☐ 3

a) One of the basic rationales underlying graduate training in research has to do with the value of the apprenticeship relationship of the doctorate candidate to his senior professor. On the whole, how satisfactory is this relationship, from your point of view?

Very satisfactory .... ☐ 5   Very unsatisfactory .... ☐ 8

Satisfactory .... ☐ 6   Can't say .... ☐ 9   52—

Unsatisfactory .... ☐ 7

37. How are most dissertation topics really selected, in your experience?

Student selects it independently .... ☐ 0

Student and sponsor jointly select it .... ☐ 1   53—

Sponsor really selects it .... ☐ 2

Can't say .... ☐ 3

38. How many doctoral candidates in your department do you get to know fairly well, on a professional basis?   54—

All of them .... ☐ 5   Only a few .... ☐ 8

Most of them .... ☐ 6   None .... ☐ 9

Several of them .... ☐ 7

Questions 39 and 40 are the same as questions 38 and 39 in Questionnaire to Graduate Deans

3. QUESTIONNAIRE TO RECENT RECIPIENTS OF THE DOCTORATE

• 1 •

BACKGROUND

1. Name .... **2.** Year of birth .... **3.** Sex: M ☐ 1   F ☐ 2   8—

9—

10—

4. Present position ....   11—
                                     (include rank and dept. where appropriate)

Institution or organization ....   12—

If in academic work: Do you teach or supervise graduate students?

0 ☐ Yes   1 ☐ No   16—

If this is not your first full-time job after receiving the doctorate, what was?

Position .... Institution 17/x

5. Educational background

	Year	Institution	Department or field
Bachelor's			
Master's			
Doctorate If not Ph.D., what was it?			

50/x

6. Marital Status:

	When you began doctorate study	*When you got the doctorate*	
Were you married?			51—
If yes: No. of children			52—

7. Your father's major occupation ....   53—

Your father's highest level of formal education ....   54—

FJ: 18-	BA: 25-	MA: 33-	O: 41-
19-	26-	34-	42-
20-			43-
21-	27-	35-	44-
22-	28-	36-	45-
23-	29-	37-	46-
24-	30-	38-	47-
	31-	39-	48-
	32-	40-	49-

• 2 •

8. About when did you really decide to go ahead for the doctorate?

By high school graduation	☐ 0
Early in college (first 2 years)	☐ 1
Late in college (last 2 years)	☐ 2
After college graduation	☐ 3
After Master's degree	☐ 4

55—

a) Who particularly influenced you to go to graduate school?

No one; decided to go pretty much on my own	☐ 0
High school teacher	☐ 1
Undergraduate teacher	☐ 2
Parents	☐ 3
College friends	☐ 4
Spouse	☐ 5
Other (specify)	☐ 6

56—

b) Did you seriously consider some other career choice? .... Yes ☐ No ☐ 0

If yes: Was your doctoral training in any sense the second choice? Yes ☐ 1 No ☐ 2

57—

9. How did you decide to go to the institution at which you took your doctorate work?

(Mark the three most important reasons — 1, 2, 3)

0 .... Location	6 .... Recommendation of undergraduate teachers
1 .... Low cost	
2 .... Prestige of institution	7 .... Employment possibilities associated with study there
3 .... Reputation of department	8 .... Special program of interest to you
4 .... Reputation of particular man or two	9 .... Just stayed on after undergraduate work there
5 .... Financial support from institution	x .... Other (specify) ....

58—

59—

a) Was this institution your first choice among those you applied to? Yes ☐ 0 No ☐ 1

60—

10. How would you now rank the department in which you took your doctorate, among other graduate departments in your field in the U.S.?

0 ☐ First or second	3 ☐ Eleventh to twentieth
1 ☐ Third to fifth	4 ☐ Lower
2 ☐ Sixth to tenth	5 ☐ Can't say

61—

11. How well pleased are you with your present position, for this stage of your career?

Thoroughly satisfied; no desire to change ...	☐ 6
Satisfied, but would consider a change	☐ 7
Somewhat dissatisfied; would change if I could	☐ 8
Thoroughly dissatisfied	☐ 9

62—

12. a) After receiving the doctorate, did you want or feel the need of a year or so of formal post-doctorate study (assuming appropriate support)?

Yes ☐ 0   No ☐ 1   Can't say ☐ 2

63—

b) Have you had, or do you plan to have, a year of post-doctorate study?

Yes, had or have now ☐ 4   Yes, plan to ☐ 5   No ☐ 6

64—

c) In your field, is post-doctoral training becoming necessary, or highly desirable, for proper advancement?

Yes ☐ 8   No ☐ 9   Can't say ☐ x

65—

• 3 •

13. How would you characterize the current state of health of your discipline—its intellectual vigor, development, progress, etc.?

Very satisfactory .... ☐ 6　　Adequate .... ☐ 8

Quite satsfactory .... ☐ 7　　Unsatisfactory .... ☐ 9　　**66—**

　　　　　　　　　　　　　　　　　　　　Can't say .... ☐ x

DURATION OF DOCTORAL PROGRAM

1/20

As you know, there is a lot of talk these days about the duration of doctoral programs. This is a difficult matter to collect information on by questionnaire because of the complicated character of many programs, but I hope the following questions will be satisfactory in your case. If not, please note below the additional information necessary to describe your situation accurately.

2—

3—

4—

5—

14. a) Number of elapsed years between your Bachelor's and Doctor's degrees (to nearest ½ year)

.... years　　**6—**

b) Number of elapsed years between your start on graduate work toward the doctorate and the award of the degree

.... years　　**9—**

c) Number of years, in <u>full-time equivalent</u>, spent in work <u>directly</u> involved in securing the degree (including work on the dissertation)—that is, how long it <u>really</u> took you to get the degree if you had been doing nothing else?

.... years　　**12—**

[If you had a research assistantship and the work was used for your dissertation, count that amount here.]

d) In your case, do you consider the amount of <u>elapsed</u> time (14.b) to be reasonable for getting the doctorate, too long or too short? How about the <u>actual</u> time (14.c)?

15—

16—
17—

	Elapsed time	Actual time
Reasonable, about right	☐ 0	☐ 5
Too long	☐ 1	☐ 6
Too short	☐ 2	☐ 7
Can't say	☐ 3	☐ 8

18—

If not reasonable: What would be?　........... years .... years

19—
20—

e) Finally, if too long, what mainly contributed to that? *(Check as many as apply.)*

	Elapsed time	Actual time
Inadequate undergraduate preparation	☐ 0	☐ 0
Family obligations, other work, money problems	☐ 1	☐ 1
Dissertation	☐ 2	☐ 2
Foreign language requirement	☐ 3	☐ 3
Unrealistic standards imposed by faculty	☐ 4	☐ 4
Unrealistic standards imposed by myself	☐ 5	☐ 5
Other *(specify)*	☐ 6	☐ 6

21—

22—

23—

• 4 •

15. a) <u>What else</u> did you do between getting the Bachelor's degree and starting graduate work toward the doctorate?

b) <u>What else</u> did you do between starting graduate work toward the doctorate and receiving the doctoral degree?

Give answers in <u>amount of time</u>, to nearest ½ year of full-time equivalent. (Incidentally, the years here and in 14.c may not add up to the elapsed time, e.g., if you were working full-time and doing your dissertation on the side.)

	a) Between Bachelor's and starting	*b) Between starting and getting degree*
Academic employment at the doctorate institution not directed to the degree (e.g., teaching assistant)	....	....
Other academic or educational employment	....	....
Non-academic employment	....	....
Other *(specify)*	....	....

24/x

Please use this space to clear up any ambiguity, apparent inconsistencies, or lack of clarity in the above account of the period in which you got the degree.

51/x

16. Now a few other data related to the duration of your doctoral program.

a) Counting from the time you started graduate work toward the doctorate, how long did you spend in <u>full-time</u> work on the degree (to nearest ½ year)?

.... years

52—

b) For the same period, how long did you spend in <u>full-time</u> employment <u>not</u> directed toward the degree?

.... years

55—

c) As a rough indication, how long did it take you to do your dissertation, in total time spent working directly on it? (Include any time as a research assistant if the work went directly into your dissertation.)

.... years

58—

d) Did you complete the doctorate in one continuous period or was your work toward it interrupted or seriously delayed by <u>full-time</u> work on something else?

Continuous ☐ 0   Interrupted ☐ 1

61—

25-27:	38-40:
28-30:	41-43:
31-33:	44-46:
34:	47:
35-37:	48-50:

• 5 ·•

CONDITIONS AND EVALUATION OF DOCTORAL WORK

17. ·During your graduate work, how much of the time did you have financial support of the following kinds (to nearest ½ year)?

Support, outside my own family, requiring no work from me, e.g., a fellowship .... years

Support requiring work that contributed directly to my degree, e.g., a research assistantship used for dissertation .... years

Support requiring work that did not contribute directly to the degree, e.g., a teaching assistantship .... years

Loans .... years

a) When you received the degree, were you $1,000 or more in debt as a result of getting the doctorate?

Yes ☐ 0   No ☐ 1

18. Among the students in your department, a number of people who started working for the doctorate never got it. Which of those reasons were involved, so far as you know?

	More important	Less important
Lack intellectual ability to do the work	☐ 0	☐ 0
Lack necessary physical or emotional stamina	☐ 1	☐ 1
Lack financial resources	☐ 2	☐ 2
Found the degree wasn't necessary for what they wanted to do	☐ 3	☐ 3
Disappointed in graduate study and quit	☐ 4	☐ 4
Lack proper motivation	☐ 5	☐ 5
Other reasons		
(specify)	☐ 6	☐ 6

19. People have different motives for seeking the doctorate—e.g., the academic objective of becoming a scholar and teacher and the practical objective of getting a job for which the degree is necessary or desirable. Recognizing that such motives are usually mixed, how would you describe why you and most of the students in your department were after the doctorate?

	Myself	Fellow students
Primarily practical	☐ 0	☐ 0
More practical than academic	☐ 1	☐ 1
Equally important	☐ 2	☐ 2
More academic than practical	☐ 3	☐ 3
Primarily academic	☐ 4	☐ 4
Can't say	☐ 5	☐ 5

20. On the whole, how would you describe the morale of yourself and your fellow students as you worked toward the doctorate?

	Myself	Fellow students
Consistently high	☐ 7	☐ 7
Consistently low	☐ 8	☐ 8
Fluctuated between high and low	☐ 9	☐ 9
Can't say	☐ x	☐ x

21. Some people say that graduate students learn a great deal from one another. In your experience, is that true?

Yes ☐ 0   No ☐ 1   Can't say ☐ 2

a) When you get right down to it, and taking everything into account, did you learn more from your fellow students or from your professors?

More from fellow students ... ☐ 4   About equal .... ☐ 6

More from professors .... ☐ 5   Can't say .... ☐ 7

• 6 •

22. How would you characterize your living arrangements and your social life while in graduate school?

	Living arrangements	Social life
Satisfactory	☐ 0	☐ 4
Unsatisfactory	☐ 1	☐ 5
Can't say	☐ 2	☐ 6

23. As a doctoral candidate, did you have a major professor who was in charge of your progress and to whom you looked for guidance, supervision, etc.?

Yes ☐   No ☐ 0   **28—**

If Yes: In effect, did you choose him or did he choose you?

I chose him .... ☐ 1   Mutual choice .... ☐ 3
He chose me .... ☐ 2   Can't say .... ☐ 4

a) How closely did your thesis advisor work with you on your doctoral dissertation; i.e., how much attention, direction, supervision, etc., did you get from him?

Too much supervision .... ☐ 0   Less, but sufficient for my
                                        purposes .... ☐ 2   **29—**
Close and continuous super-   Not enough .... ☐ 3
vision .... ☐ 1   Can't say .... ☐ 4

b) In general, how satisfactory was this "apprenticeship" relation from your point of view?

Very satisfactory .... ☐ 6   Unsatisfactory .... ☐ 8
Satisfactory .... ☐ 7   Very unsatisfactory .... ☐ 9   **30—**
                                        Can't say .... ☐ x

24. As for your dissertation:

a) How was your dissertation topic really selected?

You selected it independently .... ☐ 0   **31—**
You and your sponsor jointly selected it ...... ☐ 1
Sponsor really selected it .... ☐ 2
Can't say .... ☐ 3

b) Did you actually make a start on more than one dissertation topic?

Yes ☐ 5   No ☐ 6   **32—**

c) When did you really start work on the dissertation you submitted for the degree?

Before taking the qualifying or general ex-
amination in the subject .... ☐ 8   **33—**
After taking it .... ☐ 9

d) Did you do all or the major part of your dissertation while still at the university or did you do it away from the campus ?

At the university .... ☐ 0
Not at the university but in close contact
with my thesis sponsor .... ☐ 1   **34—**
Not at the university and not in close con-
tact with him .... ☐ 2

e) Now that it's done, how do you feel about your dissertation itself, as a piece of work (not as a requirement for the degree)—as you think of the return on your investment of time and energy?

Very satisfied with it .... ☐ 5   **35—**
Fairly satisfied with it .... ☐ 6
Rather dissatisfied with it .... ☐ 7
Very dissatisfied with it .... ☐ 8
Can't say .... ☐ 9   **36/x**

• 7 •

f) Which of the following comes closer to describing the way you now feel about the experience of writing a doctoral dissertation?

Exciting, enlightening intellectual experience	□ 0	
Tedious, pedantic drudgery; not worth the effort in itself, but necessary for the degree	□ 1	37—
In between—element of both	□ 2	

g) Regardless of what the formal requirements were, do you think that the value of your dissertation was primarily as an original contribution to knowledge in your field or primarily as an exercise in research training for yourself? In your view, which should it be?

	Was	*Should be*	
Primarily contribution to knowledge	□ 0	□ 5	38—
Primarily research training	□ 1	□ 6	
Both equally	□ 2	□ 7	39—
Can't say	□ 3	□ 8	

25. Some people say that doctoral candidates are too often subject to the political requirement of "touching base" with the important professors in their department, as a way of safeguarding the acquisition of the degree, getting good job recommendations, etc. Was this requirement bothersome or delaying in your case?

        Yes □ 0   No □ 1   Can't say □ 2   40—

26. As a graduate student, were there times when you felt you did not know where you stood with your major professor or the department —e.g., how far along you really were, how well you were doing, etc.?

Yes, often	□ 4	No .... □ 6	41—
Yes, occasionally	□ 5	Can't say .... □ 7	

27. How many faculty members in your department did you get to know fairly well, on a professional basis?

All of them	□ 0	Several of them .... □ 2	
Most of them	□ 1	Only a few .... □ 3	42—
		None .... □ 4	

28. Are you confident that you can rely on your major professor and/or the department for good recommendations, suggesting you for jobs, and otherwise helping your career?

        Yes □ 6   No □ 7   Can't say □ 8   43—

29. As it turned out, how good was each of the following aspects of your undergraduate preparation for graduate study?

	Satis-factory	*Unsatis-factory*	*Can't say*	
Foreign languages	□ 0	□ 1	□ 2	
Writing and organizing ability	□ 4	□ 5	□ 6	44—
Preparation in subject field	□ 0	□ 1	□ 2	
Preparation in related fields	□ 4	□ 5	□ 6	45—
General background of liberal education	□ 0	□ 1	□ 2	
Ability to work on your own	□ 4	□ 5	□ 6	46—
Other (....)	□ 0	□ 1	□ 2	47—

a) One of the problems of graduate education is its relation to undergraduate education. How do you feel about each of these statements: 48—

	Yes	*No*	*Can't say*	
Part of my graduate program was essentially a wasteful repetition of what I had already covered at the undergraduate level	□ 0	□ 1	□ 2	49—
The undergraduate training in my field was substantially behind the state of the field as presented at the graduate level	□ 4	□ 5	□ 6	50—
For my field of graduate study it is undesirable to have a strong undergraduate concentration in the same field	□ 8	□ 9	□ x	51—

• 8 •

30. In order to get your doctorate, you had to pass a foreign language requirement.

    a) Did you actually use the language(s) in your graduate training or in preparing your dissertation?

        Yes ☐ 0   No ☐ 1   52—

    b) Have you used them (or it) in your professional work since you got the degree?

        Yes ☐ 3   No ☐ 4   53—

    c) Do you feel you really know the language(s) in which you passed the necessary examinations?

        Yes ☐ 6   No ☐ 7   54—

31. How did you get your present job?

    Had it before I got the doctorate .... ☐ 0

    Got it primarily on my own .... ☐ 1.   55—

    Got it primarily through my major professor .... ☐ 2

    Get it primarily through the department ...... ☐ 3

    Got it primarily through the placement office of the institution .... ☐ 4

    Got it by chance .... ☐ 5.

    Other (specify ....) ☐ 6

32. As nearly as you can now tell, how good was your doctoral program in training you for the position you now hold?

    Very good .... ☐ 0   Just adequate .... ☐ 2

    Fairly good .... ☐ 1   Unsatisfactory .... ☐ 3   56—

                                        Quite poor .... ☐ 4

If only adequate or worse: Where in particular does the training fall short?   57—

33. Taking everything into account, how do you feel about the graduate work leading to your doctorate—what you got out of it compared with what it cost in time and energy and money?

    Very satisfied .... ☐ 6   Dissatisfied .... ☐ 8

    Satisfied .... ☐ 7   Very dissatisfied .... ☐ 9   58—

                                         Can't say .... ☐ x

If dissatisfied: What, briefly, are the major reasons for your dissatisfaction?

34. What do you now consider the parts of your doctoral training that were particularly valuable? Which were of relatively little value?

	Particularly valuable	Of little value
Course work	☐ 0	☐ 0
Independent reading	☐ 1	☐ 1
Relation to major professor(s)	☐ 2	☐ 2
Relation to fellow students	☐ 3	☐ 3
Teaching assistantship	☐ 4	☐ 4
Research assistantship	☐ 5	☐ 5
Preparing for general examinations	☐ 6	☐ 6
Dissertation work	☐ 7	☐ 7
Other (specify ....)	☐ 8	☐ 8

59—

60—

• 9 •

35. In the current debate over graduate education, there are two points of view about what graduate study is for—what its major aim or purpose is and ought to be. Put oversimply for sharpness, they are represented by these terms:

Professional Conception		*Academic Conception*
Training	as against	Education
Development of skills	as against	Development of wisdom
Development of depth	as against	Development of breadtth
Specialist	as against	Cultivated man
Technical expert	as against	Scholar-Teacher

In your experience, where <u>did</u> the emphasis lie? In your view, where <u>should</u> it?

	My experience	My preference	
More with professional conception	☐ 0	☐ 4	**61—**
More with academic conception	☐ 1	☐ 5	**62—**
Can't say	☐ 2	☐ 6	

36. As you think back on it, how would you compare the quality of teaching and training that you received at different levels of education? That is, compare how the high school did its job with how the college did its job and with how the graduate school did its job. How would you rank them (1, 2, 3)?

High school	....	**63—**
College	....	**64—**
Graduate school	....	**65—**

37. About when, on the way to the doctorate, did you come to think of yourself as a scholar or scientist rather than a student?

When you began graduate work	☐ 0
During period of course work	☐ 1
When you passed the preliminary examination for the doctorate	☐ 2
When you really got into the dissertation	☐ 3
When you passed the dissertation defense and were awarded the degree	☐ 4
Other (*specify when*)	☐ 5
Not yet	☐ x

66—

a) Do you now feel confident that you could creditably undertake an independent program of research?

Yes ☐ 9   Perhaps ☐ 1   No ☐ 2   Can't say ☐ 3   **67—**

38. Considering what you think a recipient of the doctorate in your field <u>ought</u> to know, how satisfied are you with what you actually did know when you got the degree?

Knew less than a doctorate should	☐ 5	**68—**
Knew about as much as he should	☐ 6	
Knew more than he is expected to	☐ 7	
Can't say	☐ 8	

39. If you had it to do over, would you still work for a doctorate?

Yes ☐ x   No ☐ 0   Can't say ☐ 5   **69—**

If yes: Would you take essentially the some program that you did take?

Yes ☐ 1   No ☐ 2   Can't say ☐ 3   **70—**

Would you go to the same institution?   **71/x**

Yes ☐ 7.   No ☐ 8   Can't say ☐ 9   **72—**

a) Would you be willing to undertake the same program if there were no degree, or its equivalent, awarded at the end—just for the learning involved?

Yes ☐ 0   No ☐ 1   Can't say ☐ 2   **73—**

What percentage of your fellow students do you think would have been willing to?

.... %   Can't say ☐ x   **74—**

• 10 •

40. If you now do any undergraduate teaching:

a) What is the normal teaching load at your institution?

.... Hours a week

75—
76—

b) Was there sufficient training in <u>how</u> to teach in your doctoral program?

Yes ☐ 4   No ☐ 5

77—

c) Was the teaching assistantship, or similar teaching experience, while in graduate school really helpful to you in your present position?

Yes ☐ 7   No ☐ 8   Had none ☐ 9

78—

d) Some say that if recent recipients of the doctorate are dissatisfied in their academic posts, that is a re-flection on their graduate training. Others say that it is more the fault of the institutions to which they go, in that they do not equal the intellectual opportunities or academic atmosphere of the graduate university. What would you say?

Graduate training primarily at fault .... ☐ 0	Both really at fault .... ☐ 2	
Local institution primarily at fault .... ☐ 1	Neither at fault .... ☐ 3	
	Can't say .... ☐ 4	

79—

If local institution: In what way?

80—

CRITICISMS AND REFORMS

Questions 41 and 42 are the same as questions 38 and 39 in Questionnaire to Graduate Deans

1/40
2—
3—
4—

4. QUESTIONNAIRE TO COLLEGE PRESIDENTS

• 1 •

BACKGROUND INFORMATION

1/1y

Name ....   2—

Position ....   5—

Institution ....   6—

Your academic field or department ....   10—

Your highest earned degree ....   12—

    From what institution? .... Year when awarded ....   13—

1. a) About how many undergraduates were enrolled at your institution in Fall 1958? ....   17—

    b) As a rough guess, how many do you anticipate or plan to have in about five years? ....

    c) Roughly what percentage of your graduates in the past few years have gone on

        to graduate school (arts and sciences) .... %   19—

        to professional school (medicine, law, etc.) .... %   20—

2. Does your college have any special programs or arrangements to encourage your students to go on to graduate school—that is, to recruit for graduate study and college teaching?

    If Yes: Please describe briefly.   Yes ☐ 0   No ☐ 1   21—

3. Does your institution regularly give graduate degrees?

                                              Yes ☐ y   No ☐ 0   22—

    If Yes: Which ones? ....

    a) About how many graduate students did you have in residence this year? 23/x

    b) Do you have any plans to expand at the graduate level, either in number of students or types of degrees?

        Yes, in numbers of students   ☐ 0   Yes, in both .... ☐ 2   24—

        Yes, in types of degrees .... ☐ 1   No .... ☐ 3

        If in types of degrees, which ones do you plan to offer, and in what fields? ....

        ....   25—

4. a) About how many regular faculty members are there at your institution? ....   26—

    b) About how many of them now have the doctorate degree? ....   27—

    c) About how many new members joined your faculty in the last four years (total)? ....   28—

    d) About how many, as a rough estimate, do you anticipate adding in the next four years? ....   29—

5. In seeking new faculty members, do you go to the graduate schools for them?

        Yes, regularly ☐ 0   Yes, occasionally ☐ 1·   Not often ☐ 2   30—

    If Yes: Which three or four schools do you generally try first?

    If Not often: Why not?   31—

    32—

    33/x

· 2 ·

6. What is considered the normal teaching load at your institution? .... hours a week **34—**

                                 35—

7. Many colleges have on their staffs some faculty members who have completed all their requirements for the doctorate except the dissertation, and who are still working on it when and as they can. About how many are there at your institution? .... **36—**

 a) Do you consider it highly desirable for most of them to complete their degrees, or do you think it doesn't matter so much, now that they're in active teaching?

     Highly desirable ☐ 4   Doesn't matter ☐ 5   Can't say ☐ 6 **37—**

 b) Would you welcome a program that would enable most of them to complete their work for the degree, even if that would take them away from campus from six months to a year?

     Would welcome ☐ 8 Would not welcome ☐ 9 Can't say ☐ x **38—**

8. About what percentage of the teaching at your institution is done **outside** the discipline in which the instructor received his highest earned degree (e.g., chemists teaching general science, or sociologists teaching psychology)?

    None .... ☐ 0   From 25% to 50% .... ☐ 3

    Less than 10% .... ☐ 1   Over 50% .... ☐ 4 **39—**

    From 10% to 25% .... ☐ 2   Can't say .... ☐ 5

9. Some colleges are finding it necessary to develop more research opportunities and facilities for the faculty in order to attract top people in competition with the major universities. What is your experience in this regard?

    Already true here .... ☐ 0   Neither true now nor likely

    Not true yet, but probably   in near future .... ☐ 2 **40—**

     coming .... ☐ 1   Can't say .... ☐ 3

 a) Do you consider this development a desirable one or not?

      Desirable ☐ 5   Undesirable ☐ 6 Can't say ☐ 7 **41—**

10. Is there a tendency at your institution for the lower academic ranks to teach proportionately more of the elementary courses and the higher ranks to teach the advanced ones, or is the load distributed pretty evenly?

  Lower ranks teach more elementary courses ☐ 0   Load distributed evenly .... ☐ 2

  Upper ranks teach more elementary courses ☐ 1   Can't say .... ☐ 3 **42—**

 a) Is there any special effort to allow the new young teacher to have some advanced courses of his own right from the start?

        Yes ☐ 5   No ☐ 6   Can't say ☐ 7 **43—**

11. Do you have any formal arrangements for introducing new faculty members to the problems of teaching at your institution—e.g., supervision by senior members, internships, seminars on teaching problems, and the like?

        Yes ☐ 0   No ☐ 1   Can't say ☐ 2 **44—**

 If Yes: What, briefly, are the arrangements?

12. Have you experienced any unusual difficulties in getting qualified college teachers for your staff in the past few years?

            Yes ☐ x   No ☐ 0 **45—**

 If Yes: In all fields .... ☐ 1

      In some fields .... ☐   Which ones? .... **46—**

                            ....

                            ....

 a) Do you anticipate such difficulties in the next few years?

        Yes ☐ 0   No ☐ 1   Can't say ☐ 2 **47—**

• 3 •

EVALUATION OF GRADUATE WORK

13. On the whole, how do you feel about the graduate school's contribution to the supply of college teachers, in both quantity and quality?

Graduate school is doing reasonably well, all things considered .... □ 4

Graduate school could do somewhat more, but not a great deal .... □ 5

Graduate school is not facing up to the problem, and could do much more □ 6   **48—**

Can't say .... □ 7

If could do more: What, briefly, should the graduate schools do?

14. By and large, how satisfied are you with the products of the graduate schools that are available to you as college teachers?

Very satisfied .... □ 0   Not satisfied .... □ 2   **49—**

Fairly satisfied .... □ 1   Can't say .... □ 3

a) How do you think their quality now compares with that before World War II, at your institution?

Better now .... □ 5   About same .... □ 7   **50—**

Better then .... □ 6   Can't say .... □ 8

15. Which three of the following qualities are most important for a college teacher, in your judgment? Which three are least important?   **51/x**

	Three most important	Three least important
Knowledge of how to teach	□ 0	□ 0	**52—**
Interest in fields outside his own	□ 1	□ 1	
Interest in young people	□ 2	□ 2	
Knowledge of subject matter of his discipline	□ 3	□ 3	
Pleasing personality	□ 4	□ 4	**53—**
Good citizen in the college and local community	□ 5	□ 5	
Ability to do research	□ 6	□ 6	
Administrative ability	□ 7	□ 7	

16. Some people argue that the Ph.D. isn't a good degree for college teachers because of its heavy research emphasis, and wonder why the colleges continue to want or even require it. Which of the following statements best represents your feeling?

All things considered, the present doctorate program is about as good training for college teachers as could be devised .... □ 0

Despite some problems with it, the present doctorate program is a good one for college teachers .... □ 1   **54—**

The doctorate program isn't really appropriate for college teachers but it's about all that's available .... □ 2

The doctorate program isn't really appropriate for college teachers but it's necessary because of accrediting requirements, institutional competition, and similar practical considerations .... □ 3

Other *(specify* ....*)* □ 4   Can't say .... □ x

17. Do you think the undergraduate teacher needs to be a productive research man (i.e., one who publishes papers in the learned journals) in order to be a good teacher?

Yes □ 0   No □ 1   Can't say □ 2   **55—**

a) Do you think the research training experience at the doctoral level, and particularly the dissertation, is necessary or desirable for the undergraduate teacher?

Necessary .... □ 4   Not necessary and not desirable .. □ 6   **56—**

Desirable but not really necessary □ 5   Can't say .... □ 7

b) Do you take publications into account in determining promotions and appointments?

Yes, as a major factor .... □ 0   Not at all, or rarely .... □ 2   **57—**

Yes, as a minor factor .... □ 1   Can't say .... □ 3

• 4 •

18. If you had to choose—as part of the preparation for college teachers in graduate school—between instruction in how-to-teach and instruction in the history, philosophy, and problems of the liberal arts college, which would you choose?

Instruction in teaching .... ☐ 5   Equally desirable .... ☐ 7

Instruction in history, philosophy, and problems of colleges .... ☐ 6   Can't say .... ☐ 8   58—

19. Many of the recent Ph.D.'s you have appointed to the faculty of your college have probably held teaching assistantships in graduate school, but some have not. So far as you can tell, does the teaching assistantship make them better teachers for your purposes?

Yes ☐ 0   No ☐ 1   Can't say ☐ 2   59—

20. As you think of the problem of faculty recruitment at your institution over the next few years, how would you rank the following qualifications or characteristics—first according to what you **would like** to have and then according to what you think you are **most likely** to have to take? (Rank from 1 to 6, and assume that other things are equal.)   60/x

	Would like	*Most likely*
Doctorate from major graduate school	.... (61)	.... (67)
Doctorate from minor graduate school	.... (62)	.... (68)
Doctorate from teachers college	.... (63)	.... (69)
Master's from university	.... (64)	.... (70)
Master's, from good college	.... (65)	.... (71)
Holder of a new 2-year degree, intermediate between Master's and Doctor's, and specially designed for college teachers, from good institution	.... (66)	.... (72)

73/x

21. In making appointments in regular academic departments, how important is the Ph.D. (or other doctorate) as a qualification for the candidate?   1/2y   2—

The Ph.D. (or other doctorate) is very important; it comes close to being a pre-requisite .... ☐ 0

The Ph.D. is among the most important qualifications, but it is not absolutely necessary .... ☐ 1

The Ph.D. is important, but other qualifications are just as important .... ☐ 2   5—

The Ph.D. isn't really important as a qualification for our staff .... ☐ 3

Other *(specify* ....) ☐ 4

22. Does your institution have some established means of regular contact with the graduate schools in your area?

Yes ☐ 9   No ☐ x   6—

If Yes: What is it?

How well does it work?

61-	67-
62-	68-
63-	69-
64-	70-
65-	71-
66-	72-

• 5 •

a) Do any graduate schools of arts and science (**not** professional schools) actively recruit for students on your campus?

Yes .... ☐   (How many? ....)   **7—**

No .... ☐ 0

23. Some people think that college teachers tend to look too much to the graduate schools as the models for educational policies—that is, that they aim primarily at getting their majors into good graduate schools and hence over-do the specialization, proliferate courses, etc. In your experience, is this a serious problem?

Happens, but is desirable .... ☐ 0

Happens, and is undesirable .... ☐ 1   **8—**

Doesn't happen much, or at all .... ☐ 2

Can't say .... ☐ 3

24. Some people believe that under the pressure of the years ahead, the liberal arts colleges will be able to attract, on the average, only the less able Ph.D.'s in competition with the universities and industry. Are you concerned about this for your institution?

Already happening .... ☐ 1 ⎫   If only in some fields,
Probably will happen .... ☐ 2 ⎬   which ones?
No sign now, and no likeli-   ....
hood .... ☐ 0   ....   **9—**
Can't say .... ☐ x   ....

25. As you know, there has been a good deal of criticism of graduate education in the past few years, especially with regard to the preparation of college teachers (e.g., the Committee of Fifteen, the report of the AGS Committee, the report of the Carnegie Foundation, etc.). On the whole, how do you feel about such criticism?

On the whole, justified .... ☐ 0

Justified in part .... ☐ 1

On the whole, not justified .... ☐ 2   **10—**

Can't say .... ☐ 3

CRITICISMS AND REFORMS

26. Following are some specific points made in criticism of the graduate schools, on the ground that they are not preparing college teachers properly at the doctorate level. What is your judgment of each of them?

	Agree strongly	Agree	Can't say	Disagree	Disagree strongly	
a) Doctoral programs are too specialized and narrow for good college teachers	☐ 0	☐ 1	☐ 2	☐ 3	☐ 4	**11—**
b) The graduate school gives too little attention to training doctoral candidates in how to teach at the undergraduate level	☐ 6	☐ 7	☐ 8	☐ 9	☐ x	**12—**
c) The graduate school does a poor job of initial selection and admission of doctoral candidates, from the standpoint of preparing good college teachers (e.g., too little attention to the non-intellectual qualifications of college teachers)	☐ 0	☐ 1	☐ 2	☐ 3	☐ 4	**13—**
d) The graduate universities tend to keep their better Ph.D.'s and recommend only the others to the colleges	☐ 6	☐ 7	☐ 8	☐ 9	☐ x	**14—**
e) The graduate school does too little to give doctoral candidates an introduction to the history, philosophy, and problems of the liberal arts college	☐ 0	☐ 1	☐ 2	☐ 3	☐ 4	**15—**

• 6 •

	Agree strongly	Agree	Can't say	Disagree	Disagree strongly	
f) Graduate work isn't well articulated with undergraduate work, making for waste, repetition, poor sequence in learning, etc.	☐ 6	☐ 7	☐ 8	☐ 9	☐ x	**16—**
g) Doctoral work suffers because many students don't really want to be researchers but have to go through research programs in order to get the "union badge" for college teaching	☐ 0	☐ 1	☐ 2	☐ 3	☐ 4	**17—**
h) Doctoral programs stress techniques and skills too much, at the expense of broad understanding, cultivation, and wisdom	☐ 6	☐ 7	☐ 8	☐ 9	☐ x	**18—**
i) Doctoral candidates should be required to get through their programs more quickly	☐ 0	☐ 1	☐ 2	☐ 3	☐ 4	**19—**
j) The atmosphere in graduate schools tends to lessen people's interest in and respect for undergraduate teaching	☐ 6	☐ 7	☐ 8	☐ 9	☐ x	**20—**
k) The graduate schools unduly stress research and research training at the cost of properly preparing college teachers	☐ 0	☐ 1	☐ 2	☐ 3	☐ 4	**21—**
l) The rigors of doctoral study tend to discourage the brightest, most imaginative students in favor of the conscientious plodders	☐ 6	☐ 7	☐ 8	☐ 9	☐ x	**22—**
m) Graduate training too often has the unfortunate effect of dampening the student's enthusiasm for learning and scholarship	☐ 0	☐ 1	☐ 2	☐ 3	☐ 4	**23—**

27. Here are a number of reforms or changes in graduate education that have been proposed in connection with the problem of preparing a sufficient number of qualified college teachers. What do you think of each of them?   **24/x**

	Agree strongly	Agree	Can't say	Disagree	Disagree strongly	
a) Train college teachers in Master's programs in good colleges	☐ 0	☐ 1	☐ 2	☐ 3	☐ 4	**25—**
b) Set up doctoral programs in broad subject fields, specially designed for college teaching (e.g., Doctor of Social Science, Doctor of Humanities, etc.), as preferable to traditional Ph.D. programs	☐ 6	☐ 7	☐ 8	☐ 9	☐ x	**26—**
c) Set up two degree programs at the Ph.D. level — one for researchers, one for college teachers	☐ 0	☐ 1	☐ 2	☐ 3	☐ 4	**27—**
d) Introduce a new, intermediate, 2-year degree between the Master's and the Ph.D., specially designed for college teachers; somewhat broader than the Ph.D. program, and with less research emphasis	☐ 6	☐ 7	☐ 8	☐ 9	☐ x	**28—**
e) Make the Ph.D. readily available for fulfillment of three years of acceptable work, and give additional training at the post-doctorate level for the few really able researchers	☐ 0	☐ 1	☐ 2	☐ 3	☐ 4	**29—**

• 7 •

	Agree strongly	Agree	Can't say	Disagree	Disagree strongly	
f) Require all doctoral candidates to do some undergraduate teaching, under supervision	☐ 6	☐ 7	☐ 8	☐ 9	☐ x	30—
g) Restore the standards of the Master's degree in the major universities, as a way to get more college teachers	☐ 0	☐ 1	☐ 2	☐ 3	☐ 4	31—

28. Finally: a) What do you consider the **single most important** problem of graduate study today, from the standpoint of preparing college teachers?

32—

  b) If you could make **only one** recommendation to the graduate school for the improvement of doctoral programs, what would it be?

33—

*   *   *   *

    As I said at the outset, I'd be glad to get any additional comments you care to make about the state of graduate education, with special reference to the preparation of college teachers—what's right and wrong in the system, what the problems are, what ought to be done about them, the points I ought to make and the policies I ought to recommend in my report, etc. Please add your comments here.

    And again, many thanks for your help.

34—

35—

36—

37—

41—

45—

49—

5. QUESTIONNAIRE TO REPRESENTATIVES OF INDUSTRY

• 1 •

Name 1/1, 7
                                                                                                                                    2—

Position ....
                                                                                                                                    5—
Firm ....

Address ....

BACKGROUND INFORMATION

1. About how many holders of graduate degrees (Master's or Doctor's) are now employed by your firm, in all   8/x
departments? About how many are primarily involved in research or educational work?

Highest earned degree		Total employed		Primarily doing research or educational work
Master's	....	....	(9)	.... (13)
Doctor's	....	....	(17)	.... (21)

a) Roughly how many of the total have their graduate degrees in each of the following fields? (Count each person only once, for his highest earned degree.)

		Master's		Doctor's
Chemistry	....	.... (25)	....	(46)
Engineering (all)	....	.... (27)	....	(48)
Mathematics	....	.... (29)	....	(50)
Metallurgy	....	.... (31)	....	(52)
Physics	....	.... (33)	....	(54)
Biology	....	.... (35)	....	(56)
Psychology	....	.... (37)	....	(58)
Social Science (including Economics)	....	.... (39)	....	(60)
Business Administration	....	.... (41)	....	(62)
Other	....	.... (43)	....	(64)

2. About how many graduate degree holders has your firm hired in each of the last few years? (Approximate figures will do.)

		Master's		Doctor's
1954	....	....	(6)	.... (15)
1956	....	....	(9)	.... (18)
1958	....	....	(12)	.... (21)

9.	29-	41-	54-
13-	31-	43-	56-
17-	33-	45/x	58-
21-	35-	46-	60-
25-	37-	48-	62-
27-	39-	50-	64-
		52-	65/x

1/2, 7
2—

6-	12-	18-
9.	15-	21-

5/x

• 2 •

a) What is the trend in employment of graduate degree holders in your firm, as compared with (a) pre-World War II and (b) five years ago?

24/x

	Pre-World War II	Five years ago
Sharply up now	☐ 0	☐ 6
Moderately up now	☐ 1	☐ 7
About same	☐ 2	☐ 8
Moderately down now	☐ 3	☐ 9
Sharply down now	☐ 4	☐ x
Can't say	☐ 5	☐ y

25—

26—

b) What do you expect the trend to be over the next five years (a) in your firm and (b) in your industry?

	In firm	In industry
Sharply up	☐ 0	☐ 6
Moderately up	☐ 1	☐ 7
Steady	☐ 2	☐ 8
Moderately down	☐ 3	☐ 9
Sharply down	☐ 4	☐ x
Can't say	☐ 5	☐ y

27—

28—

3. Has your firm experienced any unusual difficulties in getting qualified people from the graduate schools in the past few years?

Yes, in all fields ☐ x   No ☐ 0   Can't say ☐ 9   29—

Yes, in some fields ☐

Which ones, particularly? ....

....   30—

....

....

a) Do you anticipate such difficulties in the next few years?

Yes ☐ 0   No ☐ 1   Can't say ☐ 2   31—

4. In recruiting graduate degree holders for your staff, does your firm actually visit university campuses for personal interviews, recruiting talks, etc.?

Yes ☐   No ☐ 0   32—

If Yes: About how many universities do you visit annually for this purpose? ....

a) From which graduate schools do you primarily get Ph.D.'s (or other doctorates) for your staff? Please name the five from which most of your doctorates have recently come.

5. Does your firm have any formal training programs of its own at the post-baccalaureate level, in the fields in which you mainly do research?

Yes ☐ x   No ☐ 0   33—

If Yes: a) For what kinds of employees (e.g., Master's or people outside the field)?

• 3 •

b) Why do you find it necessary to give such formal training? *(check all that apply)*

Inadequacy of university training in this field .... ☐ 1
High degree of specialization of the subject .... ☐ 2
Need to bridge the gap between industrial applications to problems and university training in disciplines .... ☐ 3
Need for training in our own way of doing things .... ☐ 4
Other *(specify* ....) ☐ 5

6. In the past year, did your firm directly provide funds for the support of graduate study—e.g., fellowships, general grants to university departments, research grants, etc.?

Yes ☐ x   No ☐ 0

If Yes: To about how many institutions? ....
What, approximately, was the total amount in the past year? ...... $ ....
What were the major forms of support? ....

7. Does your firm have a regular plan by which it assists employees to pursue graduate work—e.g., time off for study, tuition payment by the firm, etc.?

Yes ☐ 0   No ☐ 1

a) Do you particularly encourage your professional people to seek or complete higher degrees, or not?

Encourage them ☐ 3   Do not encourage them ☐ 4   Can't say ☐ 5

8. Some people feel that the Master's degree has deteriorated at many universities to the point where it does not represent a really significant addition beyond the Bachelor's degree. In your employing policy, do you make the major distinction between the Bachelor's and the Master's or between the Master's and the doctorate?

Between Bachelor's and Master's .... ☐ 0
Between Master's and Doctorate .... ☐ 1
Both places .... ☐ 2
Make no distinction .... ☐ 3
Can't say .... ☐ 4

9. In the field in which your firm mainly does research, is formal post-doctoral training becoming necessary or highly desirable for proper advancement?

Yes ☐ 6   No ☐ 7   Can't say ☐ 8

10. Are new Ph.D's ready to start right away on productive work for you or do they require a "breaking-in" period before they are prepared to do so?

Ready right away .... ☐ 0   Can't say .... ☐ 2
Need breaking-in period .... ☐ 1

If so: About how long, on the average? *(in number of months)* ....

• 4 •

11. I'm interested in getting a broad picture of the extent to which the Ph.D.'s doing research in your firm have freedom to choose their research problems, with an eye to basic scientific contributions in the field, and the extent to which problems of an applied character are assigned to them. I appreciate that this is an extremely complicated and variable matter, and I'd be grateful if you would indicate briefly what the situation is in this regard at your firm.   46—

a) Do you have to provide "free time" for work on basic research problems in order to attract top people to your staff?

Yes ☐ 0   No ☐ 1   Can't say ☐ 2   47—

EVALUATION OF GRADUATE WORK

12. On the whole, how satisfied are you with recent products of the graduate schools that are available to you as industrial researchers?   48/x

Very satisfied	☐ 4	Not satisfied	☐ 6
Fairly satisfied	☐ 5	Can't say	☐ 7

49—

If only fairly or not satisfied: What are the major deficiencies?

a) How do you think their quality now compares with that (a) before World War II and (b) about five years ago?

	(a) Before World War II	(b) About five years ago	
Better then	☐ 0	☐ 5	50—
Better now	☐ 1	☐ 6	
About same	☐ 2	☐ 7	51—
Can't say	☐ 3	☐ 8	

13. In your experience in hiring people from the graduate schools, how satisfactory is each of the following aspects of doctoral training? Which of them do you consider particularly important for your purposes?

	Satis-factory	Unsatis-factory	Can't say	Particularly important for us	
Writing and speaking ability	☐ 0	☐ 1	☐ 2	☐ 4	
Preparation in major subject field	☐ 5	☐ 6	☐ 7	☐ 9	52—
Preparation in related subjects	☐ 0	☐ 1	☐ 2	☐ 4	
Ability to work on their own	☐ 5	☐ 6	☐ 7	☐ 9	53—
Organizing and administrative ability	☐ 0	☐ 1	☐ 2	☐ 4	
General background of liberal education	☐ 5	☐ 6	☐ 7	☐ 9	54—
Coverage of basic principles	☐ 0	☐ 1	☐ 2	☐ 4	
Coverage of problems in application of basic principles	☐ 5	☐ 6	☐ 7	☐ 9	55—
Other (specify ....)	☐ 0	☐ 1	☐ 2	☐ 4	56—

• 5 •

14. Some people say that too few graduate students these days are genuinely dedicated to their subject and deeply interested in it—i.e., that students aren't really willing to work hard, that they don't take pains in their work, that they don't have the pride of craftsmanship. How true is this, in your experience?

True of none, or only a very few	☐ 0	True of about 50%	☐ 3
True of about 10%	☐ 1	True of well over half	☐ 4
True of about 25%	☐ 2	Can't say	☐ 5

57—

15. Do you think the present character of the doctoral dissertation in the fields of interest to your firm—what's required and allowed, how it's done, etc.—is about right or not?

About right .... ☐ 7   Not right .... ☐ 8   Can't say .... ☐ 9

58—

If not right: What's wrong with it?

16. In the fields in which your firm is most interested, do doctoral students at different universities get essentially the same training, in quality and scope?

Yes ☐ 0   No ☐ 1   Can't say ☐ 2

59—

17. There is currently a good deal of controversy over the appropriate national distribution of the doctoral load in the next few years—that is, whether it should be carried primarily by the institutions already well established in the field or spread out to the newer graduate schools. What is your view, so far as your fields of interest are concerned?

Would be desirable to limit doctoral training to the major established institutions, if possible .... ☐ 4

Established institutions should be filled first, then other institutions should expand as necessary .... ☐ 5

Newer entrants into doctoral training should be encouraged to expand right now .... ☐ 6

Can't say .... ☐ 7

60—

a) Do you think that some institutions not really qualified for doctoral work are jeopardizing standards by expanding too rapidly?

Yes ☐ 0   No ☐ 1   Can't say ☐ 2

61—

18. Some people say that because so many Ph.D.'s in science are going into industrial research, the liberal arts colleges are having difficulty in getting qualified faculty members; and that this will result in poorer science teaching in college for the next generations of graduate students. Does this seem a real problem, in your experience?

Yes ☐ 4   No ☐ 5   Can't say ☐ 6

62—

If Yes: What, briefly, can be done about the matter, in your view?

19. Some people in the universities believe that industry should take more responsibility for the support of graduate work, especially since so many products of graduate study are going into industrial employment. What is your reaction?

Industry is doing all that can be expected of it now .... ☐ 0

Industry is doing a great deal now, but perhaps can or should do more .... ☐ 1

Industry should definitely do more .... ☐ 2

Can't say .... ☐ 3

63—

• 6 •

20. In the fields in which your firm is most active, have there been any important innovations or experiments or changes in graduate education in the past five years or so?

           Yes ☐ 5   No ☐ 6   Can't say ☐ 7   **64—**

If Yes: What were they and what do you think of them, as compared with traditional programs of training?   **65/x**

1/3, 7

21. The following specific points have been made in the criticisms directed at the graduate schools over the past few years. A few of them may overlap earlier questions but are included here for comparability with other groups. On the whole, how do you feel about each of them?   **2—**

	Agree strongly	Agree	Can't say	Disagree	Disagree strongly	
a) Doctoral work suffers because many students don't really want to be researchers but have to go through research programs in order to get the "union badge" for college teaching	☐ 0	☐ 1	☐ 2	☐ 3	☐ 4	**5—**
b) Doctoral programs should be "loosened" by placing more responsibility upon the student and encouraging him to do more independent work	☐ 6	☐ 7	☐ 8	☐ 9	☐ x	**6—**
c) Doctoral programs should be "tightened" and regularized more, like the training programs in medical and law schools	☐ 0	☐ 1	☐ 2	☐ 3	☐ 4	**7—**
d) A major trouble with graduate education is that a single program of doctoral work is given for three kinds of people — college teachers, researchers, and professional practitioners. The programs should be differentiated more	☐ 6	☐ 7	☐ 8	☐ 9	☐ x	**8—**
e) The graduate schools aren't doing a good job of initial selection of candidates for the doctorate at the time of admission	☐ 0	☐ 1	☐ 2	☐ 3	☐ 4	**9—**
f) Doctoral programs stress techniques and skills too much, at the expense of broad understanding, cultivation, and wisdom	☐ 6	☐ 7	☐ 8	☐ 9	☐ x	**10—**
g) Too many courses are offered at the graduate level by most departments	☐ 0	☐ 1	☐ 2	☐ 3	☐ 4	**11—**
h) Graduate work would be done better if the graduate faculty did not also have to handle undergraduate work	☐ 6	☐ 7	☐ 8	☐ 9	☐ x	**12—**
i) Major professors often exploit doctoral candidates by keeping them as research assistants too long, by subordinating their interests to departmental or the professor's interests in research programs, etc.	☐ 0	☐ 1	☐ 2	☐ 3	☐ 4	**13—**
j) Doctoral candidates get too little direct attention, supervision, and guidance on their dissertations from their major professors, and that makes for unnecessary prolonging of the period of doctoral study	☐ 6	☐ 7	☐ 8	☐ 9	☐ x	**14—**

• 7 •

	Agree strongly	Agree	Can't say	Disagree	Disagree strongly	
k) Doctoral programs of training for research are so onerous and distasteful that they repel almost as many people from research work as they attract	☐ 0	☐ 1	☐ 2	☐ 3	☐ 4	15—
l) Doctoral training for research is inefficient and wasteful because so few recipients of the degree become productive researchers in the field	☐ 6	☐ 7	☐ 8	☐ 9	☐ x	16—
m) With the numbers of students now involved in doctoral study, it has become almost impossible to provide the basic necessity of research training, namely, proper apprenticeship relations	☐ 0	☐ 1	☐ 2	☐ 3	☐ 4	17—
n) Under the impact of numbers, the standards of doctoral study are being jeopardized	☐ 6	☐ 7	☐ 8	☐ 9	☐ x	18—
o) Under the impact of numbers, the quality of the students in doctoral programs is declining	☐ 0	☐ 1	☐ 2	☐ 3	☐ 4	19—
p) The quality of doctoral work is limited these days by the fact that most students are motivated by the practical objective of getting a job rather than the objective of becoming a research scholar	☐ 6	☐ 7	☐ 8	☐ 9	☐ x	20—
						21/x
q) The practice of having graduate students and undergraduates in the same classes lowers the quality of graduate instruction	☐ 0	☐ 1	☐ 2	☐ 3	☐ 4	22—
r) Doctoral candidates are too often allowed or encouraged to attempt a major contribution as their dissertation rather than to take on a manageable topic that can be finished in a reasonable time	☐ 6	☐ 7	☐ 8	☐ 9	☐ x	23—
s) Doctoral candidates are being trained too much as technicians, not scientists	☐ 0	☐ 1	☐ 2	☐ 3	☐ 4	24—
t) The doctoral dissertation should be regarded more as a training instrument than as an "original contribution to knowledge"	☐ 6	☐ 7	☐ 8	☐ 9	☐ x	25—
u) The graduate schools have wrongly allowed the Master's degree to deteriorate in quality	☐ 0	☐ 1	☐ 2	☐ 3	☐ 4	26—
v) The doctoral dissertation is too often a pedantic or trivial exercise rather than an intellectual experience of genuine substance and interest	☐ 6	☐ 7	☐ 8	☐ 9	☐ x	27—
w) Doctoral candidates should be required to get through their programs more quickly	☐ 0	☐ 1	☐ 2	☐ 3	☐ 4	28—
x) The doctoral program is designed too much for the students of average competence rather than for the brilliant students	☐ 6	☐ 7	☐ 8	☐ 9	☐ x	29—
y) Doctoral work is conceived too much as professional training, oriented to practice, rather than as academic learning, oriented to scholarship	☐ 0	☐ 1	☐ 2	☐ 3	☐ 4	30—

• 8 •

	Agree strongly	Agree	Can't say	Disagree	Disagree strongly	
z) Doctoral programs are too specialized and narrow	☐ 6	☐ 7	☐ 8	☐ 9	☐ x	31—
aa) Doctoral programs are insufficiently specialized	☐ 0	☐ 1	☐ 2	☐ 3	☐ 4	32—
bb) One basic trouble with graduate school is that faculty members do not consider the students as their main responsibility (as compared to their own research, consultation and service jobs, administration, etc.)	☐ 6	☐ 7	☐ 8	☐ 9	☐ x	33—
cc) To much of what the graduate school does, and how it does it, is adversely affected by the sources of funds, e.g., contract grants supporting dissertation research in the sciences	☐ 0	☐ 1	☐ 2	☐ 3	☐ 4	34—
dd) The rigors of doctoral study tend to discourage the brightest, most imaginative students in favor of the conscientious plodders	☐ 6	☐ 7	☐ 8	☐ 9	☐ x	35—
ee) Students aren't made to work hard enough in graduate schools, especially as compared to the major professional schools	☐ 0	☐ 1	☐ 2	☐ 3	☐ 4	36—

22. Finally: a) What do you consider the **most important one or two** problems of graduate study today, from your point of view?

37—

b) If you could make **only one or two** recommendations to the graduate schools for the improvement of doctoral programs, what would they be?

38—

39—

40—

41—

•　　•　　•　　•

42—

I'd be glad to get any additional comments you care to make about the state of graduate education from your own standpoint—what's right and wrong in the system, what the problems are, what ought to be done about them, the points I ought to make and the policies I ought to recommend in my report, etc. Please add your comments on the inside cover.

And again, many thanks for your help.